Urban Outcasts

Urban Outcasts

A Comparative Sociology
of Advanced Marginality

Loïc Wacquant

polity

First published in 2008 by Polity Press.

Reprinted 2010 (twice), 2012

Polity Press
65 Bridge Street
Cambridge CB2 1UR, UK

Polity Press
350 Main Street
Malden, MA 02148, USA

ISBN-13: 978-07456-3124-0
ISBN-13: 978-07456-3125-7 (pb)

A catalogue record for this book is available from the British Library.

Typeset in 10.5 on 12 pt Plantin
by SNP Best-set Typesetter Ltd., Hong Kong
Printed and bound in Great Britain by the MPG Books Group

For further information on Polity, visit our website: www.politybooks.com

To my mother,

for teaching me the sense of social justice

Contents

Contents

Detailed Contents

Ghetto, *Banlieue*, *Favela*, et caetera
Tools For Rethinking Urban Marginality

Ghetto in the United States, *banlieue* in France, *quartieri periferici* (or *degradati*) in Italy, *problemområde* in Sweden, *favela* in Brazil and *villa miseria* in Argentina: the societies of North America, Western Europe and South America all have at their disposal in their topographic lexicon a special term for designating those stigmatized neighbourhoods situated at the very bottom of the hierarchical system of places that compose the metropolis. It is in these districts draped in a sulfurous aura, where social problems gather and fester, that the urban outcasts of the turn of the century reside, which earns them the disproportionate and disproportionately negative attention of the media, politicians and state managers. They are known, to outsiders and insiders alike, as the 'lawless zones', the 'problem estates', the 'no-go areas' or the 'wild districts' of the city, territories of deprivation and dereliction to be feared, fled from and shunned because they are – or such is their reputation, but in these matters perception contributes powerfully to fabricating reality – hotbeds of violence, vice and social dissolution. Owing to the halo of danger and dread that enshrouds them and to the scorn that afflicts their inhabitants, a variegated mix of dispossessed households, dishonoured minorities and disenfranchised immigrants, they are typically depicted from above and from afar in sombre and monochrome tones. And social life in them thus appears to be everywhere the same: barren, chaotic and brutish.

Breaking with the exoticizing cast of media discourse as well as with the semi-scholarly approximations of conventional research, this book takes the reader inside these territories of relegation in two advanced countries – namely, the black ghetto of the United States and the working-class *banlieue* of France – to show that such is not the case: urban marginality is not everywhere woven of the same cloth, and, all things considered, there is nothing surprising in that. The *generic mechanisms* that produce it, like the *specific forms* it assumes, become fully intelligible once one takes caution to embed them in the historical matrix of class, state and space characteristic of each society at a given epoch. It follows that we must work to develop more complex and more differentiated pictures of the 'wretched of the city' if we wish accurately to capture their social predicament and elucidate their collective fate in different national contexts.[1]

Ghetto, *banlieues*, state

The chapters that compose this book dissect and compare the postwar upheavals and contemporary makeup of the American 'Black Belt' with the structure, dynamics and experience of urban dispossession in France's deindustrializing 'Red Belt' (the peripheral working-class areas that were the traditional stronghold of the Communist Party). The immediate empirical thrust and ulterior analytical purpose that animate them are closely linked. The primary empirical aim is to describe and explain *the institutional transformation undergone by the African-American ghetto* caught in the undertow of the wave of riots that swept the metropolis in the 1960s, in the wake of the reorganization of the regime of racial domination, the capitalist economy and public policy in the United States in a way that integrates, rather than separates as is customary, the roles of the labour market, ethnic division and the state. The secondary analytical goal is to extract from the similarities and differences displayed by the American 'hyperghetto' and the declining French 'outer city' the elements of a sociological sketch of *advanced marginality*, i.e., the novel regime of sociospatial relegation and exclusionary closure (in Max Weber's sense[2]) that has crystallized in the post-Fordist city as a result of the

---

[1] We would likewise gain from 'broadening the horizon of our gaze' on the neighbourhoods of relegation of the First World metropolis by replacing them in the broader spectrum of variegated forms taken by the urban constellations of the dispossessed caught 'between war and city' in the countries of the global South (Agier 1999: 6–8).

[2] By closure (*Schließung*), Weber ([1918–20], 1968: 32, 33) designates the set of processes whereby a collective restricts 'access to the opportunities (social or economic) that exist in a given domain': its members 'draw on certain characteristics of their real or virtual adversaries to try and exclude them from competition. These characteristics may be race, language, confession, place of origin or social background, descent, place of domicile, etc.' A succinct and effective presentation of this approach to social and spatial stratification can be found in Mackert (2004).

uneven development of the capitalist economies and the recoiling of welfare states, according to modalities that vary with the ways in which these two forces bear upon the segments of the working class and the ethnoracial categories dwelling in the nether regions of social and physical space.

After diagnosing the unexpected resurgence of the repressed realities of collective violence, material destitution and ethnoracial division in the First World city over the past three decades, the first part of the book focuses on the nexus of racial domination, class inequality and state (in)action in the racialized core of the US metropolis. Breaking with the trope of 'disorganization' that has guided mainstream research on poverty in America since the early works of the Chicago School, I develop an institutionalist conception of the ghetto as concatenation of mechanisms of ethnoracial control founded on the history and materialized in the geography of the city.[3] Against the tale of the 'underclass' that came to dominate the scholarly and policy debate in the 1990s, I retrace the historic shift from the *communal ghetto* of the mid-twentieth century, a compact and sharply circumscribed sociospatial formation to which blacks of all classes were consigned and bound together by a broad complement of institutions specific to the group and its reserved space, to the fin-de-siècle *hyperghetto*, a novel, decentred, territorial and organizational configuration characterized by conjugated segregation on the basis of race *and* class in the context of the double retrenchment of the labour market *and* the welfare state from the urban core, necessitating and eliciting the corresponding deployment of an intrusive and omnipresent police and penal apparatus.

I draw on a range of empirical data from quantitative surveys, in-depth interviews with residents, and ethnographic observations conducted on the South Side of Chicago in 1987–1991 to delineate the fabric of everyday life in the contemporary ghetto and pinpoint the economic and political factors that have propelled its recent evolution, among them economic informalization and deproletarianization, the persistence of a rigid and all-enveloping racial segregation, the erosion of America's rump welfare state, and local measures of 'planned shrinkage' of government services in the inner city. In the final analysis, however, it is *the collapse of public institutions*, resulting from state policies of urban abandonment and leading to the punitive

---

[3] For a compressed discussion of the perennial biases and limitations of mainstream research on racial division and urban poverty in the United States, the reader is referred to Wacquant (1997a and 2002a for its ethnographic strand).

containment of the black (sub-)proletariat, that emerges as the most
potent and most distinctive cause of entrenched marginality in the
American metropolis.[4] In contrast with Wilson's (1987) *The Truly
Disadvantaged*, which prioritizes the role of the economy, and Massey
and Denton's (1993) *American Apartheid*, which stresses the weight
of racial segregation, this book highlights the gamut of racially skewed
and market-oriented state policies that have aggravated, packed and
trapped poor blacks at the bottom of the spatial order of the polarizing city. The implosion of America's dark ghetto and its flooding
by extreme marginality turn out to be economically underdetermined
and politically overdetermined: properly diagnosed, *hyperghettoization is primarily a chapter in political sociology*, not postindustrial economics, racial demography or urban geography.

The second part of the book develops a comparison of the structure, lived experience and political-economic foundations of urban
marginality in the United States and France based on an empirical
study centred on the notorious public housing estate of the Quatre
mille in La Courneuve, a depressed industrial exurb of Paris emblematic of the festering 'crisis of the *banlieue*'.[5] This comparison is motivated by the fact that, throughout Europe but especially in France,
the US ghetto has been taken as embodying the urban pattern with
which the poor neighbourhoods of the postindustrial city everywhere
are aligning. It draws out the contrasted social morphology, organi-

---

[4] The invention of the policy of penalization of social insecurity in the United States,
translating into the hyperincarceration of black subproletarians (one African-
American man in three is presently under criminal justice supervision, and two of
every three blacks without school credentials will serve a prison sentence during their
lifetime), is analysed in *Punishing the Poor: The New Government of Social Insecurity*
(Wacquant 2008, orig. 2004), and its internationalization in *Prisons of Poverty*
(Wacquant 2009, orig. 1999).
[5] Technically, the term *banlieue* designates a peripheral town or zone administratively
attached to a larger urban centre. Originally, in the French medieval city, it refered
to the ring of one league (*lieue*) falling under the *ban* or juridical authority of the city.
A *banlieue* can thus be bourgeois or working-class, affluent or impoverished. Since
the mid-1980s, however, the word has been increasingly reserved to denote lower-
class districts of the urban periphery harbouring high densities of deteriorating public
housing (projects known as *cités*) considered prime breeding grounds for the 'urban
ills' of the age, combining economic deprivation, ecological degradation, social dislocations, postcolonial immigration and youth delinquency (Boyer 2000). Such *cités*
are typically composed of large estates of cheaply built high rises that generate an
atmosphere of monotony and dread.

zational makeup and functions that neighbourhoods of relegation on Chicago's South Side and in the Parisian periphery fulfil for their respective metropolises. It highlights the desolidarizing effects of territorial stigmatization on local social structures and strategies, and it uncovers the principles of social vision and division that pattern the consciousness and practices of their residents, anchored by the pervasive opposition between blacks and whites on the American side and the vivid dualism of 'housing estate youths' against the rest of the world on the French side. This analysis reveals that the declining urban periphery of France and the African-American ghetto constitute *two disparate sociospatial formations*, produced by different institutional logics of segregation and aggregation, which result in sharply higher levels of blight, isolation and hardship in America's dark ghetto.

Social closure and spatial relegation in the Black Belt operate on the basis of race first and foremost, modulated by class position after the break of the 1960s, and both are anchored and *aggravated* by public policies of urban triage and neglect. It is just about the reverse in the Red Belt, where marginalization is primarily the product of a class logic, in part redoubled by ethnonational origin and in part *attenuated* by state action. It follows that the American hyperghetto is an ethnically and socially *homogeneous* universe characterized by low organizational density and weak penetration by the state in its social components and, by way of consequence, extreme levels of physical and social insecurity; whereas the French urban periphery is typified on the contrary by a fundamentally *heterogeneous* population according to ethnonational provenance (and, secondarily, class position), whose isolation is mitigated by the strong presence of public institutions catering to social needs. This internal heterogeneity is, moreover, redoubled by the external heterogeneity across different French working-class *banlieues*, which constrasts sharply with the social and spatial monotony exhibited by the ghettos of the major US cities. That is why we shall, whenever possible, speak of the ghetto in the *singular* and of the *banlieues* in the *plural*.

The balance sheet of similarities and differences between the 'new poverty' rooted in the French working-class periphery and its structural counterpart in the United States highlights the *specifically racial dimension* of urban marginality in the American metropolis. It directly refutes the furiously fashionable thesis of a transatlantic convergence leading to the emergence of 'ghettos' along the outer ring of

European cities.[6] And it confirms that *state structures and policies play a decisive role* in the differential stitching together of inequalities of class, place and origin (whether ethnoracial or ethnonational), and this *on both sides of the Atlantic*. At crosscurrent with the political ideologies and scholarly discourses that concur to stress the weakening of the state so as better to bring it about, it emerges that Leviathan remains the main vector commanding the genesis and trajectory of advanced marginality in each country. Even where it might at first glance seem to be absent, passive or puny, it is still the national state that, through its multisided action, shapes not only the markets for housing, employment and educational credentials, but also the distribution of basic goods and services, and through this mediation governs the conversion of social space into appropriated physical space. In the United States no less than in France, 'effects of place' (Bourdieu [1993] 1999) turn out to be essentially *effects of state projected on to the city*.

Finally, the methodical comparison of the black American ghetto with the French working-class *banlieues* enables us to discern the main properties that distinguish fin-de-siècle marginality from the 'Fordist' regime of poverty that had dominated the period of industrial consolidation during the three decades after World War II. Having refuted the thesis of transatlantic *convergence* (i.e., the 'Americanization' of the European city), I move to formulating the thesis of the *emergence* of a new regime of urban poverty. The analysis of polarization from below presented in the third part of this book is intended as both critique of and complement to the studies of urban polarization from above carried out under the banner of the 'global city' and 'dual city', which have paid insufficient attention to the processes of social fragmentation at the bottom that have accompanied processes of unification at the top.[7] It underlines, *inter alia*, the

---

[6] This thesis rests on a complete sociological misconstrual of what constitutes a ghetto, produced and perpetuated by (1) ignorance of the historical realities of the American city (whose empirical investigation is conveniently replaced by the endless rehashing of clichés which, being shared by tabloid-style journalism, political rumour and the more worldly sectors of scholarship, appear in the end to be founded on fact) and (2) a persistent conceptual confusion between ghettoization and spatial differentiation, residential segregation, economic pauperization, concentration of foreigners or immigrants, physical enclosure, degradation of the housing stock, criminal violence and so on (either taken *in seriatim* or in clusters).

[7] Among the key works charting the parameters of that current are Sassen (1991b, revised and expanded 2001), Mollenkopf and Castells (1991), Fainstein et al. (1992), Abu-Lughod (1999), Marcuse and Van Kempen (2002), and the Multi-City Study of Urban Inequality sponsored by the Russell Sage Foundation (O'Connor et al. 2001).

fact that post-Fordist poverty or 'advanced marginality' in the city is fuelled by the growing instability and heterogeneity of the wage-labour relation in the context of rising inequality; increasingly disconnected from the short-term cyclical fluctuations of the national economy and accentuated by the recoiling of the social welfare state; and tends to concentrate in defamed and desolate districts where the erosion of a sense of 'place' (referring to both a shared objective position and the subjective sentiment of having a 'place of our own') and the absence of a collective idiom of claims-making exacerbate the experience and effects of deproletarianization and destitution. Drawing on Erving Goffman's (1963) analysis of stigma and on Pierre Bourdieu's (1982/1991) theory of group-making, it stresses the distinctive weight and effects of territorial stigmatization as well as the insuperable political dilemmas posed by the material dispersion and symbolic splintering of the new urban poor.

As a new century dawns, the incapacity of the governments of the advanced countries, that is, the refusal or reticence of their ruling classes converted to neoliberalism to check the social and spatial accumulation of economic hardship, social dissolution and cultural dishonour in the deteriorating working-class and/or ethnoracial enclaves of the dualizing metropolis promises to engender abiding civic alienation and chronic unrest which pose a daunting challenge to the institution of citizenship. The deep rooting and wide reverberations of the social disorders generated by advanced marginality are major springs behind the spectacular expansion and generalized hardening of police and penal policies trained on the urban subproletariat in the United States and the European Union since the denunciation of the Fordist–Keynesian social compact (Wacquant 1999). But the penalization of urban poverty only aggravates the very ills it is supposed to treat, while traditional welfarist approaches leave largely untouched the causal mechanisms feeding the new urban poverty. So much to say that, to make a real difference, public policies aimed at combating advanced marginality will have to reach beyond the narrow perimeter of wage employment and move towards the institutionalization of a right to subsistence outside of the tutelage of the market via some variant of 'basic income' (Van Parijs 1995).

Towards a comparative sociology of urban marginality

By specifying the distinctive causal dynamics, social modalities and experiential forms that fashion relegation in the metropolis in the

United States and in France, this book endeavours to forge tools for rethinking urban marginality in the advanced societies. It intends thereby to help invigorate the *comparative sociology of social polarization from below* in the cities of the First World but also of Second World countries, such as Argentina, South Africa and Turkey, and of the nation-states that have issued out of the rubble of the Soviet empire, where the diffusion and intensification of urban poverty in recent years are even more pronounced.[8] From this comparison – provisional and subject to revision – between the American ghetto and the French working-class periphery at the close of the twentieth century arise five principles that may usefully orient future research.

First and foremost, it is imperative to establish a clearcut separation between, on the one hand, the *folk concepts* used by state decision-makers, city authorities and the residents themselves to designate neighbourhoods of exile and, on the other, the *analytical concepts* that social scientists must *construct*, against the pre-notions of urban common sense, to account for their evolving makeup and position in the sociospatial structure of the metropolis. This implies that particular attention be given to the critical examination of the categories and discourses (including those produced by social science) that, under cover of describing marginality, contribute to moulding it by organizing its collective perception and its political treatment. As a corollary, one must beware of the international circulation of phony concepts – such as that of the 'underclass' – which are not only unsuited to their contexts of *importation*, but do not even have purchase at home on the urban realities in their *exporting countries* (Wacquant 1996a). One must likewise guard against the confused and confusing invocation of notions, like that of 'ghetto', that operate as mere metaphors calling forth an emotive imagery that hides fundamental structural and functional differences, thereby stopping inquiry just where it should get going.[9]

---

[8] Cf. the extension of the problematic of the nexus of poverty and ethnicity to post-Soviet societies in Eastern Europe (Emigh and Szelényi 2001; Ladányi and Szelényi 2002), the resurgence of the debate on marginality in Latin American cities (Auyero 2000; González de la Rocha et al. 2004; Lago 2005), and the blooming of work on urban exclusion in post-apartheid South Africa (Robinson 1996; Gervais-Lambony et al. 1999) and Turkey during the phase of integration with Europe (Erder 1997; Keyder 2005). This debate is also of burning significance in China (Wu 2004).

[9] This is what I will attempt to demonstrate in *The Two Faces of the Ghetto*, the book that is the sequel and complement to this tome, by directly confronting the controversial question of the ghetto.

Secondly, it is vital to replace the state and fate of a neighbourhood (be it upscale or deprived, noble or ignoble) in the *diachronic sequence of historical transformations* of which they are the material expression and which never find their source and principle in the neighbourhood under examination. Any 'cross-sectional' slice of the metropolis is comprehensible only as a synchronous precipitate, artificially frozen by analysis, of 'longitudinal' tendencies of the long run that traverse social space and appropriated physical space. Thus the *brutal implosion* of the black American ghetto in the wake of the urban uprisings of the 1960s was propelled from the outside, by the confluence of the decentring of the national political system, the crumbling of the caste regime, the restructuring of urban capitalism, and the policy of social regression of the federal government set against the backdrop of the continued ostracization of African Americans. The same is true of the *slow decomposition* of the working-class territories of the French (and more generally European) urban periphery in the post-Fordist era which, like their consolidation during the period between 1910 and 1980, is overdetermined from above by the triangular relationships between the state, social classes and the city. To forget that urban space is a *historical and political construction* in the strong sense of the term is to risk (mis)taking for 'neighbourhood effects' what is nothing more than the spatial retranslation of economic and social differences.[10]

A third recommendation pertains to methodology: *ethnographic observation emerges as an indispensable tool*, first to pierce the screen of discourses whirling around these territories of urban perdition which lock inquiry within the biased perimeter of the pre-constructed object, and secondly to capture the lived relations and meanings that are constitutive of the everyday reality of the marginal city-dweller. But, lest one condemn oneself to monographic myopia, fieldwork cannot for a single moment do without institutional analysis, and vice versa – even if one or the other is sidelined or muted at certain moments of the research and its end-product. It must be guided at every step by the methodical knowledge, itself constantly revised and enriched by the first-person study of concrete situations, of the

[10] As Pierre Bourdieu forcefully reminds us ([1993] 1999: 123, 124, my trans.): 'One can break with falsely self-evident notions, and with the errors inscribed in substantialist thinking in terms of *places*, only on condition of effecting a rigorous analysis of the relations between the structures of social space and the structures of physical space', relations that are the historical product of 'struggles over the appropriation of space' in which the state plays a doubly decisive role as the ground of confrontation and as interested protagonist.

macrostructural determinants that, although ostensibly absent from the neighbourhood, still govern the practices and representations of its residents because they are inscribed in the material distribution of resources and social possibles as well as lodged inside bodies in the form of categories of perception, appreciation and action (Bourdieu 1980/1990). This is here a matter not of collecting 'fresh' data to compose 'lively' illustrations of theories elaborated outside sustained contact with the prosaic reality but indeed of enrolling ethnographic observation as a necessary instrument and moment of theoretical construction.

Although this book does not belong to the established genre of the ethnographic monograph, ethnography played an essential role in it. For field observation, structural analysis and theoretical construction advance in unison and mutually reinforce each other in it,[11] rather than opposing one another in a sterile conflict of priority. Without the direct information obtained through personal participation in ordinary scenes of life in Chicago's South Side ghetto, I would not have been able to validate my initial intuition of the incongruous and unconvincing import of the academic legend of the 'underclass', and I could not have rearticulated the question of race, class and state in the despised space of the *inner city* (the geographical euphemism used by normal US social science to designate the black ghetto, precisely to avoid *naming* it). Similarly, the data produced firsthand during the investigation carried out in La Courneuve and among the municipal and ministerial services charged with French urban policy in 1989–1991 were vital in helping me set aside the false problems imposed by the current political debate and its administrative focus, and then to triangulate the view from below and the view from above of the pauperized estates in the Parisian *banlieue* with the relevant economic and demographic data. The more abstract theorizations – such as the analytical sketch of 'advanced marginality' with which this research culminates – always gain from being solidly harnessed to a carnal grasp of the historical experience for which they purport to account.[12]

[11] Two models of synergistic integration of these three elements are Virgílio Pereira's book (2005), *Classes e culturas de classe das famílias portuenses* (especially Part 3, 'Cidade e Territorio', pp. 479–767), and Mario Small's (2004) study of a poor Puerto Rican enclave of Boston, *Villa Victoria*.

[12] This grasp can itself be thematized by means of *comparative* ethnography, based on parallel fieldwork conducted in two sites chosen to throw light upon theoretically relevant invariants and variations, as opposed to the currently fashionable 'multi-sited fieldwork' which is too often a handy excuse for escaping the practical drudgery of ethnography by not doing fieldwork anywhere.

Fourthly, it is useful to distinguish, at a minimum, between the social *condition* characteristic of a zone of relegation and the conditionings it entails (which can, over time, crystallize into a local culture and panoply of typical strategies; cf. Bourgois 1995); its *position* in a hierarchized structure of places, measured by the double yardstick of material and symbolic value; and the *function* it performs for the broader metropolitan system. Some such districts serve as active and resilient reservoirs of low-skill labour force; others are mere warehouses for supernumerary populations that no longer have any identifiable political or economic utility in the new polarized capitalism; and others yet are spatial containers for the ostracization of undesirable social categories and activities. This is true of the lowly neighbourhoods of different countries but also of different cities in a single society or even in the same metropolis. In Brazil, for example, the label *favela* fuses and confuses stable working-class districts that continue to provide solid harbours of proletarian integration into the city, zones in which the victims of 'regressive deindustrialization' are forsaken to their fate in an informal street economy increasingly dominated by criminal activities and the entropic violence they generate, and enclaves for *marginais* defined by the experience of group stigma and collective taint.[13] The same neighbourhood can fulfil one or the other of these functions in succession or, depending upon the sector, simultaneously for different categories, according to proportions set by the history of its composition and position in the objective and subjective hierarchy of the districts that make up the city.

Lastly, one needs to specify the *degree and form of state penetration* in neighbourhoods of relegation as well as the changing – and often contradictory – relations that their inhabitants maintain with different public officials and agencies, schools and hospitals, housing and social welfare, firefighting and transportation, the courts and the police. These relationships cannot be assumed to be static, uniform, univocal or adequately summed up by the catch-all phrase of 'clientism' or by the familiar figures of conflict and complaint. On the one hand, indeed, even when poor city-dwellers fail to overturn the 'rituals of marginality' that bind them to the governing elite, their collective action continually engenders new meanings and multistranded exchanges that open up a possible space for collective demands and

---

[13] It suffices, to realize this, to contrast Ribeiro (1996) with Pamuk and Cavallieri (1998), Pino (1997) with Goldstein (2003), and, from a historical and biographical viewpoint, the works assembled by Zaluar and Alvito (1998). The same demonstration could be made for the *Problemquartier* in Germany, the *bairro degradado* in Portugal, the *ciudad perdida* in Mexico or the *varoş* in Turkey, and so on.

social critique (Vélez-Ibañez 1983). On the other hand, there exists a wide gulf between government policies 'on paper', decided and articulated by the centres of state power, and the ordinary practices of the street-level bureaucracies (Lipski 1980) that provide (or fail to provide) public services in a manner that is always differentiated and differentiating according to client category and location, a gulf that we can bridge only by empirical analysis of specific and prosaic cases.[14]

Among the institutions that stamp their imprint on the daily life of the populations and on the climate of 'problem' neighbourhoods, special attention must be accorded to the police. As the 'frontline' agency and frowning face of the state directly turned down towards precarious and marginal categories, the police are everywhere confronted with a deep crisis of legitimacy, mission and recruitment that the recent managerial turn can neither contain nor mask, since it finds its source in the overall reconfiguration of the state, the erosion of the public monopoly over systems of surveillance and sanction of deviancy, and the broad diffusion of a feeling of *social* insecurity to which political leaders have chosen to respond with the all-out politicization of *criminal* insecurity, which sets off an upward spiralling of expectations that the forces of order cannot but betray in the end.

Yet, while the social foundations of 'police fetishism' – the ideological illusion that would make it the 'solution' to the 'crime problem' (Reiner 1997: 1003) – are crumbling, the police have again been entrusted, not only with maintaining public order, but also, in a very concrete sense that returns it to the historic mission of its origin, with buttressing the new social order woven out of vertiginous inequalities and with checking the turbulences born of the explosive conjunction of rampant poverty and stupendous affluence engendered by neoliberal capitalism in the cities of the advanced and advancing countries around the globe.[15] And if putting working-class districts left economically and socially fallow under police restraint has recently become so popular among rulers, it is because it enables the high state nobility to give itself the comforting feeling that it is responding to the demands of the 'people' while at the same time exculpating its own historic responsibility in the making of the urban outcasts of the new century.

[14] For a fine-grained study of 'the regulation of tensions and of the production of consent' by state administrations responsible for the everyday management of urban poverty (in the case at hand, two family benefits offices in two French towns), read Dubois (1999).
[15] On this issue, see Chevigny (1995), Palidda (2000), Jobard (2002) and Binder (2004), respectively, on the Americas, Italy, France and Argentina.

Prologue: An Old Problem in a New World?

1

The Return of the Repressed
Riots, 'Race' and Dualization in Three Advanced Societies

In the expansionary decades following the mid-twentieth-century traumas of depression and war, the rich countries of the capitalist West came to think of themselves as peaceful, cohesive and egalitarian societies – in a word, as *civilized* in both the ordinary, morally effusive, meaning of the term denoting the most accomplished form of culture and human life, and in Norbert Elias's ([1937] 1978) sense of 'civilizing' as engaged in a long-term process of restructuring of social relations entailing the extension of chains of interdependencies, the multiplication of organizations, and the pacification of social exchange via the monopolization of the use of public violence by a centralized bureaucratic state.

Advanced nation-states such as the United States, France and Great Britain also embraced a vision of themselves as increasingly *democratic* in Tocqueville's understanding of the term, that is, oriented towards the ineluctable reduction of inequalities of condition, particularly those derived from 'ascribed' positions and identities. Indeed, one of the most salient dimensions of the self-understanding of First World societies during the immediate postwar period was that inherited statuses, such as class, ethnicity or 'race', were increasingly irrelevant for access to valued social locations and the attendant bundle of life chances.[1] Mass consumption, the supposed *embourgeoisement* of the working class, the growing weight of educational credentials in the competitive allocation of persons in an increasingly

---

[1] This broad-brush portrait does not allow recognition of significant variations among what are cursorily labelled 'First World' societies. For a pointed presentation of differences in the sociopolitical construction of inequality and poverty in France, Great Britain and the United States, see Silver (1993: esp. 342–8).

differentiated occupational structure, the diffusion of liberal individualism: together these factors promised to usher in an unprecedented
era of personal well-being and social comity. Two books, published
simultaneously in 1960 in the United States, may be taken as emblematic projections of this emerging societal vision, as revealed by their
titles: Walt W. Rostow's (1960) *The Stages of Economic Growth: A
Non-Communist Manifesto* and Daniel Bell's (1960) *The End of Ideology*. Sociology gave a scholarly expression to this belief by elaborating
the notion of 'meritocracy'. In the United States, a whole school of
stratification research (based at the University of Wisconsin, Madison)
laboured to formalize this vision of an increasingly fluid and porous
class structure by making 'status attainment' the conceptual backbone of countless studies of 'opportunity'.[2]

During the same period, it became widely accepted that the more
extreme forms of inequality in basic life circumstances had been or
were about to be alleviated, if not eradicated, by the wide provision
of public goods, such as education, health and housing, through the
arm of the welfare state – in the case of Western European countries
– or via the trickle-down effects of sustained free-market growth and
targeted programmes of assistance – in the United States. Buoyed
by industrial consolidation and by the continued expansion of newer
services sectors, First World societies came to construe poverty as a
mere *residue* of past inequities and backwardness or as the product
of *individual deficiencies* liable to remedy – at any rate, as a phenomenon bound to recede and disappear with the full 'modernization' of
the country.[3] Thus, on the eve of the contentious 1960s, the economist John Kenneth Galbraith (1958) called poverty an 'afterthought'
and an anomaly in US society, characterizing it as pertaining only to
'case poverty' and 'insular poverty'. True, the so-called islands of

---

[2] The terminology itself is revealing of the ideological presuppositions of such
research. Knotterus (1987) dissects the image of society underlying 'status attainment' research, carried out in particular by members of the Wisconsin School. One
could show that the ideology of *social meritocracy* (as embodied by the writings of
Talcott Parsons, Peter Blau and Otis Dudley Duncan, on the American side, and
Raymond Aron and Henri Mendras, on the French side) fulfilled for Euro-American
societies a function similar to that performed for Brazil by the national myth of 'racial
democracy', as formulated by Gilberto Freyre ([1938] 1946).

[3] Castel (1978) offers a historical account of this problematic in the case of the
United States, while Wilson and Aponte (1985) record the cyclical 'disappearance'
and 'rediscovery' of the question of poverty in American society over the twentieth
century. On the corresponding gyrations of the French debate (around the theme of
'exclusion' after the late 1980s), consult Paugam (1993); on the British discussion,
L. Morris (1994).

poverty were rather populous, since there were still tens of millions of poor people in America, among whom were a disproportionate number of blacks, but they would not remain so for long: when he launched the 'War on Poverty' in 1964, President Lyndon B. Johnson proudly announced that the United States would eradicate poverty by the year 1976, so that the bicentennial of the country would also herald the birth of the first 'society of affluence' in history. In France, at about the same time, the equally rosy horizon of a 'new society' was being beamed by the hegemonic Gaullist party under Jacques Chaban-Delmas's leadership, later to be refurbished as the promise of 'advanced liberal society' by President Giscard d'Estaing, whose Labour Minister had published a best-seller proclaiming that one can 'vanquish poverty in the rich countries' (Stoléru 1974). As Sinfield (1980: 93) notes, through the 1970s, there was 'no poverty debate in France', no political mobilization around the issue, as well as no official policy to combat it.

The obsolescence of class was presumed to apply equally to ethnicity and 'race' (or postcolonial divisions).[4] To varying degrees, First World societies also took to seeing themselves as 'nonethnic' social formations, increasingly homogeneous and unified as *gemeinschaftliche* relations founded on ancestry, region and culture gave way to instrumental affiliations based on interest, occupational specialization and the functional imperatives of a complex technological economy. *Assimilation for all* was the order of the day (Gordon 1961), and adoption of the national cultural patterns seemingly the only available course for outgroups that lived in, or entered into, these societies (Hirschman 1983).

By thus eliding the question of ethnicity, the ideologues of advanced society marched in the steps of classical and contemporary social science. Did not Karl Marx and Emile Durkheim, progenitors of the two main rival currents of sociology, agree that capitalist industrialization would result in the replacement of traditional social bonds by impersonal forms of identification and belonging rooted in commodity relations and increasingly abstract civic ideals? Likewise, the two paradigms of social change that dominated social science in the

---

[4] 'Race' is put in quotation marks to stress that (i) racial identity is but a particular case of ethnicity (one that falsely presents itself as, and is believed to be based on, biological inheritance), i.e., a historically constructed principle of social classification; (ii) the gamut of social and symbolic relations designated by 'race' (or 'colour') varies significantly from one society to the next and from one historical conjuncture to another; and with it (iii) the mechanisms of (re)production of racism as a mode of domination invoking nature as principle of legitimation.

postwar era, structural-functionalism (and its offshoot modernization theory) and developmental Marxism (led by the work of the Latin American *dependistas* and world-system theory), postulated that ethnicity and race were fated to be eroded and eventually disappear. Thus, for the advocates of modernization such as David McLelland, Alex Inkeles and Daniel Lerner (1958), the 'passing of traditional society' logically implied the dissolution of ascribed social ties and the concurrent emergence of the free, enterprising, 'achieving' individual, due to the rise of literacy, technology and the mass media.[5] For defenders of various Marxist theories of societal transformation, from André Gunder Frank and Fernando Enríque Cardoso to Immanuel Wallerstein, class formation was to wash away ethnicity and create a global class structure – eventuating, in the vision proposed by Wallerstein (1983), in a transition towards a 'socialist world order'. Various theories of postindustrial society shared these assumptions and similarly conceived ethnoracial divisions, not as enduring bases of social structuring endowed with their own dynamic, but as 'backward', reactive or derivative principles of grouping, transitory impediments in the natural course of modern society towards universalism (Kumar 1995).[6]

Violence from below: race riots or bread revolts?

Over the last two decades of the century, this self-image of the First World was shattered by spectacular outbursts of public unrest, rising ethnic tensions, and mounting destitution and distress at the heart of large cities. Far from witnessing a resorption of poverty and an erosion of ethnonational affiliations, advanced societies have been plagued by the concurrent spread of 'new poverty' and the surge – or

[5] The opposition between 'ascription' and 'achievement' is one of the founding antinomies of the structural-functionalist theory elaborated by Talcott Parsons (1971), which portrayed the United States as the historical incarnation of the supposedly universal ideal of the meritocratic society. For a curt and acerbic critique of the shortcomings of this theory, read Bourdieu (1975).

[6] Florestan Fernandes (1978: 7) offers a capsule expression of this widespread view in his appraisal of the nature and fate of ethnic divisions issuing from slavery in Brazilian society: 'The Brazilian racial dilemma constitutes a pathological social phenomenon, which can only be corrected by processes that would remove the obstruction of racial inequality from the competitive social order.' This position is of course much older: recall that the 'race relation cycle' of the early Chicago School, with its ordered progression from conflict and competition to accommodation and assimilation, pointed to the gradual resorption of ethnoracial divisions.

resurgence – of racializing ideologies often accompanied by violent conflicts directly involving youths in lower-class neighbourhoods (Wilson 1987; Mingione 1993). Three instances of urban disruption in France, England and the United States among many illustrate the phenomenon.[7]

October 1990 in Vaulx-en-Velin, a drab, quiet working-class town on the periphery of Lyons, France: several hundred youths, many of them the offspring of immigrants from the Maghreb, take to the streets to confront police after a neighbourhood teenager dies in a motorcycle accident caused by a patrol car. For three days and nights, they clash with law enforcement officials and the *Compagnies Républicaines de Sécurité* (CRS, riot brigades) hastily dispatched by the government, pelting police vans with rocks, ransacking shops, and setting 200 cars on fire. When calm finally returns, tens of injured are counted, damage is estimated at some 120 million dollars, and the country is in a state of shock. The long-simmering rage of the *banlieues* – declining peripheral areas with high densities of degraded public housing – zooms to the top of the political agenda and will dominate public debate for years on end.[8]

July 1992 in Bristol, England: a nearly identical chain of events triggers several nights of rioting on the Hartcliffe estate, a dilapidated industrial district on the southern edge of town. Violence breaks out after two local teenagers joyriding on a stolen police motorcycle are killed in a collision with an unmarked police car. Later that night, some hundred youths go on a rampage through the local shopping centre. When police counterattack, they are showered with bricks and stones, steel balls, scaffolding and gasoline bombs. The confrontation quickly spills throughout the neighbourhood. More than 500 elite troops have to be called in to restore order to a one-

[7] I can give only the briefest sketch of such incidents here. For a fuller account of the rise of collective violence and ethnoracial tensions in the housing projects of France's urban periphery during the 1980s, see Adil Jazouli's (1992) *Les Années banlieues*; for an exemplary American case, Bruce Porter and Marvin Dunn's (1984) analysis of *The Miami Riot of 1980*; for an overview of the British riots of the early 1980s, read the Scarman Report and its offshoots (Benyon 1984).

[8] Clashes continued throughout the summer of 1991, forcing the central government to expand and institutionalize various programmes of 'incident prevention', in particular during the summer vacation (the so-called *Opérations anti-été chaud*). Similar outbursts of collective violence would occur periodically over the ensuing decade, culminating in the wave of simultaneous riots that rocked France for three long weeks in November 2005 (in reaction, again, to the death of two marginalized youths during an encounter with the police, aggravated by the scornful public statements of Interior Minister Nicolas Sarkozy).

square-kilometre area temporarily turned urban guerrilla zone. Similar large-scale incidents break out that same summer in Coventry, Manchester, Salford, Blackburn and Birmingham.[9]

April 1992 in Los Angeles: the acquittal of four white police officers implicated in the brutal videotaped beating of Rodney King, a defenceless black motorist arrested after a car chase, sets off an explosion of civil violence unmatched in American history in the twentieth century. In the ghetto of South Central, white motorists are snatched out of their cars and beaten, shops are vandalized, police cars are overturned and set aflame. The Korean-owned liquor outlets, swap-meets and markets that dot the area are targeted for systematic destruction. So overwhelming is the eruption that neither firefighters nor the police can prevent the torching of thousands of buildings. Rioting promptly mushrooms outwards as scenes of mass looting multiply. A state of emergency is proclaimed, and 7,000 federal troops, including 1,200 Marines, are drafted in and deployed. Sniper fire and gun battles between rioters, police and storeowners who take up arms to defend their shops bring the death toll to forty-five. By the end of the third day of upheaval, nearly 2,400 have suffered injury, and over 10,000 are under arrest; 1,000 families have lost their homes and 20,000 their jobs. Total destruction is estimated at a staggering one billion dollars.

These outbursts of collective violence are but three drawn from a list of urban disturbances too long to enumerate.[10] Most of the disorders, big and small, that have shaken up the French working-class *banlieues*, the British inner city, and the ghettos and adjacent *barrios* of North America have involved chiefly the youths of impoverished, segregated and often dilapidated urban neighbourhoods caught in a spiral of decline; they appear to have been fuelled by growing ethnoracial tensions in and around those areas. Thus the dominant interpretation in media accounts, as in political debates, has been that they are essentially 'race riots' expressive of animosity against, or between, the ethnic and/or immigrant 'minorities' of these countries (Cross and Keith 1993; Gooding-Williams 1993).

[9] In 1980, 1981 and 1985, major riots erupted in 'inner-city' areas of Bristol, London, Liverpool, Birmingham and a host of other declining working-class municipalities. Incidents resumed in the early 2000s, this time prominently involving youths of Asian descent (Amin 2003).

[10] One should add to incidents in France, Britain and the United States the rash of violent attacks on foreigners and asylum seekers in Germany and repeated incidents involving North African immigrants in northern Italy and southern Spain.

There is much, on the surface of things, to support this view. The Europe of the 1980s was indeed swept by a seemingly unstoppable wave of xenophobic sentiment in the public sphere if not in everyday life.[11] In France, long-covert anti-'Arab' hostility burst out into the open (Silverman 1990) and fuelled a reported increase in racist assaults. It found a political expression in the xenophobic populism of the National Front (Husbands 1991), which in turn stimulated the growth of a wide 'anti-racist' movement, symbolized by the irruption on the public scene of the activist group *SOS-Racisme* (incubated under the wing of the Socialist Party). In Great Britain, antagonism between black West Indians, South Asians and whites flared up in repeated street confrontations and has grown more acrimonious. Debates about street crime and police brutality have been racialized to the extent that public unrest and violence are increasingly openly perceived and treated as essentially 'black problems' (Solomos 1988). Meanwhile in the United States a society-wide backlash against the gains made by so-called minorities (mainly African Americans but also, secondarily, Latinos and some Native and Asian groups) in the wake of the Civil Rights confrontations of the 1960s has led to a noticeable deterioration of race relations signalled *inter alia* by an escalation in racially motivated or 'hate' crime, a generalized fear of black males in public space (E. Anderson 1990), interethnic incidents on university campuses, and the blatant exploitation of anti-black feelings in local and national political campaigns (Franklin 1991; D. Anderson 1995). And, while Europe has become haunted by the spectre of the crystallization of American-style 'ghettos' on its soil, the United States has been consumed by nightmarish visions of a so-called 'underclass', a fearsome group said to have coalesced at the heart of the segregated metropolis which epitomizes all the urban pathologies of North America.[12]

---

[11] On the rise (or resurgence) of racism on a European scale and its various national manifestations, see Allen and Macey (1990), Miles (1992) and Holzner (1993).

[12] Mingling social science, journalism and common sense, empirical analysis and ordinary preconceptions, the academic-cum-policy myth of the 'underclass' has fused and given new life to age-old prejudices against African Americans, the poor and state intervention by demonizing the black urban subproletariat (Wacquant 1992a). Its invention partakes of a broader reconfiguring of the ideological map of 'race' in the United States, along with the legend of Asians as 'model minority', the symbolic unification of diverse population streams coming from Central and South America under the administrative category of 'Hispanics', and the growing demands for official recognition made by the self-proclaimed representatives of 'multiracial' persons.

In all three countries, then, urban violence and collective unrest have come to be closely linked, if not equated, in the public mind with ethnoracial division and/or immigration. In the United States, this association is a long-standing one, dating from the era of black urbanization after Emancipation, if not further back, and it is periodically reactivated during periods of economic contraction or social conflict (Lane 1986). In Europe, this connection is more recent, even as it has proved ideologically powerful in the rocky socioeconomic conjuncture opened by the sweep of deindustrialization and economic recessions in the mid-1970s. Nonetheless, several elements suggest that the label 'race riot' is misleading and hides another, deeper phenomenon, mixed with it in different proportions, and this on both sides of the Atlantic.

The collective urban disorders of the 1980s and 1990s are not a simple extension of traditional racial uprisings such as the United States has experienced throughout the last century (Young 1970). Contrary to the ambient discourse of journalism and certain magazine-inspired sociology, we are not witnessing an 'Americanization' of urban poverty and protest, a mutation in the regime of urban marginality that would herald an epochal transatlantic convergence between the two continents on the US pattern, as will be shown in the second part of this book. A closer look at their anatomy suggests that these urban disorders led by lower-class youths have, to a varying extent depending on the country, *combined two logics*: a logic of protest against *ethnoracial injustice* rooted in discriminatory treatment – of a stigmatized quasi-caste in the United States, of 'Arab' and other 'coloured' migrants or citizens come from the former colonies in France and Great Britain – and a class logic pushing the impoverished fractions of the working class to rise up against *economic deprivation and widening social inequalities* with the most effective, if not the only, weapon at their disposal, namely, direct confrontation with the authorities and forcible disruption of civil life.[13]

As a period of neoliberal restructuring following the throes of stagflation, the 1980s were the decade of the slow maturing of *mixed riots* – mixed in terms of their dynamics and goals as well as by virtue of their multiethnic composition. For, contrary to media portrayals, neither the declining French *banlieues* nor the degraded British inner cities are solely or even predominantly populated by immigrants, and those who partook in unrest in them were more often than not

---

[13] On the logic and social conditions of the political efficacy of such popular disruptions, see Piven and Cloward's (1977) classic study, *Poor People's Movements*, a very topical book in the current phase of rightward recentring of progressive political parties.

recruited across a kaleidoscope of ethnic categories. While youths from Maghrebine or West Indian immigration assumed the lead in the urban clashes that rocked France and England during those years, they acted in concert with, and with the active support of, the offspring of native European families residing in formerly industrial neighbourhoods now lying fallow. In the case of the British 'summer disturbances' of 1981, for instance, even though the triggering incidents typically entailed a confrontation between the police and black youth, 'an estimated 60% of the rioters involved in the worst anti-police violence at Toxteth and many of those who participated in the so-called 'copy-cat' riots were white' (Unsworth 1982: 69). Moreover, the demands of the rioting youths were those of working-class youths everywhere: decent jobs, good schools, affordable or improved housing, access to basic public services, and fair treatment by the police and other agencies of the state (Jazouli 1992). There is nothing 'ethnic' about them – save the demand that the state, precisely, cease to treat them as such.

Similarly, during the riots of South Central Los Angeles, the thousands who pilfered merchandise from burning supermarkets and mini-malls were far from being all black: more than half of the first 5,000 arrests were Latinos, and another 10 per cent whites. The uprising was not exclusively an Afro-American outcry against gross racial discrimination perpetrated by the police and further affirmed by an egregious miscarriage of justice (the blanket acquittal of the white policemen involved in the beating of Rodney King by a lily-white suburban jury). It was also, and inseparably, a 'bread revolt' against grinding poverty and the severe aggravation of daily living conditions brought on by economic recession and cutbacks in government programmes, as testified by the televised scenes of Latinos but also Asians and whites milling about ransacked stores in search of free goods. As one of the city's seasoned observers put it, 'the nation's first multiracial riot was as much about empty bellies and broken hearts as it was about police batons and Rodney King'.[14]

---

[14] Mike Davis, 'In L.A., Burning All Illusions', in Hazen (1992: 43–54); for further materials, see the excellent selection of press reports compiled by the Institute for Alternative Journalism (Hazen 1992) and some of the essays in Gooding-Williams (1993) and Baldassare (1994). This interpretation was later validated by Pastor (1995), who shows that the active participation of Latinos and poverty rates were central to the outbreak and spread of the riot, and by Murty et al. (1994), who report, based on street interviews with 227 residents and workers in South Central Los Angeles, that participants in the outbreak perceived themselves as 'freedom fighters' over the issues of poverty, unemployment, police brutality and racial discrimination, a mix of motives that fits well the confluence of structural forces determining the clash.

Violence from above: deproletarianization, relegation, stigmatization

It is tempting to view outbreaks of collective violence 'from below' as symptoms of moral crisis, pathologies of the lower class, or as so many signs of the impending societal breakdown of 'law and order' (e.g., Banfield 1970). Thus the typical response of the English authorities to the wave of violent incidents that rocked the cities of the Midlands in the summer of 1992 was to bemoan the deviant behaviour and amorality of lower elements of the working class. After the Bristol riots, politicians vied to blame 'mindless hooliganism' fuelled by alcohol, even though the residents of Hartcliffe agreed that hostility between youths and police had been building up for months if not years; no 'hooligan' was ever spotted or arrested during the riots; and consumption of alcohol on the nights of the clash was not above normal. In 1981, the skinheads were also singled out for special condemnation and were 'diabolized as bestial marionettes of Right-wing extremism' by the press (Unsworth 1982: 76). Similarly, in the United States, the loathsome tale of the 'underclass' has provided a low-cost, depoliticized, ready-made discourse with which to account for the relentless rise of violence in and around the ghetto since the mass upheavals of the 1960s. Indeed, such violence has been widely seen as definitive proof of the existence of that group defined precisely by its antisocial behaviours.

Yet close comparative analysis of their timing, makeup and unfolding shows that, far from being irrational expressions of impenitent incivility or pathological atavism, the public disorders caused by dispossessed youths in the cities of Europe and the United States over these past dozen years constitute a (socio)logical response to the massive *structural violence* unleashed upon them by a set of mutually reinforcing economic and sociopolitical changes. These changes have resulted in a polarization of the class structure which, combined with ethnoracial segregation and welfare state retrenchment, has produced a *dualization of the social and physical structure of the metropolis* that has consigned large sections of the unskilled labour force to economic redundancy and social marginality.[15] This violence 'from above' has three main components:

[15] For a view from above of the roots and dynamics of this process of dualization, see Sassen (1991b), Mollenkopf and Castells (1991), Fainstein et al. (1992); a call for analytical caution on this front is sounded by Marcuse (1989).

1 *Mass unemployment*, both chronic and persistent, amounting, for entire segments of the working class, to *deproletarianization* and the diffusion of *labour precariousness*, bringing in their wake a whole train of material deprivation, family hardship, temporal uncertainty and personal anxiety.
2 *Relegation to decaying neighbourhoods* in which public and private resources diminish just as the social fall of working-class households and the settlement of immigrant populations intensify competition for access to scarce public goods.
3 Heightened *stigmatization* in daily life as well as in public discourse, increasingly linked not only to class and ethnic origin but also to the fact of residing in a degraded and degrading neighbourhood.

These three forces have proved all the more noxious for combining against the backdrop of a general upswing in inequality. Far from representing a peripheral by-product of a 'Third-worldization' of rich countries or regressions towards premodern forms of sociopolitical conflict, this return of the repressed realities of poverty, collective violence and ethnoracial divisions issuing from the colonial past at the heart of the First World city must be understood as the result of the uneven, disarticulating development of the *most advanced sectors* of capitalist societies, whose manifestations are therefore quite unlikely to abate soon (as I shall stress in the third part of the book).

Unlike previous phases of economic growth, the uneven expansion of the 1980s and 1990s, where it occurred at all, failed to 'lift all boats' and resulted instead in a deepening schism between rich and poor, and between those stably employed in the core, skilled sectors of the economy and individuals trapped at the margins of an increasingly insecure, low-skill, service labour market, and first among them the youths of neighbourhoods of relegation.[16] In the United States, this gap has grown so pronouncedly that it is readily palpable on the streets of big cities, where beggars and the homeless became a common sight in the 1980s even in lavish business districts, and in the extremes of luxury and destitution, high society and dark ghetto, that have flourished and decayed side by side. Thus, while the share of national wealth owned by the richest 1 per cent of Americans

[16] Statistical data on the rise of income inequality in England, France and the United States for that period are in Townsend (1993), CERC (1989 and 1997) and Danziger and Gottschalk (1993) respectively.

doubled in a decade, jumping from 17.6 per cent in 1976 to 36.3 per cent in 1989, more people lived under the official 'poverty line' in 1992 than at any time since 1964: thirty-six million, including one of every three black or Latino households.

In France, income inequality grew for the first time in the postwar era in spite of a host of social transfer measures targeted on deprived categories implemented by successive Socialist governments. As the ranks of the 'Golden Boys' bulged at the Palais Brogniard along with the unprecedented appreciation in stocks and real estate values, so too did those of the unemployed, the homeless and the destitute. By the close of the 1990s, according to official estimates regularly broadcast by the media, over four million French people lived in poverty, 300,000 were deprived of regular housing, and over half a million were recipients of the national guaranteed minimum income plan (RMI) hastily instituted in 1988 in an effort to curb rising destitution. On the national news, reports of conflicts between 'bosses' and 'workers' going on strike to defend their wages and social rights have been replaced by stories about delinquency and somber assessments of the predicament of *érémistes* (recipients of the RMI, a term coined to capture the new reality of quasi-permanent rejection from the wage labour sphere). In Great Britain supply-side economics and rollbacks in social expenditures by the state have likewise caused a redistribution of wealth upwards and a sharp divergence of living standards between working class and upper class as well as between provinces (Dunford 1995). The northern sections of the country have been dramatically impoverished, as the regional economies of major industrial centres such as Manchester, Liverpool and Glasgow crumbled. So much so that some analysts took to comparing the provinces of the North of England to the Italian *mezzogiorno* to highlight the growing national dualism.[17]

Employment shifts from manufacturing to education-intensive jobs, on the one side, and to deskilled service positions on the other, the impact of electronic and automation technologies in factories and even in white-collar sectors such as insurance and banking, the erosion of unions and social protection have combined to produce a simultaneous destruction, casualization and degradation of work for the residents of the dispossessed districts of the large cities. For many of them, economic restructuring has brought not simply loss of

---

[17] For broader discussion of the mechanisms whereby the breakdown of the Fordist regime of accumulation and regulation fed deflationary adjustment and regional inequality throughout Britain, see Dunford and Perrons (1994).

income or erratic employment: it has meant outright denial of access to wage-earning activities, that is, *deproletarianization*. Thus most West European countries have witnessed a steady rise not only in unemployment – the average rate in the European Community increased from 2.9 per cent in 1974 to nearly 11 per cent in 1987 – but also, more significantly, in the number of the *long-term* unemployed who come overwhelmingly from the lower class. By the early 1990s, the proportion of jobless without employ for a year or more exceeded three-quarters in Belgium, one-half in the Netherlands, and 45 per cent in France and the United Kingdom. The comparable figure of 8 per cent for the United States is misleading because its measurement is different (it suffices to work one hour in a month to be counted as 'employed'), and it hides enormous variations across categories and locations: in many inner-city areas, effective jobless rates among adults hover well above 50 per cent, and for many exclusion from formal employment lasts for years and even decades. Survival based on a mix of casual labour, welfare support and illegal activities trumps regular wage labour participation.[18]

The persistent, nay permanent, exclusion from wage labour of a segment of the working class and the correlative growth of the informal economy in declining urban areas are two converging indicators of the formation, at the core of First World cities, of what Fernando Henríque Cardoso and Enzo Faletto (1979) called an 'excess reserve army of labour', for whom economic advancement translates into a regression of material conditions and a curtailment of life chances. Witness the spread of hunger or malnutrition (attested by the prosperity of 'soup kitchens' and assorted food banks) and the reappearance of bygone contagious diseases such as tuberculosis in the flagging neighbourhoods of relegation of Los Angeles, Lyons and Leeds.

Just as their economies underwent deindustrialization and globalization, advanced countries have absorbed a fresh influx (or the definitive settlement) of immigrants from the Third World who are typically channelled into those very neighbourhoods where economic opportunities and collective resources are steadily diminishing.[19] The formation of a worldwide space of circulation of capital over the past

[18] At the core of Chicago's ghetto in 1988, for instance, nearly six adults in ten lived off meagre welfare payments, and fully 80 per cent of recipients expected to remain on public aid for more than a year (see ch. 3 *infra*, pp. 109–11).

[19] On the causes and role of international migration in activating or amplifying social transformations in advanced societies, see the conceptual précis by Zolberg (1991) and the empirical analyses of Sassen (1989a), Tarrius (1992) and Castles (1993).

three decades has led to the knitting of a global network of labour circulation that has reshaped the population and brought large numbers of fresh migrants into the big cities of Europe and North America (Fassman and Münz 1996; Portes 1999). These 'new immigrants', as they are often called to distinguish them from the transatlantic migration chains that primarily connected the Old and the New Worlds until the middle of the twentieth century, originate mainly in former colonies of Western Europe or in the economic and political satellite countries of the United States. They tend to congregate in the poorer neighbourhoods of large urban centres, those where housing is cheaper, where they can more easily gain a foothold in the informal and entrepreneurial sectors of the economy, and where networks of compatriots or coethnics provide critical assistance in the process of adaptation to life in the new country (Portes and Rumbaut 1990; Castles 1993).

Whether or not the arrival of the new immigrants has accelerated the partial deproletarianization of the native working classes by providing a substitute pool of pliable labour needed by the expanding deskilled service sectors is unclear. What is beyond doubt is that their concentration in the segregated and degraded lower-income neighbourhoods has accentuated the social and spatial polarization in the city because it occurred at a time when, thanks largely to state support of individual housing through urban planning and fiscal policy, the middle classes were fleeing mixed urban areas and relocating in protected territories where they benefit from a higher level of public services (France), provision their basic household needs on the private market (United States), or enjoy a mix of superior public and private goods (United Kingdom).

Spatial segregation intensifies hardship by accumulating in isolated urban enclaves downwardly mobile families of the native working class and immigrant populations of mixed nationalities who are young, economically fragile and equally deprived of readily marketable skills in the core of the new economy. Thus, more than half of Vaulx-en-Velin's 45,000 residents in 1990 lived in large, cheerless public housing projects, and one in four were of foreign origin; more than 40 per cent were under age 20, and one-third of all adults could not find employment. Government programmes of training and job search assistance are unable to help youths gain a firm foothold in the shrinking and fragmenting labour market, and sports and cultural activities can provide only so much diversion. Similarly, joblessness among inhabitants of south Bristol aged 16 to 25 at the time of the riots stood at 50 per cent and had risen with the increased presence of foreign families. The crime rate in Hartcliffe – reputed to be among the highest in England at the time – was in no small part due to the severe dearth of community resources and of recreational facilities needed to keep youths occupied when trapped in the social void between school and work. Turning to the United States, between 1978 and 1990, the county of Los Angeles lost 200,000 jobs, most of them high-wage unionized positions in industry, just as it received an infusion of nearly one million immigrants. Many of these jobs were lost by minority residents of South Central and inner-city communities where public investment and programmes were being aggressively curtailed (Johnson et al. 1992). As a consequence, in 1992 unemployment in South Central exceeded 60 per cent among young Latinos and blacks, and the illegal drug economy had become the most reliable source of employment for many of them.

Such cumulation of social ills and the narrowing of the economic horizon explain the atmosphere of drabness, ennui and despair that pervades poor communities in large Western cities and the oppressive climate of insecurity and fear that poisons daily life in the black American ghetto (Wacquant 1992a and chs 2 and 4, *infra*). Residents of these derelict districts feel that they and their children have little chance of knowing a future other than the poverty and exclusion to which they are consigned at present. Added to this sense of social closure is the rage felt by unemployed urban youths due to the taint befalling residents of decaying urban areas as their neighbourhoods become denigrated as hellish breeding grounds of 'social pathologies'. Youths of Maghrebine origins in the northern district of Marseilles, their counterparts originating in Jamaica and Pakistan in London's Brixton, and blacks trapped on Chicago's South Side do not suffer only from material deprivation – shared, in the ethnically mixed areas of urban Europe, with their white neighbours – and from the ambiant ethnoracial or ethnonational enmity: they must also bear the weight of the public scorn that is now everywhere attached to living in locales widely labelled as 'no-go areas', fearsome redoubts rife with crime, lawlessness and moral degeneracy where only the rejects of society could bear to dwell.

As I shall demonstrate in chapter 6, the reality and potency of the territorial stigma imposed upon the new urban outcasts of advanced society should not be underestimated. First, the sense of personal indignity it carries is a highly salient dimension of everyday life that colours interpersonal relations and negatively affects opportunities in social circles, school and the labour market. Second, there exists a strong correlation between the symbolic degradation and the

ecological disrepair of urban neighbourhoods: areas commonly perceived as dumpsters for the poor, the deviant and the misfit tend to
be avoided by outsiders, 'redlined' by banks and real estate investors,
shunned by commercial firms, all of which accelerates decline and
abandonment. They can be overlooked at little cost by politicians –
except, precisely, when they become the site of visible unrest and
street clashes. Third, territorial stigmatization encourages amongst
residents sociofugal strategies of mutual avoidance and distancing
which exacerbate processes of social fission, feed interpersonal mis-
trust, and undermine the sense of collectivity necessary to engage in
community-building and collective action.

Lastly, there is the curse of being poor in the midst of a rich society
in which participation in the sphere of consumption has become
a *sine qua non* of social dignity – a passport to personhood if not
citizenship (especially among the most dispossessed, who have
little else at their disposal to signal membership). As testified by the
proliferation of 'mugging' in the British inner city, *dépouille* (the stripping of fancy clothes under threat of force) in the estates of
the French *banlieues*, and gold-chain snatching and drug dealing
on the streets of the black American ghetto, violence and crime are
often the only means that youths of proletarian background with
no employment prospects have of acquiring the money and the
consumer goods indispensable for acceding to socially recognized
existence.[20]

Political alienation and the dilemmas of penalization

If direct and spontaneous forms of *infra-political protest* by way of
popular disruption of public order, outright seizure of goods, and
destruction of property have spread in the declining urban boroughs
of advanced society, it is also the case that formal means of pressure
on the state have declined along with the disruption and then decomposition of traditional machineries of political representation of the
poor.

In France, the crumbling of the Communist Party and the centrist
turn of the successive Socialist governments have left the working
class in deep political disarray (Masclet 2003) – a disarray upon

[20] For illustrations in the American context, see Taylor (1989) and Padilla (1992).
One suspects that a similar logic was at work, *mutatis mutandis*, in the fright-
ful weekend irruptions of 'funkers' on the wealthy, white beaches of Ipanema and
Copacabana in Rio de Janeiro in the mid-1990s.

which the extreme Right-wing party of Le Pen was quick to capitalize with an ideology scapegoating immigrants that, for lack of something better, has the virtue of offering a crystal-clear picture of society, a coherent diagnosis of its main ills, and a radical cure that promises to restore workers' sense of dignity as citizens (redefined as 'nationals'). In Great Britain, a decade and a half of Thatcherism prolonged by the neoliberal policies of Tony Blair has speeded up the long-term decline of trade unions and the ideological revamping of the Labour Party (Allmendinger and Tewdwr-Jones 2000), while the breakup of working-class communities undercut the local mobilizing capacity of their grass-roots organizations. In the United States, where the lower class has never had much of a political voice, the mass exodus of whites and the middle class to the urban periphery, the nationalization of political campaigns under the tutelage of corporate funders, the demise of big-city electoral 'machines', and the administrative fragmentation of the metropolis have converged to marginalize poor minorities in the political field (Weir 1993). Stripped of the institutional means to formulate collective demands in a language comprehensible by state managers, what are poor urban youths to do if not take to the streets? A teenage rioter from Bristol speaks for many of his peers in East Harlem, the Red Belt boroughs of Paris, and Toxteth in Liverpool when he exclaims:[21]

> I don't have a job and I'll never have one. Nobody wants to help us get out of this shit. If the government can spend so much money to build a nuclear submarine, why not for the inner cities? If fighting cops is the only way to get heard, then we'll fight them.

The widening gulf between rich and poor, the increased closure of political elites onto themselves and the media, the increasing distance between the lower class and the dominant institutions of society all breed disaffection and distrust. They converge to undermine the legitimacy of the social order and to redirect hostility toward the one state organization that has come to symbolize its unresponsiveness and naked repressiveness: the police. In the vacuum created by the lack of political linkages and the absence of recognized mediations between marginalized urban populations and a society from which they feel ejected, it is no wonder that relations with the police have everywhere become both salient and bellicose, and that incidents with the 'forces of order' are invariably the detonator of the

[21] Cited in The *Guardian*, 20 July 1992, in a report in the wake of the Bristol riot.

explosions of popular violence that have rocked poor neighbourhoods over the past two decades in the city (Cashmore and McLaughlin 1992; *Cultures et Conflits* 1992).[22]

In the French working-class *banlieues*, the police are regarded by the youths of the housing projects (of North-African and French origins alike) as an undesirable presence sent for the express purpose of intimidating and harassing them, and nearly all instances of collective unrest over the past two decades have at their start an incident opposing them to agents of law enforcement. It is not a coincidence if the police invented the bureaucratic category of *violences urbaines* (plural) in those years, based on a pseudo-scientific scale of levels of aggression (of which the 'gathering of youngsters in the building stairways' is the first stage!), in order better to depoliticize these confrontations and make them liable to a strictly penal treatment (Bonelli 2001). The Scarman Report on the riots that shook British cities in the the early 1980s noted likewise that inner-city youths are 'hostile and vindictive towards the police and no longer have any confidence in them' (Benyon 1984: 126). Most careful observers concurred that the police were the primary target as well as active participants in the erupting street violence, responding vigorously to the attack of youths, making the riots a vivid expression of the '*mutual* alienation of police and sections of multi-racial working-class inner-city communities' (Unsworth 1982: 73).

But it is in the segregated black and Latino areas of the American urban core that relations with the police are the most antagonistic and the most virulent. Residents of the ghetto are torn between their need for protection from rampant crime and their fear that police intervention will add to the violence, not diminish it, due to their discriminatory and brutal behaviour. In the desolate districts of the Los Angeles ghetto, the forces of order act as if they were waging a trench war with the residents, treating them as an army of occupation would its enemies (Davis 1992; Herbert 1997). In June 1992, Amnesty International released a report compiling evidence of a deep-seated pattern of routine police brutality against poor African Americans and Hispanics in Los Angeles going on unchecked for

---

[22] The other dominant institution which is perceived with enormous ambivalence, as both platform of opportunity and vehicle of official intrusion and external imposition, is the school, due to the long-overdue universalization of secondary education. Balazs and Sayad (1991) explore the range of reactions to the symbolic violence of public education in the French working-class *banlieue* of Vaulx-en-Velin, including rude behaviours (relabelled 'incivilities' in the idiom of official criminology), vandalism, avoidance and physical violence.

years with near-complete impunity from local and federal authorities.[23] Expanding on the scathing report of the Christopher Commission (1991) set up to inquire into the widespread use of 'excessive police force in the inner city' in reaction to the Rodney King videotaped beating, the sixty-page document details heinous incidents of abuse of force, often 'amounting to torture or other cruel, inhumane or degrading treatment', that involve the unwarranted use of firearms 'in violation of international standards', shootings or beatings of compliant suspects and even innocent bystanders, the routine overuse of electric 'tazer' guns,[24] and the unleashing of attack dogs on suspects (including juveniles and minor offenders, some of them already in custody) who had surrendered and posed no threat.

For the disaffected youths of declining urban districts, then, the police constitute the last 'buffer' between them and a society that rejects them, and which they therefore view as 'the enemy', trespassers in a territory where their rule is often openly contested and incites defiance and hostility that can extend to verbal and physical aggression – as illustrated by the controversial song 'Cop Killer' by the rap singer Ice T. (whose namesake Ice Cube played a germane role in John Singleton's cult movie *Boyz N the Hood*). In all advanced countries, whenever the police come to be considered as an alien force by the population they are supposed to protect, they become unable to fulfil any role other than a purely repressive one and, under such circumstances, they can only add to discord and disorder, often fuelling the very violence they are trusted to curb (Wacquant 1993).

---

[23] The entire report entitled *Police Brutality in Los Angeles, California, United States of America* (Amnesty International USA 1992) is recommended reading. That such a scathing study should fail to elicit any meaningful reaction from local and national authorities testifies to their remarkable indifference to endemic and routine police abuse in the neighbourhoods of relegation. The Rodney King affair was eclipsed a few years later by the so-called Rampart Division scandal, in which seventy officers from a special gang unit were found to engage routinely in gross criminal misconduct and abuse (deliberate beatings and shootings of criminal suspects, writing false reports and lying in court, and planting drugs and guns on gang members). As a result, scores of criminal convictions were overturned, and the city of Los Angeles entered into a consent decree with the US Department of Justice granting a federal judge the power to monitor the LA Police Department for a period of five years.

[24] A tazer gun is a hand-held electro-shock weapon. It allows police to neutralize potential or actual assailants by subjecting them to a powerful electric jolt from a distance. It can easily be abused since it leaves few if any external physical traces. Its deployment by police departments in the United States has been controversial: several studies have shown that the supposedly 'safe' electric shocks have caused the death of dozens of targets.

Political responses to the return of urban marginality and collective violence have varied significantly from country to country depending on national ideologies of citizenship, state structures and capacities, and political conjuncture. They span the *spectrum between the criminalization of poverty* and dispossessed populations, at one end, and *politicization of the problem* via the collective renegotiation of social and economic rights, at the other. The two tendencies, symbolized by the prison and the ballot box, can be observed to operate simultaneously in all three societies considered here, albeit in different combinations and trained on different categories, as various fractions of their respective ruling classes vie to steer state policy towards one or the other pole.[25] No country has fully avoided increased recourse to the criminal justice apparatus (irrespective of the evolution of crime), and all have had to reconsider some citizenship rights and the range of social entitlements, whether to restrict or expand them selectively. Yet it remains that, overall, the question has been most fully politicized in France and most completely depoliticized in the United States, with the United Kingdom occupying a sort of median way between these two paths.[26]

Through a decade of urban strife, the French government passed legislation creating a guaranteed minimum income for those fallen through the cracks of the work and welfare grid. It expanded unemployment benefits and training schemes for unskilled youths; and it established a mechanism to transfer wealth from rich to poor cities (albeit a very limited one). The state also deployed a comprehensive urban redevelopment programme officially designed to improve conditions first in 400 and then in 751 'sensitive neighbourhoods'

---

[25] I have shown elsewhere how, over the decade that followed this initial diagnosis (1993), the solution consisting in penalizing social insecurity through the glorification and amplification of the penal state has diffused and generalized across the First World and even parts of the Second World (Wacquant 1999).

[26] The following characterization of patterns of policy reactions to urban marginality and disorder in the advanced societies is an analytic simplification that exaggerates the homogeneity and consistency of state responses in each country. One would need to distinguish in each case between different levels (central and local) and domains (ideological, legislative, judiciary, welfare, etc.) of response as well as between different sites of intervention (e.g., homelessness or collective violence), and between target groups (foreigners or citizens, welfare recipients or criminal offenders, etc.). Because states are highly differentiated and imperfectly co-ordinated organizational machineries, they often engage in policies that are either inconsistent or operate at cross purposes with one another. In addition, there exists a yawning gap between the proclaimed purposes and effective aims of a given policy, its bureaucratic implementation, and its effects at ground level.

throughout the country.[27] Renewed government activism was officialized by the nomination, at the end of 1990, of a Minister of the City (with rank of state minister, highest in the French administrative hierarchy) and by the political commitment of both President and Prime Minister to winning the battle of 'urban renewal'. Over the ensuing decade, new plans kept being concocted, and layers of measures added, combining spatially targeted interventions in the areas of housing rehabilitation, crime prevention, education, transportation and access to culture. The number of cities involved in such state-sponsored 'contracts' grew from 27 in 1977 to 247 in 2000. Yet urban disturbances continued, if in muffled fashion, as testified for instance by a string of incidents in the declining public housing estates of Argenteuil, Sartrouville and Mantes-la-Jolie in the Parisian periphery in 1994. Gradually, collective clashes between *cité* youths and the police have become a routine feature of life in the declining Red Belt – barely noticed by the media and tacitly accepted by city managers, unless and until they jump outside their usual range in sheer intensity and geographic spread, as they did in November 2005. The so-called social treatment of persistent urban marginality by means of 'urban policy' aimed chiefly at housing may alleviate some of its symptoms and please state elites, who can thereby continue to pay lip service to the doctrine of republican equality. It does nothing to attack its root causes: the fragmentation of wage labour feeding unemployment and casual employment.[28]

The response of the American authorities to the Los Angeles upheaval took a diametrically opposed tack. Once open rioting was checked by the prompt proclamation of a state of emergency, putting military 'boots on the ground', and aggressive police reaction, the first priority of the Bush Administration was to send a team of special prosecutors and to boost funds available to bring the full force of the law to bear on the thousands arrested during the disturbance. (A highly publicized and equally unsuccessful effort was made to identify and charge suspects of looting and assorted crimes based on evidence adduced by the thousands of hours of amateur video shot

---

[27] See Paugam's *La Société française et ses pauvres* (1993) for a detailed discussion of the centrepiece of this policy, viz., the creation of 'a national guaranteed minimum income' programme, its political rationale, foibles and actual impact, and Bachmann and Le Guennec (1996) for a recapitulation of a half-century of French urban policy.

[28] By the close of the 1990s, the predictable failure of 'urban policy' to remedy relegation in the French urban periphery had led the central government to roll out an aggressive policing campaign to contain its ramifying effects (Wacquant 1999).

during the riots.) Mayor Bradley loudly called for the hiring of more police officers and the building of more jails. The Los Angeles District Attorney stridently announced that the county would seek a minimum sentence of one year in prison for all those caught committing disturbance-related offences. And the US Attorney General William Barr used the riots as yet another pretext to push his platform of prison expansion as 'the solution to crime'. The local, state and federal goverments thus joined in accelerating penal repression, even though the surging incarceration rate in Los Angeles, California and the nation had already been shown to have had no detectable impact on stagnating crime rates (Petersilia 1993).[29]

Unlike in cases of meteorological disasters (such as the hurricanes and floods that periodically ravage the coastal areas of the South or the plains of the Midwest), in which the federal government extends prompt and generous material and financial assistance to victims (who are essentially property owners of the middle and upper classes), in South-Central Los Angeles Washington was content to co-ordinate charity relief and to encourage private rebuilding and reinvestment efforts. And, although the riot had erupted at the outset of the 1992 presidential campaign, the fate of the urban poor was not deemed worthy of mention by any of the three major candidates for the White House. Stubborn refusal to acknowledge the structural mooring and political import of the uprising gave warrant to continue the policy of state neglect that helped provoke it in the first place (Johnson et al. 1993), and all but guaranteed that the human toll – in terms of fear and despair, crime, incarceration and excess mortality – exacted by urban marginalization would continue to mount unchecked.

The United Kingdom positioned itself about midway between these two poles of politicization and criminalization. The inclination to attribute disorder to a predominantly black 'criminal minority' is always strong; yet, even the staunchly *laissez-faire* governments of Thatcher and Major decided to re-establish a degree of state oversight

[29] Another indicator of the American emphasis on the penal sanction of urban disorders is the lopsided approach to narcotics control in the inner city: two-thirds of the 12 billion dollars expended annually by the federal government in its much-vaunted 'War on Drugs' around the turn of the 1990s was allotted to law enforcement, filling custodial establishments to overflowing with petty drug consumers and dealers, while education and treatment services fell behind for lack of funding. The result was a quadrupling of the population incarcerated for drug offences in a decade with no detectable impact on the street commerce and use of narcotics, and a grossly disparate impact on lower-class African-American men (Tonry 1994).

over urban zoning and housing improvement (Cameron and Doling 1994). At the local level, many British cities opted for a two-pronged approach, elaborating more effective policing techniques in order to regain control of the streets at the very outset of a putative riot, on the one hand, and engaging in establishing connections and building trust between the forces of order and the resident populations (under the aegis of 'community policing'), on the other. After the Handsworth riots, for instance, the Birmingham police developed a series of indicators of tension designed to pre-empt the outbreak of violence, and they were able, in collaboration with neighbourhood leaders, to keep young men off the streets when incidents threatened again. But one wonders how long such policies of 'papering over' widening social cleavages can be expected to dampen discontent, especially when the state policy of 'urban regeneration' fostering market mechanisms deepens inequalities within as well as between cities (Le Galès and Parkinson 1993).

Coda: a challenge to citizenship

The popular disorders and urban protests that have shaken the advanced societies of the capitalist West over the past two decades find their roots in the epochal transformation of their economies (deregulation of financial markets, desocialization of wage work, revamping of labour to impose 'flexibility'), the social polarization of their cities, and state policies that have more or less overtly promoted corporate expansion over social redistribution and commodification to the detriment of social protection.[30] The ruling classes and government elites of rich nations have, to varying degrees, proved unable or unwilling to stem the rise of inequality and marginality. And they have failed to curb the social and spatial cumulation of economic hardship, hopelessness and stigma in the deteriorating working-class neighbourhoods of the dual metropolis. The conjugation of (real or perceived) ethnic divisions and deproletarianization, in declining

---

[30] As Mollenkopf and Castells (1991: 404) note in the case of the United States, 'the public sector did not play a redistributive and corrective role but amplified the trends toward income inequality, spatial segregation, and lack of adequate services for a large part of the population.' This observation applies in the main to British public policy during that period, though starting from a stronger cushioning role for public institutions. The record for France is more mixed on this count, with different sectors of state action evolving in opposite directions, and indicators of segregation and inequality changing more slowly and modestly.

urban districts deprived of the organizational means needed to forge
an emergent identity and formulate collective demands in the political field, promises to produce more unrest and to pose a daunting
challenge to the institution of modern citizenship for decades to
come.

Citizenship, in T. H. Marshall's ([1949] 1964) famous formulation, serves essentially to mitigate the class divisions generated by the
marketplace: it is its extension, from the civil to the political to the
socioeconomic realm, that has 'altered the pattern of social inequality' and helped make advanced society relatively pacified and democratic by historical standards.[31] During the postwar era of steady and
protected growth, well-bounded and sovereign nation-states were
able to establish a clear separation between members and non-
members and to guarantee a relatively high degree of congruence
between the basic dimensions of membership – with the spectacular
exception of African Americans in US society. Today, that ability
and congruence are both deeply reduced, so that the hitherto hidden
fractures of the space of citizenship are appearing in full light. As the
external boundaries and the (real or imagined) internal homogeneity
of advanced societies are eroded, from above by high-velocity capital
flows and from below by the confluence of the decomposition of the
industrial working class and increased immigrant inflows, it becomes
increasingly clear that citizenship is not a status achieved or granted
once and equally for all, but a contentious and uneven 'instituted
process' (to use the language of Karl Polanyi) that must continually
be struggled for and secured anew.

Thus the question facing First World countries at the threshold of
the new millennium is whether their polities have the capacity to
prevent the further contraction and fragmentation of the sphere of
citizenship fuelled by the desocialization of labour and, correspond-
ingly, what new mediating institutions they need to invent to provide
full access to and active participation in the city, in the double sense
of urban setting and *polis*. Failing which, we may witness not only
continued urban disorder, collective violence and ethnoracial conflict
(actual or imagined) at the heart of the advanced societies, but a
protracted process of societal fission and a capillary ramification of

---

[31] Turner (1986) makes a terse but strong case for the significance of citizenship in
dampening the built-in contradictions of advanced society and offers an insightful
critical exegesis of Marshall's influential thesis. For a provocative historical recon-
ceptualization of citizenship as an 'instituted process' *à la* Polanyi, see Somers (1993).
An exemplary study of cross-national variation in patterns of immigrant incorporation due to differences in the political definition of citizenship is Brubaker (1992).

inequalities and insecurities at the bottom of the order of classes and places.

It is urgent, then, for both scientific and political reasons, to properly diagnose the emerging forms of urban marginality coalescing in districts of dereliction since the breakup of the Fordist–Keynesian compact, which is what this book sets out to do in three steps. The first is to return to the United States, the urban backdrop and model against which European developments have been consistently set and evaluated, to dissect the involution of the black American ghetto after the peaking of the progressive movements of the 1960s. The second is to compare and contrast the forms and experience of persistent poverty in the US metropolis and the French city, so as to examine empirically and clarify theoretically the thesis of the transcontinental convergence of regimes of marginality. The third is to characterize properly the logics of urban polarization from below and to clarify the policy options available to stem it on the threshold of the twenty-first century.

Part I

From Communal Ghetto to Hyperghetto

2

The State and Fate of the Dark Ghetto at Century's Close

> Tryin' to survive, tryin' to stay alive
> The ghetto, talkin' 'bout the ghetto
> Even though the streets are bumpy, lights burnt out
> Dope fiends die with a pipe in their mouth
> Old school buddies not doin' it right
> Every day it's the same and it's the same every night
> I wouldn't shoot you bro' but I'd shoot that fool
> If he played me close and tried to test my cool
> Every day I wonder just how I'll die
> The only thing I know is how to survive.
>
> Too Short, 'The Ghetto'[1]

Twenty years after the uprisings that lit fires of rage in the black sections of the American metropolis in the mid-1960s, the ghetto returned to the frontline of national issues. Only, this time, the spectacular turmoil that tore through the African-American community of big cities in revolt against white authority had given way to the 'slow rioting' (Curtis 1985) of endemic crime, collective destitution and internal social decay. On the nightly news, the scenes of white policemen unleashing state violence upon peaceful black demonstrators demanding recognition of their elemental rights have been replaced by grisly reports of drive-by shootings, 'welfare dependency' and the crisis of inner-city 'teen pregnancy'. Black ministers, politicians and concerned parents still agitate and demonstrate at the local level, but

[1] From the album *Short Dog's in the House*, 1990, Zomba Recording Corp. by Leroy Hutson, Donna Hathaway, Al Eaton and Todd Shaw, copyright © 1990 Don Pow Music; administered by Peer International Music Corporation, all rights reserved; used by permission.

now their pleas and marches are less often directed at the government than at the drug dealers and gangs who have turned so many ghetto neighbourhoods into macabre theatres of dread and death.

From race riots to silent riots

The vision of Negro looters and Black Power activists reclaiming forceful control over their community's fate (Boskin 1970), riding the crest of a wave of racial pride and self-assertion, has given way to the fearsome imagery of a vile 'underclass', a term purporting to denote a new segment of the black poor allegedly characterized by the behavioural deficiency and cultural deviance of its members (Auletta 1982; Sawhill 1989). This menacing urban hydra is personi-fied, on the masculine side, by the defiant and aggressive 'gang banger' and, on the feminine side, by the dissolute and passive 'welfare mother', two twin figures whose (self-)destructive behaviour is felt to represent the one a physical threat and the other a moral assault on American values.

The surging social movements that accompanied the mobilization of the black community and helped lift its hopes during the decade of the 1960s (McAdam 1981; A. Morris 1984) have receded and, with them, the country's commitment to combating racial inequality. This ebbing is well reflected in the changing idiom of public debate on the ghetto. As the 'War on Poverty' of Lyndon B. Johnson gave way to the 'War on Welfare' of Ronald Reagan and his successors (Katz 1989), the question of the societal connection between racial domination, class inequality and poverty was reformulated in terms of the personal motivations, family norms and values of the residents of the 'inner city', with welfare playing the part of the villain. The goals of public policy were downgraded accordingly: rather than pursue the eradication of poverty – the grandiose target that the Great Society programme was set to reach by 1976 as a tribute to the nation's bicentennial – and the resolute reduction of racial dis-parities, at century's close the state is content to oversee the contain-ment of the first in crumbling urban enclaves reserved to lower-class blacks (and in the prisons that were built at an astounding pace during the 1980s to absorb the most disruptive of their occupants) and a policy of 'benign neglect' of the second.[2]

---

[2] Going against the recommendations of the Kerner Commission (1968), which advocated massive state intervention to dismantle the structure of racial inequalities

By the same token, the focus of social science research shifted from the urban colour line to the individual defects of the black poor, from the ghetto as a mechanism of ethnoracial domination and economic oppression (Clark 1965; Liebow 1967; Blauner 1972), and the structural political and economic impediments blocking the full participation of urban proletarians in the national collectivity, to the 'pathologies' of the 'underclass' said to inhabit it and to the punitive measures that must urgently be deployed to minimize their abusive resort to public resources and to push them on to the peripheral segments of a fast-expanding low-wage labour market (e.g., Ricketts and Sawhill 1988; Mead 1989).[3]

But this drift in the symbolic representation and political treatment of the ghetto cannot efface the fact that the ominous forewarning of the 1968 National Advisory Commission on Civil Disorders (Kerner Commission 1968, 1988: 396, 389), charged with scrutinizing the causes and implications of the riots of 1964–1968, has become reality: 'The country [has moved] toward two societies, separate and unequal' as a consequence of 'the accelerating segregation of low-income, disadvantaged Negroes within the ghettos of the largest American cities.' While the black middle class experienced spectacular growth and real advances – albeit fragile ones, since they rest largely on governmental efforts and (secondarily) on increased legal pressure upon corporate employers (Collins 1983; Landry 1987; Son et al. 1989), the poverty of black urbanites has grown more intense, more tenacious and more concentrated than it was in the 1960s (Wilson 1996). And the economic, social and cultural distance

---

inherited from the era of legal segregation, Nixon's Under Secretary for Labour Daniel Patrick Moynihan (1969: 9) had called for 'a period of benign neglect' of the racial question, on the pretext that the 1960s had seen a 'breakthrough' so that 'in quantitative terms, which can be trusted, the American Negro is making extraordinary advances'. Although it was immediately refuted by social researchers (e.g., Cook 1970), this thesis served as guiding principle for federal policies over the ensuing three decades.

[3] Thus research on 'urban poverty' during the 1980s was fixated on issues of family, welfare and deviance, at the cost of neglecting both the deepening class disparities and the continuing racial division that properly characterize American society and the political shifts that led to the implementation of an array of public policies (in education, housing, health, urban development, criminal justice, etc.) that have gravely curtailed the life chances of ghetto residents. The issues of family structure, race and poverty were conflated to the point of becoming synonymous with each other (Zinn 1989), as if they were linked by some congenital causality. Likewise, urban decline and race became amalgamated (R. Franklin 1991: ch. 4), so that the adjective 'urban' has become a euphemism to designate issues related to poor blacks and other subordinate ethnoracial categories present in the city.

between the people locked in the vestiges of the historic ghetto and the rest of society has reached an amplitude unprecedented in recent American history as well as unknown in other advanced societies.

Farewell to the eternal ghetto

Is this to say, borrowing the words of historian Gilbert Osofsky (1968: 244), that there is an 'unending and tragic sameness about black life in the metropolis', that of the 'enduring ghetto', which perpetuates itself unchanged across the decades, unaffected by societal trends and political forces as momentous as the onset of a postindustrial economy, the enactment of broad civil rights legislation and affirmative action programmes, and the reorganization of metropolitan space under the twin pressures of suburban deconcentration and central-city gentrification? Quite the contrary. For beyond the persistence of economic subordination and racial entrapment, the ghetto of the 1980s and 1990s is quite different from its predecessor of the mid-twentieth century. The *communal ghetto* of the immediate postwar era, compact, sharply bounded and comprising the full complement of black classes bound together by a unified collective consciousness, a near-complete social division of labour, and broad-based agencies of mobilization and representation, has been superseded by what we may call the *hyperghetto* of the fin de siècle (Wacquant 1989), whose spatial configuration, institutional and demographic makeup, structural position and function in urban society are quite novel. Furthermore, the separation of the ghetto from American society is only apparent: it pertains to the level of the 'life-world' and not the 'system', to use a conceptual distinction elaborated by Habermas ([1981] 1984). It refers to the concrete experiences and relationships of its occupants, not to the underlying ties that firmly anchor them in the metropolitan ensemble – albeit in exclusionary fashion. Indeed, I shall argue in this and the next two chapters that there exist deep-seated causal and functional linkages between the transformation of the ghetto and structural changes that have redrawn the visage of the US economy, social space and field of power in reaction to the shock of the progressive movements of the 1960s.

Instead of repeating or extending previous analyses of racial domination in the Fordist–Keynesian era as if it were some timeless institutional contraption, we must *historicize the state and function of the ghetto* in the US metropolis and reach beyond its physical perimeter to elucidate its fate after the climax of the Civil Rights movement. Dissecting the economic and political forces that have combined to turn them into veritable domestic 'Bantustans' reveals that ghettos are not autonomous sociospatial constellations that contain within themselves the principle of their evolution. It demonstrates likewise that the parlous state of America's Black Belt at century's end is not the simple mechanical result of deindustrialization, demographic shifts or of a skills or spatial 'mismatch' between the supply and demand for labour governed by ecological processes, and still less the spawn of the coming of a 'new underclass', *in statu nascendi* or already 'crystallized' into a permanent fixture of the American urban landscape (Loewenstein 1985; Nathan 1987; Marks 1991), whether defined by its deviant behaviours, income level, cultural proclivities or social isolation. Rather, it is the product of a novel *political* articulation of racial cleavage, class inequality and urban space in both dominant discourse and objective reality.

The ghetto as instrument of exclusionary closure (as defined by Max Weber [[1918–20] 1968]) is still with us, but it is a different type of ghetto: its internal makeup has changed along with its environment and with the institutional processes that simultaneously chain it to the rest of American society and ensure its dependent and marginal location within it. To understand these differences, what the ghetto is and means to both insiders and outsiders at century's close, one must sweep aside the scholarly tale of the 'underclass' that has crowded the stage of the resurging debate on the intersection of race and poverty in the city and reconstruct instead the linked relations between the transformation of everyday life and social relations inside the racialized urban core, on the one hand, and the restructuring of the system of forces, economic, social and political, that account for the particular configuration of caste and class of which the hyperghetto is the materialization. Accordingly, this chapter gives pride of place to the *external* factors that have reshaped the material and symbolic territory within which ghetto residents (re)define themselves, and it addresses the *internal* production of its specific social order and consciousness only indirectly. This emphasis is not born of the belief that structural determination constitutes the alpha and omega of group formation and trajectory, far from it. It rests, rather, on two premises, the one theoretical and the other empirical.

The first premise is that elucidation of the objective conditions under which a collectivity comes to be constructed and identity asserted in the metropolitan core constitutes a socio-logical prerequisite to the analysis of the *Lebenswelt* of the ghetto and the forms of practice and signification embedded in it. It is in this objective space of material and symbolic positions and resources that are rooted the strategies deployed by ghetto residents to figure out who they are and who they can be. While it is true that such an analysis remains unfinished absent the complement of an 'indigenous perspective' (advocated by Aldon Morris (1984)) throwing light on the complexities of signification and action from below (or, to be more precise, from within), it remains that the populist celebration of 'the value of blackness' and the richness of 'oppositional black culture' (hooks 1992: 17) offers neither a substitute nor a viable launching pad for a rigorous assessment of the state and fate of the ghetto after the close of the Fordist–Keynesian era.

The second premiss of this chapter is that the reality of the ghetto as a physical, social and symbolic place in American society is, whether one likes it or not, being shaped – indeed imposed – from the outside, as its residents are increasingly stripped of the means to produce their own collective and individual identities. A brief contrast between the opposed provenance, uses and semantic charge of the vocabularies of 'soul' and 'underclass' is instructive in this respect. The notion of soul, which gained wide appeal during the ghetto uprisings of the 1960s, was a 'folk conception of the lower-class urban Negro's own "national character"' (Hannerz 1968: 454). Produced from within for in-group consumption, it served as a symbol of solidarity and a badge of personal and group pride. By contrast, 'underclass' status is assigned wholly from the outside (and from above); it is forced upon its putative 'members' by specialists in symbolic production – journalists, politicians, academics and government experts – for purposes of control and disciplining (in Foucault's sense of the term, entailing both subjection and subjectivation) and without the slightest concern for the self-understandings of those who are arbitrarily lumped into this analytical fiction. Whereas the folk concept of soul, as part of an 'internal ghetto dialogue' toward an indigenous reassessment of black identity (Keil 1966), was appraisive, the idiom of underclass is derogatory, a negative label that nobody claims or invokes except to pin it on to others. That even 'insurgent' black intellectuals such as Cornel West (1994) should embrace the idiom of underclass is revealing of the degree to which the ghetto has become an *alien object*, at once strange and estranged, on the social and symbolic landscape of the United States.

Three preliminary caveats

Three caveats are in order before we draw a portrait of social conditions and everyday life in the black ghetto of Chicago at century's end. First, one must stress that the ghetto is not simply a topographic entity or an aggregation of poor families and individuals but an *institutional form*, that is, a distinctive, spatially based, concatenation of mechanisms of *ethnoracial closure and control*. Briefly put, a ghetto can be characterized ideal-typically as a bounded, ethnically uniform sociospatial formation born of the forcible relegation of a negatively typed population – such as Jews in the principalities of Renaissance Europe and African Americans in the United States during the age of Fordist consolidation – to a reserved territory within which this population develops an array of specific institutions operating both as a functional substitute for, and as a protective buffer against, the dominant institutions of the encompassing society (Wacquant 1991). The fact that most ghettos have *historically* been places of widespread and sometimes acute material misery does not mean that a ghetto is necessarily poor – certainly, the 'Bronzeville' of the 1940s (as residents of Chicago's ghetto called it then) was more prosperous than the vast majority of Southern black communities – or that it has to be uniformly deprived.[4] This implies that the ghetto is not a social monolith. Notwithstanding their extreme dilapidation, many inner-city neighbourhoods still contain a modicum of occupational and familial variety. Neither is the ghetto entirely barren: amidst its desolate landscape, scattered islets of relative economic and social stability persist, which offer fragile but crucial launching pads for the strategies of coping and escape of its residents; and new forms of sociability continually develop in the cracks of the crumbling system.

Second, one must resist the tendency to treat the ghetto as an alien space, to see in it only what deviates from the common norm, in short to *exoticize it*, as proponents of the scholarly myth of the 'underclass' have been wont to do in their grisly tales of 'antisocial' behaviour that resonate so well with journalistic reports (from which they are often drawn in the first place) and with ordinary class and ethnoracial prejudice against poor blacks. A rudimentary sociology of

[4] Conversely, not all low-income areas are ghettos, however extreme the destitution of their residents. Think of declining white cities of the deindustrializing Midwest such as Kenosha (Wisconsin) or Pontiac (Michigan) in the 1980s, rural counties of the Mississipi delta, Native American reservations, or large portions of the United States during the Great Depression. To label as 'ghetto' any area exhibiting a high rate or concentration of poverty is not only arbitrary (what is the appropriate cut-off point and for what unit of measurement?). It robs the term of its historical meaning and empties it of its sociological contents, which thwarts the investigation of the precise mechanisms and criteria whereby the exclusion of which it is the product operates (Wacquant 2002b).

sociology would show that most descriptions of the 'underclass' reveal more about the *relation* of the analyst to the motley populations it designates, and about his or her racial and class preconceptions, fears and fantasies, than they do about their putative object; and that representations of 'underclass areas' bear the distinctive mark of the ostensibly 'neutral' (that is, dominant) gaze set upon them from a distance by analysts who, all too often, have never set foot in them.[5] Contrary to appearances reinforced by the biased perception of the media and certain sociology inspired by them, ghetto-dwellers are not a distinctive breed of men and women in need of a special denomination; they are ordinary people trying to make a life and to improve their lot as best they can under the unusually oppressive and depressed circumstances thrust upon them. And while their cultural codes and patterns of conduct may, from the standpoint of a hurried outside commentator, appear peculiar, quixotic or even 'aberrant' (an adjective so often reiterated in discourses on the post-Fordist ghetto that it has become virtually pleonasmatic with it), upon close and methodical observation, they turn out to obey a social rationality that takes due stock of past experiences and is well suited to the constraints and facilitations of their proximate milieu.[6]

The third caveat stresses, against the core assumption of American poverty research, that the contemporary ghetto does not suffer from 'social disorganization' – another moralizing concept that would deserve to be retired from social science, considering the rampant abuse to which it has been put (Wacquant 1997a). Rather, it is *organized differently* in response to the relentless press of economic necessity, generalized social insecurity, abiding racial hostility or indifference, and political denigration. We shall see in the first part of this book that the hyperghetto comprises a particular type of social order, premissed upon the rigid racial segmentation of space, 'orga-

---

[5] Perhaps it was necessary, to produce this odd discursive formation woven of moral sermonizing and political incantations dressed up as empirical investigation – whose primary purpose is to insulate and shelter 'mainstream' society (another equally vague designation) from the threat and taint of poor blacks by symbolically extirpating them from the national body – for the proponents of the 'underclass' legend to stand studiously removed from the ghetto in order to 'theorize' it from afar and from above, through the reassuring sights of their bureaucratic research apparatus. One indicator among many of this distance: of the twenty-seven authors who contributed to the canonical volume bringing together the papers presented at a major conference on the topic pithily entitled *The Urban Underclass* (Jencks and Peterson 1991), *only one* had carried out extensive firsthand observation inside the ghetto.

[6] I tried to demonstrate this elsewhere by analysing the everyday worldview and income-generating strategies of a professional 'hustler' who works the streets on the South Side of Chicago (Wacquant 1998).

nized around an intense competition for, and conflict over, the scarce resources' that suffuse an environment replete with 'social predators' (Sánchez-Jankowski 1991: 22, 183–92), and constituted as inferior and inferiorizing by the ordinary functioning of the political and bureaucratic fields. Relatedly, those who dwell in it are not part of a separate group closed in on itself, as advocates of the 'underclass' thesis would have us believe (in spite of the absence of data showing a change in patterns of recruitment and mobility at the bottom of the class structure). They belong, rather, to unskilled and socially disqualified fractions of the black working class, by virtue of their unstable position at the margins of the wage-labour sphere as well as their kinship links, social ties and cultural connections to the other components of the African-American community (Aschenbrenner 1975; Pétonnet 1985).[7]

From the 'communal ghetto' of the 1950s to the 'hyperghetto' of the 1990s

The process of black ghettoization – from initial spatial confinement in a reserved perimeter on pain of violence, piling up and then expansion on the heels of white flight, followed by the formation of a parallel network of institutions enveloping the life of its residents in the manner of a shield but also a trap, leading in turn to increases in joblessness, crime and assorted social dislocations – is old and well documented. It goes back to the original formation of the Black Belt as an institution of *ethnoracial exclusion* in the early decades of the twentieth century.[8] It is less well known that blacks are the only

[7] In an overlooked network-analytic study, Melvin Oliver (1988) provides a suggestive portrait of the urban black community as linked clusters of interpersonal ties belying its common representation as a hotbed of social disaffiliation and pathologies. He shows that the residents of Los Angeles's historic ghetto of Watts and those of the newer segregated middle-class district of Crenshaw–Baldwin Hills have similar network structures (as characterized by size, relational context, spatial distribution, density, strandedness and reciprocity) and that extralocal ties with kin are equally prevalent in both areas.

[8] See Spear (1968), Philpott (1978), and Drake and Cayton ([1945] 1993) in the case of Chicago's ghetto, and Kusmer (1986) and Franklin (1980) for a broader historical overview of black incorporation into the cities of the industrial North in the Fordist age. It is not possible here to give an adequate treatment of the historical roots of the trajectory of the dark ghetto in the *longue durée* of its lifespan. Suffice it to emphasize that, although its motor causes are situated outside it, the transformation of the ghetto is, as with every social form, mediated by its internal structure, so that a full elucidation of its recent evolution should start a century ago, in the decades of its incubation.

category to have experienced ghettoization in American society. So-called ethnic whites (that is, European immigrants of ethnonational origins other than the Anglo-Saxon founders of the country: Italians, Irish, Polish, Slavs, Jews, etc.) initially lived, for most of them, in heterogenous *ethnic clusters* which, though they may have been slums, were temporary and, for the most part, voluntary way-stations on the road to integration into a composite white society. They were not, *pace* Wirth (1927), ghettos in any sense other than an impressionistic one. Segregation in them was partial and based on a mixture of class, nationality and citizenship. The confinement of blacks, on the other hand, was (and still is) unique in that only African Americans were constrained to reside in zones where 'segregation was practically total, essentially unvoluntary, and also perpetual' (Philpott 1978: p. xvi).[9] Moreover, the forced separation of blacks spilled beyond housing to encompass basic institutional arenas, from schooling and employment to public services, political representation, and the sphere of intimate contacts, which caused them to develop a near-complete parallel social structure staffed by and turned toward blacks without counterpart among 'ethnic whites'.

What is distinctive about the current phase of black marginaliza-tion in the metropolis is, first, that the ghetto has become spatially *decentred* as well as institutionally *differentiated*, split, as it were, between a subproletarian core that deteriorates as it expands, on the one hand, and satellite working-class and bourgeois neighbourhoods located along the internal periphery of the city and, increasingly, in segregated suburbs (often contiguous with the historic Black Belt), on the other. The second novel feature of black ghettoization in post-Fordist America is its sheer scale and 'the intensity of the collapse at the centre of the ghetto', as well as the fact that 'the cycle still oper-ates two decades after fair housing laws have been in effect' (Orfield 1985: 163). Indeed, it is in the very period when legal reforms were presumed to bring about its amelioration that the heart of the Black Belt in the American metropolis has been undermined by accelerat-ing physical degradation, street violence and endemic insecurity, as well as by levels of economic exclusion and social hardship compa-rable only to those of the worst years of the Great Depression.

[9] For instance, in 1930, when the all-black South Side ghetto already contained more than 90 per cent of the city's African-American population, Chicago's 'Little Ireland' was a hodgepodge of twenty-five nationalities composed of only one-third Irish persons and housing a bare 3 per cent of the city's residents of Irish descent (Philpott 1978: 141–2).

Physical decay and danger in the urban core

Walk down 63rd Street in Woodlawn, on the South Side of Chicago, within a stone's throw of the University of Chicago campus, along what used to be the one of the city's most vibrant commercial strips, and you will discover a lunar landscape replicated across the black ghettos of the United States[10] – in Harlem and the Brownsville district of Brooklyn in New York City, in north Philadelphia, on the East Side of Cleveland and Detroit, or in Boston's Roxbury and Paradise Valley in Pittsburgh. Abandoned buildings, vacant lots strewn with debris and garbage, broken sidewalks, boarded-up storefront churches, and the charred remains of shops line up miles and miles of decaying neighbourhoods left to rot by the authorities since the big riots of the 1960s.

On the morrow of World War II, 63rd Street was nicknamed the 'Miracle Mile' by local merchants vying for space and a piece of the pie.[11] The neighbourhood counted nearly 800 businesses and not a single vacant lot in an 18-by-4-block area. Woodlawn was overflowing with life as people streamed in from the four corners of the city, composing throngs so dense at rush hour that one was literally swept off one's feet upon getting out of the elevated train station. Large restaurants were teeming with clients around the clock; no fewer than five banks and six hotels shared the two main thoroughfares near the intersection with Cottage Grove Avenue; and cinemas, taverns and ballrooms never seemed to empty. Here is a description of the street given to me by the only white shopkeeper left from that era in August of 1991:

> It looks like Berlin after the war and that's sad. The street is bombed out, decaying. Seventy-five per cent of it is vacant. It's very unfortunate but it seems that all that really grows here is liquor stores. And they're not contributin' anything to the community: (groaning) it's all 'take, take, take!' Very depressing. (He sighs heavily) It's an area devoid of hope, it's an area devoid of investments. People don't come into Woodlawn.

[10] Unless otherwise indicated, observations and quotes from interviews come from fieldwork I conducted on Chicago's South Side between 1988 and 1991 in the course of an ethnographic study of the culture and economy of boxing in the ghetto.

[11] The nickname 'Miracle Mile' was intended to echo the 'Magnificent Mile', the public moniker of the section of Michigan Avenue running north of the Chicago river parallel to Lake Michigan, the beacon of tourism where city landmarks and upscale shops are concentrated.

Now the street's nickname has taken an ironic and bitter twist, for it takes a miracle for a business to survive on it. Not a single theatre, bank, jazz or blues club, or repair shop has outlived the 1970s. The lumber yards, print shops, garages and light manufacturing enterprises that used to dot the neighbourhood have disappeared as well (during the three years of my fieldwork, two gas stations located within ten blocks of each other on 63rd Street went belly up, as did two dozen stores). Fewer than ninety commercial establishments remain, most of them tiny eating places, food stores huddled behind heavy metal grates, small beauty parlours and cheap laundromats, barber shops, apparel outlets and secondhand furniture stores, not to mention the ubiquitous 'currency exchanges' and liquor stores also operating as lotto stations, all of which employ at best a handful of workers.[12]

Yet the most significant brute fact of every daily life in the fin-de-siècle ghetto is without contest the extraordinary *prevalence of physical danger and the acute sense of insecurity* that pervade its streets. Violence is a vexed aspect of the politics of race and class in America that is difficult to broach without activating the sordid images of stereotypical media descriptions of lawlessness. Yet ethnographic fieldwork conducted on Chicago's South Side convinced me that any account of the hyperghetto must start with it, because of its acute experiential salience and its wide reverberations across the social fabric. At the same time, one must stress that this violence is, in its forms and effects, quite different from what journalistic accounts suggest, in that it is at once patterned, routinized and entropic. What is more, such internecine violence 'from below' must be analysed not as an expression of the senseless 'pathology' of residents of the hyperghetto but as a function of the degree of penetration and mode of regulation of this territory by the state. It is a reasoned response (in the double sense of echo and retort) to various kinds of violence 'from above' and an intelligible by-product of the policy of abandonment of the urban core.[13]

---

[12] A currency exchange is an outlet providing retail banking services for the poor. It makes up for the absence of mainstream financial institutions in deprived neighbourhoods by enabling residents to cash cheques, pay utility and telephone bills, and effect money transfers to third parties, but also to access certain public services that the local state subcontracts to them (e.g., payment of the yearly car tax). All these operations are charged at prohibitive rates which can reach 10 per cent of the sums cashed or transferred. The presence of currency exchanges is an excellent visual indicator that one is in or near a district of urban destitution.

[13] This point is an extension of the argument on rioting made in ch. 1 and further elaborated in ch. 4 *infra*.

Between 1980 and 1985 alone, violent crime reported to the Chicago police grew fourfold to reach the astonishing rate of 1,300 offences per 1,000 residents. Most of these crimes were committed by and upon residents of the ghetto. Over 70 per cent of the 849 homicide victims recorded in Chicago in 1990 were young African-American men, most of them shot to death in poor all-black neighbourhoods. Mortality in the segregated core of the country's major cities reached 'rates that justify special consideration analogous to that given to "natural disaster areas"' (McCord and Freeman 1990: 174). As a result, males in Bangladesh had a higher probability of survival after age 35 than their counterparts of Harlem in the early 1990s. The availability of handguns, lasting exclusion from wage labour and pervasiveness of the drug trade have combined to alter the rules of masculine confrontation on the streets in ways that fuel the escalation of deadly assault. A former leader of the Black Gangster Disciples muses:

> See, back then, if two gang guys wanna fight, they let'em two guys fight *one-on-one*. But it's not like that now: if you wanna fight me, I'mma git me a gun an' shoot you, you see what I'm sayin'? Whenever you got a gun, tha's the first thin' you think about – not about *peace treaties* an' let dese two guys fight and settle their disagreement as real grown men. It's *scary now* because dese guys, they don' have – (his voice rising in a spike of indignation) I mean they don't have *no value for life* – *no value*!

Residences are scarcely safer than the streets. The windows and doors of apartments and houses are commonly barricaded behind heavy metal gates and burglar bars. Public facilities and spaces are not spared. Elderly ghetto-dwellers nostalgically evoke a time when they used to sleep in municipal parks in the summer, rolled into mosquito nets, or on rooftops and balconies in search of relief from the summer heat. Nowadays, most parks are 'no-go areas', especially after nightfall. Many are off limits even to the youths who live in their immediate vicinity because they fall within the territory of a rival gang, so that to go and play in them would amount to risking one's life. Buses of the Chicago Transit Authority running routes from the downtown Loop through the length of the South Side are escorted by special police squad cars to deter assaults, yet still register several hundred violent incidents every month. A half-dozen CTA train stations on the Jackson Park line have been closed to entry in a last-ditch attempt to limit crime, at the cost of denying local residents access to public transportation (they can get off but not get on the train at these stops). Insecurity is so pervasive that simply manoeuvring one's way through public space has become a major dilemma in the daily round of ghetto residents, as averred by this plaintive comment from an elderly South Sider on a sunny day in late June:

> Oh, I hate to see this hot weather back. I mean I do like warm weather, *it's the people it bring out I don't like*: punks an' dope fiends, you're beginnin' to see them outa the buildings now, on the streets. That ain't no good.

Schools are no exception to this pattern. Designed and outfitted in the manner of military fortresses, with bricked-up windows and reinforced metal doors, many public establishments in Chicago's ghetto organize parent militias or hire off-duty police to bolster security. They commonly deploy metal detectors to try to limit the number of guns and other hand-weapons circulating on school grounds. A South Side elementary school on 55th Street briefly made the headlines in the winter of 1990 after five youths were gunned down and killed within a few blocks in the course of a single year. Its students were found to be living in 'numbing fear' of the gang violence that awaits them outside the school and pursues them all the way inside. Children 'say they are afraid for their lives to go to school', confessed one teacher. 'It seems like every year somebody's child loses their life and can't get out of 8th grade,' complained a mother. And the principal could only regret that the school security guards were unable to provide protection once pupils leave the premises (*Chicago Tribune* 1990).

The fin-de-siècle hyperghetto is truly 'no place to be a child', as suggested by the title of a book comparing Chicago's inner city to refugee camps in war-torn Cambodia (Garbarino et al. 1991). Youngsters raised in this environment of pandemic violence suffer serious emotional damage and display post-traumatic stress disorders similar to those endured by veterans. A tenant of a South Side high-rise complex (cited in Brune and Camacho 1983: 13) concurs that this part of Chicago 'is no place to raise a family. It's like a three-ring circus around here during the hot weather. There's constantly fighting. They've been times when we had to take all the kids and put 'em in the hallway on the floor, so much gunfire around here.' By age 5, virtually all children living in public housing projects have had firsthand encounters with shootings and death. Many mothers opt to send their offspring away to stay in the suburbs or with family back in the South to shelter them from the neighbourhood's brutality.

The incidence of crime in the ghetto is exacerbated by the ethnoracial closure of space in American cities. If so much violence is of the 'black-on-black' variety, it is not only because the residents of the declining districts of the metropolitan core suffer extreme levels of economic redundancy and social alienation. It is also that anonymous black males have become widely recognized symbols of criminal violence and urban danger (E. Anderson 1990: ch. 6). So that, unless they display the trappings of middle-class culture, they are *de facto* barred from bordering white areas where their skin colour causes them to be immediately viewed as potential criminals or troublemakers:

> You can't go over to the white community to do anything, because when you're seen over there, you're already stopped on suspicion. So you got to prey in your den, because you're less noticeable over there. You got to burglarize your own people. (Cited in Blauner 1989: 223; see also Pettiway 1985)

Depopulation, deproletarianization and organizational folding

Yet the continued physical and commercial decline, rising street violence and multisided insecurity that pervade the ghetto are themselves but surface manifestations of a deeper transformation of its socioeconomic and institutional fabric. First, whereas the Bronzeville of the 1950s was overpopulated due to the swelling influx of black migrants coming from the South triggered by the wartime boom of World War II and the mechanization of agriculture in that economically retarded region, the contemporary ghetto has been afflicted by steady depopulation as better-off families moved out in search of more congenial surroundings to the districts ringing the historic Bronzeville left vacant by whites gone to take refuge in the suburbs. For instance, the heart of Chicago's South Side lost close to one-half of its inhabitants: the population of Oakland, Grand Boulevard and Washington Park dropped from 200,000 in 1950 to 102,000 in 1980, before slipping further down to 64,000 in 1990. During this period, moreover, despite the construction of massive low-income high rises, the number of housing units decreased by one-third due to arson (generally perpetrated by absentee landlords seeking to collect insurance money and then deduct the amortization of the remaining ruins) and to the destruction brought about by an 'urban renewal' campaign (christened 'Negro removal' in the black community) that razed more dwellings than it built, so that overcrowding and substandard housing are still widespread at the heart of the ghetto.

Yet the most dramatic change in the demography of Bronzeville remains the precipitous collapse of the employed population caused by two mutually reinforcing trends: the continuing exodus of upwardly mobile black families and the rising joblessness of those left behind. In 1950 over half of the adults living at the heart of the South Side were gainfully employed, an employment rate equal to the city average. Chicago was still a dominant industrial centre, and one-half of employed blacks held blue-collar jobs. By 1980, the number of working residents had fallen by a staggering 77 per cent, leaving jobless nearly three out of every four persons over the age of 16. In thirty years, the number of operatives and labourers crumbled from 35,808 to 4,963; the ranks of craftsmen plummeted from 6,564 to 1,338, while the corresponding figure for private household and service workers plunged from 25,181 to 5,203. And whereas the black middle class grew fivefold in greater Chicagoland between 1950 and 1980, the number of white-collar employees, managers and professionals residing in the historic centre of Bronzeville was cut by half, falling from 15,341 to 7,394. A long-time resident of Woodlawn (who, ironically, recently moved to the city's North Side to shelter his children from the violence and temptations of the streets) complains about the vanishing of better-off families from his old South Side neighbourhood:

> It [used to] be tonsa teachers livin' in d'neighborhood, but now they movin', *everybody move up*. . . . If you look at d'community, Louie, it's *decayin': ain't nobody here*. Ain't no teachers on 63rd Street, over here on Maryland, *ain't none*, know what I'm sayin'? Everybody that's got a lil' knowledge, they leavin' it. If these people would stay in an' help reshape it, *they can reshape it*. Like teachers, policemen, firemen, business leaders, all-a 'em *responsible: everybody leavin' out*. An' they takin' the money with them.

How could such a dramatic collapse of the class structure happen? At the close of World War II, *all* blacks in Chicago, irrespective of their social status, were forcibly assigned to the same compressed enclave, and they had no choice but to coexist in it. Then, as whites fled *en masse* from the central city to rally the suburbs with the blessing and help of the federal government, they opened up adjacent areas into which black families from the (petty) bourgeoisie and the upper strata of the working class moved to create new, soon to be exclusively black, outlying neighbourhoods. The spatial dispersal of the African-American population, in turn, dispersed the established institutions of the ghetto and increased their class differentiation.[14] Simultaneously, in a systematic and deliberate effort to maintain the prevailing pattern of racial segregation, the city ensured that all of its new public housing was built exclusively inside the historic perimeter of the ghetto (Hirsch 1983), where only the most dispossessed would tolerate dwelling. By the late 1970s, then, *the urban colour line between blacks and whites had effectively been redrawn along a class fracture* at the behest of government, with the historic core of the Black Belt containing inordinate concentrations of the jobless and welfare-reliant, while the brunt of the black middle and stabler working class resided in segregated neighbourhoods along the outer rim of the historic ghetto.

The consequence of this threefold movement – the out-migration of stably employed African-American families made possible by state-sponsored white flight to the suburbs; the crowding of public housing in black areas already plagued by slums; the rapid deproletarianization of the remaining ghetto residents – was soaring and endemic poverty. In Grand Boulevard, a section of the South Side containing some 50,000 people, 64 per cent of the population lived under the poverty line in 1990, up from 37 per cent only a decade earlier, and three out of every four households was headed by a single mother. With a median family income below $8,500 per annum (less than one-third the citywide figure), the majority of households did not even reach *half the official poverty line*. Six residents in ten had to rely on one or another form of public assistance in order to subsist.[15]

The social and economic desolation of the contemporary ghetto has not escaped its inhabitants, as data from the Urban Family Life

---

[14] To be sure, this class differentiation existed in attenuated forms since the origin of the Black Belt. The latter was never the *gemeinschaftliche* constellation oft invoked by analysts nostalgic for a 'golden age' of the ghetto that never existed. The caste division imposed by whites never obliterated internal cleavages along class lines (closely overlapping with differentiation by skin colour) among African Americans, as can be seen, for instance, in the spreading of 'storefront churches' vying with old-line Baptist and Methodist churches in the 1920s (Spear 1968: ch. 9) or in the bifurcation of the 'jook continuum' and the 'urban-commercial complex' in the realm of dance and entertainment (Hazzard-Gordon 1991).

[15] A fuller statistical profile of Grand Boulevard can be found in table 3.1 below, p. 96.

Survey reveal.[16] When asked how many men are working steadily in their neighbourhood, 55 per cent of the residents of Chicago's traditional Black Belt (South Side and West Side together) answer 'very few or none at all', compared to 21 per cent in peripheral black areas harbouring a mix of subproletarian, working-class and middle-class families. Fully one-half also declare that the proportion of employed males in their area has diminished over the preceding years. One adult in four belongs to a household without a working telephone (compared to one in ten in outlying black areas), and 86 per cent to a household that rents its living quarters (as against about one-half among blacks in districts ringing the historic ghetto); nearly one-third reside in buildings managed by the Chicago Housing Authority (CHA), although the latter oversees only 4 per cent of the city's housing stock.

It is clear that, by the close of the twentieth century, the vestiges of the historic ghetto of Chicago contain mostly the dispossessed fractions of the black (sub)proletariat unable to escape its blighted conditions. Given a choice, fewer than one in four residents of the South Side and West Side would stay in their neighbourhood – as against four in ten in black tracts situated alongside their perimeter. Only 18 per cent rate their neighbourhood as a 'good or very good' place to live, contrasted with 42 per cent in black districts around the ghetto, and nearly one-half report that the state of their surroundings has worsened over the past few years. Not surprisingly, gang activity is more prevalent at the heart of the ghetto: one-half of its inhabitants consider that gangs pose a 'big problem' in their area, compared to fewer than one-third in outlying black tracts. As for the future, nearly one-third of our respondents foresee no improvement in their neighbourhood, while 30 per cent expect it to continue to deteriorate.

Residents of the fin-de-siècle ghetto are thus not only *individually poorer* than their counterparts of three decades ago in the sense that they have borne a reduction in their standard of living and that the distance between them and the rest of society has increased – the federal poverty line came to one-half of the median national family

[16] This questionnaire-based survey was carried out in 1986–7 (under the direction of William Julius Wilson) on a multistage, random probability sample of residents of Chicago's poor neighbourhoods (defined as census tracts containing at least 20 per cent of individuals living below the 1980 federal poverty threshold, 20 per cent being the rate for the whole city). The survey covered 1,184 blacks, with a completion rate of about 80 per cent, of whom one-third lived on the city's South Side and West Side.

income in 1960 but to only one-third by 1980 (Beeghley 1984: 325). They are also considerably *poorer collectively* in several respects. First, they reside among an overwhelmingly deprived and downwardly mobile or immobile population, so that they have become organizationally isolated from other components of the African-American community: the black middle class has fled the historic Bronzeville after the 1960s, and, above all, it has grown and reproduced itself outside of its perimeter in the ensuing decades.[17] Second, and as a consequence, they can no longer rely on the dense nexus of institutions that conferred upon the ghetto of yesteryear its internal coherence and cohesion. The 'Black Metropolis' of the mid-century finely dissected by Drake and Cayton ([1945] 1993) was a 'unique and distinctive city within a city' containing a near-complete division of labour and the full gamut of black social classes. The 'proliferation of institutions' that made Bronzeville the 'capital of black America' enabled it to duplicate (albeit at an incomplete and markedly inferior level) the organizational structure of the surrounding white society and to provide limited but real avenues of mobility within its internal order.

By contrast, the hyperghetto of the late century has weathered such organizational depletion that it contains neither an extended division of labour and the spectrum of black classes, nor functioning duplicates of the central institutions of the broader urban society. The organizational infrastructure – the black press and church, the black lodges and social clubs, the black businesses and professional services, and the illegal street lottery known by the name of 'numbers game' – that gave the ghetto of the 1950s its communal character and strength, and made it an instrument of collective solidarity and mobilization, has become impoverished and withered away, and along with it the networks of reciprocity and co-operation that used to crisscross the city (Mithun 1973). And whereas, in the context of the full employment and industrial prosperity brought by the Korean War, 'the entire institutional structure of Bronzeville [was] providing

---

[17] The fact that an increasing number of urban blacks from the middle and upper classes have never experienced ghetto life firsthand (even as they continue to endure discriminatory practices and other routine manifestations of ethnoracial domination, as most of them live in sharply segregated, all-black areas) is bound to affect processes of identity formation. The meanings that bourgeois blacks attach to a range of idioms and expressive symbols characteristic of the ghetto (corporeal and linguistic hexis, musical styles, hairdos and dress codes) is likely to change when exposure to them comes indirectly from formal sources such as the popular media and the school system rather than through native immersion and familial connection.

basic satisfactions for the "reasonable expectations" shared by people at various class levels' (Drake and Cayton [1945] 1993: xliii), the prevalence of joblessness and the organizational void of the contemporary hyperghetto prevent it from satisfying even the basic needs of its residents.

Oppressive as it was, the traditional ghetto formed 'a milieu for Negro Americans in which they [could] imbue their lives with meaning' (Drake and Cayton [1945] 1993: p. xlvi) and which elicited attachment and pride. By contrast, the hyperghetto of century's end is a despised and loathed space from which nearly everyone is desperately trying to escape, 'a place of stunted hopes and blighted aspirations, a city of limits in which the reach of realistic ambition is to survive' (Monroe and Goldman 1988: 251).

'Hustling' and everyday subsistence in the informal economy

Mass unemployment and chronic underemployment in the hyperghetto compel its residents to seek public assistance. The egregious inadequacy of welfare support even for sheer subsistence, in turn, forces them to pursue additional unreported or unreportable income-generating activities (Scharf 1987: 20; Edin 1991).[18] Most ghetto residents thus have little choice but to 'moonlight' on jobs, to 'hustle' for money through a diversity of schemes, or to engage in illegal commerce of various kinds (including the most dangerous and potentially lucrative of them, drug retail sale), in order to 'make that dollar' day to day. The frenetic growth of the informal and criminal economy observed at the heart of large cities in the United States over the last two decades of the century is directly explained by the combined closing of access to unskilled jobs, the organizational desertification of the urban core, and the failings of welfare coverage (a topic to which we return in the next section).

Subsistence strategies in the ghetto vary as a function of the social, economic and cultural resources, as well as the composition, of precarious families. When strapped for cash, as is common among welfare recipients whose monthly aid cheque is usually expended within two weeks of receipt, a favourite strategy of single mothers is to borrow small sums of money (from $5 to $40) from parents,

---

[18] In keeping with the doctrine of 'less eligibility', levels of public aid in the United States are set extremely low, at about half the federal poverty line. In Illinois, the maximum AFDC package for a family of three in 1996 was $377 per month, 15 per cent below the national average; and the real-dollar value of this aid had dropped by 60 per cent in a quarter-century (Committee on Ways and Means 1997: 443–5).

partners or close friends. For many, female kin networks are the most reliable, if not the only, source of financial support they can draw on in case of emergency (Stack 1970; Edin 1991). An unemployed mother subsisting on AFDC with her four children on the city's West Side explains:[19]

> If I get much down, then I can go to mama, and my mama, she help me a little bit. Can't do it too much, but she say to keep my kids from starvin', she help me a little. So now and then . . . she help me out for a few days. Well, if it gets too much . . . I tell her . . . I tell her, 'Well, we ain't got nothin' over here.' So she try to get me somethin'.

Another prevalent option is to seek free food from a pantry, a church or a city agency. In 1987, over 70 per cent of the adults aged 18 to 48 living in Chicago's historic Black Belt had to call on such outside assistance to feed themselves and their family. Chronic malnutrition is a fact of life in the ghetto that is plain to see for those who care to look, notwithstanding government programmes such as food stamps and the occasional free distribution of agricultural surpluses and dairy products unfit for commercialization. Soup kitchens run by churches on the South Side cannot keep up with demand and regularly turn away hungry families. Many ghetto residents periodically pawn goods (jewellery, clothing, musical instruments, kitchenware and home electronics) to raise the cash needed to bridge a period of dearth. Others take in boarders, sell the food stamps they receive from the public aid office (the going rate on the streets is one-half of their face value), or dig into their meagre savings if they have any. But 82 per cent of adults in Chicago's ghetto had no savings account at the close of the 1980s, and only one in ten could muster the means to maintain a checking account (as we shall see in the next chapter). Currency exchanges and pawn shops function as high-cost substitutes for the banks that do not exist (or reject ghetto residents where they still operate), as this unemployed mother of three living on the South Side indicates:

> I pawn my wedding rings and get a lil' money and when I get some money I go back and get my rings. They're gone now. I could have

---

[19] The interview excerpts in this section are drawn from data produced as part of the Urban Family Life Project, especially a set of forty-eight in-depth interviews conducted by the author in their domicile with residents of the West Side and South Side, which extended the quantitative survey by focusing on ordinary classifications and perceptions of inequality and opportunity (see n. 16 above for further detail).

gone back and got them but I just forgot about them – *I pawn them so much*, I pawn them every month. . . . The man at the pawn shop see me comin', he sees me, he knows me! Yeah, it's been like that for a couple of years now, he know what I'm bringing and he starts writin' it up [in his registry] before I even get there. And I get them out every month and pawn them every month. That's terrible. Twenty-five dollars is not that much. It can buy some cigarettes when I need it and that's a habit right there, definitely. It helps out a lot, a whole lot.

The mainstay of daily subsistence, however, is furnished by the odd jobs and marginal trades that have flourished in the ghetto over the past two decades. Many residents babysit the children of neighbours or run errands for them in exchange for victuals; they cut hair or repair electrical appliances; they mow grass in the summer and shovel snow in the winter; they collect pop cans for small sums of money, or 'pick up junk outa the alley' for resale to those even less fortunate than themselves. Others become occasional street peddlers or vendors (Jones 1988) by purchasing clothes and perfumes, meat or toiletry supplies, at wholesale price on Maxwell Street that they then try to sell at retail. Others sell their blood to plasma-collecting firms or hang about day-labour agencies in the hope of obtaining any kind of stopgap employment. A chronically unemployed single mother from the West Side says about her neighbours:

They go to Handy Andy [a day-labour agency]. That's like a job, you can go up North and you get twenty dollars a day for working eight hours or something. That's what I did before but it's not worth it, just temporary stuff.

At 31 years of age, Robert, who resides in his mother's apartment in a large and severely dilapidated housing project on the Near West Side, has never known anything other than this ill-paid, short-term, casual work: 'I work for Just Jobs, they send you to different places nearly every day, it's not so bad really, when they like find you a job', washing dishes in restaurants, working on an assembly line in a factory, moving goods in a chemical products warehouse or clearing a building site after the main construction work has been completed. During the seven months of the professional basketball season, Robert does day-labour setting up the basketball court for the Chicago Bulls when they play home games (in shifts of four hours paid $8, two to three times a week). He would like to be a janitor and dreams of some day finding a job that would pay him $8 an hour. But without an education – he left high school before graduating to escape the deadly gang fights around the school grounds – he must get by on intermittent side jobs paying barely $3 an hour.

Those who do not wish to rent themselves out on the margins of the wage-labour economy can find irregular employ at an 'after-hours' club operating illegally in a private residence, drive a 'gypsy cab', become a 'jack-leg' mechanic or plasterer, sell cooked food or home-made T-shirts, or become one of those 'insurance artists' who contrive (especially in foul weather) to provoke automobile or bus accidents in which they deliberately get injured so as to collect monetary damages from the entrapped driver. More hardened and desperate individuals may commit petty crimes for the express purpose of getting themselves incarcerated: the county jail is famously violent and punitive, but it offers a sure bed, three free meals a day, and basic medical care – all things that the outside world is hard pressed to deliver for many subproletarians confined to the ghetto. In this turbulent setting awash with unending economic uncertainty, children represent vital resources and are under constant pressure to generate income as soon as they near their teens (whether it is to help their household or for their personal consumption). Thus, in the dead of winter, boys aged 8 to 10 years old can be seen at all hours of the day or night at gas stations on Chicago's South Side offering to pump gas or to wipe windshields for petty change, or found waiting at the exit of supermarkets to carry grocery bags in exchange for a few coins or some food.

The subsistence strategy of last resort – or first resort for those intent not simply on subsisting but on escaping the daily press of grinding poverty – involves a wide gamut of illegal activites, ranging from gambling, theft in stores and warehouses, fencing and selling stolen ('hot') merchandise to extortion, insurance arson, street stick-ups, armed robbery, prostitution and drug dealing. When I asked her what people in her neighbourhood of Grand Boulevard do to survive, a 47-year-old packer for a mailing company answered:

> Steal, knock old ladies down and take their pension checks. Like on the 'El' [elevated train] station there. Especially when they get their Social Security checks, *they be out there*, waitin' for them, grab their purses and everything. Lot of that happenin' around here. . . . They broke in on me when I first moved in here so I put bars in. They got my stereo. But I haven't had any trouble since I put my bars up.

A 28-year-old jobless single mother from the adjacent district of Washington Park candidly adds:

Shit! Turn tricks, sell drugs, anything . . . *any and every thing*. Mind you: everyone is not the stick-up man, you know, but any and every-thing. Me myself, I have sold marijuana. I'm not a drug pusher, but I'm just tryin' to make ends . . . I'm tryin' to keep bread on the table: I have two babies.

For those who are repeatedly rejected from the labour market or who balk at taking dead-end 'slave jobs' in the deregulated service sectors that strip them of their dignity by requiring that they execute menial tasks paid at poverty wages with no benefits, vacation or retirement attached, underground activities offer a bounty of full-time employment opportunities. For them, predatory crime consti-tutes a form of *petty entrepreneurialism* in which they put to use the only valuable assets they possesss: physical prowess and a working knowledge of the demi-monde of the streets (Wacquant 1998). The sums that can be grossed in the drug trade in the ghetto are extrava-gant in relation to the crushing poverty of the local population and the miserly level of wages and public aid. Even though low-level participants in the commerce make a fraction of the monies churning through the narcotics mill, often earning little more than minimum wage, the certainty of getting one's hands on fresh cash and the pos-sibility of rapidly earning large sums make it seem like an economic lottery worth playing to those hardened or desperate enough to put up with the acute psychological stress and high physical risks it carries. Here is an excerpt from a long interview I conducted with Five, a 28-year-old street hustler who, after having run the gamut of illegal pursuits, works intermittently as a dish-washer at a community college and runs dice games (a craft he learned from his father) in pool halls, livery cabs and after-hours clubs:

LW: What drug is most common today, the easiest to sell?
Five: Rock [crack cocaine]. Ten dollars.
LW: You can get a rock for ten dollars?
F: Yeah.
LW: Who buys that stuff?
F: Every guy, old guy, young guy. Inside the neighbourhood, outside the neighbourhood. More outside, that's the highest drug outlet, the best.
LW: How much can you make today?
F: *Ooooh, man!* Much! Fifty thousan', a hundred thousan'. I say a month's time, they might make like 10 G's [ten grands = 10,000] in a month's time. You take that every month in a year, *that's a loootttaaa money.*

The main attraction of gangs for young subproletarian men in the hyperghetto is precisely that they are, among other things, queer business concerns that increase their chances of securing income in cash and thus offer a modicum of financial security (Sánchez-Jankowski 1991: 40–1). In the void created by the withdrawal of legitimate firms, illegal lines of work such as the theft and resale of goods, trafficking in counterfeit documents (such as Medicaid cards), and 'stripping' of stolen cars, and especially drug dealing have evolved complex organizational structures that come to mirror those of firms operating in the official economy. Besides, the drug trade is often the only form of business known to adolescents, and one which has the immense virtue of being a genuine 'equal opportunity employer' (Williams 1989; Sullivan 1989: ch. 7). In addition, contrary to so many service establishments where one toils for famine wages with little chance of promotion, drug-retail employment promises immediate and tangible rewards for those who display a solid work ethic.[20] A 34-year-old woman who shares a decrepit South Side apartment with her janitor brother is considering this employment option for that very reason: 'The fellah told me: you make 250 dollars a week, okay – in this neighbourhood, he's got so many people working for him for 250 dollars a week – and if you're good enough you might make 400 dollars a week.'

It goes without saying that the overall impact of the drug economy on the ghetto is tremendously destructive. While it provides stopgap employment and income to many, in effect serving as a subterranean welfare system of sorts, it also saps the willingness of young men to work at low-level wages by offering apparently attractive, if risky, alternative economic opportunities.[21] It creates an environment of high morbidity and constitutes a major factor of premature mortality.

---

[20] It follows from this that the economic standing and social status of the deproletarianized residents of the ghetto living by the informal (and largely illegal) economy of the street may be higher than those of the unskilled workers in the formal sector, as in the big cities of Latin America before the period of industrial expansion (Peattie 1968).

[21] But these low-wage jobs are more often than not inaccessible: unlike the wage-labour economy, the informal or illegal street economy constantly offers *some* opportunity for both 'action' and income (especially after the explosive growth of retail trade in drugs caused by the introduction of 'crack' in Chicago in 1989), whereas the former periodically dries up. So that the conventional contrast between these two sectors of activity has become inverted: official employment is irregular and unreliable, whereas underground activities, taken collectively, are regular and dependable: 'You can *always* rack up somethin' off a back-alley and hustle some money on the street, Louie: *always*.'

It subjects kin relationships to intolerable strain and weakens local social cohesion. Finally, the trade in narcotics engenders ramifying violence that installs rampant insecurity in the neighbourhood (Johnson et al. 1990) as the pall of sudden death hovers everywhere. Five, the dice-thrower interviewed above, saw his father die from a bullet through the head. He tried to enrol in the military after 'seein' my homeys started getting' killed, I said I'm gonna go to d'army. (What happened?) I couldn't pass the test.' He would gladly settle for a stable and dignified job like 'carpenter or brick-layin'' if he could get one, and he nearly breaks down in tears upon evoking that scenario:

> That'd be a blessin'! Ooooh! please help me! (in an imploring tone, loudly, joining his hands as if in prayer) Please show me that one, I want that so badly, hopin' it'll come at night, see what I'm sayin'? . . . 'Cause when you live by the sword, you also die by the sword, an' I don't wanna die: I got a daughter, right? I hope all this make sense, I mean I hope all this what I'm sayin' to you is very simple. Because what I'm sayin' is, when a person don't finish school, he be livin' like that.

This pervasive and acute insecurity, in turn, accelerates the retraction of the wage-labour market and further pushes ghetto residents away from the regular economy and society. It also undermines neighbourhood cohesion and accelerates the exodus of those families who possess the minimal resources to move out of the historic core of the ghetto, but not to migrate far away from its percussive ambit. The relentless press of predatory crime, then, helps to account for the steep depopulation of Bronzeville as well as the filling out of areas immediately adjacent to it by poor black households (Morenoff and Sampson 1997).[22]

The *explosive growth of the criminal economy* dominated by street-level drug trafficking also accounts for the crystallization of a 'culture of terror' that now engulfs the streets of the hyperghetto. Anthropologist Philippe Bourgois has shown that, in this shady commerce, routine displays of violence are a business requirement: they serve to establish commercial credibility and avert being taken over by competitors or robbed by intruders, customers or police (some of whom are not the last to partake of the trafficking, as evidenced in chapter

---

[22] I compare the sociodemographic profiles of the core and periphery of the ghetto in the next chapter, to show that the social differentiation of the black population is mirrored by its spatial redistribution in a two-tier urban constellation replicating the opposition between blacks and whites among African Americans.

4 below). In a universe depleted of the most basic resources and characterized by a high density of social predators, trust is simply not a viable option, so that everyone must protect themselves from violence by being ready to wield it at any time: 'Inner-city street violence is not limited solely to drug sellers or to street criminals; to a certain extent, everyone living in the neighbourhood who wants to maintain a sense of autonomy . . . finds it useful to participate, at least passively, in some corner of the culture of terror' (Bourgois 1989: 647).

Economic and political roots of hyperghettoization

Why have physical decay and violence reached levels such that public space has nearly entirely withered away in the ghetto? Why are so many adults in it deprived of a secure foothold in the regular economy and forced instead to rely on a mix of underground and predatory activities and on the stigmatizing and flagrantly insufficient support of welfare to subsist? Why have public and private organizations declined so markedly in the racialized core of the American metropolis after the mid-1970s? And what explains the bunching of poor blacks in these continually deteriorating enclaves?

The causes of the 'hyperghettoization' of the inner city involve a complex and dynamic concatenation of economic and political factors operating over the whole postwar era that belies the simplistic, short-term plot of the 'underclass' tale. The most obvious – but not necessarily the most potent – of these factors is the transition of the American economy from a closed, tightly integrated, factory-centred, Fordist system of production catering to a uniform mass market to a more open, decentralized, service-intensive system geared to increasingly differentiated consumption patterns. This structural shift was accompanied by a dualization of the occupational structure and a hardening of the racial segmentation of the peripheral segments of the labour market. A second factor, too often overlooked as it is so deeply rooted that it can be taken for granted, is the persistence of the rigid residential segregation of African Americans and the deliberate stacking of public housing in the poorest black areas of large cities, amounting to establishing a system of *de facto* urban apartheid. In the third place, the swift and wide retrenchment of an already miserly welfare state combined with the cyclical downturns of the American economy to help ensure a steady increase in poverty in the Black Belt after the mid-1970s. A fourth and last major factor is the turnaround in federal and local urban policies over the past two decades as expressed in the 'planned shrinkage' of public services in historically black districts.

For the sake of analytic clarity, I consider each of these factors separately and sequentially, even though their full impact can be adequately assessed only by taking into account the interaction effects arising out of their changing synchronic and diachronic articulation.[23] I conclude by arguing that, on balance, it is not so much the impersonal workings of broad macroeconomic and demographic forces as the will of urban elites, i.e., their *decision to abandon the ghetto* to these forces (as they had themselves been politically channelled) that best accounts for the *implosion* of the Black Belt and the gloomy life prospects offered to its residents on the threshold of the new century.

Disinvestment, polarized growth and the racial segmentation of deskilled labour

In the mid-1960s, the US economy found itself caught in the pincers of the saturation of domestic markets and intensifying international competition. It shifted toward a new type of capitalist organization characterized by the vertiginous mobility of capital, the autonomization of the financial sector, 'flexible specialization', and generalized reduction of the protections of wage-earners (Scott and Storper 1986; Piore and Sabel 1984; Bluestone and Harrison 1988). The old economic system anchored in standardized industrial production, mass consumption, strong unions and the corresponding 'social contract' between corporations and their stable workforce was gradually replaced by a new regime based on the predominance of service occupations, the bifurcation of financial and industrial capital, the erosion of integrated regional economies, and a sweeping reorganization of labour markets and earnings scales.

During the last quarter of the twentieth century, a polarized labour demand, characterized by a widening gulf between high-wage, credentialled positions and routinized low-paying jobs, set on variable schedules, offering few benefits and no employment security, became a structural feature of the American economy (Thurow 1987; Sassen

---

[23] For instance, racial segregation, though roughly constant over the postwar era, operates to varying degrees both in the manner of a Keynesian 'accelerator' amplifying the effect of external economic changes and as an enabling political precondition for (and consequence of) the curtailment of public services in the urban core.

1991a). Of the 23 million jobs created in the country between 1970 and 1984, a full 22 million were in the service sector, so that by 1990 upwards of three-fourths of all employment was in services. But nearly one-third of all jobs generated in the 1980s were part-time positions, and 75 per cent of these were filled by people who would have preferred to work full-time. Furthermore, many of these service jobs paid between $4 and $6 an hour, a far cry from the hourly rate of $12–15 common in the unionized branches of durable-goods manufacturing. Indeed, half of the jobs added in the United States between 1970 and 1983 paid less than $8,000 a year (Bureau of the Census 1985: table 40), equal to $2,100 less than the official poverty threshold for a family of four.

This change in the structure of labour markets is not the product of some inevitable, technologically preordained trend but results from the decisions of large US firms to favour strategies of short-term profit-making that make their wage bill a variable of adjustment and demand that they relentlessly reduce their operating costs. One study reported by Squires et al. (1987: 28) estimates that two-thirds of the 203,700 manufacturing jobs lost by greater Chicagoland between 1977 and 1981 following firm shutdown or 'downsizing' were due to corporate disinvestment aimed at *transferring* activities to sites with lower land costs, cheaper labour pools and low unionization rates, such as the southern US states and Second World countries like Mexico, Turkey and Brazil. Federal policies of government deregulation (in sectors such as transport and communication) and high interest rates, together with the *laissez-faire* stance of the National Labour Relations Board, assisted in this reorganization of the workforce by furthering the decline of unions and undercutting the protection of peripheral wage earners (Rosenberg 1983). This paved the way for the explosive growth of 'contingent labour' and subcontracting, as well as for the resurgence of homework, piecework and sweatshops in light industry. These changes were most consequential for black workers, whose social condition has historically depended more on protections granted by federal policies than on the operation of the market.

Of the many crisscrossing forces that have reshaped the face of urban labour markets over the past thirty years, three are particularly relevant to the fate of the ghetto because they have converged to eliminate the role of reservoir of cheap industrial labour that it played in the previous state of the racial division of labour. First, the *sectoral shift* toward service employment spelled massive cutbacks in those job categories traditionally most accessible to urban blacks with a generally low level of skills. Like other major northern cities such as New York, Detroit, Philadelphia and Baltimore, Chicago saw its manufacturing base cut in half between 1950 and the early 1980s. In 1947, the city harboured nearly 670,000 manufacturing jobs (corresponding to 70 per cent of the region's total); by 1982, this figure had dwindled to 277,000, representing only one-third of the metropolitan total (Wacquant and Wilson 1989). The loss of factory employment accelerated as the decades wore on, rising from 52,000 jobs lost between 1947 and 1954 to 169,000 lost for the period 1967–82. Because ghetto blacks were overrepresented among factory workers as late as the mid-1970s, and because in addition they tended to be employed in the lowest industrial occupations and in the least protected firms of declining sectors (Stearns and Coleman 1990), they were disproportionately hurt by this sectoral reshuffling. And they continue to be the primary bearers of the costs of deindustrialization in Chicago: a full 43 per cent of the residents of Bronzeville questioned by the Urban Family Life Project reported that most of their friends had become unemployed due to a plant shutdown in the previous few years (as against 31 per cent of respondents in peripheral black neighbourhoods). A 32-year-old mother of three, laid off ten years ago from her job on an assembly line who now lives in a South Side public housing project, reports: 'There just ain't enough [jobs]. Used to be . . . used to have the steel industry and all that. But they closed it down. Reagan closed that down and sent it to other states.'

Secondly, the *spatial redistribution* of jobs correlative of the disagglomeration of the urban economy has also reduced the options of unskilled blacks on the labour market, as business moved out of central cities in search of cheaper land, tax abatements and more flexible labour. In the 1970s alone, while its suburban ring gained employment in every occupational category, adding half a million positions to their payroll, the city of Chicago posted a net loss of 119,000 blue-collar positions and 90,000 clerical and sales jobs. The only categories for which the city recorded increases in employment were those of managers, professionals, technical and administrative support personnel, that is, jobs requiring at least some college education (Kasarda 1989: 29) and therefore beyond the reach of ghetto residents left uneducated and untrained by the city's crumbling school system. The geographical shift in employment to the suburbs and exurbs also had a disproportionate impact on ghetto residents due to the gross deficiencies of public transportation. Blacks in Chicago are twice as likely as whites to use public transportation because the cost of owning and operating an automobile exceeds their means. But the underfunded and underdeveloped municipal bus and train network is configured in such a way that it isolates the suburbs from the inner city so that, 'for all practical purposes, the jobs in the outer suburban areas are not accessible by public transportation from the high unemployment areas' (Orfield 1985: 179).

Thirdly, the occupational shift to *higher-education jobs* has severely restricted the employment chances of ghetto residents, given the incapacity of public institutions – public schools, but also job training schemes and federal and local employment programmes – to prepare them for this change. In Grand Boulevard, 65 per cent of adults over 25 years of age did not finish high school, and fewer than 3 per cent attended a four-year college. Only 16 per cent of a cohort entering 8th grade in public establishments in the city graduates four years later at or above the national reading average. Yet, between 1970 and 1980, the number of jobs held by city workers with less than a high-school education dropped by 42 per cent, and the ranks of workers who were high-school graduates diminished by nearly one-fifth. By contrast, the volume of jobs requiring some college training rose by 44 per cent, and that for jobs mandating a four-year university degree grew by 56 per cent (Kasarda 1989).

A fourth critical factor in the economic marginalization of ghetto residents is the *continued racial segmentation of low-wage labour* (Fainstein 1987; Bailey and Waldinger 1991; Tomaskovic-Devey 1993). In the manufacturing and service sectors, most blacks are employed in specific 'occupational niches' which contain heavy concentrations of African Americans and they are routinely excluded from other occupational networks effectively reserved to whites and other minorities considered more docile (especially Hispanics coming from Mexico and other countries in Central America). In many service subsectors which have experienced rapid employment growth, such as restaurants and catering places, blacks tend to be channelled into the least attractive jobs and stacked in entry-level positions cut off from career ladders. A detailed analysis of job quality in the US economy from 1973 to 1990 confirms that the declining position of black men on the national labour market stems from 'both a worsening job mix relative to white men and a sharp drop in the quality of low-skill jobs' (Gittleman and Howell 1995: 420). Moreover, ghetto residents with low education, few skills, and scattered job experience have been pushed further down the job queue by stepped-up competition from women and the 'new immigration', legal and illegal, which has flooded America's metropolitan core with cheap, pliable, unskilled labour as a consequence of the reforms in immigration law of the mid-1960s (Sassen 1989b). A divorced mother of 38 with two children who works as a hotel cashier on the South Side complains: 'Too many people, too few jobs. A thousand people go out and try for one hundred jobs. Machinery and computers are taking a lot of jobs.'

Thus, at the foot of the new postindustrial order, the growth of unskilled, service positions and downgraded manufacturing largely bypassed ghetto blacks, as employers turned to other sources of pliable labour less likely to balk or protest at unstable and super-exploitative work conditions. And because the contemporary ghetto has become ever more closely associated, in the public mind, with depravity and lawlessness, the mere fact of dwelling in a district of the historic Black Belt has become an additional handicap, a signal that many employers use to separate 'good' (educated, middle-class-oriented) blacks and 'bad' (unreliable and unruly) blacks, and thereby select ghetto-dwellers out of their pool of applicants. As I shall show later in chapter 6, the *stigma attached to residing in the decaying core of Bronzeville* is yet another hurdle over which inner-city blacks have to jump in their quest for employment: 'I think that if you have a decent address, it helps a lot,' sighs an unemployed mother of 37 living on the South Side. 'Like when you apply to jobs, *they see it's not the heart of the ghetto.*'[24] All in all, the polarization of the occupational and wage structure, the generalized downgrading of unskilled jobs, and enduring ethnoracial segmentation on the secondary labour market have effectively dried up the work options of miseducated blacks, pushing more of them into the only employment sector to which they readily have access: the informal and often illegal economy of the street.

---

[24] The two stigmata born by ghetto residents on the labour market (and in other institutional settings), that attached to skin colour and that linked to dwelling in a place publicly regarded as a repository of 'social pathology', are not independent of each other. But neither are they confounded in their nature or identical in their effects. Racial markers are impossible to shed for most African Americans, but their signification can at least be inverted and revalorized from within (according to the paradigm 'Black is beautiful'). Territorial taint may, in many situations, be shed by adept techniques of impression management. But having to hide one's place of residence from outsiders (including other blacks), especially when these are official agents of dominant institutions such as firms, schools and other government bureaucracies, who often have the means to uncover it at some point, constantly reactivates the sense of indignity. Additionally, one cannot effect a reversal of the symbolic valence of ghetto dwelling (few today could effectively advocate 'Living in the ghetto is beautiful').

Racial segregation, housing policy and the concentration of black poverty

But transformations of the production apparatus and labour recruitment cannot by themselves account for the accumulation of social dislocations that destabilized the ghetto after the heyday of the Civil Rights movement. Racial segregation is the crucial intervening variable that explains how so many lower-class blacks have been severed from the new job openings of the decentralized service economy and disabled from pursuing social mobility through spatial mobility. The persistence of the residential enclosure of poor African Americans in the historic ghetto plays a pivotal role in its involutive decline because, in tandem with the suburban exodus of hundreds of thousands of whites (followed in later years by middle-class blacks), it underlies a distribution of employment opportunities, school chances, taxable wealth and political influence that has stripped them of the supports needed to preserve or improve their social and economic condition (Orfield 1985). Spatial isolation operates in the manner of a prism that intensifies and concentrates hardship inside the hyperghetto. The resurging debate over the fate of the inner city in the 1980s and 1990s has largely minimized the causal weight of racial segregation, sometimes to the point of total eclipse, as when the term 'ghetto' is used to designate any area of extreme poverty without reference to its population and institutional makeup (e.g., Jargowsky and Bane 1991).[25] Yet, *the perpetuation of the exclusionary mission of the ghetto is first and foremost the concrete expression of the persistence of the 'colour line'* in the metropolis even as it became overlaid by a class divide to produce a dual structure of black entrapment composed of a (sub)proletarian core and a middle-class periphery.

Although it elected a black mayor for the first time in its history in 1982, Chicago enjoys the dubious privilege of being the most ethnically segregated metropolis in America. In 1980, over two-thirds of the city's 1.2 million blacks lived in tracts *over 95 per cent black*. The segregation or dissimilarity index for African Americans

---

[25] For a thorough critique of the inconsistencies of this redefinition of the ghetto (fashionable among policy-oriented scholars in the United States), which empties the concept of its historic meaning and reduces it to a synonym for 'slum', see Wacquant (2002b). Massey and Denton's (1993) pivotal tome on the racial underpinnings of extreme poverty in the American metropolis was an outlier in that regard – and a disturbing one, as indicated by the exclusion of Douglas Massey from Jencks and Peterson's (1991) edited volume on *The Urban Underclass* even though he gave a paper at the conference on which the book is based.

has barely budged since 1950; it even rose from 89 in 1970 to 92 in 1980 (the maximum of 100 indicating complete separation).[26] The 'exposure index', another instrument commonly used to gauge segregation, reveals that the typical black Chicagoan lives on a block that is barely 4.5 per cent white (although whites make up close to half of the city's population), while the block of the typical white resident is a paltry 2.6 per cent black. At the residential level, African Americans are virtually as separated from other groups – including Hispanics, whose settlements tend to function as 'buffer zones' between white and black neighbourhoods (Squires et al. 1987: 111) – as if they lived under a regime of legal apartheid. Moreover, blacks are the *only ethnic category to suffer such intense separation*, as households of Hispanic and Oriental descent display comparatively moderate to low levels of segregation: in the thirty largest metropolitan areas of the country, Latinos and Asians are more likely to have whites for neighbours than families from their own ethnic group,[27] whereas the probability of white–black contact based on residence rarely exceeds 5 per cent (Massey and Denton 1987).

It is important to stress that the exceptional residential isolation of African Americans is *not an expression of cultural affinity or ethnic choice,* for, in both principle and conduct, blacks overwhelmingly prefer to live in racially mixed neighbourhoods (Farley et al. 1978; Streitweiser and Goodman 1983). Their enveloping segregation is also *not due to class differences* between black and white families. Were that the case, the rapid expansion of the black middle class after the 1960s would have been accompanied by a steep decrease of racial disjunction in space. Indeed, if the African-American population were distributed in a colour-blind housing market driven solely by

[26] The segregation index reaches 100 when two ethnic groups are totally disjoint (i.e., when all city blocks are racially homogeneous, either 100 per cent black or 100 per cent white) and 0 when every block sports the same black–white composition as the city as a whole. Other measures of segregation turn up the same pattern, confirming that African Americans are the sole category to suffer extreme segregation in every possible dimension simultaneously: unevenness, isolation, clustering, centralization and concentration (Massey and Denton 1989).

[27] These populations themselves are not homogeneous in this regard. The category 'Hispanic' (coined by the Census Bureau for administrative purposes), for instance, lumps together different ethnonational and immigration streams that face varying conditions of entry and incorporation into America's social and physical space. The integration paths of Cubans, Mexicans and Puerto Ricans differ widely, the situation of the latter being closer to that of African Americans due to antipathy based on skin colour – though Puerto Ricans in Chicago are not cut of one cloth, as shown by Padilla (1987).

income level, the percentage of blacks in the census tracts making up Chicago would range from a low of 10 per cent to a high of 27 per cent instead of the 90 per cent which is the norm for their neighbourhoods (Berry 1979: 9). Unlike other subordinate ethnic categories in US society such as Mexican Americans (Massey and Mullan 1984), the residential ostracization of African Americans does not decrease as they climb the class ladder.

The colour line bisecting the city is the result, first, of the inflexible *dualization of the housing market along ethnoracial lines* (Foley 1973; Berry 1979; Tobin 1987). Systematic racial steering by rental and sales agents, as well as bias in mortgage financing and informal white obstruction to the housing search – all of them condoned by the reticence of Congress and the federal government to enforce Fair Housing laws passed since 1968 – are still prevalent in large cities such as Chicago (Schlay 1987; Yinger 1997). Blacks who attempt to move out of the perimeter effectively set apart for them encounter reticence, unease, if not outright hostility and violent resistance. While sizable majorities of whites agree on principle that everyone has a right to reside wherever they wish, in practice they continue to reserve this right for themselves: most whites would refuse to live in a neighbourhood containing more than a small percentage of blacks, and few support local ordinances designed to implement racial mixing (Massey and Gross 1991).[28]

A second major cause of continued racial segregation is found on the side of the *housing and urban renewal policies* implemented by federal and municipal governments after World War II, which have intentionally trapped and packed poor African Americans in the poorest all-black areas of the central city. The historical myopia of the debate on the 'underclass' has obscured the fact that the crumbling of the ghetto at the close of the century is but the tailspin of a downward spiral whose initial impetus was given some five decades earlier by Washington's housing programmes.[29] As Kenneth

---

[28] A survey of Detroit conducted in the mid-1970s found that 42 per cent of whites would feel uncomfortable in a neighbourhood comprising as few as one-fifth blacks and that fully one-half of the whites interviewed would be unwilling to move into such an area (Farley et al. 1978). These tendencies have not fundamentally changed since in Detroit, where blacks who managed to move to the suburbs are more segregated and isolated from whites than their brethen in the city (Darden and Kamel 2000), and at the national level (Meyer 2000).

[29] Most theories of the 'underclass' go no further back than 1970 and focus on the 1970s as the decade of its putative 'emergence', for the simple reason that tract-level census data on poverty rates and associated variables needed to 'measure' the group are not readily available for previous years.

Jackson has shown in his authoritative history of American suburbanization, from the Wagner–Steagall Act of 1937, which legally established government responsibility to aid low-cost housing, to the present,

> the result, if not the intent, of the public housing program in the United States [has been] to segregate the races, to concentrate the disadvantaged in inner cities, and to reinforce the image of suburbia as a place of refuge for the problems of race, crime and poverty. (Jackson 1985: 219)

The state's approach to resolving the tensions of race and class in the struggle over scarce urban space and resources in the postwar era was two-pronged. On the one side, at the top of the metropolitan order, the federal government underwrote the massive subsidization of *middle- and upper-class* housing in the suburbs through a combination of tax deductions, federal mortgage guarantees, and construction of a vast web of highways enabling prosperous families to work in the city but live away from it, while at the local level zoning ordinances and racial restrictions enforced or tolerated by the Federal Housing Agency (FHA) ensured that *only whites* would move to the suburbs in large numbers. Until 1949, it was the official policy of the FHA to refuse to insure any housing unit that disrupted 'community composition', and this agency did not require nondiscriminatory pledges from loan applicants until 1962.[30] To this day, the Fair Housing legislation passed by Congress in 1968 has been given no enforcement apparatus. Every year, the Department of Justice litigates but a handful of cases nationwide, and under the administrations of Reagan and Bush (the father), it even reduced requests for compensation in cases of grievous and repeated infractions.

On the other side, at the bottom end of the urban hierarchy, the state also embarked on a vast scheme of support for low-income housing but with two major differences. First, in sharp contrast with middle-class, white suburban construction, state aid for housing the poor proved remarkably stingy: between 1937 and 1968, 10 million middle- and upper-income private units sprang up with the backing

---

[30] Until that date, property titles could legally contain clauses called 'restrictive covenants' which forbid one to rent or sell the housing unit in question to blacks (or Jews).

of the FHA, while only 800,000 cheaply built public units were erected with federal subsidies (Kerner Commission 1968, 1988: 474). Second, the federal government granted municipalities discretion over whether or not to build low-income housing and where to locate it, so that federal projects invariably reinforced existing segregation. White localities at the city's edge refused to create public housing authorities, and white neighbourhoods inside the city ferociously resisted the penetration of blacks into their exclusive perimeters. In Chicago, white racial violence from below and white political manipulation from above converged to constrict the placement of Chicago Housing Authority (CHA) housing *exclusively within the established boundaries of the historic ghetto*, 'thus fixing and institutionalizing its borders like never before' (Hirsch 1983: 409). Nearly all public housing developed in the 1950s and 1960s was located squarely inside or immediately adjacent to the traditional Black Belts of the South Side and West Side. As a result, in 1981 fully *95 per cent of all Chicago Housing Authority family rental units were occupied by blacks*. Instead of building low-density housing on cheaper and less congested land outside the central cities, as Western European countries did during the same period, the US government fostered the dumping of shoddy high rises into the most poverty-impacted neighbourhoods, which amounted to making public housing over into 'a federally built and supported slum' (Hirsch 1983: 226).

The consequences of this racially and socially skewed public policy were not difficult to foresee. Indeed, as early as 1968, the Kerner Commission (1968, 1988: 474) pointed out that 'federal housing programs concentrate the most impoverished and dependent segments of the population into the central-city ghettos where there is already a critical gap between the needs of the population and the public resources to deal with them'. This gap was due to widen in the following two decades as funds for public housing dried up after the turbulent 1960s and the city stopped building and even maintaining CHA units after it was found guilty of racial discrimination and ordered by the courts to construct scattered-site social housing in ethnically mixed neighbourhoods. To this day, the United States remains the only advanced country in the world without significant state support for low-income housing, despite the glaring fact that nowhere have private developers built for the poor – in 1980, publicly owned or managed housing represented about *1 per cent* of the US housing supply, compared to some 46 per cent in England and 37 per cent in France (Harloe 1985). It is also the only postindustrial nation to have erected a state-run 'vertical ghetto' doubly segregated on the basis of race and class.[31]

The federal government and local authorities are thus doubly responsible for the extraordinary social and spatial concentration of the black subproletariat in the fin-de-siècle hyperghetto. First, they actively supported the rigid racial segmentation of the housing market at the level of the metropolis, and they then perpetuated it through housing policies that locked poor blacks in the dilapidated perimeter of the Black Belt by eliminating every other option in the public housing stock and by artificially raising the cost of rental and owner-ship in peripheral African-American neighbourhoods. Secondly, at both the central and the local level, the state produced a grossly insufficient quantity of dwellings of shoddy quality destined for poor households that it deliberately implanted exclusively in the run-down core of the city. In short, the highly peculiar physical and demo-graphic configuration of the urban purgatory that is the US hyper-ghetto is a political creature of the state – and not the product of some ecological dynamic creating 'mismatches' or of the free choice, culture or behaviour of its residents.

The retrenchment of the miserly welfare state

The gradual retrenchment of the social welfare state after the mid-1970s is another major political cause of the continued deterioration of the life chances of the urban (sub)proletariat in the United States. Contrary to popular neoconservative rhetoric (Murray 1984; Mead 1992), the last quarter of the century was not a period of expansion and generosity for welfare but one of blanket retraction. Aid to Fami-lies with Dependent Children became steadily less helpful to poor families due to the woefully low level of grants and the failure to index them on inflation. Programme outlays peaked at 1.6 per cent of the federal budget in 1973 and declined steadily until the abolition

---

[31] Owing to massive cutbacks in federal funding, not to mention the shameless plundering of public coffers by senior federal and local officials, most large cities are financially unable to ensure the upkeep of their already insufficient stock of low-income housing. Their oversight bureaucracies have also lost control over the day-to-day management of their property. The crowning of this state policy of abandonment consisted in proposing (as did G. W. H. Bush's Secretary of Housing and Urban Development, Jack Kemp) that public housing tenants be 'promoted' to ownership of housing that is so run-down and unsafe that public authority cannot establish itself over it, save by means of a quasi-military occupation riding roughshod over the basic civil rights of tenants.

of AFDC in 1996 and its replacement by Temporary Aid to Needy Families, which further cut grants and enforces stringent 'workfare' provisions. Not only was public aid rationed via legal and bureaucratic restrictions on eligibility (Susser and Kreniske 1987); the real dollar value of the average cash grant to families on public aid in the state of Illinois diminished by more than one-half between 1970 and 1990. By 1995, a family of three on AFDC received, under the best of circumstances, a maximum of $645 a month, including food stamps, a sum barely equal to the rent of an average one-bedroom apartment in Chicago.

Based on a detailed quantitative analysis of the ability of welfare programmes to lift recipients above the poverty line, Axinn and Stern (1988: 102) contend that 'the explosion of central city poverty was much more the result of declining program effectiveness than economic breakdown'. Indeed, it is in the central cities that this rate reached its lowest level and where it also decreased the most over time: in 1983, 30 per cent of urban households nationwide were poor before transfer as against 18.4 per cent after transfer, for an effectiveness rate of 38 per cent; this is a drop from an effectiveness of 50 per cent in 1973 when the corresponding poverty rates were 27.5 per cent and 14 per cent. A simple computation shows that if aid programmes had retained their limited effectiveness of the mid-1970s, they would have absorbed the brunt of the short-term effect of deindustrialization and polarized economic growth so that the poverty rate in cities would have grown by only one percentage point, from 14 per cent to 15 per cent (instead of reaching 21 per cent by 1990). The deficiencies of US social policy aimed at the poor are even more glaring when one contrasts them with similar programmes in neighbouring Canada – hardly a world leader in welfare generosity. Economists Rebecca Blank and Maria Hanratty (1991) demonstrated that if the United States adopted the Canadian system of anti-poverty transfer measures, the poverty rate for single-parent families would decrease from 43 per cent to between 2 and 16 per cent depending on a range of assumptions about participation rates and labour supply. This means that a social policy genuinely aimed at the 'welfare' of its target population would nearly eradicate poverty among female-headed households, which account for the majority of the ghetto poor today.

Those pushed out of the labour market have also been adversely affected by the *increased shortcomings of social insurance*. In theory, jobless benefits are designed to meet cyclical needs and provide twenty-six weeks of coverage at about 40 per cent of the last wage

rate at the time of layoff. But, under the weight of high rates of joblessness for two decades after the mid-1970s, the system has been
coming apart. Business lobbying and political concern with costs
reduction conspired to produce a severe tightening of eligibility and
a multiplication of administrative obstacles to benefits delivery. As a
result, the share of the unemployed covered nationwide declined
from 50 to 30 percent between 1975 and 1990. Again, this decline
was particularly pronounced in large cities and was especially detri-
mental to the residents of the racialized urban core who, being confined in the lowest segments of the secondary labour market, have
short work tenures and experience frequent changes of employer. In
point of fact, most intermittently employed ghetto residents rarely
become eligible for unemployment benefits when they lose their jobs.

The welfare system also worsens the living conditions of ghetto
residents and indirectly contributes to the profusion of insalubrious
accommodations by insisting on paying its housing subsidies for
rental on the private market directly to building owners. Slum landlords – the largest of which is the Chicago Housing Authority, the
municipal bureaucracy in charge of social housing – know that their
tenants are a captive clientele, devoid of alternatives and means of
pressure. So they can charge high rents and neglect necessary maintenance and repairs since they always receive full rent for apartments
that only welfare recipients would tolerate occupying (Susser and
Kreniske 1987: 57). Thus in Chicago most public housing buildings
are literally crumbling, and nearly all of them sport multiple viola-
tions of municipal housing codes. They are commonly infested with
roaches, rats and maggots. High-rise projects such as the Henry
Horner Homes on the city's West Side or Stateway Gardens on the
South Side have no entry halls and no security guards; their lifts are
broken, their walls covered with graffiti, and their stairwells unlit and
reeking of human and animal excrements. Apartments on the ground
floor and first floor are nearly always abandoned and boarded up
because they present too high a risk of repeat burglary. Most units
in Henry Horner had not seen a coat of paint since 1970 and were
in such a state of disrepair in June of 1991 that the Henry Horner
Mothers Guild was able to file a suit against the Chicago Housing
Authority for carrying out a 'de facto demolition' of their site: half
of the 1,760 units of the complex were vacant for lack of funds to
renovate or clean them for rental.

Lastly, the *fiscal policies of the state and federal governments have also
added* to the plight of ghetto residents. The adverse repercussions of
Reagan's regressive tax policies on the urban poor are amply docu-

mented, since these reductions of government tax revenues were compensated primarily by the reduction of public budgets devoted to aiding the most dispossessed Americans (Caraley 1992). Less well known is the fact that about three dozen states implemented similar tax reforms that resulted in the further destabilization of precarious families in the 1980s. According to figures compiled by the advocacy group Voices for Illinois Children, nearly one million households saw their income cut significantly by the rise in state taxes. In 1992, Illinois had the second heaviest combined state and local tax burden on the poor in the country after Kentucky: the state's poorest 20 per cent households paid nearly 11 per cent of their meagre income in total taxes, twice the percentage borne by the richest 1 per cent of households. A preponderance of evidence thus confirms that it is a policy of malign neglect by the state on the housing, welfare and taxation fronts, not the emergence of a self-destructive 'underclass', that best explains rising poverty and deepening exclusion in the racialized core of the American metropolis.

Political marginality and the 'planned shrinkage' of the inner city

The neglect of the ghetto orchestrated by federal and local authorities does not stop at welfare policy but extends to the gamut of services aimed at disadvantaged populations. In the two decades after World War II, the steady expansion of the economy and the spectacular swelling of younger age cohorts created a context propitious to oppositional movements, and black demands for a less unequal sharing of public resources in the city led to the growth of federal and local programs (Katz 1989; Quadagno 1994). The economic retrenchment of the 1970s, characterized by the conjoint flaring up of unemployment and inflation, and the polarized growth of the 1980s, by contrast, fuelled a sweeping political and budgetary backlash against programmes geared to ameliorating the inner city.[32]

At the federal level, after Nixon's landslide re-election in 1972, a sudden *turnaround in urban policies* was effected by the federal government that practically annulled and then reversed the modest gains of

---

[32] A full analysis of this backlash, its social roots and racial imagery, its political mediations, and differential impact upon the various state programmes and bureaucracies that supervise the diverse components of the ghetto population is needed here. The reader is referred to George Lipsitz's (1988: ch. 8) fascinating account of its onset in the city of St Louis for a case study and to Edsall and Edsall (1991) for a suggestive discussion of the noxious nexus of 'race, rights, and taxes' at the national level.

the War on Poverty launched under Lyndon Johnson in response to black mobilization (Caraley 1992). Public housing funds were first frozen and then replaced with federal sharing grants controlled by local elites who redirected them to the benefit of the real estate industry and property owners. A whole array of compensatory programmes keeping inner-city institutions afloat, originally set up under the umbrella of the Great Society, were also cut and dropped. Federal resources directed at cities declined steadily under the aegis of Reagan and Bush the father, culminating with the termination of the CETA job training programme (Comprehensive Employment and Training Act), of General Revenue Sharing, and of Urban Development Grants. As urban political machines and local parties lost sway in the recomposed national electoral space, the web of intergovernmental grants between the four levels of the US bureaucratic field (federal government, states, counties and municipalities) that had cushioned the hardships of the urban poor across political boundaries became unhinged. The political isolation of cities, in turn, reinforced their role as entrepreneurs at the expense of their mission as social services providers, further fragmenting the revenue base on which the financing of public institutions rests (Weir 1994).

At the local level, a coalition of industrial, banking and commercial interests used the pretext of the fiscal crisis of cities to press for the dismantling of social programmes that sustained ghetto residents and their neighbourhoods. They were joined by managers of the local state who saw in the methodical rolling back of municipal services an efficient means of reducing public expenditures and of pushing the poor outside of areas in decline or slated for revitalization. This vision was materialized by what urban planners called the policy of 'planned shrinkage' or 'triage' of inner-city neighbourhoods (Beauregard 1993: 224–32; Marcuse et al. 1982): the selective curtailment or closing of public schools and libraries, hospitals and clinics, police stations and firehouses, bus routes and subway stations, aimed at pushing impoverished households to leave the heart of the metropolis and free up government funding for the 'redevelopment' of their neighbourhoods thus desertified (and/or other, better-located districts) for the benefit of business and the middle classes, whose presence conditions the fiscal health of the city.[33] Thus, in

---

[33] The expression 'planned shrinkage' was made famous in 1976 by Roger Starr, the former director of public housing for the city of New York who, ironically, had become Henry Luce Professor of Urban Values at New York University, in a resounding article published in the *New York Times Magazine* under the title 'Making New York Smaller'. In it, Starr (1976) proposed in particular that 'federal housing

Chicago, since the middle of the 1970s, the siting of public facilities and infrastructural outlays, land clearance decisions and tax abatements have increasingly served to attract and boost private capital and to stimulate the development of a new downtown dedicated to finance, business services and their higher-ranking employees. This diversion of city resources from households to firms and from the bottom to the top of the class structure effectively dried up public investment in the ghetto neighbourhoods of the West Side and South Side, sentencing them to stasis and decrepitude.

Few organizations are more revealing of the degree of institutional abandonment suffered by Chicago's hyperghetto than public schools. For they have in effect been reduced to *custodial* – as distinct from educational – facilities that serve to warehouse the offspring of the poor rather than to open an escape hatch out of their cramped life sphere. The city's public schools are rigidly stratified by both ethnicity and income, with racial segregation untouched and class segregation rising sharply since the 1960s. By the 1990s, the children of the historic Black Belt attended class in establishments whose student body was generally 100 per cent minority and more than 80 per cent from families living below the poverty line. They were educated in decrepit and overcrowded facilities, in larger classes led by teachers trained in the least selective colleges, and with fewer counsellors than either suburban or private city schools. For instance, all of the 601 pupils attending the Julia Lathrop elementary school on the city's West Side were black, and 592 of them qualified for free breakfast and lunch due to the extreme poverty of their family. The school had gone two decades without a library (the books rescued were left to gather mould in the lunchroom) and had no Parent Teacher Association. Most of its windows were boarded up or broken, and its walls covered with graffiti; its basketball courts had no hoops, and its main playground was littered with broken glass. All of its teachers came from the outside and rarely ventured into the

---

subsidies be used to encourage movement away from deteriorating areas'. The 'stretches of empty blocks may then be knocked down, services can be stopped, subway stations closed, and the land left to lie fallow until a change in economic and demographic assumptions makes land useful again'. Starr acknowledged that 'to advocate control of the shrinking population' via internal displacement and external 'resettlement' of the poor 'treads perilously near the tolerable limit of infringement on the rights of the people to be moved'. But he deemed it necessary to avert the collapse of the metropolis, and 'the problems connected with inaction are worse' anyway: 'The social disorganization that follows the concentration of dependent families in the older cities presents the greatest risk of all.'

neighbourhood for fear of violent crime. Indeed, it was difficult to get substitute teachers to come at all once they found out the location and condition of the school: 'When they see the building and the neighbourhood,' the principal lamented, 'they just keep on driving. You can't even get a taxi to bring you here' (Chicago Tribune 1986: 151–2).

The segregated public high schools of the city feed into a system of community colleges also defined by the double segregation of its student body based on race and class.[34] And with 'dropout' rates soaring well above 50 per cent (compared to 2.5 per cent in the schools of affluent suburbs) and three in four schools unequipped to train students for entrance to a college requiring a minimal scholastic level, higher education is out of the realm of the possible for the mass of adolescents from the South Side and West Side of Chicago. This leads political scientist Gary Orfield (1985: 176), one of the country's foremost authorities on public education in the metropolis, to insist that ghetto youth face

> a separate and unequal set of educational opportunities that continues throughout their schooling. One could easily argue that their educational experiences are not intended to and cannot prepare [them] to function in the same society and the same economy.

Because they (dis)serve a population that federal and local officials consider devoid of electoral value (given that the poor hardly vote), ghetto schools are also on the frontline of the budget cuts periodically imposed by a Board of Education perpetually strapped for funds. In summer of 1991, the Chicago school superintendent announced plans to close down sixteen schools in response to an unexpected revenue shortfall of $200 million: fourteen of the sixteen doomed establishments were located in poor black neighbourhoods (*Chicago Tribune*, 5 July 1991). As for parochial schools, they are no longer able to fill the gaping void created by the breakdown of public education: just a year earlier, the Chicago archdiocese had announced its own plan to close down seventeen establishments due to severe

---

[34] Community colleges (or junior colleges) are establishments of postsecondary education attended mainly by the children of the working class and ethnic minorities. They are supposed to give access to four-year university courses but serve mostly to provide remedial courses at the secondary school level, awarding a devalued credential (the 'associate degree') after two or three years of study (for a historical and sociological analysis of their role in the American academic field and social space, read Brint and Karabel 1989).

financial difficulties, eleven of them in the city's historic Black Belt.

The degradation of public schools is matched only by that of medical facilities. In 1990 the Acting Health Commissioner of Chicago publicly acknowledged that the city's public health system 'is a nonsystem . . . that is falling short and close to falling apart' (*Chicago Tribune*, 16 January 1990). Because of very low and tardy reimbursements by Medicaid (the federal programme providing health care for the indigent), a dozen inner-city clinics and hospitals went bankrupt during the 1980s. In September 1987, Provident Hospital, the nation's oldest black hospital, founded nearly a century earlier as part of the emergence of the 'institutional ghetto' (Spear 1968: 126), closed its doors, leaving the South Side without a full-service medical facility accessible to the poor. Six years later, local government had yet to fulfil its solemn promise to put it back in operation, in spite of mounting community demands.[35] Other than the grossly overburdened and gigantic Cook County Hospital (Lewis 1995), no private health care provider in greater Chicagoland offers prenatal and neonatal care to uninsured women. Poor women with no health insurance likely to have high-risk pregnancies are regularly turned away by private hospitals that do not hesitate to violate the law by transferring them to Cook County Hospital even during active labour (*Chicago Tribune* 1989) so as to rid themselves of 'clients' who would turn out to be financial burdens. The practice is so common that medical researchers coined the gruesome name of 'perinatal dumping' to describe and measure it (Handler et al. 1991).

Ghetto residents clamour not for high-tech therapies but for the most basic medical care such as immunizations for children, pap tests for women, high blood pressure and cholesterol screening, as well as nurses to visit patients too poor or too ill to travel, or who cannot lose entire days waiting in the emergency services of the public hospital to receive routine care. As a consequence of this 'medical gridlock', the infant mortality rate for blacks in the state of Illinois stood at 21.4 per 1,000 live births in 1985, compared to 9.3 per 1,000 for whites (*Statistical Abstract of the United States*, table 116). And in many sections of the ghetto, this rate exceeded 30 per thousand, a

---

[35] In 1993, Cook County finally purchased the building and reopened it as a satellite facility for the municipal hospital network in an effort to improve medical services to the South Side. Provident thus went from being a black-run hospital to a state institution.

figure comparable to those sported by such Third World countries as Costa Rica and Mali, in spite of the rapid progress in medical technology for the care of low-birthweight infants. Every year, over 1,000 newborns die in Chicago's historic Bronzeville, and another 3,000 are born with brain damage and other serious neurological ailments, and in most cases these ailments were fully preventable with better public health services. This excess infant mortality and morbidity cannot be explained except as a direct result of 'the deterioration of the medical infrastructure' in the racialized core of the capital of the Midwest as in other major cities nationwide (Guest et al. 1998: 31; also Whiteis 1992).

A series of empirical studies in urban and medical ecology conducted in New York City on the synergistic patterns of increased health care inequality, violent death and homelessness, the spread of AIDS and substance abuse, has established a direct causal relation between the urban desertification, social disintegration and sanitary worsening of ghetto neighbourhoods, on the one hand, and reductions in municipal services such as fire control, police protection and sanitation to levels far below those needed to maintain urban population densities, on the other (Wallace and Wallace 1990). Wherever city services have been cut or terminated, in keeping with the policy of 'planned shrinkage', rates of morbidity and social dereliction have shot up, setting off a self-reinforcing cycle of urban decay and lethal violence thrusting entire neighbourhoods into a fatal tailspin of deterioration. A germane statistical study of the links between race, neighbourhood distress and mortality in Chicago around 1990 'paint[s] a particularly stark picture of the human toll of residential and socioeconomic apartheid': infants born in the poorest black districts of the city are three times more likely to die than those born in the wealthiest white districts, while black men aged 15–45 die at six times the rate of men in affluent nonwhite neighbourhoods (Guest et al. 1998). This picture confirms the direct connection between the reduction of health services and the amputation of literal life chances in the hyperghetto at century's end.

The collapse of public institutions in the racialized urban core and the deepening marginality of its population are thus the product of public policies that, working against the backdrop of rigid racial division, have fragmented the public sphere, weakened black political capacities (Fainstein and Fainstein 1989), and stimulated the exit into the private sector of all those who could escape it, leaving the most dispossessed fractions of the African-American working class to rot in the social purgatory of the hyperghetto.

Conclusion: political reconfigurations of racial domination

In a famous article on the shanty-towns of Latin America, Alejandro Portes remarked that 'the *grave mistake of theories on the urban slum has been to transform sociological conditions into psychological traits* and to impute to the victims the distorted characteristics of their victimizers' (Portes 1972: 286, emphasis added). This is an apt characterization of the policy and scholarly debate on the dark ghetto that resurfaced in the United States after the mid-1980s. By focusing narrowly on the presumed behavioural deficiencies and cultural deviance of inner-city residents or the aggregate impact of the consolidation of a postindustrial economic order without paying due attention to the historical structures of racial segmentation, class inequality and governmental (in)action that refract and amplify their impact as well as distribute them in space, the thematics of the 'underclass' has hidden the political roots of the institutional implosion and material collapse of the ghetto, and it has contributed to accentuating the stigmatization and political isolation of its residents.

This is not the place to address the multiple analytical inconsistencies, empirical flaws and policy dangers of the *demi-savant* concept of 'underclass',[36] other than to point out (i) its internal heterogeneity and instability, which enable those who advocate it to redraw its boundaries at will to fit their ideological interests; (ii) its essentialism, which, through a slippage from substantive to substance, from measurement to reality, leads one to mistake a *statistical artefact* for a realized social group; (iii) its heavily negative moral connotations which reactivate the century-old opposition between the 'deserving' and the 'undeserving' poor; and (iv) its falsely deracialized ring, allowing those who use it to speak about race without appearing to do so. Suffice it, by way of coda, to spotlight its built-in propensity to sever the (hyper)ghetto from the broader sociopolitical structures of caste and class domination of which it is both instrument and product.

By reviving and modernizing the multi-secular notion that urban poverty is the result of the personal vices and collective pathologies of the poor (Boyer 1978), the rhetoric of the 'underclass' has conferred a veneer of scientific legitimacy on upper- and middle-class fears of the black subproletariat trapped at the bottom of the dualiz-

---

[36] See Wacquant (1992a) for an analysis of the functions of this scholarly myth at the intersection of the academic, political and journalistic fields and of the (extra-scientific) reasons for its social success, and Gans (1991) for a pugnacious discussion of its policy liabilities.

ing urban order. It has impeded, if not paralysed, a rigorous, historically grounded analysis of the changing articulation of racial
segmentation, rising class inequality and state abandonment in the
American metropolis. It has diverted attention away from the institutional arrangements in education, housing, welfare, transportation,
health and human services, and police and criminal justice that
produce and perpetuate the concentration of casualized and deproletarianized African Americans in the ruins of the historic ghetto.

Even the powerful structural theories elaborated by progressive
scholars intent on undercutting the behaviourist and moralizing cast
of the dominant strand of the 'underclass' tale dramatically downplay
the responsibility of the state in the dereliction of the dark ghetto.
Thus, for William Julius Wilson (1987 and 1996: p. xix), the main
woe befalling the inner city at century's close is 'the disappearance
of work and the consequences of that disappearance for both social
and cultural life'. Wilson considers public policies chiefly as a restor-
ative mechanism, responses by the state to undesirable conditions
produced essentially by blind market mechanisms and inert structures of spatial isolation.[37] Massey and Denton (1993: 2) make segregation their primary focus and show that the enduring residential
cloistering of blacks 'concentrates poverty to build a set of mutually
self-reinforcing and self-feeding spirals of decline in black neighborhoods'. But they isolate housing from the gamut of public (in)actions
that operate to compact and intensify marginality in America's racialized urban core. And, because they analytically conflate segregation
and ghettoization, they miss the structural and functional shift from
the communal ghetto of the Fordist age to the hyperghetto of the
post-Keynesian and post-welfare era.[38] By contrast, in the analysis
proposed here, the disapparance of a minimal social state is a self-
standing source of marginalization, and the range of state policies
oriented towards the populations trapped in the bottom tier of social

---

[37] Wilson (1996: 49–50) does acknowledge in passing that 'since 1980, a fundamental shift in the federal government's support for basic urban programs has aggravated
the problems of joblessness and social organization in the new poverty neighborhoods', but he devotes less than two pages of his 300-page study to this 'fundamental
shift'.
[38] Massey and Denton (1993: ch. 7) characterize as a 'failure of public policy' what
is diagnosed here as a functional product of state action. In the closing chapter of
American Apartheid (ibid. ch. 9), they offer recommendations for 'dismantling the
ghetto' that concern, nearly exclusively, housing and overlook the fact that the ghetto
of yesteryear has already been dismantled – only to make room for a different and
more deadly apparatus of exclusionary closure.

and physical space is treated as a full-fledged causative force before it can be discussed as possible curative answer.

By failing to link the implosion of the ghetto to the systematic debasement of the public sector and to *government policies amounting to the organized dumping of poor blacks*, the tale of the 'underclass' masks and thus absolves regressive choices made by the federal and local authorities (irrespective of party affiliation) in the wake of the political turnaround of the mid-1970s. Yet it is this policy of state abandonment and punitive containment of the marginalized fractions of the black working class that best explains why, a full century after its creation and three decades after the country's aborted and ill-named 'War on Poverty', the vestiges of the American ghetto remain, to borrow a premonitory phrase from the preface to the *Kerner Report* (1968, 1988: p. xx), 'the personification of that nation's shame, of its deepest failure, and its greatest challenge'.

3

The Cost of Racial and Class Exclusion in 'Bronzeville'

After a long eclipse, the ghetto made a stunning comeback onto the political stage and into the collective consciousness of America in the mid-1980s. Not since the riots of the 'long hot summers' of 1964–8 (Fogelson 1971) had the black poor of the metropolis attracted so much conjoined attention from the media, scholars and policymakers.[1] The relentless rise of persistent poverty (especially notable among women and children) and street crime, the crumbling of the patriarchal family, the continuing degradation of public housing and public schools, the sudden erosion of the tax base of cities afflicted by large ghettos and the dilemmas of gentrification, the disillusion of liberals over welfare and the sweeping political offensive of the New Right, all converged to thrust the residents of the segregated core of the large cities to the centre of public debate (Wilson 1987). But, owing to the growing hegemony of neoconservative ideology in the United States, discussions of the plight of ghetto blacks have been typically cast in individualistic and moralistic terms: the poor are presented in them as a formless aggregate of pathological cases, each with its own logic and self-contained causes, as the creatures of a noxious ethnic culture, or yet as the beneficiaries of a profligate welfare state that perpetuates the very misery it is supposed to combat by rewarding sloth and vice.[2]

[1] e.g., Kornblum (1984), Holdt (1985), Danziger and Weinberg (1986), *Chicago Tribune* (1986), Brewer (1987), Harris and Wilkins (1988) and Wilson (1993). Gephart and Pearson (1988) review the emerging wave of investigations into the remaking of the ghetto and its population on behalf of the Social Science Research Council, as prelude to a new research programme on the 'underclass' which would make its mark in the 1990s.

[2] An excellent overview of the springs, parameters and limitations of the resurging debate on poverty, welfare and racial division during the 1980s can be found in Katz (1989: ch. 4).

Severed from the structural changes and collective struggles that determined them, the social dislocations roiling the ghetto were then portrayed as a spontaneous, self-inflicted and self-perpetuating phenomenon. This marginalist vision of poverty found perhaps its most accomplished expression in the lurid descriptions of the black subproletariat that flourished in the pages of popular magazines, congressional hearings, and on televised programmes devoted to the emergence of an 'underclass'[3] characterized by its antisocial behaviours that would henceforth ravage the core of the US metropolis. Depictions and explanations of the predicament in which this group was said to find itself stressed the individual attributes of its presumed members and the alleged grip of a 'culture of poverty', reactualized through the idiom of 'moral poverty' or the 'culture of dependence' (Himmelfarb 1994).

Breaking with this moralistic and individualistic vision, this chapter draws attention to the specific features of the *proximate social structure* within which ghetto residents evolve and strive, despite the accumulation of obstacles, to live and, as much as possible, escape the crushing poverty and personal degradation that is their daily lot. To do so, I draw up a sociological profile of blacks who dwell within the despised perimeter of Chicago's 'inner city', or, to be more precise, I contrast the social condition of the inhabitants of the heart of the historic ghetto of the South Side and West Side (formed in the years between 1920 and 1940) with that of the residents of the adjacent black neighbourhoods (which arose in the post-World War II period and expanded in the wake of the Civil Rights revolution). Beyond its sociographic contribution, the central argument of this chapter is that the vague and morally pernicious neologism of 'underclass' and its behavioural-cum-cultural slant mask a phenomenon pertaining to the macrostructural order: the ghetto has experienced a 'crisis' not because the microstructures of the family and individual conduct have suddenly collapsed or because a 'welfare ethos' has mysteriously taken hold of its residents,[4] but because joblessness and economic

---

[3] See Wilson (1988) for an efficient dissection of the sensationalistic portraits of this new bogeyman category in the mass media and Wacquant (1996a) for a theoretical and empirical critique advocating that it enter into the sociology of urban marginality as object and not instrument of analysis.

[4] On the morrow of the Los Angeles riots of May 1992, Vice-President Dan Quayle declared in a speech that was to remain famous (in it he reproached the TV series *Murphy Brown* for presenting out-of-wedlock motherhood, the root cause of all the ills of the age, in a favourable light): 'The lawless social anarchy which we saw is directly related to the breakdown of family structure, personal responsibility and

exclusion, by rising to extreme levels against the backdrop of rigid racial segregation and state abandonment, have triggered a process of 'hyperghettoization' – in the sense of an exacerbation of the exclusionary logic of the ghetto as an instrument of ethnoracial control.

Indeed, the precarized strata of the black proletariat of the fin-de-siècle metropolis differ both from their counterparts of earlier epochs and from the white poor, in that they have grown increasingly concentrated in dilapidated territorial enclaves that are the receptacle and paroxystic concretization of racial and socioeconomic marginalization. Thus in Chicago the proportion of all poor blacks residing in extreme-poverty areas (i.e., census tracts containing more than 40 per cent persons living in households below the official poverty line) shot up from 24 per cent to 47 per cent between 1970 and 1980. By this date, fully 38 per cent of all poor African Americans in the country's ten largest cities lived in extreme-poverty tracts, compared to 22 per cent a decade earlier and only 6 per cent among poor non-Hispanic whites.[5]

This growing social and spatial concentration of extreme poverty has created an unprecedented mesh of obstacles for blacks residing in the imploding urban core. As we shall see in the next section, the social structure of the postindustrial ghetto has been radically recomposed by the mass destruction of manual jobs and the exodus of stable wage-earning households, as well as by the rapid deterioration of housing, schools, commerce, recreational facilities and other community organizations. This involutive process was abetted, amplified and exacerbated by government policies of industrial and urban *laissez-faire* that have channelled a disproportionate share of federal, state and municipal resources toward the more affluent classes and neighbourhoods (Squires et al. 1987; Caraley 1992). The economic

---

social order in too many areas of our society. For the poor the situation is compounded by a welfare ethos that impedes individual efforts to move ahead in society, and hampers their ability to take advantage of the opportunities America offers. . . . During this period of progress [since the ghetto riots of the 1960s], we have also developed a culture of poverty – some call it an underclass – that is far more violent and harder to escape than it was a generation ago. . . . The intergenerational poverty that troubles us so much today is predominantly a poverty of values. Our inner cities are filled with children having children; with people who have not been able to take advantage of educational opportunities; with people who are dependent on drugs or the narcotic of welfare.' This mishmash of false received ideas on the new urban poverty can be found, with minor variations, in newspaper reports, academic studies and policy debates from the mid-1980s onward.

[5] A detailed analysis of trends in the economy, social morphology and poverty concentration in these ten cities is laid out in Wacquant and Wilson (1989).

and social buffer provided by the presence of an established black working class and a visible, if small, black middle class which cushioned the impact of downswings in the economy and tied ghetto residents to the world of work during the decades of triumphant Fordism, have all but disappeared. And, like the tissue of local institutions, the social networks of kin, friends and neighbours have seen their resources gradually depleted. In sum, the residents of the fin-de-siècle ghetto find themselves facing a *closed opportunity structure*, shorn of the support of the institutions that used to ensure social stability and even mobility within the closed order of the Black Belt.

The purpose of this chapter is to highlight this specifically sociological dimension of the evolution of marginality in the historic core of Chicago's Black Belt. Data drawn from from a multistage, random sample of black citizens of Chicago's poor districts reveal that residents of the hyperghetto are indeed confronted with unique obstacles owing to the properties of the proximate social structure they compose.[6] But I must first set the historical backdrop by providing a skech of the accelerating degradation of Chicago's ghetto connecting the accumulation of social dislocations on the South Side and West Side to changes in the city's economy over the three decades after World War II.

Deindustrialization and hyperghettoization

Social conditions in the ghettos of the big cities of the Northeast and Midwest have never been enviable by metropolitan standards (Clark 1965; Rainwater 1970), but after the 1970s they descended into new depths of deprivation and suffering. The state of Chicago's racialized urban core is emblematic of the social changes that have sown marginality and despair in these declining districts. As table 3.1 indicates,

[6] The data used in this chapter come from a questionnaire survey of 2,490 adults living in poor neighbourhoods of Chicago carried out by the National Opinion Research Center in 1986–7 for the University of Chicago's Urban Family Life Project (directed by William Julius Wilson). The sample for blacks was drawn randomly from among the residents of 377 census tracts with at least 20 per cent inhabitants living below the federal poverty line (equal to the municipal average in the 1980 census). It was stratified by parental status and included 1,184 respondent, of whom 35 per cent lived in low-poverty tracts (with poverty rates between 20 per cent and 29.9 per cent), 31 per cent lived in zones of high poverty (30–39.9 per cent), and 30 per cent dwelled in extreme-poverty areas (including 10 per cent in tracts where the poverty rate exceeded 50 per cent).

TABLE 3.1
Selected characteristics of Chicago's ghetto neighbourhood, 1970–80

Area	Families below poverty line (%)			Unemployment rate (%)			Single-parent households (%)			Median family income*			Residents with 4-year college degree (%)	
	1970	1980	1990	1970	1980	1990	1970	1980	1990	1970	1980	1990	1970	1980
West Side														
Near West Side	35	47	51	8	16	21	37	56	60	6.0	7.5	10.3	5	13†
East Garfield Park	32	40	46	8	21	28	34	55	61	6.4	9.7	14.3	1	2
North Lawndale	30	40	44	9	20	27	33	52	60	7.0	9.9	14.2	2	3
West Garfield Park	25	37	36	8	21	27	29	49	55	7.5	10.9	17.1	1	2
South Side														
Oakland	44	61	70	13	30	45	48	74	77	4.9	5.5	5.9	2	3
Grand Boulevard	37	51	64	10	24	34	40	60	72	5.6	6.9	8.4	2	3
Washington Park	28	43	57	8	21	31	35	57	70	6.5	8.1	9.1	2	3
Near South Side	37	43	61	7	20	25	41	71	75	5.2	7.3	7.6	5	9†

Source: Chicago Fact Book Consortium, *Local Community Fact Book: Chicago Metropolitan Area* (Chicago: Chicago Review Press, 1984 and 1995).

* In thousands of dollars annually.

† Increase due to the partial gentrification of these areas.

an unprecedented tangle of social woes has gripped the black residents of the city's South Side and West Side. In the wake of the race riots that rocked the capital of the Midwest (whose peak was reached on the morrow of the announcement of Martin Luther King's assassination in April 1968), these enclaves have experienced vertiginous increases in the number and percentage of poor families, massive out-migration of working- and middle-class households, stagnation (if not regression) of income, and record levels of joblessness approaching those witnessed during the Great Depression. According to the 1990 census, the official unemployment rate reached 27 per cent in North Lawndale and East Garfield Park and neared one-third in Washington Park and Grand Boulevard, with a spike at 45 per cent in Oakland (just north of the prosperous neighbourhood of Hyde Park, home of the University of Chicago). The poverty rate approached the 50 per cent mark on the West Side and commonly surpassed 60 per cent on the South Side; two-thirds of all families living in these dilapidated zones were headed by lone mothers; about one-half of the population relied on public aid, for most adults were out of a job, and only a tiny minority of them (about 3 per cent in most districts) had completed college.

The most powerful vector behind the irresistible economic pauperization and social marginalization of large segments of the population penned in the segregated heart of Chicago is a set of mutually reinforcing spatial and industrial changes in the country's urban political economy[7] that converged during the 1960s and 1970s to undercut the material foundations of the ghetto by stripping it of its traditional role as reservoir of unskilled labour. Among these structural shifts are the decentralization of industrial plants (which commenced right after World War I but accelerated sharply after 1950) and the flight of manufacturing jobs abroad, to the Sunbelt states or to the suburbs and exurbs at a time when blacks were continuing to migrate *en masse* into Rustbelt central cities; the general deconcentration of metropolitan economies and the turn toward service sectors and occupations, fostered by the growing separation of banks and industry; the rise of the financial sector and the emergence of

[7] Space does not allow me to do more than allude to the main transformations of the US economy bearing on the composition and trajectory of the ghetto. One can find in-depth analyses of the systemic disorganization of advanced capitalist economies and polities and the impact, actual and potential, of 'postindustrial' and 'flexible specialization' trends upon cities and their labour markets in Lash and Urry (1987), Offe (1985), Block (1987), Hicks (1985), Bluestone and Harrison (1988), and Piore and Sabel (1984).

post-Taylorist, 'flexible' forms of productive organization; and, lastly, generalized corporate attacks on unions (expressed, among other things, by mass layoffs, severe wage cutbacks, the reduction of 'benefits' attached to jobs, and the spread of 'two-tier' wage and promotion scales and labour outsourcing) which have intensified job competition and triggered an explosion of low-pay, part-time work. It follows that even moderate forms of ethnoracial discrimination (by the city's historical standards) have a bigger impact on those caught at the bottom of the urban class order. In the labour surplus environment of the late 1970s and 1980s, the weakening of unions and the retrenchment of policies of reduction of racial inequality (including civil rights enforcement) hardened the segmentation of unskilled labour markets along ethnic lines (see, for instance, Wintermute 1983; Fainstein 1987; Williams 1987), marking vast numbers of ghetto blacks with the stamp of economic redundancy.   .

In 1954, Chicago was still near the apogee of its industrial power. Over 10,000 manufacturing establishments operated within city limits, employing a total of 616,000, including nearly half a million production workers. By 1982, the number of plants had been cut by half, providing a mere 277,000 jobs for fewer than 162,000 blue-collar employees (a loss of 63 per cent, in sharp contrast to the overall growth of manufacturing employment in the country, which added nearly one million production jobs in the quarter-century starting in 1958). Five years later, the city sported only 4,377 factories for 135,000 production jobs.[8] This crumbling of Chicago's industrial base was accompanied by substantial cuts in trade employment, with more than 120,000 jobs deleted in retail and wholesale from 1963 to 1982. The comparatively moderate growth of services (which created an additional 57,000 jobs during the same period outside health, financial and social services) came nowhere near compensating for this collapse of the city's low-skill employment pool.

Because blacks have historically relied heavily on manufacturing and blue-collar employment for economic sustenance,[9] the upshot of these structural changes for ghetto residents has been a steep and exponential *rise in labour market exclusion*. On the morrow of World War II, the residents of 'Bronzeville' – as the denizens of the city's

[8] These figures come from periodic reports by US Census Bureau, *County and City Data Book* (Washington, DC: Government Printing Office, 1955, 1983, 1988).

[9] In 1950, fully 60 per cent of employed black men and 43 per cent of black women in Chicago had blue-collar occupations (skilled and unskilled combined), compared to 48 per cent and 28 per cent of white men and women respectively. See 'Black Metropolis 1961, Appendix', in Drake and Cayton ([1945] 1993: 807–25).

TABLE 3.2
Rise of labour market exclusion in Chicago's ghetto neighbourhoods,
1950–80

	Adults not employed (%)		
	1950	1970	1980
City of Chicago	43.4	41.5	44.8
West Side			
Near West Side	49.8	51.2	64.8
East Garfield Park	38.7	51.9	67.2
North Lawndale	43.7	56.0	62.2
South Side			
Oakland	49.1	64.3	76.0
Grand Boulevard	47.5	58.2	74.4
Washington Park	45.3	52.0	67.1

Source: Computed from Chicago Fact Book Consortium, *Local Community Fact Book: Chicago Metropolitan Area, 1990* (Chicago: Chicago Academy Publishers, 1995); Philip M. Hauser and Evelyn M. Kitagawa, *Local Community Fact Book for Chicago, 1950* (Chicago: University of Chicago, Chicago Community Inventory, 1953).
Note: Labour market exclusion is measured by the percentage of adults not employed, aged 16 years and older for 1970 and 1980, 14 years and older for 1950.

main ghetto used to call it then – sported roughly the same employment ratio as the city overall, with some six adults in ten working (see table 3.2). While this ratio did not change citywide over the ensuing three decades, by the closing decade of the century most residents of the historic Black Belt could not find employment in the wage sector and had to resort to welfare, participation in the informal economy, or illegal activities in order to survive and thrive (as described in chapter 2). In 1980, two adults in three did not hold a job in the ghetto neighbourhoods of East Garfield Park and Washington Park, and three in four were not employed in Grand Boulevard and Oakland.[10]

[10] Rates of joblessness after the 1970s rose at a much faster pace in the perimeter of the historic ghetto than for African Americans as a whole, due to the growing class differentiation and spatial dispersal of the black community. For comparative data on the long-term decline of black labour force participation during the close of the industrial era, especially among males, see Farley and Allen (1987) and Bradbury and Brown (1986).

As the metropolitan economy shed its smokestack industries and redeployed outside Chicago, emptying the Black Belt of most of its manufacturing jobs and employed residents, the gap between the ghetto and the rest of the city – not to mention its white suburbs – widened dramatically. By 1980, median family income on the South and West Sides had dropped to around one-third and one-half of the city average respectively, compared with two-thirds and near parity thirty years earlier. Meanwhile, some of the city's white bourgeois neighbourhoods and upper-class suburbs had reached more than twice the citywide figure. Thus one-half of the households of Oakland on the historic South Side had to make do with less than $5,500 a year in 1980, while one-half of the households of Highland Park (in the northern periphery of the city) enjoyed incomes in excess of $43,000.

An ethnographic account of changes in North Kenwood, one of the poorest sections of the city's South Side, nudged between Cottage Grove Avenue, Lake Michigan and 35th Street, vividly encapsulates the accelerating physical and social decay of the ghetto and is worth quoting *in extenso*:

> In the 1960s, 47th Street was still the social hub of the South Side black community. Sue's eyes light up when she describes how the street used to be filled with stores, theaters and nightclubs in which one could listen to jazz bands well into the evening. Sue remembers the street as 'soulful.' Today the street might be better characterized as soulless. Some stores, currency exchanges, bars and liquor stores continue to exist on 47th. Yet, as one walks down the street, one is struck more by the death of the street than by its life. Quite literally, the destruction of human life occurs frequently on 47th. In terms of physical structures, many stores are boarded up and abandoned. A few buildings have bars across the front and are closed to the public, but they are not empty. They are used, not so secretly, by people involved in illegal activities. Other stretches of the street are simply barren, empty lots. Whatever buildings once stood on the lots are long gone. Nothing gets built on 47th. . . . Over the years one apartment building after another has been condemned by the city and torn down. Today many blocks have the bombed-out look of Berlin after World War II. There are huge, barren areas of Kenwood, covered by weeds, bricks, and broken bottles. (Duncan 1987: 18–19)

Duncan recounts how the disappearance of businesses and loss of housing stimulated the influx of drugs and criminal activities, which, in turn, undermined the sense of solidarity that once permeated the neighbourhood. With no activities or organizations left to bring them together or to represent them as a collectivity, with half the population evaporated in fifteen years, the remaining residents, some of whom now refer to North Kenwood as the 'Wild West', seem to be caught in a perpetual *bellum omnium contra omnes* for daily survival. One informant expresses this succinctly: 'It's gotten worse. They tore down all the buildings, deterioratin' the neighbourhood. All your friends have to leave. They are just spreading out your mellahs [close friends]. *It's not no neighbourhood anymore*' (cited by Duncan 1987: 21, italics added). The future of the community appears gloomy, given the ever-present threat of gentrification. For much of North Kenwood is composed of abandoned lots sitting on prime lake-front property that would bring in fabulous profits if they could be turned into upper-class condominiums and luxury apartment complexes to cater to the needs of the higher-income clientele of Hyde Park which lies just to the south. One long-time resident explains:

> They want to put all the blacks in the projects [on State Street, a corridor filled with gigantic and degraded public housing estates at the epicenter of the ghetto, only a few miles west].[11] They want to build buildings for the rich, and not us poor people. They are trying to move us all out. In four or five years we will all be gone. (Cited by Duncan 1987: 28)

Fundamental changes in the organization of the advanced capitalist economy of the United States have unleashed irresistible centrifugal pressures that have combined with black rejection of the caste regime through the Civil Rights movement to break up the social structure of the traditional ghetto and set off a process of *hyperghettoization*. By introducing this new term, I wish to indicate that, in shedding its economic function as a 'reservoir' of industrial manpower, the ghetto also lost its organizational capacity to embrace and protect its residents. The 'pulpit and the press', which formed the symbolic armature of the mid-twentieth-century Bronzeville according to Drake and Cayton ([1945] 1993), virtually collapsed as agencies for collective unification and action. Everyday life inside the South Side no longer unfolds in a parallel and relatively autonomous social space that duplicates the institutional structure of the broader society, albeit at an inferior level, and provides its inhabitants with the basic minimal resources to deploy their strategies of social reproduction or mobility (within the truncated black class structure). And

---

[11] For a fine-grained description of the history, informal economy of, and daily life in the high-rise project of the Robert Taylor Homes in the 1990s, read Venkatesh (2000).

the social ills that have long been associated with segregated poverty in the United States – violent crime, drug consumption and trafficking, housing blight, family disruption, educational failure, and the degeneration of the associational and commercial fabric – have reached qualitatively different proportions and become articulated into a new configuration that endows each of them with a more deadly impact than before.

The historian Allan Spear (1968) has introduced a useful distinction between what he calls the 'physical ghetto', a mere material structure of exclusion born out of white hostility and which keeps blacks apart in an enclosed and reserved space, and the 'institutional ghetto', the network of organizational and cultural forms elaborated by African Americans in reaction to their virulent ostracization by whites in the industrial city.[12]

> The rise of the new middle-class leadership was closely interrelated with the development of Chicago's black ghetto. White hostility and population growth combined to create the physical ghetto on the South Side. The response of Negro leadership, on the other hand, created the institutional ghetto. Between 1900 and 1915, Chicago's Negro leaders built a complex of community organizations, institutions, and enterprises that made the South Side not simply an area of Negro concentration but a city within the city. (Spear 1968: 91)

According to this schema, the hyperghettoization of the postindustrial era can be construed in part as a *retrogression towards the physical ghetto*, a retrogression resulting in an intensification of exclusionary social closure, since it now combines racial division with class segmentation against the backdrop of deproletarianization without the compensating action of a canvas of strong homespun organizations. If the 'organized' (or institutional) ghetto of the mid-twentieth century admirably described by St Clair Drake and Horace Cayton ([1945] 1993) imposed a colossal cost on blacks collectively,[13] the

---

[12] While useful descriptively to capture the main transformation of the structure and function of the reserved black districts of the early twentieth-century metropolis, the distinction between physical and institutional ghetto is nonetheless conceptually confusing (since the ghetto is itself an institution). It is more accurate to say that black Chicagoans moved from forcible *segregation* to full-fledged *ghettoization*, with the latter representing a distinct and novel urban constellation. This question will be addressed in another study devoted specifically to clarifying what makes a ghetto; see Wacquant (2005) for a preliminary statement.

[13] Let me emphasize here that the analytical contrast between the 'communal' or traditional ghetto and the contemporary 'hyper' ghetto implies no moral value judgement or nostalgic celebration of the Bronzeville of yesteryear. If the latter was

'disorganized' ghetto or hyperghetto of the fin de siècle carries an even steeper price. For now not only are residents of Bronzeville, as before, subject to the dictates of outside agents that rule the field of power (the white economic and political elite, banks and real estate agencies, the managers of state bureaucracies of social control). They also have no sway over the public services and private institutions, massively inferior to those of the wider society, upon which they depend day by day. The denizens of the contemporary hyperghetto comprise almost exclusively the most vulnerable and marginalized segments of the black community, devoid of the resources to escape the urban inferno that the collapsing ghetto has become.

Having lost the economic underpinnings and most of the fine texture of organizations and patterned collective activities that enabled previous generations of black urbanites to sustain their family and to (re)produce themselves as a collectivity in the face of continuing economic hardship and unflinching racial subordination, the Bronzeville of the close of century is the spawn of radical *class and racial exclusion*. It is to a sociographic assessment of this twofold exclusion that the second part of this chapter is devoted.

The cost of living in the hyperghetto

For reasons of ideological and practical convenience, students of urban poverty in the United States have accepted the ready-made categories of the US policy debate and state bureaucracy – starting with the artificial 'poverty line' created in 1963 for administrative and not scientific purposes. This has saddled them with a narrow, income-based, economistic model that provides both an inaccurate and an incomplete picture of social life, constraints and opportunities at the bottom of the social and spatial structure of the US metropolis.[14] Income is a thin and unreliable variable, especially difficult to

---

organizationally and socially integrated, it was not by free choice but under the yoke of total black subjugation and with the permanent threat of direct and overt violence from whites. By contrast with the transitory 'ethnic neighbourhoods' wherein lower-class immigrants of European origin clustered, black separation was never a voluntary development, but a protection against unyielding pressures from without (as demonstrated by Spear (1968) in his account of the genesis of Chicago's primary ghetto and Kusmer (1976) in the case of Cleveland).

[14] Surveying the intellectual foundations and scientific legacy of the 'War on Poverty' launched in the 1960s, Michael Katz (1989: 122) notes: 'The capture of the social science agenda by government combined with the capture of poverty by economists to confine the scope of the debate within market models of human behavior and interaction.'

measure when dealing with populations that are both marginal to the regular wage-labour economy and subjected to intensive state surveillance (through the regulations of welfare offices in particular). Moreover, aggregates of individuals characterized by the income level of their households or census tract give us little handle on the texture of social relations and on the springs and possibilities of action in their corner of social space. To gain a clearer picture of extant material conditions and fully document the depletion of collective resources at the core of the dark ghetto than can be done by reciting the standard statistics used in the first part of this chapter, I develop *multiple measures of economic and social vulnerability*, including the surrounding class composition, welfare trajectory, economic and financial assets, and social capital.

To capture and characterize the proximate milieu in which the residents of the contemporary hyperghetto evolve, I proceed by comparing the social structure of the neighbourhoods composing the historic core of Chicago's 'Bronzeville', solidified during the period 1910–1940, with that of the zones of black settlement that grew up around its perimeter after the uprisings of the 1960s. It so happens that, empirically, this distinction overlaps closely with that between black neighbourhoods of extreme poverty, defined as those areas of the city in which over 40 per cent of the population live below the federal poverty threshold according to the 1980 census, and black neighbourhoods of moderate poverty, comprising 20–30 per cent poor persons, which are broadly representative of the average black neighbourhood in Chicago, since the overall poverty rate of the African-American community in the city is about one-third.[15] In point of fact, nearly all (97 per cent) of the respondents in the latter category resided outside the historic perimeter of the Black Belt, whereas over 82 per cent of the respondents in extreme poverty dwelled on the West Side and the South Side, and an additional 13 per cent lived in immediately adjacent tracts. Thus, when we counterpose extreme-poverty areas with moderate-poverty areas, we are in effect comparing the historic heart of the ghetto, born in the industrial era, with its postindustrial periphery. Although this com-

---

[15] There are no white neighbourhoods of extreme poverty in Chicago or in any other US metropolitan area (Jargowsky 1997). Intense urban destitution is a phenomenon that affects exclusively African Americans (and to a lesser extent Puerto Ricans, to the degree that they sport a kindred phenotype), proof that the specific forms taken by urban marginality in the United States cannot be disassociated from the dichotomous ethnoracial division organizing that society.

parison involves a truncated spectrum of types of neighbourhoods,[16] it reveals a systematic and pronounced contrast between the hyper-ghetto and the adjacent black neighbourhoods (in which the African-American bourgeoisie has sought refuge and grown).

It should be noted first that this distinction between the districts of the core and the periphery of the ghetto, or between moderate- and extreme-poverty areas, is not merely an analytical or statistical distinction, but captures differences that are clearly perceived by social agents at ground level. First, the folk category of 'ghetto' does, in Chicago, refer to the South Side and the West Side, not just any area of black settlement inside the city; mundane usages of the term entail a sociohistorical and spatial referent that goes beyond the sole racial dimension. Furthermore, the residents of the historic Bronzeville have a diverging – and noticeably more negative – opinion of their neighbourhood compared to that of the residents of the surrounding black districts. Only 16 per cent rate their sector of the ghetto as a 'good' to 'very good' place to live in, compared to 41 per cent among inhabitants of low-poverty tracts; at the heart of the ghetto, nearly one respondent in four finds their neighbourhood 'bad or very bad', compared to fewer than one in ten among their counterparts on the outer perimeter of the ghetto. In short, the opposition between the zones of extreme poverty of the historic Bronzeville and other black areas where poverty remains moderate is one that is socially meaning-ful to their residents.

1   Class structure at the core and rim of the ghetto

The first major difference between the historic core of the ghetto and its rim areas pertains to their class structure (see figure 3.1). A sizable majority of the residents of the peripheral zones of the Black Belt are integrated into the wage-labour economy: two-thirds hold a job, including 11 per cent in middle-class occupations and 55 per cent in working-class positions, while one-third do not work.[17] These

[16] Because the sampling protocol excluded census tracts with poverty rate below 20 per cent, the survey excludes the black bourgeois neighbourhoods which would further accentuate the contrast between the historic heart of the ghetto and the new African-American middle class residing outside it.

[17] Class categories are defined on the basis of the respondent's current occupation as follows: the middle class comprises managers, administrators, executives, profes-sional specialists and technical staff; the working class includes both blue-collar (craft and skilled labour, operatives and labourers) and non-credentialled white-collar workers (sales, clerical and service employees); in the jobless category fall all those who did not hold a job at the time of the interview (regardless of their usual

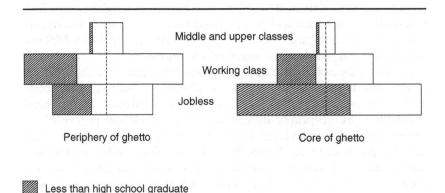

FIGURE 3.1   The black class structure in the core and periphery of Chicago's ghetto

proportions are exactly the opposite at the heart of the ghetto, where fully 61 per cent of adults are without employment, one-third hold working-class jobs, and a mere 6 per cent enjoy a middle-class occupational status. For those who reside in the vestiges of Bronzeville, then, *deproletarianization* is far and away the most common situation while having a stable job in the regular wage-labour economy is the exception. Controlling for sex does not affect this contrast except to confirm the greater economic vulnerability of women, who are twice as likely as men to be jobless. Men in both types of neighbourhoods feature a more favourable class mix resulting from their better rates

---

occupation when they held it). Our dividing line between the middle and working classes, cutting through 'white-collar' occupations, is consistent with recent theory and research on class (e.g., Abercrombie and Urry 1983; Wright 1985) and with contemporary perceptions of class in the black community (Vanneman and Cannon Weber 1987: ch. 10). The category of the jobless is admittedly heterogeneous – as it should be, since the identity of those without an occupational position is unstable and ambiguous in reality itself. It includes people actively looking for work (one-half of the men and one woman in ten), keeping house (13 per cent of the men and 61 per cent of the women), and a minority of respondents who also attend school part- or full-time (16 per cent of the males, 14 per cent of the females). A few respondents without jobs declared themselves physically unable to work (6 per cent of the men, 3 per cent of the women).

of employment (78 per cent at the rim of the ghetto and 66 per cent at its core). If women are much less frequently employed (42 per cent and 69 per cent respectively do not hold a formal job), they have comparable – that is, severely limited – overall access to middle-class status. Only 10 per cent hold a job requiring a postsecondary degree in both types of districts.

There is nothing surprising in these data. They stand as a stark reminder that, absent a protective welfare state, joblessness and poverty are the two sides of the same economic coin. The poorer the neighbourhood, the more prevalent unemployment and the lower the class distribution of its residents. But these results also reveal that the degree of economic exclusion observed in the remnants of the historic ghetto during the period of stagflation of the late 1970s had become more accentuated a decade later, despite a period of economic expansion among the most rapid in recent American economic history.

As one would expect, there is a close association between class position and educational titles: virtually all members of the middle class (93 per cent) have at least graduated from high school; nearly two-thirds of working-class blacks also completed their secondary education; but fewer than half (44 per cent) of the jobless obtained their high-school diploma. Looked at from another angle, 15 per cent of our educated respondents (i.e., high-school graduates or better) made it into the middle class, one-half have become white-collar or blue-collar wage-earners, and 36 per cent are without a job. By comparison, those without a high-school education are distributed as follows: 2 per cent in the middle class, 38 per cent in the working class, and a substantial majority of 60.5 per cent in the jobless category. In other words, for Chicago blacks, a high-school diploma is an indispensable credential for acceding to the world of work, let alone that of stable employment generally reserved to the middle class. Not finishing secondary education is synonymous with economic redundancy and paves the way for deproletarianization.

Residents of the core of the Black Belt are, on the whole, notably less educated than their counterparts in the neighbourhoods situated at its periphery. This results in part from their lower class composition, but also from the much more modest academic background of the jobless there: fewer than four in ten jobless respondents on the city's South Side and West Side graduated from high school, compared to nearly six in ten at the outer margins of the ghetto. One should note in passing that education is one of the few areas in which women do not fare worse than men: they are as likely to hold a high-school diploma (50 per cent) as their male counterparts in Bronzeville and more likely to do so in moderate-poverty areas (69 per cent versus 62 per cent). Yet this modest credential edge does not prevent them from suffering more acutely from poverty.

Moreover, residents of the heart of the Black Belt sport lower class origins overall, if one judges by the economic assets of their family of orientation and by the educational level of their father (only 36 per cent of residents of the ghetto core have a father with at least a high-school education, compared to 43 per cent among those who live around its outer rim). Fewer than four Bronzeville dwellers in ten come from a family that owned its home, and six in ten have parents who owned no assets (home, business or land). In the districts at the periphery of the ghetto, 55 per cent of inhabitants grew up in a home-owning family while only 40 per cent had no assets at all a generation ago. At both the heart and the periphery of Chicago's ghetto, women are less likely to come from a household possessing a home or any other asset (46 per cent and 37 per cent respectively). This difference in class origins is also captured by differential rates of welfare receipt during childhood: the proportion of respondents whose parents were on public aid at some point when they were growing up is 30 per cent at the outer edge of the ghetto and 41 per cent at its core. Women inside the perimeter of Bronzeville are by far the most likely to come from a family with a welfare record.

2 Class, gender and welfare trajectories

If they are more likely to have been raised in a household that received public aid, the residents of historic Bronzeville are also much more likely to rely or to have relied on welfare themselves. Differences of class, gender and neighbourhood cumulate at each juncture of the 'welfare trajectory' to produce considerably higher levels of aid receipt among the population at the core of the ghetto (table 3.3).

In the peripheral zones of moderate poverty, only one respondent in four is currently on aid at the time of the survey, while almost one-half have never personally received assistance. At the core of the ghetto, by contrast, over half of the residents are current welfare recipients, and only one in five have never received aid in the past. These differences are consistent with what we know from censuses and other studies: in 1980, about half of the black population of most districts of the South Side and West Side were officially receiving welfare benefits, while working-class and bourgeois black neighbour-

TABLE 3.3
Welfare receipt and food assistance in the periphery and core
of Chicago's ghetto (%)

	All Respondents		Males		Females	
	Periphery	Core	Periphery	Core	Periphery	Core
On aid when child	30.5	41.4	26.3	36.4	33.5	43.8
Currently on aid	25.2	57.6	13.4	31.8	32.4	68.9
Never had own grant	45.9	22.0	68.6	44.5	31.3	11.9
Expects to remain on aid*						
Less than 1 year	52.9	29.5	75.0	56.6	46.1	25.0
More than 5 years	9.4	21.1	5.0	13.0	10.8	22.0
Receives food stamps	33.5	60.2	22.2	39.1	40.4	70.0
Receives at least one of five forms of food assistance†	51.1	71.1	37.8	45.0	59.6	85.2

Source: Urban Family Life Survey, University of Chicago.
*Asked of current public aid recipients only.
†Including pantry or soup kitchen, government food surplus program, food stamps, Special Supplemental Food Program for Women, Infants and Children, free or reduced-cost school lunches.

hoods further out on the southern quadrant of the city, such as South Shore, Chatham or Roseland, had rates of welfare receipt ranging between one-fifth and one-fourth.

None of the middle-class respondents living in census tracts bordering the ghetto was on welfare at the time they were interviewed, and only one in five had ever been on aid in their life. Among working-class residents, a mere 7 per cent were currently on welfare, and just over one-half had never relied on welfare assistance. The same relationship between class and welfare receipt is found among Chicagoans at the core of the historic ghetto, but with significantly higher rates of public aid receipt at all class levels: 12 per cent of working-class respondents are currently on aid, and 39 per cent received welfare before; even a few (9 per cent) middle-class blacks are drawing public assistance, and only one-third were never on public assistance before, instead of three-quarters at the periphery of Bronzeville. But it is among the jobless that the difference between the heart and the rim of the ghetto is the widest: fully 86 per cent of those residing inside the perimeter of the historic Black Belt currently rely on welfare, and only 7 per cent have never had recourse to public aid, compared with 62 per cent and 20 per cent respectively among those who live at its border. Along with chronic joblessness, then, resort to public aid has become a majority experience for two generations of residents of the hyperghetto.

Neighbourhood differences in patterns of welfare receipt are robust across genders, with women exhibiting noticeably higher rates than men in both types of areas and at all class levels.[18] The handful of black middle-class women who reside at the heart of the ghetto are much more likely to admit to having received aid in the past than their male counterparts (one-third versus one-tenth). Among working-class respondents, levels of current welfare receipt are similar for both sexes (5 per cent and 8.5 per cent respectively), whereas levels of past receipt again display the greater economic vulnerability of women (one in two received aid in the past as against one man in five). This gender differential is somewhat attenuated inside Bronzeville by the general prevalence of public aid associated with acute economic marginalization, with two-thirds of all jobless males and nine in ten jobless women currently receiving public aid (typically General Assistance for the former and Aid to Families with Dependent Children for the latter).

The high incidence and persistence of joblessness and welfare reliance inside the hyperghetto, reflecting the drying up of viable options for employment, take a heavy toll on those who are on aid by severely depressing their subjective hope of finding a route to economic self-sufficiency.[19] Whereas a slim majority of welfare recipients living in low-poverty tracts at the margins of Bronzeville expect to be self-supporting within a year, and only a small minority anticipate resort-

---

[18] This gap reveals the 'maternalist' slant of the public assistance sector of the American state (Gordon 1990): the major means-tested programmes are aimed at women with very young children (as with Aid to Families with Dependent Children, the most commonly received aid until its abolition by the 'welfare reform' endorsed by Clinton in 1996), with the objective of reproducing the established structure of family and gender relations.

[19] This is consistent with other studies of welfare receipt that have repeatedly shown that being on aid is accompanied not only by anxiety and embarrassment but also by a sense of depression and entrapment among recipients (Rank 1994: 134–41).

ing to assistance for longer than five years, in the dilapidated districts of the historic ghetto, by contrast, fewer than one public aid recipient in three expects to be off the rolls within a year, and fully one in five anticipate needing assistance for longer than five years. This difference in the profile of expectations is more pronounced among the jobless of both genders. For instance, unemployed women at the heart of the ghetto are twice as likely as unemployed women at its periphery to think that they will remain on aid for more than five years and one-half as likely to anticipate getting off the rolls within a year.

Thus, if the likelihood of tapping public aid increases sharply as one crosses the line between the employed and the jobless, it remains the case that, at each level of the class structure, welfare receipt is notably more frequent at the core of the ghetto than at its rim, especially among the unemployed and among women. This spatial pattern is confirmed by data on the incidence of food assistance presented in table 3.3, with 85 per cent of women and 45 per cent of men in historic Bronzeville relying on a neighbourhood soup kitchen or receiving food aid from the government for themselves or their children (against 60 per cent and 38 per cent on the outer edges of the ghetto). This strongly suggests that those unable to secure jobs on the periphery of the Black Belt have access to social and economic supports that enable them to avoid welfare that their counterparts living at the heart of the ghetto lack, due to the fact that they are surrounded nearly exclusively by other (sub)proletarians shorn of resources. Chief among those are their financial and economic assets.

3 Differences in economic and financial capital

A quick survey of the economic and financial assets of the residents of Chicago's poor black neighbourhoods (table 3.4) reveals the appalling degree of economic hardship and economic insecurity that they confront day in, day out.[20] The picture in the peripheral zones of the ghetto is grim; inside Bronzeville, the situation is one of near-total dispossession.

[20] Again, I stress that this comparison excludes by sampling fiat the black upper- and middle-class neighbourhoods that have mushroomed in Chicago since the 'relaxation' of racial relations in the 1960s. Bart Landry (1987) surveys the development of this 'new black middle class' and Mary Pattillo-McCoy (1999) describes its vulnerabilities on Chicago's South Side.

TABLE 3.4

Economic and financial assets of residents in the periphery and core
of Chicago's ghetto (%)

	All Respondents		Males		Females	
	Periphery	Core	Periphery	Core	Periphery	Core
Household income						
Less than $7,500	27.2	51.1	16.1	33.6	34.5	59.0
More than $25,000	34.1	14.3	41.4	22.7	29.8	10.5
Finances have						
improved	32.3	21.1	35.7	23.4	30.4	20.1
Financial assets						
Has checking						
account	34.8	12.2	33.3	17.6	36.4	9.9
Has savings						
account	35.4	17.8	40.4	26.6	33.1	14.1
Has none of six						
assets*	48.2	73.6	40.7	63.1	52.6	78.3
Has at least three						
of six assets*	23.3	8.3	26.8	13.5	21.3	5.8
Respondent owns						
nothing†	78.7	96.6	75.6	93.7	80.5	98.0
Material assets of household						
Owns home	44.7	11.5	49.7	19.8	41.5	7.8
Has a car	64.8	33.9	75.9	51.4	57.7	25.7

Source: Urban Family Life Survey, University of Chicago.
*Including personal checking account, savings account, individual retirement
account, pension plan, money in stocks and bonds, and prepaid burial.
†Home, business, or real estate.

In 1986, the annual median family income for blacks nationally
was pegged at $18,000, compared to $31,000 for white families.
African-American households dwelling at the border of the historic
ghetto sport roughly equivalent incomes, with 52 per cent declaring
more than $20,000 per year. Those residing at the heart of the
ghetto, by contrast, command but a fraction of this figure: half of all
Bronzeville respondents live in households that dispose of less than
$7,500 annually, twice the figure for residents at the rim of the Black
Belt. Women assign their households to much lower income brackets

in both areas, with fewer than one in three at the border of the ghetto and one in ten at its core enjoying annual incomes exceeding $25,000. Even those who work report significantly lower incomes inside Bronzeville: the proportion of working-class and middle-class households falling under the $7,500 mark on the South Side and West Side (12.5 per cent and 6.5 per cent respectively) is double that for other black neighbourhoods, while fully one-half of jobless respondents in extreme-poverty tracts do not reach the $5,000 mark. Not surprisingly, residents of the historic ghetto are also less likely to report an improvement of the financial situation of their household, with women again in the least enviable position. These figures reflect sharp class differences: 42 per cent of middle-class respondents and 36 per cent of working-class blacks report a financial amelioration, as against 13 per cent of the jobless.

Due to their paltry and irregular income, the financial and banking services that most Americans take for granted are, to put it mildly, not of obvious access to poor blacks in the metropolis. Barely one-third of the residents of the outer edge of the ghetto maintain a personal checking account (which requires a fee); only one in nine manage to do so at the core of the ghetto, where nearly three of every four respondents report no financial assets whatsoever from a possible list of six (checking, savings or retirement accounts, stocks and bonds or burial insurance), and only 8 per cent possess at least three of those six assets (see table 3.4). Here, again, class and neighbourhood lines are sharply drawn: in low-poverty zones at the border of the ghetto, 10 per cent of the jobless and 48 per cent of working-class blacks have a personal checking account compared to 3 per cent and 37 per cent respectively inside the historic Black Belt; but the proportion for members of the middle class is similar (63 per cent) in both areas.

The American dream of owning one's home remains well out of reach for the overwhelming majority of our black respondents, especially those at the heart of the ghetto, where barely one adult in ten belongs to a home-owning household, compared to more than four in ten at the outskirts of Bronzeville – and this difference is just as pronounced within each gender. The considerably more modest dream of owning an automobile is also one that has yet to materialize for residents of the historic ghetto, of whom only one-third live in a household with a car in running order. Again, this figure expresses the cumulation of sharp class and neighbourhood differences: 79 per cent of middle-class respondents and 62 per cent of working-class blacks have an automobile in their household, contrasted with merely

28 per cent of the jobless. But, inside Bronzeville, only 18 per cent of the jobless have domestic access to a car (34 per cent for men and 13 per cent for women).

The social consequences of the radical paucity of income and assets suffered by blacks living in the hyperghetto cannot be overemphasized. Just as the lack of financial resources or possession of a home represents a critical handicap when one can find only low-paying and casual employment or when one loses one's job, in that it literally forces you to go on the welfare rolls, not owning a car severely curtails one's chances of competing for available jobs that are not located in the immediately vicinity or are not readily accessible by public transportation.

4 Social capital and poverty concentration

Among the resources that individuals can draw upon to implement strategies of social reproduction and mobility are those potentially provided by their lovers, kin and friends and by the contacts they develop within the formal organizations to which they belong – in sum, the resources they have access to by virtue of being socially integrated into solidary networks or associations, what Pierre Bourdieu (1986) calls 'social capital'.[21] To capture this dimension of the local structure, we asked our respondents to list their membership in various organizations and inquired about key social properties of their loved ones and three best friends (employment, education, welfare receipt and residence). The survey data indicate that not only do residents of the ghetto core have fewer and less dense social ties but also that they tend to have ties of lesser social worth, as measured by the lower social position of their partners, parents, siblings and best friend. In short, residents of fin-de-siècle Bronzeville possess lesser volumes of all three major forms of capital: economic, cultural and social.

Living in the hyperghetto means being more socially isolated: nearly half of the residents of extreme-poverty tracts have no current 'partner' at the time of the survey (defined here as a person they are

[21] Carol Stack (1974) has documented the pivotal role played by relatives, friends and lovers in strategies of subsistence among the urban black working class. On the management of personal relationships and the influence of friends in the ghetto specifically, see Liebow (1967), Hannerz (1969), Anderson (1978) and Williams and Kornblum (1985). But see also Patterson (1998) for a severe critique of the view that such interpersonal relations are either prevalent or effective in buffering urban African Americans.

TABLE 3.5

Social capital of residents in the periphery and core
of Chicago's ghetto (%)

	All Respondents		Males		Females	
	Periphery	Core	Periphery	Core	Periphery	Core
Current partner						
Respondent has no current partner	32.4	42.0	23.3	39.1	38.0	43.1
Respondent married*	35.2	18.6	40.9	27.0	31.2	14.9
Partner completed high school	80.9	72.1	83.8	83.0	88.4	71.5
Partner works steadily	69.0	54.3	50.0	34.8	83.8	62.2
Partner is on public aid	20.4	34.2	38.6	45.5	16.2	28.6
Best friend						
Respondent has no best friend	12.2	19.0	14.3	21.1	10.7	18.1
Best friend completed high school	87.4	76.4	83.7	76.3	87.2	76.3
Best friend works steadily	72.3	60.4	77.2	72.8	65.6	54.8
Best friend is on public aid	14.0	28.6	3.0	13.6	20.5	35.3

Source: Urban Family Life Survey, University of Chicago.
*And not separated from his or her spouse.

married to, live with or are dating steadily), and one in five confess
to having no one who would qualify as a 'best friend' – compared to
32 per cent and 12 per cent respectively in the neighbourhoods
adjacent to the ghetto. This means also that intact marriages are
much less common in the remnants of the historic ghetto (table 3.5).
Jobless men are much less likely than working males to have current
partners in both areas (44 per cent in Bronzeville and 62 per cent in
adjacent neighbourhoods). Black women have a slightly better chance
of having a companion, and this partner is more likely to have completed high school and to work steadily, if they live in a low-poverty

area along the rim of the ghetto. Residing in Bronzeville strongly impacts the class position of these men: the partners of women living at the heart of the ghetto are less likely to be stably employed than those of female respondents at its periphery (62 per cent work regularly in the former case, and 84 per cent in the latter). The remarkable fact that most male companions *have jobs* even in neighbourhoods where the vast majority of men are jobless confirms that being unemployed radically devalues men on the partnership market in the eyes of lower-class women.[22]

Friends often play a crucial role in life in that they provide moral and material support, help construct one's identity, and open up opportunities that would not materialize if not for their intercession, particularly in the area of jobs for members of the lower class (Fischer 1982; Sheppard 1966). We noted above that the residents of Bronzeville are more likely than other black Chicagoans to have no close friend. Moreover, when they do have a 'best friend', he or she is less likely to work; he or she is less educated; and he or she is twice as likely to receive public aid. Since friendships tend to develop primarily within genders and women have much higher rates of economic exclusion, female respondents are much more likely than men to have a best friend who does not work and relies on welfare support. Both of these characteristics, in turn, tend to be more prevalent among women living at the heart of the ghetto.

These differences in social capital are also evidenced by different rates and profiles of organizational participation. While being a member of a formal organization (such as a block club or a community organization, a political party, a school-related association, a sports, fraternal or other social outfit) is a rare occurrence as a rule – with the notable exception of middle-class blacks, two-thirds of whom belong to at least one such group – it is more common for residents of the historic ghetto (64 per cent versus 50 per cent in peripheral zones), especially among females (64 per cent versus 46 per cent), to belong to no organization. As for church membership, the small minority who profess to be, in Max Weber's felicitous expression, 'religiously unmusical' is twice as large at the heart of the ghetto as along its rim (12 per cent versus 5 per cent). For those

---

[22] Moreover, those who do have jobs are not for that reason necessarily attractive partners. In a detailed qualitative study of 292 low-income women in three US cities, Kathryn Edin (2000) further explores this devaluation by showing that the 'affordability' of men as marriage partners depends also on the stability and pay level of the jobs they hold, in addition to factors such as respectability and control over household decisions.

who declare a religion, residence in Bronzeville tends to depress church attendance slightly (29 per cent against 37 per cent attend service at least once weekly), even though women tend to attend more regularly than men in both areas. Finally, black women who inhabit the historic ghetto are also slightly less likely to know most of their neighbours than their counterparts in outlying low-poverty areas. All in all, then, the concentration of poverty at the core of the crumbling ghetto has the effect of systematically devaluing the social capital of those who live in its midst. This cannot but severely hamper the ability of residents of Bronzeville to search for, find and obtain employment in the regular wage economy.[23]

Conclusion: social structuring of poverty in the hyperghetto

The inordinate levels of material blight, economic deprivation and social hardship plaguing Chicago's historic Black Belt in the mid-1970s did not abate over the ensuing decade, quite the contrary. Bronzeville went unaffected by the economic resurgence of the 1980s, and neighbourhood conditions continued to deteriorate even as aggregate income and employment turned upwards in the city, which indicates an asymmetric linkage between the crumbling ghetto and national economic trends.[24] This underlines the pressing need to study *the public policies and the social structures that refract their relationship* and foster the continuing isolation of the racialized urban core and its residents.

The significant and systematic differences we have uncovered between the heart and the rim of Chicago's ghetto are a reflection of their diverging class mix and of the prevalence of economic exclusion inside the historic perimeter of the Black Belt. The contrasting class composition and organizational fabric of these two zones, in turn, point to the *implosion of the communal ghetto* which used to contain the full complement of social classes and ethnic

---

[23] Elliott and Sims (2001) found, moreover, that inner-city blacks use personal networks less than their Latino counterparts and that, when they are employed, they are 'less likely to risk their reputations by recommending friends and neighbours' due to the precariousness of their employment status.

[24] By that I mean that material conditions in the ghetto worsen significantly when the economy goes through a recessive phase but do not return to the *status quo ante* during the ensuing expansion, so that cyclical fluctuations in the national economy lead to stepwise increases in social dislocations inside the Black Belt (I return to this point in chapter 8, where I argue that this functional disconnection is a distinctive characteristic of advanced marginality).

institutions, and its incipient *replacement by a dual sociospatial structure* composed, on the one hand, of a hyperghetto harbouring the most precarious fractions of the black proletariat trapped at the core by collapsing public institutions and, on the other, the segregated neighbourhoods formed at the periphery by the growing black middle and upper classes.

The sociography of the Black Belt at century's end presented in this chapter suggests that social analysts of the nexus of racial division and urban poverty in the American metropolis must pay closer attention to the growing spatial and social differentiation of a black 'community' that can no longer be treated as a sociological monolith. They must fully reckon with the extraordinary intensity of socioeconomic marginality at the core of the crumbling ghetto before they resuscitate and spread tales about the stranglehold of a 'culture of poverty' or 'culture of dependency' that have yet to receive rigorous conceptual specification and firm empirical documentation.[25] The scholars and commentators who have been pushing moral and cultural or individualistic and behavioural explanations of the social dislocations that have ravaged the neighbourhoods of the historic Black Belt after the close of the Fordist–Keynesian era have created a fictitious axiological divide among urban blacks which, even if it turned out to be grounded (which has never been ascertained), cannot but pale when compared with the objective structural schism that sets the hyperghetto apart from the rest of the city and the brute material constraints that bear on its residents.[26]

[25] One could easily show that these notions are but scholarly capsules expressing the national folk conception of poverty that assigns its origins to the moral failings or psychological weaknesses of *individual poor persons*. Castel (1978) offers a cogent historical analysis of the moral(istic) tenets underlying the prevalent vision of poverty in the American mind and welfare policy.

[26] I am emphatically not proposing that differences between the denizens of the hyperghetto and the poor urbanites from other districts can be *explained by* their place of residence. Absent a theory of the socially selective processes whereby individuals and families get allocated across districts, separating 'neighbourhood effects' (the specific impact of location inside Bronzeville) from the social forces that operate jointly with, or independently of, them cannot be done by simple controls such as I have used here for descriptive purposes. On the thorny methodological complications posed by such socially selective effects and the theoretical difficulties entailed in specifying place-specific mechanisms, read Lieberson (1985: 14–43 and *passim*) and Sampson et al. (2002).

4

West Side Story: A High-Insecurity Ward in Chicago

> In such condition, there is no place for Industry; because the fruit thereof is uncertain: and consequently no Culture of the Earth; . . . no account of Time; no Arts; no Letters; no Society; and which is worst of all, continuall feare, and danger of violent death; and the life of man, solitary, poore, nasty, brutish, and short.
>
> Hobbes, *Leviathan* (1651)

The United States can rightfully lay claim to being the *first society of advanced insecurity* in history. Not just because it engenders – and tolerates – levels of lethal criminality incomparably greater than those prevailing in other postindustrial societies (its homicide rate in 1990 was ten times that of the major countries of the European Union, and its rate of incarceration four to ten times higher), but in the sense that it has elevated insecurity as an *organizing principle* of collective life and a key mode of regulation of individual conduct and socio-economic exchanges.

At every level of the social edifice and in every sector of existence, whether it be work, education, housing, family or health care, precariousness is omnipresent, and professional, material or moral downfall looms either as a common condition taken for granted for those at the bottom of the ladder or as the imminent sanction inflicted upon those who fail or fall short in the relentless and endless race for the 'American dream'.[1] True privilege, in today's United

[1] It is striking that Americans of the middle and managerial classes who have tasted the bitter dish of downward mobility following a job loss invariably consider themselves personally responsible for their fall. One gains the measure of the utter moral misery induced by their tribulations in reading Katherine Newman's (1988) revealing book *Falling from Grace*. On the pervasiveness of the national mythology of the 'American dream' of social advancement as the product of individual exertion at the bottom of the ethnic and class hierarchy, see Hochschild (1995: ch. 5).

States, consists in enjoying a social position situated outside – that is to say, high above – this vast *system of social insecurity* which continuously generates a diffuse anxiety and feeds a sort of frantic (and often frightened) *fuite en avant* from which only the higher reaches of the corporate and state nobility fully escape.[2]

But it is in the vestiges of the dark ghetto, that segregated and degraded enclave of the metropolis, that the insecurity which permeates and enwraps US society attains its paroxysm and that its characteristic social forms and effects are therefore concentrated and exposed to full scrutiny, as if through a magnifying lens. This chapter extends the two preceding ones by anatomizing a slice of the texture of daily life in a *high-insecurity ward* located within that immense open sore of dispossession that is the West Side ghetto of Chicago, among the largest and most infamous in the country. In it we come down from the abstract sky of aggregate statistics to take the reader to ground level to palpate the concrete meshing of spatial enclosure, deproletarianization, state abandonment and physical danger, and feel firsthand the abiding sense of peril and trepidation they create for those entangled in it.

West of Douglas Park, between Ogden Avenue and Roosevelt Avenue some five miles from the futuristic and opulent towers of downtown Chicago, lies a trapezoid-like district of ten square kilometres, bounded on three sides by railway tracks, containing some 62,000 people, 98 per cent of whom are African American and more than one-half under 20 years of age. This is the neighbourhood of North Lawndale on Chicago's West Side, one of the two historic 'Black Belts' of the capital of the Midwest. North Lawndale does not enjoy the historic renown of 'Bronzeville', its older and larger cousin of the South Side (Drake and Cayton [1945] 1993). But it has a distinguished industrial and cultural history of its own. Through its transition from a Jewish stronghold christened 'Chicago's Jerusalem' in the 1910s to a growing and populous African-American district after World War II, it was the cradle of Sears, Roebuck and Co. when it occupied the largest mercantile plant in the world and of G. E.'s Hawthorne Works when Elton Mayo conducted his path-breaking studies of factory productivity. Jazz clarinettist Benny Goodman,

---

[2] During the decade between 1985 and 1995, capital mobility, the stranglehold of financial logic and job insecurity all increased in tandem (Harrison 1994). Job precariousness 'democratized' (relatively speaking) as mass layoffs and the deterioration of employment terms struck white-collar workers and middle management, especially in the wake of corporate mergers and the stock-market machinations of their top executives (Wacquant 1996b).

blues guitarist Buddy Guy, and heavyweight world champion Ernie Terrell once called it home, as did a young Zionist militant by the name of Golda Meir before them. But by the time the neighbourhood erupted in five days of rioting in April 1968 in reaction to Martin Luther King's assassination, prompting Mayor Daley to give the national guards his infamous order to 'shoot to kill' looters, its industrial base had began to crumble, its social fabric to fray, and its historical fate to capsize.[3]

State poverty and street capitalism

It is an understatement to say that poverty is endemic in North Lawndale and that daily life there is harsh and insecure. It suffices to take a drive along its scraggy avenues lined with rubbish-strewn vacant lots and burnt-out or crumbled buildings to realize *de visu* the scale of the disaster that has befallen this sector of the ghetto. The carcasses of storefront churches (small independent chapels set up by the hundreds in the wake of the two great waves of African-American migration to the city in the 1920s and 1940s)[4] alternate with closed-down factories and warehouses condemned by the deindustrialization that battered the city's black working class head on. Western Electric, Island Stub, Sunbeam, Zenith, Ryerson Steel and

[3] A detailed historical account of the swift emergence and sudden decline of the West Side ghetto from World War II to the mid-1970s is Seligman (2005); an insightful analysis of everyday perceptions of poverty, social (im)mobility and opportunity among younger black men living on the Near West Side in the mid-1990s is offered by Young (2004).

In the summer of 1987, I spent six weeks conducting interviews in North Lawndale and adjacent areas (West Garfield Park, Austin, Near West Side) with participants in the Social Opportunity component of the Urban Family Life Project, including a dozen torrid days in the same public housing project of Ogden Court, where I was able to strike up cordial relations with a number of respondents who provided detailed descriptions of their daily round. In addition, several informants of my study of boxing grew up or were current residents of this section of the West Side and validated (or corrected) my firsthand observations as well as residents' accounts.

[4] On the social roots, cultural place and polyvalent role of these religious outlets in the black American ghetto at its apogee, see the classic study of Arthur Fauset, *Black Gods of the Metropolis* (1944), which gives an idea of the vertiginous decline of churches in the Black Belt after World War II. Their changing missions and effects in the 1990s are explored by Omar McRoberts (2003) in *Streets of Glory*, who reveals that contemporary churches in the inner city are run and attended mostly by outsiders to the neighbourhood, and therefore disconnected from the needs and interests of local residents.

Alex Paper Box are a few of the many big names of American industry that deserted North Lawndale for the far suburbs, southern states
and Third World countries in search of cheaper and less recalcitrant
labour.[5] The distribution centre of the retail chain Sears, Roebuck
and Co. employed 10,000 in 1970. By 1985 its staff had been halved,
and in 1989 Sears closed the site to relocate in a prosperous white
suburb in return for free land, ready access to a skilled workforce,
and tax breaks fit to make the most finicky corporate chief drool. The
title of largest employer in the neighbourhood was then turned over
to Mount Sinai Hospital, with a staff of some 2,000. Economically,
North Lawndale is not even the shadow of its former self: a desert
whose few oases now consist of unskilled, underpaid jobs in commercial and personal services, and of the criminal economy whose
control the three main gangs of the neighbourhood – the Vice Lords,
the Latin Kings and the Disciples – battle over.

The deterioration of the built environment is no less spectacular.
A third of the 16,000 dwellings in the neighbourhood are categorized
as unsound or unfit for human habitation by the city's housing
department. More than 12,000 of them predate World War II, and
another 2,000 were destroyed by fire or razed during the 1970s. At
the intersection of Hamlin Street and 16th Street, where Martin
Luther King had come to rent a two-bedroom unit in January 1966
to attract media attention to the criminal decrepitude of the housing
stock of the times and to launch a campaign to mobilize people
against enclosure in the ghetto (Lewis 1970: 315), there remains
nothing but a vacant lot strewn with broken glass and garbage. In
the early 1990s, the city implemented a demolition policy that led to
the razing of thousands of abandoned buildings deemed structurally
unsound or serving as dens of vice and crime. Streets and blocks
dotted with crumbling structures thus gave way to naked corridors
and vacant lots.

Commercial establishments are as scarce as abandoned buildings
are plentiful. North Lawndale has but a single supermarket, a single
bank and a single hospital, as against fifty-four lottery outlets and an
equal number of 'currency exchanges', those check-cashing and bill-
paying counters that, for usurious commissions, provide the poor

---

[5] According to a detailed econometric study, 106,000 of the 152,000 industrial jobs
lost by the greater Chicago area during the 1980s were the result of 'factory closures
and mass layoffs by Chicago firms taken over by multinationals' (Ranney 1993: 91–
3). These 106,000 lost jobs reduced the city's aggregate income by $3.2 billion.
During the same period, the state of Illinois lost 67,000 jobs transferred to *maquila-
doras* on the Mexican border alone.

with the financial services they cannot otherwise access.[6] And no fewer than one hundred liquor stores. The majority of the local shops are run by immigrants come from countries of the Middle East (especially Palestinians, Lebanese and Syrians, generically categorized by their black customers as 'Arabs') and of South-East Asia (mainly Koreans but also Filipinos). They distribute second-rate merchandise – for instance, the faded fruits and vegetables and cuts of meat unsuited for the butchers of the bourgeois neighbourhoods of the city – at prices considerably higher than usual.[7] Aside from its assortment of victuals, Fadi's Food Mart on Ogden Avenue and Homan Street sells $3,000 worth of lottery tickets every week. And three-quarters of its sales come from transactions effected by means of food stamps (*Chicago Tribune* 1986: 29, 52).

The reason why commerce in good fortune and alcohol – to say nothing of narcotics – is the most reliable sector of the local economy is that North Lawndale contains only the most marginalized fractions of the city's black proletariat. All those who could do so have fled this accursed territory in an attempt to escape the multiform insecurity that reigns in it. The neighbourhood lost one-third of its population between 1970 and 1980, and another quarter during the following decade; despite this exodus, the ranks of the destitute have remained roughly constant. Fully 44 per cent of the residents lived below the 'poverty line' (about $12,000 annually for a family of four) in 1990 owing to astronomical unemployment. The official jobless rate exceeded 20 per cent in 1980, after having doubled over the previous decade. The mini-boom of the close of that decade had practically

---

[6] Like pawn shops, currency exchanges have experienced booming expansion over the past two decades (Caskey 1994), due to the erosion of the economic base of the working class and the increased cost of access to banking services (all banking operations entail a charge in the USA, except for customers who keep large sums in their accounts). The unavailability of regular financial services further increases the cost of living for poor families: 40 per cent of American households declaring annual incomes of less than $12,000 in 1991 did not have bank accounts.

[7] David Caplowitz's (1967) demonstration that ghetto stores systematically overcharge their customers for merchandise of inferior quality still holds good a quarter of a century later (Eitzen and Smith 2003). The causes have remained the same: lack of competition, underinvestment, high costs of theft and insurance, failure to display prices, sales on credit at egregious interest rates and higher profit margins. In the meantime, thanks to economic deregulation, a veritable industry specializing in the financial exploitation of poor households has developed in the realm of credit cards, housing and automobile loans, and educational loans, worth over $200 billion (Hudson 1996).

no repercussions in this sector of the ghetto, as unemployment rose to 27 per cent in 1990 – but tallying adults who have given up on looking for jobs that do not exist reveals that nearly seven out of every ten residents are without work. During the 1970s alone, the neighbourhood lost 7,519 jobs for manual workers, amounting to 80 per cent of its industrial base. Over the same period the number of jobs in retail and wholesale trade fell by one-half, while the service sector lost more than 1,000 positions (Chicago Fact Book Consortium 1995: 107).

The brutal retraction of the labour market simultaneously accelerated the erosion of the patriarchal family and forced a good half of the residents of North Lawndale to resort to public aid to make ends meet. In 1980, 42 per cent of the 17,815 households tallied by the census were headed by a single mother; in 1990 that share had reached 60 per cent, and almost all were compelled to subsist on the meagre subsidies provided by the US 'semi-welfare state' – to borrow the acerbic expression of historian Michael Katz (1986, 1996). For those who managed to plough their way through the administrative jungle that hampers access to them, welfare benefits, whose value has diminished steadily over the years (they are not indexed on inflation), came up to a maximum of $385 per month for a family of four in 1990, to which could be added up to $219 in food stamps and $18 in home energy credit (to cover one's gas or electricity bill). Hardly enough to survive, then, since the average monthly rent in Chicago exceeded $400, and the heating bill for a typical apartment could easily reach $100 a month during the winter. According to the convoluted and cynical computations of the welfare services of the state of Illinois, the standard aid package fell 16 per cent below the 'survival threshold'.

This is to say that welfare recipients – who are forbidden to work for pay on pain of seeing this miserly aid withdrawn – are sentenced to a long term of *state poverty*. By the same token, they are fated, whether they want it or not, to turn to the informal economy, legal and illegal, which has experienced spectacular development of late.[8] Everything can be bought and sold on the streets of North Lawndale as in the rest of the ghetto; there is no profit too small, no trade too petty or too dangerous, no transaction too incongruous, when day-

---

[8] The growth of the informal sector in the big cities of postindustrial societies is not a conjunctural phenomenon, tied to deindustrialization alone, but a structural characteristic of their economies that has emerged in direct connection with the growth of the most advanced sectors (Portes and Sassen-Koob 1987).

to-day survival is at stake. Food stamps, false Medicaid cards and the public transport tokens distributed by the welfare office are the objects of endless trafficking. Even CTA bus receipts, which can be used for a return trip, are resold for 50 cents (twice their face value at purchase but still half the cost of full fare). A whole parallel economy has grown up around the picking up and recycling of cardboard, paper and garbage, similar to that observed in the shanty-towns of Latin America (Lomnitz [1975] 1977; Cross 1998): some collect aluminium cans, sold by the kilo to DMS Metal on Fairfield Avenue, or bricks from collapsed buildings (40 cents each) and metal from pipes, or paving slabs prised up from back alleys (those can fetch up to $5 a piece from a good contractor). One sells one's labour force at a day-labour agency to whomever wants it for the vilest tasks, one's time and blood (commercial plasma banks do a booming business in the hyperghetto),[9] one's personal belongings and those of others – the 'hot' merchandise that arrives in whole suitcases from the Chicago-O'Hare international airport, some fifteen miles away, is distributed within the hour. From disposable diapers to expensive cameras, to VCRs, clothing, liquor, weapons, car radios, cooked foods, jewellery, cosmetics and medicines: everything is available at unbeatable prices to those who know to show patience in the super-market of the streets.

Everyone tries to capitalize on their skills and abilities as best they can, and to transform themselves into a child-care worker or gardener, hairdresser or mechanic, plumber or taxi driver, plasterer or nurse, body guard (for men) or body for hire (for women). Brothels and gambling dens vie bitterly for the lean money, clean or dirty, circulating in the neighbourhood, along with the shady night spots (known as 'after-hours clubs')[10] where people can drink and buy drugs and sexual favours of every stripe. Anything goes in the battle to haul in that dollar, as ardently desired as it is cruelly lacking. But the spearhead of the new street economy is, without contest, the retail trade in drugs. With the invention of 'crack', the narcotics market moved for good into the democratic era: even the poorest of the poor can get their fix of low-grade cocaine, and if not, their 'Karachi stick', a few capsules of PCP or a couple of grams of 'Angel

[9] The subproletarians of the metropolis are the main suppliers of the flourishing industry of the collection of blood for hospitals and medical research (Snow and Anderson 1994).

[10] The place of these illegal nocturnal clubs and establishments in the history of the black American diaspora is explored by Hazzard-Gordon (1991); their specific sociability and functions are described by Roebuck and Frese (1977).

Dust'. In the three years that followed its introduction to Chicago at the end of 1989, the price of a bag of crack, commonly known as 'ready rock', fell from $20 to $5. Crack-addicted prostitutes, designated by the ultra-pejorative term of 'skeezers', offer the most varied and *outré* sexual services for barely a handful of dollars: the price of the trick is indexed on that of a dose of crack.[11]

Dope is everywhere, inside and outside, around the edge of North Lawndale as well as at its heart. You can buy it from neighbours or on the street, or in this burnt-out store with only the canopy left standing or this abandoned storefront church, that video arcade or this dry-cleaner which everyone knows launders more than just linen. And with drugs comes the silent procession of deathly infections and illnesses, of which hepatitis C, tuberculosis and AIDS are but the most visible (Walker and Small 1991; Chitwood et al. 1995). Nowadays everyone, or nearly everyone, in the hyperghetto is more or less directly impacted by the drug economy, whether as consumer or seller, employer or employee, kin, lover or friend of a dealer or a 'crackhead'; or again as neighbour and victim of the daily turbulence and violence that this poor man's savage capitalism sows in its wake (Harrell and Peterson 1992; Adler 1995).

The grisly lottery of homicides

The 'informalization' of the economy led by the retail trade in drugs and the weakening (if not outright collapse) of public institutions, from education to health to low-income housing and the most basic city services, added to the chronic penury and material distress of families, explains why physical insecurity has flung its net into the smallest crevices of North Lawndale and imposes itself nearly everywhere in its most acute forms. Like entrenched social marginality, violence tends to concentrate in the historic African-American neighbourhoods of the US metropolis.[12] Thus, the residents of the five

[11] For a portrait of the highly peculiar economy of sexual services linked to crack, see Ratner (1992) and Bourgois (1995: ch. 7), and, for a broader view of the 'hustling' strategies of women in the streets of the Milwaukee ghetto, read Miller (1987).

[12] The statistics that follow are computed on the basis of crimes reported in each district by the Chicago police for the year 1985 (provided by the Chicago Police Department). The extreme concentration of homicides in the racialized urban core of the United States is well documented, as are its linkages to intense segregation, poverty and inequality – see, e.g., Lauritzen and Sampson (1998) and Parker and McCall (1999).

African-American police districts in Chicago (four on the South Side and the fifth covering the West Side, housing some 550,000 souls, 96 per cent black) are *eleven times more likely* to be victims of violent crime than the 404,000 residents of the two white districts (91 per cent white) covering the north and south-west sectors of the city. Measured against their area, the black districts record twenty-four times more violent crimes than the white ones, even though they have twice as many police officers as their white equivalents. The homicide rate in North Lawndale is five times the national average, the frequency of sex offences six times higher, and the incidence of assaults more than tenfold. Violent death is an ordinary occurrence, a sort of grisly lottery, as documented by this excerpt from the murder roster kept by the neighbourhood police between August and December 1983 (and serialized by the *Chicago Tribune* in the autumn of 1985):

13 August: Fred Jones, 42, stabbed at 1:40 am in his apartment on South Albany Avenue.

13 August: Keith Perkins, 21, shot in the entrance hall of his building at 4300 W. 19th Street.

15 August: Edgar Thomas, 19, shot dead at 11:20 pm at 3200 W. 16th Street.

24 August: Charles Jackson, 36, a double amputee, beaten to death with his own wheelchair at 3:20 am in a vacant lot at 1500 South Kedzie Avenue.

3 September: Elvis Allen, 25, shot at about midnight in his apartment on South Tripp Avenue.

10 September: Graylin Moses, 21, shot at 1:30 am at 2600 Ogden Avenue.

11 September: Joyce Partridge, 31, shot at 3:30 am during an attempted robbery while sitting with her boyfriend in his car parked near 1400 South Millard Avenue.

12 September: Timothy Chapple, 27, shot dead at 2:00 pm on 3600 West Greenshaw Avenue.

23 September: Allen Bates, 23, found stabbed at about 6:00 am in a vacant lot at 1500 South Lawndale Avenue.

29 September: Charles House, 20, shot at 2:20 pm in an alley at 1600 South Homan.

3 October: Kenneth Price, 20, shot dead at about 9:00 pm at 2200 South Avers Avenue.

5 October: Kevin Foster, 21, shot dead at about 9:00 pm at the corner of South Homan and W. 16th Street.

15 October: Lionel Jones, 34, found shot at 9:00 pm in a vacant lot at 3300 W. 16th Street.

22 October: Gloria Mitchell, 24, stabbed at about 2:00 am in front of her home at 1100 South Springfield Avenue.

13 November: Raul Muggia, 23, shot at 3300 West Douglas Avenue.

4 December: Marie Stevens, 34, of Calumet Park, stabbed at 10:00 am in her car at 3900 W. 19th Street.

18 December: James Collins, 50, shot at about midnight in a tavern at 3700 West Ogden Avenue.

20 December: Jay Jackson, 46, found stabbed at 9:30 pm in his apartment at 1600 South Springfield Avenue.

28 December: Dorsey Dickson, 19, shot dead at 8:40 pm in a poolhall at 4200 West Roosevelt.

The second son of a working-class family that came up from Mississippi a generation ago, 'Jazzy' Ike, 27, has lived in North Lawndale all of his life. He has knocked about the different ill-reputed housing projects on Chicago Avenue, Central Park and Lexington Boulevard. In his youth, like many neighbourhood teenagers, he hung out with two of the local gangs turfing along Ogden Avenue for a while. But the street has changed a lot since then, and the risks have become too severe. Today the money is too 'fast' and the rules of manly honour that used to regulate confrontations no longer apply. Because sidewalk clashes, once involving individuals, have become increasingly collective: they pit gangs, or rival factions of a gang ('crews' and 'posses'), which fight over control of the economy of predation in the neighbourhood.[13] The result is a sort of free-for-all, a perpetual latent mini-guerrilla war of the dispossessed among themselves in which, as Thomas Hobbes wrote of the state of nature – that is, the state of culture and social relations characteristic of seventeenth-century English society under strain from the rise of mercantile capitalism (Macpherson 1964) – 'the notions of Right and Wrong, Justice and Injustice have there no place', because 'where there is no common power, there is no Law; where no Law, no Injustice'. And, as in war, 'Force, and Fraud, are . . . the two Cardinall vertues' of daily life. Despite his gruelling schedule (he normally works sixty-six hours a week but often puts in more than ninety hours), Ike is delighted to

---

[13] The logic of these struggles for the appropriation of territory and control of the predatory economy that develops in it is unpacked by Vigil (1988), Sánchez-Jankowski (1991) and Venkatesh (1997).

have scrounged a job as night watchman at the Sutherland hotel, a nondescript establishment on the edge of the ghetto, because his previous job as part-time security guard in a local shop proved to be much too risky.

Ike: I witnessed killin's *several times*. Matter of fact, I was held at gunpoint, coupla times. They was tryin' to force a coupla us to be involved in the gang. An' uh, two guys, I guess tied to another gang, went and blew their head off right by the tracks. It was on Lawndale, no it was on Avers, by Archer.

LW: So it could have been you?

Ike: Yeah! That's what I'm sayin': *it coulda been me a lotta times*. But see, it's the same witchyou, you could be walkin' around, down the street, somebody shoot you.

The junction of Kedzie Avenue and 16th Street is the epicentre of a zone known to the local police by the revealing moniker 'The Bucket of Blood', for being the site of frequent assaults and murders. The driver of the municipal bus that shuttles up and down Ogden Avenue always carries a revolver under his uniform; some shopkeepers in the area wear holstered guns openly on their belts to discourage potential robbers. Others serve their customers from behind steel gates or thick sheets of bulletproof glass, a sawn-off shotgun lying on the counter within easy reach. Everyone takes care not to tempt providence by avoiding public places such as parks and bus or train stations as much as possible. Special vigilance is exercised by all when the end of the month nears: it is a period of heightened danger since it is when recipients of public aid receive their cheques and inject new cash into the anaemic economy of the neighbourhood.

The presence of the police is of little help in such a social context of generalized suspicion and dread. Worse yet: the police themselves are feared, not because they represent the secular arm of the law but because they are an additional vector of violence and insecurity. 'I seen crooked poh-lice officers dealin' drugs', Ike says:

I've seen poh-lice *shoot people*, y'know, for no reason. I've seen poh-lice *beat up* people for no reason. It's jus' part of . . . If they will shoot the poh-lice jus' as [inaudible] the poh-lice will shoot them (brief smirk), it's like that. . . . No, it's no different, if it's a black or a white poh-lice, to me it's no different. They do their job, they do they job accordin' to their report sheet, or how they have to handle they job. Now if they have to deal with it to save their life, or how they feel best the situation, then they *do it like that*. That's *anybody* who's out there will do it [i.e., shoot first], even the drug dealer: if you mess up his stuff, he'll send somebody for you. Now if that boy don't do it, he'll come an' do it hisself, or have somebody else do it.

An informant from the adjacent neighbourhood of Austin (also exclusively black and nearly as poor as North Lawndale) who works as an exercise instructor at the local YMCA fitness club adds:

Tubby: Why a guy gonna go work a job and be makin' three hun'red dollars a week when he can make three, four hun'red dollars a day sellin' drugs? He don't wanna do it, he en' up sellin' drugs. (whispering, very earnest) And the way I look at it, *it's not illegal to sell drugs* – it's illegal if you don't wanna cooperate [with the police].

You know, I was with frien's of mine playin' basketball yesterday and they all police officers and they say the same thin'. Because it's everywhere. They say when they call [the police precinct], you don't even get the backup. What he's tellin' me, the ones that really they bust is someone who hasn't been *cooperatin'* . . .

You out there bustin', *you know everybody's sellin' drugs*. People call the police station, 'Hey, these people sellin' drugs' you know, 'this house is sellin'.' They don't bust 'em.

LW: And why is that?

Tubby: Because they lack the manpower and somebody's gittin' paid.

LW: Who is that?

Tubby: Politicians, police, someone, they coul' be payin' off an alderman or somethin', 'Keep the police off my back.' So he pays off the alderman, the alderman pays off the commander, *whoever, whoever, whoever*, you know. So, it's like uh, it's jus' a *ugly-ass scene* out there.

'Six feet under the ground or in jail'

As violence and fear spread and intensify in the hyperghetto, social relations unravel, zones of sociability shrivel, and the institutions embodying citizenship turn into so many hulks empty of content and meaning or, worse yet, into additional implements of marginalization.

In North Lawndale, children (and even more so their teachers) fear going to school, where playground confrontations and fracas at the end of classes threaten to degenerate at any moment into deadly shoot-outs. Many youths give up their studies, reasoning that if they have to risk their lives, they might as well do it 'working the street' and contribute their due to the family budget or crash the doors of the culture of teenage consumption. Senior residents no longer dare to venture outdoors even in broad daylight, especially on the day – known to all – when they must go to fetch their pension cheques, which makes them conspicuous prey, with the result that they cannot benefit from the few social services to which they are entitled. The health services are teetering on the edge of ruin: half of the 25,000 patients treated by the emergency services of Mount Sinai Hospital in 1985 were seriously injured (categorized 'with trauma') as a result of wilful violence in the vast majority of cases, and 60 per cent of emergency cases had to be funded (niggardly and with long delays) by Medicaid, leaving an unpaid bill totalling $1.6 million. With barely 2 per cent of Chicago's population, North Lawndale accounts for 10 per cent of calls to the city's fire department ambulances, which are unable to keep up with demand. Similarly, how can the plague of drugs be turned back when policemen play an active part in the trade (some officers keep all or part of the narcotics they seize when they arrest dealers, for their personal use or for later resale at their own profit), and the justice system is incapable of protecting witnesses who would have the courage to testify against traffickers?

It is clear that the different forms of insecurity – economic, physical, civil and social – which manifest themselves to varying but rarely small degrees in the different segments of American society, and of which the contemporary ghetto is a sort of hyperbolic incarnation, are closely interconnected. It is clear also that these interconnections are all the tighter for being woven through the double prism of rigid racial segregation and steep class inequality, both of which are particularly pronounced in the big cities abandoned by the state in the era of neoliberal reconfiguration. And it is equally patent that, whenever it reaches the extreme levels it displays on the West Side of Chicago, insecurity becomes a veritable social and financial millstone for the city and, by extension, for the country, over and beyond the tragic human waste and bottomless (and politically censored) suffering it forces on those who have to experience it day by day. The policing of North Lawndale, carried out by a contingent of 150 officers and aimed mainly at preventing violence from spilling over the neighbourhood's perimeter, alone cost the city more than $40,000 a day in 1985, even though the official rate of theft there hardly exceeded the city average (*Chicago Tribune* 1986: 47). The state of Illinois paid out to the neighbourhood a daily 'subsidy' of $247,000 in public assistance, amounting to four times the average welfare layout per capita for the state as a whole, and another $13,400 for free medical care (equal to five times the Illinois average). In 1985, Chicago spent nearly $500 million on law enforcement and $300 million to run the county criminal court. A resident of the Windy City spent an average of $600 on protecting himself or herself against crime, while the state of Illinois allocated a budget of $400 million to the construction of new penitentiaries. Between 1980 and 1995, the state's prison population jumped from 12,500 to 37,000 inmates, but the number of black convicts behind bars quadrupled to reach 24,600 (Hartner 1998), the overwhelming majority of them coming from the devastated neighbourhoods of the South Side and the West Side.[14] The annual cost of holding a run-of-the-mill felon in the Midwest was in the vicinity of $22,000, equivalent to the median annual income of an African-American family. One cannot but wonder how high a tribute of misery, violence and money American society is prepared to lay each year on the altar of insecurity.

Whatever 'optimism of the will' one might manage to muster as a matter of principle, it is difficult to not give in to the 'pessimism of the intellect' (to borrow Romain Rolland's formula made famous by Antonio Gramsci) when one considers the future that such systemic insecurity promises to those who have grown up with it day and night in the hyperghetto. That so many youth of the West Side find themselves caught in the economy of drugs and violent predation, which marginalizes them still further when it does not lead them to a tragic and premature end, leaves Ike puzzled and even slightly angry:

Ike (puzzled and agitated): It's a *trip! I dunno* an' I tell 'em 'Hey! Man, that ain't the right way to go!' They say (defensively, but firmly, as if to reluctantly concede that they might not be wrong after all): 'What, you want us to *starve* an' be *nothin'*?' I say, 'you bein' a nothin' anyway 'cause you only have but two ways to go, *six feet under the ground or in jail.*'

LW: Do they know it, do they recognize it?

Ike: Yeah, yeah, they know. But they said they not gonna let themselves not have anything. For a young guy stuck in the ghetto, today, it's hard, real hard, y'know. Yeah, bein' black, if you don' have a education, you're not gonna get anywhere.

[14] In 2001, half the 15,500 prisoners released by the Illinois Department of Corrections after serving their sentences came from Chicago. North Lawndale headed the roster of six dilapidated and segregated districts (out of the seventy-seven districts composing the city) that welcomed home a full third of the ex-convicts returning to the Midwest capital. Three of the others were the adjacent and contiguous districts of Austin, East Garfield Park and Humboldt Park on the West Side, the remaining two being the adjoining South Side neighbourhoods of Englewood and West Englewood (La Vigne et al. 2003).

Part II

Black Belt, Red Belt

Part II

Black Belt, Red Belt

5

From Conflation to Comparison
How *Banlieues* and Ghetto Converge and Contrast

Having mapped out the position and transformation of the dark ghetto in the American metropolis after the acme of the Civil Rights movement, we now turn to laying the rudiments of a comparative sociology of the structures and mechanisms of urban marginalization in France and the United States. This chapter examines not the substance but the *substrate* of the racialized urban tensions that have manifested themselves with increased virulence in these two societies at the close of the century – the sociological soil in which they have lately sprung forth with astonishing vigour in the one case and taken root over the run of decades in the other, namely, the *cités* (housing projects) of the French working-class *banlieues* and the black ghetto of the US metropolis. Whence it emerges that, beyond surface similarities in the lived experiences of their residents and certain recent trends of their economic and demographic structures, the reality of urban seclusion and marginality pertains to two profoundly different processes and scales on the two sides of the Atlantic.

To anticipate my thesis: the *banlieue*, or rather the *banlieues* (plural), said to be *deprived* (in so far as this term designates a sociologically meaningful entity and not just an object of ordinary or political-cum-journalistic common sense)[1] are not *ghettos* in the sense acquired by that notion in the US context in reference to African Americans.

---

[1] Let me emphasize at the outset that, if there is a signal characteristic of the French *banlieues*, it is their extreme heterogeneity as regards their urban texture and economic activities as well as their population and occupational composition – as Soulignac (1993) shows in the case of 'the' Parisian periphery in *La Banlieue parisienne. Cent cinquante ans de transformations*. The 'sensitive neighbourhoods' targeted by France's urban policy since the early 1990s are themselves just as diverse and dispersed (Tabard 1993; Goldberger et al. 1998).

On the one hand, the cumulative incidence of segregation, poverty, isolation and violence assumes a wholly different intensity in the United States. On the other hand, and this is the more crucial point, *banlieues* and ghettos are the legacies of different urban trajectories and arise from disparate criteria of classification and forms of social sorting: sorting operates first and foremost on the basis of class position (modulated by ethnic provenance or appearance) in the first case, and of ethnoracial membership in a historically pariah group (irrespective of class position) in the second. Finally, the French Red Belt and the American Black Belt have been the object of diametrically opposed political constructions and bureaucratic managements in the 1980s and 1990s. This is to say that the chasm that separates these two sociospatial constellations is not only of a quantitative order but pertains more fundamentally to the *sociohistorical and institutional* registers.

This diagnosis, refuting the thesis of a transatlantic 'convergence' on the pattern of the black American ghetto, in no way implies that the declining working-class districts of the French urban periphery have not seriously deteriorated since the postindustrial turn,[2] to the point where their predicament calls for a multisided intervention of public authorities much more vigorous and coherent than the ones, largely media-oriented and reactive, that it has elicited thus far. Nor does it rule out the possibility that, absent a sustained corrective action, it might *eventually* evolve toward a situation *approximating* in certain respects the ethnic patterns of urban America. Simply, in the current state of these two universes and of the empirical knowledge that we have of their functions and functioning, the parallel with the black American contour – especially when it takes the form of an emotive amalgamation rather than of a reasoned comparison – is sure to obscure the social transformations of which the margins of the French city and the racialized core of the American metropolis are at once the locus, product and symbol.

The analysis that follows draws mainly, on the US side, on a series of studies conducted in Chicago's black ghetto between 1987 and 1991 by means of a varied panoply of methods (a quantitative survey of a large representative sample of residents, in-depth interviews with a subsample of inhabitants and with local employers, analysis of official statistics, participant observation and neighbourhood ethnog-

---

[2] The same structural decline has afflicted the working-class districts of the industrial cities of other European countries (Jacquier 1991), such as the United Kingdom, the Netherlands and Germany, following the sudden rise of long-term unemployment and its destructive effects on the urban fabric from the close of the 1970s onwards (Cross 1992; Engbersen et al. 1993; Kronauer et al. 1993).

raphy) and, on the French side, on a systematic reading of available urban monographs, complemented by interviews with government experts and officials in charge of urban policy for greater Paris (Île-de-France), the scrutiny of administrative documents, along with a field study carried out in La Courneuve, a working-class town of the proximate ring of the Parisian suburbs in 1989–1991. Its goal is not to close the raging debate about the 'Americanization' of poverty in the European city and its linkages, structural or conjunctural, with the rise of racism and xenophobia across the Old World, but to contribute to better formulating the vexed question of 'ghettoization' by clarifying the main terms of a Franco-American rapprochement. By laying out the rudiments of a provisional comparative schema, I wish above all to *urge the utmost caution in the transatlantic transfer of concepts* and theories pertaining to the articulation of racial domination, class inequality, and the structuration of space. And thereby to help prevent the errors of public policy that follow from analytic slip-ups fostered by the political and journalistic hype to which this confused and controversial issue is subject.[3]

In this chapter, I set out the framework for a rigorous analysis of the structural similarities and functional differences between the black American ghetto and the declining working-class *banlieues* of France before addressing in the next two chapters four salient dimensions of everyday life in these two spaces of urban exile: the experience of territorial indignity and the cleavages that organize ordinary perceptions and relations (chapter 6); delinquency and violence, both real and perceived, and the role of formal institutions and public bureaucracies in feeding or thwarting them (chapter 7). This point-by-point comparison will allow us, in the third part of the book, to recast the question of urban marginality on the threshold of the new century and to exorcize once and for all the spectre of the 'ghettoization' of the European city.

The moral panic of the '*cités*-ghettos'

On the threshold of the 1990s, France witnessed the swift rise and crystallization of what South African sociologist Stanley Cohen

---

[3] The same errors of diagnosis of the nature and dynamics of the black ghetto led, in combination with an adverse balance of political forces, to the gross inadequacy and, as a consequence, the stunning failure of urban policies aimed at improving the fate of its residents in the wake of the uprisings of the 1960s (Harris and Wilkins 1988).

(1972) calls a *moral panic* over the '*banlieues*'.[4] Until then, the bland and banal universe of the degraded housing projects of the urban periphery hardly interested anyone, whether in the microcosm of politics or in that of the media, and to a lesser degree in the arena of social research. In the span of a few years, however, in the changing political climate caused by the breakthrough of the National Front in the mid-1980s and a series of incidents and events of various kinds and degrees of seriousness – brawls among youths, racist or non-racist assaults, tensions between families of different origins dwelling in large housing projects, skirmishes or open confrontations between local youths and the police, protests against the ongoing deterioration of the estates hastily thrown up in the 1960s, the political mobilization of young '*beurs*' (French-born children of North African provenance), etc. – to which, for reasons that are partly their own, the media gave considerable play, the *cités* became one of the main topics of preoccupation of journalists, politicians and experts in urban planning. This sudden rise of '*la banlieue*' – typically in a homogenizing singular and without specification of its location or makeup – in the hierarchy of so-called current issues was accompanied by the lightning-quick promotion of the theme of the 'ghetto'[5] and, with it, the blossoming of an imagery of presumed American origin (Chicago, Harlem, the Bronx, 'gangs,' etc.), suggesting, in a more or less articulated manner, that the condition of the residents of the peripheral public housing estates of France was growing increasingly akin to that of blacks trapped in the abandoned urban core of the United States.

[4] 'A condition, episode, person, or group of persons emerges to become defined as a threat to societal values and interests; its nature is presented in a stylized and stereotypical fashion by the mass media; the moral barricades are manned by editors, bishops, politicians, and other right-thinking people; socially accredited experts pronounce their diagnoses and solutions; ways of coping are evolved or (more often) resorted to; the condition then disappears, submerges or deteriorates and becomes more visible' (Cohen 1972: 9). Three characteristics point to a moral panic: the suddenness and disproportion of the public reaction to the phenomenon; the designation of a 'folk devil', i.e., a wicked category taken to be responsible for the collective ill in question; and the rise of hostility against this guilty party. A theoretical and empirical review of the large body of research inspired by this concept is Goode and Ben-Yehuda (1994).

[5] This would have to be nuanced: the theme of the 'ghettoization' of the *banlieues* is not as new as would seem at first glance, as Christian Bachmann and Luc Basier (1989) note in their analysis of the media construction of the *cité* of the Quatre mille in La Courneuve. But, in quantitative terms, the contrast in the frequency of its invocation in the mainstream media between the early 1980s and 1990s is clear and massive.

One would need, drawing on the works of the American school of 'constructivism' which has done much to advance our understanding of the specific logic of production of this sort of artefact founded in reality (*cum fundamento in rei*) that are 'social problems', to analyse the process whereby '*la banlieue*' was manufactured as a public issue,[6] deserving of the attention of specialists – administrative or scientific – and calling for the actual or proclaimed intervention of political decision-makers; by what route this object, with its fuzzy contours and variable geometry, and for this reason well suited to espousing the disparate ideological and professional interests of those who invoke it, came to occupy the first rank in the 'arena of social problems' (Hilgartner and Bosk 1988); who are the agents that have worked to make it recognized as such and with what aims; what rhetorical stratagems and strategies they have deployed and with what effects, intended or unintended, positive or perverse; and who, at the end of this ongoing collective work of production, can claim 'ownership' of the problem.[7] I will content myself here with sketching in broad strokes, and without claiming to comprehensiveness, its image in the recent public debate by picking out a few salient examples in journalistic, political-administrative, and intellectual discourse.

The core of this composite discursive nebula is made up of what took on the air of a veritable campaign, conducted by weekly magazines and daily newspapers in the early 1990s, around the growing menace posed by the '*banlieues*' and their now overly familiar procession of deprivation and vice, despondency and despair, to public order and the integrity of the national society. Both cause and effect of this media build-up, the belief that the country's declining working-class *cités* are swimming in anomie and on the brink of constant rioting due to an unprecedented combination of geographic isolation, physical deterioration of the housing stock, and the concentration of 'immigrants', have spread very widely. Whether founded or not, the notion that they have already turned into 'ethnic ghettos' (the hard

---

[6] See Spector and Kitsuse (1987) for a theoretical panorama, and Best (1989) for a varied range of illustrative case studies.

[7] Joseph Gusfield (1981) shows, using the example of drunk driving, that the process of production of a 'social problem' typically culminates in the granting of a sort of 'ownership right' to those competing agents who have succeeded in defining with authority its nature and remedies. In the case of the *banlieues* 'in crisis', the pre-eminence initially accorded to architects and urban planners, educators and experts in social matters was quickly overtaken by police discourse and the consolidation of a flourishing industry of private expertise in 'urban security'.

version) or are on their way to becoming such (the soft version) is now shared, with minor nuances, by the leading media outlets, the executives of the state bureaucracies entrusted with the day-to-day management of these urban estates, some representatives of the populations concerned, and even a good many researchers.

Proof is the epidemic of articles with alarming and alarmist titles, such as 'Ghetto Stories', 'Long Live the Ghetto', 'These *Banlieues* where the Worst is Possible',[8] triggered at the beginning of the 1980s by the infamous 'rodeos' in the Minguettes neighbourhood of Vénissieux (a waning industrial suburb of Lyons) and the firearm death of little Toufik Ouanès in the *cité* of the Quatre mille in La Courneuve in July 1983, which was suddenly accelerated and greatly amplified following the incidents in Vaulx-en-Velin in October 1990, variously described by the press as 'a riot', a 'revolt', an 'uprising' (as one says of a subject people), and even a 'veritable urban guerrilla [war]'. Since then, apocalyptic prophecies have multiplied, according to a logic well known to analysts of the journalistic construction of social problems, according to which, leaning upon one another and backed by the notions of the political *doxa* of the moment, which they share with the officials of the established parties and senior civil service, each news organization 'frames' its reporting after that of its competitors and draws from them part of its materials and its interpretive schemata – whence the convergence of journalistic 'analyses' of the phenomenon and its concomitant appearance on the scene of 'current events', well suited to produce a strong *effect of objectivity*.[9] To the point where the French government felt compelled, in the spring of 1991, to assemble hastily a package of emergency measures aimed to anticipate and avert a 'hot summer' – the *Nouvel Observateur* granted its precious cover for the week of 20–26 June 1991 to a 'Special on the *Banlieues*: Before the Fire . . .' – , after which it put in motion an 'Anti-Ghetto Act' whose implementation would be supported by nothing less than a 'Marshall Plan for the *banlieues*'.

[8] In *L'Évènement du jeudi*, 10–16 May 1990; *Politis*, 8 February 1990; and *Le Figaro*, 9 October 1990, respectively. One could cite countless other news reports and show that the themes, images and warnings they sounded are remarkably homogeneous across the newspapers and magazines politically identified as Right and Left.
[9] The workings of this self-reinforcing process are explored by Best (1990) with respect to the 'problem' of 'child victims' in the United States, and by Reinerman and Levine (1997) about the panic around 'crack' cocaine; see also the remarks of Champagne ([1993] 1999).

Citations could easily be multiplied *ad lib*. 'Let's call the tragedy of Vaulx-en-Velin by its proper name,' wrote *L'Express* in an October 1990 article entitled 'The Powderkeg of the *Banlieues*': 'an *American-style* urban revolt, the revolt of a social *ghetto* featuring 50% of youths and 20% unemployed among its population of 45,000' (11 October 1990, my emphases). Several months before this episode, the weekly *Politis* was already sounding the alarm about an 'American-style evolution' leading straight to the establishment of 'a soft apartheid' in the *banlieues* of the national territory (8 February 1990). Even a newspaper that prides itself on being so staid and circumspect as *Le Monde* entered the round. In the February 1991 edition of its *Dossiers et documents* devoted to 'The City and its *Banlieues*', the daily of the Rue des Italiens worried about 'badly managed immigration that takes the form of ethnic "ghettos"' and about bands of youths 'modelled after the teens of Los Angeles or Harlem who fascinated them in cult-films like *Warriors* or *Colors*' (*Le Monde* 1991). And the Minister of the Interior (in charge of law enforcement) in person sought to reassure what is customarily called public opinion by declaring, with much grandstanding but at little expense, that his government would not permit the blossoming of 'Bronxes' in French cities.[10]

Let us clearly assert, to avoid any ambiguity, that it is not a matter of reducing the 'problem' of the peripheral *cités* to the sole symbolic construction of it that the press, television and other specialists in representation are putting forth. There is no question that the objective reality of urban inequalities and their distribution in space has changed significantly in France since the historic rupture of the mid-1970s and that the social misery and daily malaise of the residents of the popular neighbourhoods gone fallow have gained in both depth and intensity, if only due to the relentless rise of unemployment and assorted forms of underemployment linked to the 'flexibilization' of the labour market (Boyer 1988) in the course of a decade otherwise marked by an unprecedented celebration of the values of money and individual 'success' – and this under the aegis of successive Socialist governments. It is a matter, first and by way of methodological precaution, of questioning the hasty equation too often made between transformations of discourse and transformations of reality, and of emphasizing the wide discrepancy that can exist

---

[10] In a statement published in the issue of *Paris Match* dated 15 June 1991, and featured as a title on the colour cover.

between a phenomenon and its media projection.[11] Next, it is an opportunity to recall that, far from reflecting the movements of society, albeit in the manner of a distorting mirror, the representations that circulate in the journalistic field contribute to fashioning reality to the extent – which is never negligible – that they influence the ways in which the latter is perceived, managed and experienced, both by those in charge of the bureaucratic oversight of 'social problems' and by those who are the targets of their interventions. And the well-known effect of self-fulfilling prophecy that can be observed every time a discourse is invested with the power to bring into being what it claims is already there (Bourdieu 1982: 157–61) can turn out to be especially powerful in the case of populations which, over and beyond their economic deprivation, suffer from being dispossessed of the mastery of their own public representation.

Finally, much as with the question of immigration (Noiriel 1988: 124), there is every reason to think that the greater recent *visibility* of the *banlieues*, like their lesser *readability*, is explained in part by the increase in the number and dispersion of the agents with a professional interest in their existence and problematization. This increase is itself related to a set of broader cultural and political transformations, among them (i) the pre-eminent place that the school now occupies in the system of instruments of social reproduction and mobility for categories that were until recently largely excluded from it, especially the children of the lower fractions of the working class which find themselves concentrated precisely in these defamed districts; (ii) the multiplication of means and channels of mass communication, with the appearance of new private radio and television channels and the proliferation of specialized publications, all oriented toward the quest for maximum audience, for whom the *banlieue* provides a topic propitious for dramatic reporting; (iii) the gradual devaluation of the dirigist tradition of state planning and decentralization of public administrations, which gave a plethora of new bureaucratic agents a parcel of authority to negotiate with regard to urban problems;[12] and (iv) the work of autonomization and valoriza-

---

[11] Read Sánchez-Jankowski's (1994) exemplary dissection of this discrepancy as concerns gangs in the US metropolis. The subsequent importation into France of the US media mythology of gangs is sketched by Wacquant (1994).

[12] For an insider's view of the intertwined relationships of competition and collaboration arising among bureaucratic operators intervening within the framework of the new urban policy, see Bourdieu (1991a). Bachmann and Le Guennec (1996) trace the bureaucratic piling on and entanglement of the programmes put in place by successive governments of the Left and Right.

tion of these 'urban issues' inside the state, stimulated by the sudden rise of the idiom of 'exclusion' at the intersection of the political, intellectual and journalistic fields (Tissot 2005).

But isn't the thematics of *'cités-ghettos'* just a discourse of journalists for journalists that allows them to create a media splash, to manufacture on the cheap a homegrown exoticism geared to increasing circulation or viewership ratings? Not solely, since politicians and para-politicians (members of the higher civil service, heads of public bureaucracies, leaders and co-ordinators of local associations and pressure groups interested in issues relating to the city) have taken up this discourse for themselves and fuelled it with their own contributions. Here again, I will limit myself to three significant examples. The first is the evaluation report on the Neighbourhood Social Development programme (*Développement Social des Quartiers*) produced by experts from the Commissariat général du plan and published by La Documentation française in 1988, which assigns to this vast state undertaking the objective of stopping in their tracks 'ghetto phenomena and the risk of social explosion they induce' (Lenoir et al. 1989: 31).[13] This point of view is shared by certain (real or supposed) representatives of the populations concerned, such as Farid Aïchoune, who sums up this vast topic in his book of interviews with youths of immigrant origins in the Parisian industrial suburbs, generously peppered with street slang, *Born in the Banlieue* (*Nés en banlieue*), in these terms:

> The worst is yet to come: it is not only violence but the risk of a drift toward the constitution of American-style 'ghettos' – long denounced – that threatens France. The temptation of Islam as a sheltering value and the phenomenon of gangs are its telltale signs. (Aïchoune 1991: 173)

Similarly, countless mayors have rushed to invoke the spectre of *'quartiers-ghettos'*, either with the aim of justifying *ex post* a policy of urban development undertaken for completely unrelated reasons, or, on the contrary, to dress up in falsely generous intentions their refusal to see public housing built in their boroughs, or, finally, to clamour for the creation of a municipal police force in order to reinforce the surveillance of the populations confined to their problem *cités*. But,

[13] Another illustration on this front: the 'Loi d'orientation sur la ville' (Omnibus Act on City Policy) voted in 1991 by parliament was likewise known as the 'anti-ghetto law' – the coarseness of the label is presumed to indicate the sturdy determination of the national representatives to stop the plague dead in its tracks.

in this competition to exploit the ghetto label, the first prize goes without contest to architect Roland Castro, founder and figurehead of Mission Banlieues 89, an administrative venture launched by the French presidency in 1983 to steer the rehabilitation of public housing around the rim of Paris and 'to make the *banlieues* as beautiful as the cities'. Castro does not hesitate to claim – without anyone knowing on what criteria he does so – that there now exist no fewer than '600 ghettos' on French territory, which shelter 'two million people living in abject exclusion and another five to six million "at risk"', who, owing to their very vulnerability, are on the brink of descending into a 'civil war' with which the 'France-*banlieue*' is said to be pregnant.[14]

Even social scientists have contributed to the swelling of this panic discourse by encouraging the uncontrolled analogy with the United States, thus decisively bolstering the process of officialization of the problem, in both contents and effect, since the media-political representation can then deck itself out in the authority of science. Thus demographer Hervé Le Bras (1989) put Europe on guard against the 'American trap' represented by the formation of ethnic 'ghettos', which he claims is already under way in several countries of the continent. Sociologist Alain Touraine (1990) is still more affirmative and urgent in his evocation of what he calls 'the American syndrome':

> We are rapidly sliding toward the American model. . . . We are heading toward segregation in its harshest form, the ghetto. . . . In view of the general logic of the growth of segregation, we can expect that our big cities will take the path of Chicago.[15]

[14] In an interview cited in the colourful (and fanciful) special report 'Racisme: enquête sur la ségrégation en France' (Racism: An Inquiry into Segregation in France), *Le Nouvel Observateur*, 22–8 March 1990.

[15] Touraine (1991a) seemed to revise this opinion in an article that appeared a few months later in *Le Monde* (17 July 1991) under the title 'La France perd-elle la tête?' (Is France Losing its Mind?), in which he writes in particular: 'In France, there exist in practice no ghettos – with the exception of the camps for families of *harkis* [Algerians who fought in the French Army during the Algerian war of independence] – but instead zones with high populations of various foreign origins, which is quite different.' But in an interview given that same year to the magazine *Sciences Humaines*, Touraine (1991b) again jumps on the bandwagon of the US drift: 'We are living in a society that is no longer structured by relations of production, an American-style society defined by consumption, by opposition to a society structured around class conflict. . . . The theme of exclusion or integration has superseded that of social class. There is no longer a pyramidal vision of society. The discontinuity within reality and the idea of the ghetto are imposing themselves upon us.'

This is asserted without the support of the slightest empirical inquiry or an ounce of statistical data, because the unanimity of journalists, politicians and administrative officials who summon the word on every occasion suffices to establish the reality of this 'harsh segregation'. We will now demonstrate that such assimilation is in several respects fraudulent, even dangerous. It proceeds simultareously from ignorance about the black American ghetto and its historical trajectory (especially in the period following the Civil Rights revolution and the great riots of 1965–8) and from an incomplete and incorrect diagnosis of the 'crisis' of the French working-class *banlieues*.

Working-class *banlieues* are not US-style ghettos

The empirical comparison between the ghetto of Chicago and the large *cités* of the Parisian *banlieue*, such as can be characterized through the 'exemplary' site of La Courneuve and its infamous project of *Les Quatre mille*,[16] reveals a number of parallels that seem at first to support the convergence thesis. For the sake of clarity of exposition, I will group these parallels under two headings: that of social morphology and that of the lived experience and representations of their residents.

Surface similarities in morphological evolution and lived experience . . .

The first similarity pertains to recent trends in demographic and economic structures. One observes without doubt several *common evolutions* at the level of the *composition, distribution and dynamics of the populations* concerned. First of all, *banlieue* and ghetto have in common that they are enclaves with high concentrations of 'minorities' or ethnically marked populations – blacks on the American side, immigrants (that is, immigrants phenotypically identifiable as being of extra-European origin) and their descendants on the French side – and enclaves that are clearly identified as such, by those who live

---

[16] La Courneuve is a sort of empirically realized ideal-type of the traditional 'working-class territory' in decomposition that presents in an accentuated form most of the characteristics of the 'problem *banlieues*'. The Quatre mille (thus named after the 4,100 units it originally contained) is a large public housing estate notorious in the country for concentrating all the urban ills of the age. A more detailed comparative sociography of the neighbourhood of Woodlawn in Chicago's ghetto and La Courneuve can be found in Wacquant (1995a).

in them as well as those who flee or fear them. It is well established that the concentration of foreigners in the Parisian suburbs has grown more pronounced over the years (Leray 1989: 94–8). Thus the share of non-nationals in the population of La Courneuve doubled after the 1960s, jumping from 11 per cent in 1968 to 25 per cent in the 1990 census. As for African Americans, they have held a monopoly over the perimeter of the 'Black Belt' from its inception. And the areas adjoining the ghetto themselves count fewer and fewer white families, as 'buffer zones' populated mainly by families of so-called Hispanic origin (Puerto Ricans, Mexicans and other Caribbean and South Americans) as well as Asians consolidate.

On both sides of the Atlantic, *cités* and ghettos have experienced significant depopulation over the last decades of the century. The project of the Quatre mille in La Courneuve lost nearly 15 per cent of its residents between 1975 and 1982 alone, while the population of the town declined by one-fifth between 1968 and 1988. Phenomena of comparable scale can be noted in a number of large working-class projects in the Parisian Red Belt and around older industrial cities in the provinces. Similarly, black American ghettos have seen their populations thin rapidly even as their borders expanded. After their ranks more than doubled between 1930 and 1950, to the point of reaching levels of overcrowding worthy of the Third World right after World War II (Hirsch 1983), the historic core of Chicago's South Side was gradually emptied of its inhabitants during the ensuing three decades: some 200,000 lived in the three districts of Grand Boulevard, Oakland and Fuller Park in 1950, as against 100,000 thirty years later and fewer than 70,000 in 1990.

The age structure and household composition of the French working-class *banlieues* and the American ghetto present a number of similar distortions in relation to their immediate urban environment. The profile of the age pyramid of Chicago's South Side reveals a pronounced dip in the intermediate categories: the area harbours more young people (nearly half of its residents are under age 20) and more seniors than figure in the black population of the metropolitan area. The same is true of the Quatre mille, the infamous *cité* of La Courneuve, where young people represent fully 46 per cent of the population (as against 30 per cent for the city as a whole). In addition to an unusually high number of children per household, the family structure sports a notable overrepresentation of single-parent families on both sides of the Atlantic.

If these neighbourhoods have suffered such demographic haemorrhaging, it is essentially because they have been emptied of their economic activities and because they have borne the full brunt of skyrocketing unemployment tied to the deindustrialization of the advanced economies. Between 1968 and 1984, La Courneuve lost more than 10,000 of its 18,000 manual labour jobs, while the number of factory positions in the Greater Paris area declined by 280,000 (for a cut of 20 per cent between 1968 and 1982). For nearly two decades now, the fief of former French Communist Party Secretary General Waldeck-Rochet has sported one of the highest rates of job-seekers in the country: it exceeded 16 per cent in 1986, almost twice the average for the Île-de-France region, at which time it approached 30 per cent in the Quatre mille. Similarly, we have seen in chapter 3 that the official unemployment rate on Chicago's South Side oscillated between 25 and 45 per cent in 1990, depending on the district, corresponding to five to nine times the city average. The shift to the service economy and the relocation of industrial activity (to the suburbs, to southern states where social legislation severely limits the prerogatives of unions, and abroad in cheap-labour countries) have struck Chicago even harder than the Paris region: the capital of the Midwest recorded a net loss of 269,000 industrial jobs and 111,000 trade jobs between 1963 and 1982 (Wacquant and Wilson 1989). These deep cuts in the industrial fabric caused the collapse of secondary-sector employment in the ghetto, with the number of manual workers in the historic core of the South Side falling from 36,000 in 1950 to 5,000 in 1980. Ghetto and *banlieue* are thus both territories ravaged by deindustrialization, where ethnically marked populations tend to be concentrated, and where households suffering from unemployment and low income accumulate, translating into high rates of poverty and social dislocation.

A second important feature common to *banlieue* and ghetto (to which we return for a more in-depth analysis in the next chapter) is *the bleak and oppressive atmosphere that suffuses them and the potent stigma* associated with living in a bounded urban area publicly regarded as a place of relegation, and widely equated with social failure, destitution and crime. The residents of La Courneuve are quick to take up the media representations that describe the Quatre mille as a 'chicken coop', a 'reservation' or 'the *cité* of fear' (Avery 1987: 13). For many youths, the estates are a detested universe (the adjective that comes most often to their lips when they describe it to outsiders is *pourri* (rotten)) that weighs on their entire existence like a fatality that is not easily ignored, for the contempt that enshrouds the *cité* is omnipresent and tenacious. A teenager who recently left the shabby buildings of the Quatre mille explodes with rage when asked if he would agree to return and live there after the ongoing renovation is completed:

> For us, to go back there is to be submitted to insult again. The Quatre mille is an insult. We take it like a slap smack in the face. And then there's the poverty, and if you're going to do it, you might as well choose your poverty. There are people who are more or less poor. This poverty [in the Quatre mille] is hideous and shameful. For many people, the Quatre mille is experienced as a shame. It is *a shame*. (Euvremer and Euvremer 1985: 7)

This vision is not unanimous because of the very heterogeneity of *banlieues*: many of their residents remain attached to their *cité*, especially among the younger residents, for whom it is the anchor of adolescent identity, and older tenants, for whom access to the low-income estates meant an improvement in their housing and who seek instead to defend it against the vituperative view from the outside.[17] But, whether they accept it or resist it, all concur in acknowledging the disgrace that affects the residents of the declining housing estates.

One encounters a germane feeling of collective inferiority and indignity in the American ghetto. All the more so as the exodus of middle-class and stable working-class black families, who migrated to the adjoining neighbourhoods abandoned by whites fleeing to the suburbs, has left behind only the most destitute strata of the African-American community to live in the historic heart of the Black Belt (Wilson 1987). We noted in chapter 3 that over 80 per cent of the residents of Chicago's South Side and West Side find their neighbourhood 'bad' or 'very bad', and that three-quarters of them would wish to move out as soon as possible. The ghetto has become a loathed place whose mere mention suffices to evoke lurid images of drugs, violence, and social and moral dissolution. The ambivalent yet strong feeling of attachment, connected to pride in having a space with institutions of one's own that offer protection and the possibility of upward mobility within the internal hierarchy of the ghetto, expressed in the 1940s at the apogee of 'Bronzeville' (Drake and Cayton [1945] 1993: 383–97), has been erased to give way to rejec-

---

[17] Such attachment is vividly revealed during the demolition of large towers carried out with a view toward 'rehabilitating' degraded *cités*. The residents then express an acute nostalgia, even regret tinged with bitterness, at losing buildings that were also nodes of sociability and the physical supports of their individual and collective history.

tion and bitter distantiation.[18] Here is how a young man from Woodlawn describes the main street of his neighbourhood, which had been one of the liveliest commercial arteries of the South Side in the postwar decade, now reduced to a barren strip of burnt-out stores and abandoned buildings:

> You have a lotta street walkers, you have yo' gang-bangers, you have yo' *dope dealers*, yo' *dope users* – I mean [a tad defensive] that's in every neighbourhood, I'm not jus' sayin' this neighbourhood, I mean you have dat around here.
>
> And it's *bad for the kids* that's comin' up in the neighbourhood 'cause that's who they have to look up to. They got people like *dese guys* [gesturing towards a group of men 'shooting the breeze' by the entrance of a liquor store] tha's doin' *everythin' wrong* to look up to. I mean! Is that anythin' to try to teach a kid, to be a dope dealer or a dope user, or to be a pimp? . . . It's *bad* ya know, that dese guys, they messed up they lives and stuff, ya know, or they don't *care* too much about how dey life gonna turn out to be. . . .
>
> People that don't know nuttin' about the Southeast side, comin' 'roun' here and see this, and the first thin' they think about, [mockingly, in an exaggeratedly scared voice] *'Aw! I'm not getting' out my car!* I'm not gon' leave my car. I don't want my kids to be 'roun' here . . .'

Nowadays the first indicator and symbol of success in the ghetto is to leave it behind, and the dearest wish of South Side mothers is to see their children escape as soon as possible. Some do not hesitate to exile their progeny to live with kin in the suburbs or in small towns in the southern states to protect them from the daily dangers of the street.

The similarity in the reactions of the residents of France's forlorn *cités* and America's crumbling ghetto in this regard is explained by the fact that they belong to subordinate categories, relegated to penalized and penalizing territories situated at the very bottom of the symbolic hierarchy of neighbourhoods and bearing a residential stigma that is all the stronger as the vituperative discourse on 'cités-ghettos' on the French side and the degrading rhetoric of the 'underclass' on the American side balloon and spread (Bachmann and

---

[18] This bitterness finds a vitriolic expression in the songs of rappers such as Niggers With Attitude (NWA) and Public Enemy Number One (and in those of their rivals in the 'gangsta rap' genre), whose stage names and attire reveal as well as their lyrics the pervasiveness of the equation 'ghetto youth = danger'.

Basier 1989; Kornblum 1984; Wacquant 1992a). From the homology between the position that each occupies in the sociosymbolic and physical space of their respective country follows the homology of their points of view as views taken from points similarly situated in the structure of these spaces (Bourdieu [1987] 1989).

. . . mask deep differences of scale, structure and function

But these two families of shared features in the registers of social morphology and collective representation conceal deep structural and functional differences such that one is compelled to assert that this is but a surface convergence and that we are in fact comparing sociospatial specimens of different species – urban 'apples and oranges' as it were. Here I will briefly emphasize five of these differences which, together, demonstrate that, if the working-class French *banlieues* and the black American ghetto are both 'forced settlements' (Pétonnet 1982: 126) that combine economic hardship, social dislocations and an ethnicized and degraded image, the mode of (re)production of these groupings, their composition and the constraint from which they issue are neither of the same nature nor operating on the same scale.

1 Disparate organizational ecologies

First of all, when it comes to size, assimilating US ghettos and French *cités* amounts to matching heavyweights with flyweights. Notwithstanding its postwar devolution, Chicago's historic ghetto still harbours some 300,000 inhabitants and extends over 110 square kilometers. The ghettos of New York (in such areas as Harlem, Brownsville and East New York in Brooklyn, and the South Bronx) hold nearly a million blacks, and those of South Central and Watts in Los Angeles (or yet Compton just to the south) several hundred thousand – not counting Latinos and other immigrants of colour, whose numbers are fast growing, segregated in their own ethnic neighbourhoods, and whose social condition is often nearly as precarious. Against this yardstick, the largest French *cités* – those of the close ring around Paris, the industrial periphery of Lyons, Lille and Toulouse, or the northern wards of Marseilles – cut a very modest figure. In 1982, the Quatre mille housed about 13,000 people, occupying some 0.35 square kilometers, close to the average for a Red Belt suburb. The cluster of towers of Les Minguettes in Vénissieux, one of the highest concentrations of public housing estates in the country, held 35,000. No *cité* in France reaches one-tenth the size of one of the American ghettos with which the '*cité*-ghetto' discourse rashly identifies them.

One might object that this size differential only translates the difference of scale between the typical French city and the US metropolis: isn't America a country-continent where everything is stamped by gigantism? Not solely. For this scale discrepancy is primarily an expression of deep *functional and ecological differences* between *banlieue* and ghetto. Isolated though they may be, the French *cités* are not multifunctional ensembles endowed with an extended division of labour enabling them to reproduce themselves without ongoing exchanges with their urban surroundings. Far from being autonomous centres of economic and cultural production, they are *residential islands*, copses of public housing sprinkled at the periphery of a composite urban-industrial landscape with which they necessarily maintain regular functional relations tending to mix the social uses of space and thereby to draw populations closer together – whence the frictions between them, especially conflicts arising at the borderline between *pavillons* (individual tract housing) and *cités*. The majority of the residents of the Quatre mille work and consume outside the estate; they have for immediate neighbours the owners of working-class or petty-bourgeois single homes; and they need only walk out of the project to enter into contact with other strata of the population and to escape, be it only for a few hours of the day, the claustrophobic atmosphere of their estate.[19] They have not developed a network of parallel institutions of their own that would allow them to organize their daily round inside a restricted space and compensate for the failings of the external institutions from which they have been debarred.

Conversely, the American ghetto is not simply a residential concentration of poor families relegated to a dilapidated and isolated habitat, but a continent endowed with its own social division of labour and (relative) institutional autonomy, such that it functions largely as a self-contained unit. In the manner of a veritable 'black city within the city',[20] Chicago's South Side harbours within itself a

---

[19] Besides, it is one of the favourite activities of youths, as noted by Calogirou (1989) and Avery (1987). One of the common complaints voiced by teenagers against the police is precisely that the forces of order restrict this mobility with repeated and abusive identity checks at the perimeter of the *cité* and on the public transport routes leading there.

[20] To recall the title of the classic work of Drake and Cayton, *Black Metropolis* ([1945] 1993), which dissects the social structure and culture of Chicago's black ghetto at mid-century.

whole network of organizations specific to the group it isolates –
stores and currency exchanges, schools and churches, media outlets
and mutual help associations, clinics and political organizations, etc.
– parallel to mainstream institutions from which blacks have historically been excluded. While they are massively inferior to those of the
surrounding white society, and in a terminal phase of decomposition
for many of them, these institutions still ensure that the ghetto clasps
most of the everyday activities of its residents within its mesh. The
majority of them have little contact with the outside, as their relations
unfold essentially within the homogeneous social space of the ghetto,
especially when it comes to 'household', 'provisioning' and 'traffic'.[21]
This explains why large segments of the youth of Chicago's South
Side live in total ethnic and social isolation: not only do they personally not know a single white person, but they also rarely leave their
neighbourhood and have but remote and episodic contacts with
dominant institutions, save for state agencies of social control –
welfare, public schools operating as quasi-custodial institutions, the
police, the criminal courts and correctional officers.

The spatial enclosure and ethnoracial homogeneity of the black
ghetto are further reinforced by the rigid endogamy that continues
to regulate matrimonial strategies within the African-American community: three decades after the revocation of the last state law barring
marriages between blacks and whites (with the *Loving v. Virginia*
Supreme Court decision in 1967), nearly all black women (97 per
cent) marry black men (Farley 1996: 265), a pattern sharply divergent from that of North African immigrant women and their daughters in France, the majority of whom take a partner or spouse outside
their group (Tribalat 1995: 126).

2 Racial cloistering and uniformity versus ethnic dispersion and diversity

This urban continent, moreover, presents the highly distinctive property of being entirely and exclusively black. Whereas the popular
banlieues of France are *fundamentally pluri-ethnic* zones where a mul-
tiplicity of nationalities rub elbows – resulting in well-documented
frictions – the US ghetto is *totally homogeneous in ethnoracial terms*.

[21] Anthropologist Ulf Hannerz (1980: 102–6) distinguishes five domains that
combine to make up the panoply of roles of modern urban life: household and
kinship, provisioning ('the asymmetric relationships which regulate people's access
to material resources'), recreation, neighbouring and traffic.

For the primordial criterion of rejection in the accursed territory of the Black Belt, the barrier that separates it from the outside and forbids its inhabitants from blending with the rest of society on pain of (physical or economic) violence, is descent from an enslaved lineage, marked by the outward sign of skin colour (Davis 1991). As the historical legacy of the era of slavery and the product of the inscription of the founding division of US social space into physical space, that between 'whites' and 'blacks' (Myrdal 1944; Horsman 1986; Fields 1990), the ghetto is before all else a mechanism of *racial confinement*, an apparatus aimed at enclosing a stigmatized category in a reserved physical and social space that will prevent it from mixing with others and thus risk 'tainting' them. Whence its ambition to encompass the entirety of the subordinate group and the near-total separation of the 'communities' fictively figured as mutually exclusive blood filiations, close to those that would obtain under a regime of legal apartheid in Chicago, where the segregation index reaches 91 (out of a maximum of 100) and has practically not budged for a half-century.[22]

One of the most striking characteristics of the large estates of the French urban periphery in this regard, placing them at the antipode of the American ghetto, is precisely the fluidity and astonishing diversity of their ethnic composition. Paradoxically, one of the effects of the panic discourse about 'ghettoization' has been to erase the fact that, with few local exceptions,[23] the *banlieues* have a *heterogeneous ethnonational and even social recruitment*. In the outer rim around Paris, at the close of the 1980s, one-third of public housing was still occupied by families whose head was a white-collar employee, as against one-fifth for all dwellings in this zone; in the inner rim around the capital, white-collar workers held 22 per cent of the total housing

---

[22] The segregation (or 'dissimilarity') index measures the percentage of the population that would have to change neighbourhood for the residents of various backgrounds to be uniformly distributed across the city. It reaches 100 when the categories are perfectly segregated and zero when all blocks have the same ethnoracial composition as the metropolis. In 1980 the dissimilarity index for blacks (from whites) in the thirty largest US cities was 75, that for Hispanics was 49, and that for Asians 34 (Massey and Denton 1987). For purposes of comparison, dissimilarity indexes for the most segregated immigrants in public housing in continental Europe rarely reach the 40s, rates that US researchers regard as characteristic of 'integrated neighbourhoods' (Huttman 1991).

[23] The exceptions, such as some neighbourhoods of north Marseilles and inner Roubaix, are tied to local particularities of industrial history that call for an ideographic analysis and cannot serve as a guide to describe the general evolution of popular urban districts.

stock and 28 per cent of public housing (Barrou 1992: 108–9). This is to say that, in spite of the continual lowering of the class recruitment of social housing, which made it conform belatedly to its stated mission after the exodus of the middle classes and stable working-class families to single-home tracts and the influx of foreign households fostered by state policies supporting individuals renters ('*aide à la personne*', as opposed to support for building, '*aide à la pierre*'), the *cités* dotting the edge of French cities are far from being uniformly proletarian.

On the ethnic front, the concentrations of large projects on the periphery of French cities are more sundry still. They typically bring together persons of West African, European and Maghrebine descent – '*black, blanc, beur*', as they are sometimes referred to stereotypically – but also of a wide range of other origins. It is common for them to count fifteen to forty nationalities, even if, demographically, recent immigrants from France's former African colonies have tended to predominate among foreigners since the early 1990s. But, above all, and contrary to the vision given by the media, the dispossessed *banlieues* are not monopolized by foreign families, far from it. In La Courneuve, nearly 80 per cent of the residents of public housing estates are French nationals; even in the southern section of the Quatre mille, where 40 per cent of families are foreign, French households remain in the majority, as is the case in most large projects commonly perceived as 'immigrant ghettos', such as those of the Minguettes in the suburbs of Lyons: in 1982 their population of 25,000 was 60 per cent French and 20 per cent foreigners of North African origin. In fact, aside from circumscribed pockets of high density centred on a few buildings in such public housing complexes, nowhere on French territory is there a zone occupied exclusively by one ethnic community (whether foreign or national, or a mix of both).

There are three reasons for this. First, as Lapeyronnie and Frybes (1990: 145 and 154) note, 'in the large French metropolitan areas, but also in small towns, populations of foreign origin are rather dispersed across the *banlieues*, and, often, within the *banlieues*', with the result that 'on the whole, concentrations of foreigners are relatively low'. Second, public housing agencies have worked diligently, with varying degrees of efficacy and not without controversy and slip-ups, to prevent the constitution of these notorious 'immigrant ghettos' so often decried, through a meticulous management, down to the level of the stairway, aiming to scatter foreign tenants and so-called problem families (deemed in need of various forms of support).

Finally, and above all, the concentration of immigrants in the degraded projects of the *banlieue* is not the product of a communal segmentation of the housing market. It is due primarily to their over-representation in the lower fractions of the working class and to the fact that, as they became incorporated into French society, they could improve their housing status only by way of entering public housing at the time when it was becoming devalued both materially and symbolically (Barrou 1992: 117–18). By contrast, the confinement of blacks inside the ghetto is the expression of a racial dualism that cuts across the gamut of institutions of US society and is barely inflected as they climb up the class ladder: increasing education and income did not significantly lower the isolation of African Americans from whites after the 1960s.[24] In French urban space, ethnic discrimination in access to housing is very real, but it is strongly attenuated when the members of families of colour improve their economic and cultural capital. Proof is the absence of middle-class neighbourhoods of North African or black tenor on French territory.

3 Divergent rates and degrees of poverty

The racial basis of their exclusion, reinforced by the extreme exiguity of the social protection granted by the national 'semi-welfare state',[25] explains why ghetto residents experience poverty rates and degrees of destitution with no equivalent in France (or in any other postindustrial country in Western Europe). The converging unemployment statistics cited in the previous section are deceptive in this regard. If we go beyond the official jobless rate to compute the ratio of the working population to total population, we discover that, despite the continual rise of unemployment, nearly half of the adult residents of La Courneuve held a job in the early 1990s; in the *cité* of the Quatre mille, the employment ratio was 48 per cent in the northern estate and broached the 40s in the southern estate. Most families in one of the most notorious Red Belt projects thus participated in economic and social life, which is far from being the case on the American side, as we previously noted in chapters 3 and 4.

---

[24] In the top 207 Metropolitan Statistical Areas of the United States in 1990, the black-to-white dissimilarity index was 72 for African Americans earning less than $15,000 a year and 62 for those with incomes exceeding $50,000 (74 and 67 for central cities). In the Midwest, the historic cradle of the dark ghetto, these indices reached 83 and 72 respectively (Massey and Fischer 1999).

[25] For a synthetic analysis of the differences between the French and US systems of welfare, see Esping-Andersen (1990) and McFate et al. (1995).

In the district of Grand Boulevard, at the heart of Chicago's ghetto, barely 16 per cent of the 50,000 residents had a paying job in those years. Almost one-half of the households lived below the official poverty line (about $12,500 for a household of four in 1989), and the median family income barely reached one-half of the city average. In 1987, this figure was around $7,000, far behind the national average income of $31,000 for a white family. Of the total adult population of the South Side and West Side, 57 per cent lived mainly on public assistance, and 60 per cent had to resort to food stamps to feed their families. Only 12 per cent possessed a checking account and 17 per cent a savings account; one household in ten owned its home, and two-thirds did not have a car despite the crying failings of public transportation. And thousands of families – a growing number of them single mothers with young children – were doubled-up in the homes of kin or homeless, even as the city's public housing stock was teeming with empty apartments.

Two statistics aptly sum up the impact of the failings of social and medical coverage on the residents of the US ghetto and the abyss that separates their condition from that of the residents of the French *banlieue*: the rates of fatherless families and infant mortality. Six per cent of households in La Courneuve comprise only one parent as against 60–80 per cent depending on the district in Chicago's ghetto, the vast majority of whom live *below half* of the federal poverty line. Infant mortality in the projects of Paris's inner ring is no higher than that for the Île-de-France region (8 per 1,000), and this rate has decreased by one-half in twenty years. On Chicago's South Side, the figure for infant mortality is on the rise and exceeded 30 per 1,000 in the early 1990s, three times the official rate for white children in the state of Illinois.

4 Criminality and dangerousness

According to proponents of the thesis of the 'ghettoization' of the *banlieues*, the insecurity that is now said to reign in the *cités* would be a major indicator of their convergence with the American inner city. If we are to believe certain media outlets, the large declining working-class projects of the French urban periphery have suddenly turned into dens of vice and violence, 'crucibles of delinquency' that flout the republican legal order to the point of posing a grave threat to civil peace. The weekly magazine *L'Express* thus titled a cover feature of November 1990 'Thugs: The Drift of the Ghetto'. Here again, empirical observation reveals a yawning gap between the everyday reality of the *cités* and this media projection, not to speak of the situation in the black American ghetto in the early 1990s, where violent crime reached pandemic levels worthy of an incipient civil war without parallel on the European continent (as well as extreme by historical standards in the United States).

What the media rashly describe as random public violence in the dispossessed *banlieues* refers mostly to aggressive behaviour at the borderline of the law, petty theft (break-ins into vehicles, thefts of cars and motorcycles, and later cell phones as they became common), the degradation of public facilities, burglary and low-level drug trafficking centred on some buildings, as well as scuffles among teenagers that partake in forms of working-class masculine sociability that should not be too quickly assimilated to criminal conduct (Mauger and Fossé-Polliak 1983). As I shall show in chapter 7, the feeling of insecurity that suffuses the Quatre mille, for example, is fed mostly by the sense of seclusion of its residents, the degraded ecology of the neighbourhood, and the nagging petty delinquency that makes youths the scapegoats for all the ills of the city. Armed robberies are rare (around twenty for the entire town in an average year), and the most serious crimes result in death only extraordinarily. Indeed, La Courneuve's overall crime rate is barely above the national average, and the incidence of burglaries and other property crime is well below the rates for Paris (Avery 1987: ch. 7).

In the American ghetto, physical violence is a palpable reality that overturns all the parameters of ordinary existence.[26] It is inconceivable to take the subway and stroll quietly on Chicago's South Side to talk to people on the street or near their homes, as one can do in La Courneuve or any *cité* of the *banlieues* of Paris, Lyons or Toulouse. For the frequency of robberies, assaults and homicides is such that it has caused the virtual disappearance of public space. I described in chapters 2 and 4 how the residents of the dark ghetto organize their daily routine so as to avoid leaving their home, taking public transportation, or crossing through parks as much as possible. Heavy metal gates and bars protect the windows and doors of their homes, similar to those used by shops (nearly all of which employ private security guards to screen customers). At the heart of the South Side, the incessant clashes between gangs and drug dealers have spawned

---

[26] For more detail, in addition to chapters 4 and 7 of this book, the reader is referred to Wacquant (1992a) and Adler (1995); on the historical roots of what may appear as a 'culture of violence' in the black American ghetto, but is fully accountable for in terms of persistent social closure, read Lane (1986).

a murderous urban guerrilla war due to the abundance of firearms – handguns, shotguns and even Uzi submachine guns are not hard to find on ghetto streets. In 1990, the homicide rate passed the astronomical figure of 100 per 100,000 inhabitants, ten times the national average, and 75 times the rate for France or neighbouring European countries. Murder is the leading cause of mortality among black youths in the city. In the big projects, shootings are so common that children learn early on to throw themselves on the ground and crawl to avoid bullets. Public facilities such as schools are not spared. Even the installation of metal detectors at the entrance of establishments, body searches between buildings, and police patrols in the hallways have failed to stop the diffusion of violence: every year several dozen students are gunned down in the yard or the vicinity of their high school.[27]

5   Urban policy and the degradation of daily surroundings

A final striking contrast between ghetto and *banlieue* in the closing decades of the twentieth century is the parlous state of the housing stock, public infrastructure and everyday surroundings characteristic of the former. The urban fabric of the average inner city in America is incomparably more deteriorated than the most wretched *banlieues* of France; to the point where it is difficult, from Europe, to form an accurate idea of the multisided process of urban desertification of which the dark ghetto of the fin de siècle is the product.

Twenty-five years after the great race riots of 1965–8, the historic African-American neighbourhoods of New York, Chicago, Philadelphia or Detroit have the look of 'war zones' – it is the term invoked by their residents – that have been subjected to an intensive bombing campaign: thousands of abandoned or crumbling buildings, carcasses of burnt-out stores, factories rotting or rusting away, and boarded-up houses that line miles of streets dotted by vacant lots covered with garbage and rubble, shattered sidewalks, ill-lit at night and empty of all life. Streets, bridges, tunnels, sewers and rail lines, as well as firehouses, police stations, hospitals and schools, are all too often in the same state of utter decrepitude, when they have not been closed down as part of the policy of 'planned shrinkage', inaugurated in the mid-1970s in response to the fiscal crisis of the big

[27] For an instructive analysis and contrast of the media, judicial and sociological construction of one such deadly shooting incident in Chicago, see Hagan et al. (2002).

cities, which caused the ghetto to bear a disproportionate share of brutal budget cuts. Not to mention that, over the past two decades, federal funding devoted to housing and urban development has declined sharply and continuously (Slessarev 1997). By the early 1990s, most of the public programmes supporting the ghetto launched under the aegis of Lyndon Johnson's Great Society had been emptied of their substance or simply eliminated.

The formation of such urban wastelands, leading to the resurgence of stretches of greenery or 'rural landscapes' at the heart of the metropolis,[28] is unthinkable in France, where the management of space is the object of strict (some would even say stifling) political-administrative oversight mobilizing a dense network of local, regional and national agencies and for which public officials are held accountable. To consider housing: the simple fact that 45 per cent of rental units in the country are in the public sector makes it difficult for housing dilapidation to occur and spread on a vast scale. In the Red Belt towns surrounding Paris and similar industrial suburbs of French provincial cities, the share of social rented housing exceeds two-thirds of the housing stock, giving the local state a direct stake in the maintenance and management of the habitat of the lower class.

Moreover, since the middle of the 1980s, degraded working-class *banlieues*, renamed 'sensitive neighbourhoods', have been the target of a concerted renovation plan under the heading 'Neighbourhood Social Development' (Développement social des quartiers, DSQ), which has pushed back insalubrious housing and even, in some areas, stemmed the departure of the lower-middle class from public housing estates.[29] In La Courneuve, an ambitious rehabilitation operation of the Quatre mille under way since 1983 has aimed to improve the physical state of the *cité*. Buildings have been repainted, refitted or demolished to open up the horizon and provide light in the court-yards. The apartments of the concierges have been remodelled. And lawns, shrubbery and playgrounds have been laid near the main towers. To be sure, these improvements of the housing frontage and exterior spaces, like the many activities sponsored by the city as part of its effort to enliven neighbourhoods (computer workshops, meeting places for women's groups, music clubs, after-school programmes, support services for young immigrants, etc.), are little more than

[28] Camilo José Vergara (1995) draws a stunning visual portrait of the sprouting of a country-like 'green ghetto' in the crumbling core of major industrial cities.
[29] See Lenoir et al. (1989) on the launching and early phase of this state programme, and Damon (2004) for a survey of the subsequent decade of French urban policy.

band-aids on gaping social wounds, in so far as they fail to touch the root of the ills suffered by the residents of the Quatre mille: chronic un(der)employment and rising social insecurity foiling the ability of the working class to reproduce itself. But, aside from having the merit of checking the process of social marginalization among some of the residents, these interventions bear witness to a collective will and sense of political responsibility that is diametrically opposed to the attitude of 'benign neglect' adopted by the American authorities – which, we saw in the first part of this book, produced utterly malign outcomes. Whatever their inadequacies and intricacies, the DSQ programme and its successors of the 1990s launched under the aegis of the Ministry of the City, as well as their counterpart on the welfare front, the establishment of a guaranteed minimum income pro-gramme (Revenu Minimum d'Insertion, RMI) (Paugam 1993), and on the education front, with the creation of ZEP (Zones d'Education Prioritaire), cannot but contrast stridently with Washington's policy of urban abandonment, which, combined with the persistence of rigid racial segregation, constitutes one of the two major causes of the accumulation of social dislocations in the black ghetto along with neoliberal economic restructuring.

Conclusion: the 'French ghetto', a sociological absurdity

Comparative analysis of the ecology, organizational structure, popu-lation and everyday life in these two territories of relegation that are the US ghetto and the French working-class *banlieue* suggests that we are dealing here with two sociospatial forms with different makeups and functions, even as they are in some respects close at the phe-nomenal level. If both are, each in its national order, deprived zones where various forms of inequality are superimposed and where social hardship and personal difficulties accumulate, the mechanisms of aggregation and segregation that determine their constitution and govern the marginalization of their residents are not the same. Unlike the black American ghetto, the French *banlieue* is not a *homogeneous* social formation, bearing a *unitary cultural identity*, endowed with an advanced *organizational autonomy and institutional duplication*, based on a *dichotomous cleavage between races* (i.e., fictively biologized ethnic categories) officially *recognized by the state*. The popular *cités* on the fringes of French cities have never had, nor do they have today, the task of containing a specific group deemed undesirable, contrary to the Black Belt of the US metropolis, which has always been a manner of urban container reserved for a dishonoured category before it came to serve as reservoir for labour power and as dumpster for social detritus (after unskilled labour became expendable).

To speak of 'ghetto' in France, under cover of the transatlantic smuggling of American concepts that are all the more easily diffused as they are less well defined and understood,[30] only makes more difficult a rigorous diagnosis of the predicament of the black American urban community after the Civil Rights revolution and the postindustrial trajectory of the marginalized populations of the rim of French cities. It is, first of all, to obfuscate the historical specificity of the ethnoracial division of US society, a cleavage anchored over the course of four centuries that have inscribed it in space as well as in institutions and bodies, and which, admitting of no middle term,[31] finds its extension in racially polarized and polarizing social strategies and state programmes. It is, next, to erase all the differences between France and the United States bequeathed by urban history and continually reactivated by the profoundly disparate state structures and policies of the two countries. It is, finally, to unduly conflate immigration and the dislocation of the low-income housing projects in the postindustrial era when everything indicates that these two 'problems' obey social logics that cannot be confounded, even as they cannot be disjoined (Wacquant 1995b). France's working-class *banlieues* are the repository of the *second generation of mass unemployment* before they are the crucible of the second generation of immigrants suffering from 'failed integration', a diagnosis belied both by the upward trajectory of the offspring of postcolonial migrants who have

---

[30] The latest avatar of this fad is the booklet by Éric Maurin (2004), vigorously promoted by *Le Monde* as a 'must-read' for France's governing elite, which uses the term 'ghetto' incoherently, as a *mot choc* to refer to supposed 'separatist tensions traversing the whole society' and to the 'silent and generalized war over territory' allegedly roiling France. Maurin's confused and confusing discussion of the spatial dimension of inequality rehashes the standard US thematics of 'neighbourhood effects' while ignoring the extensive research on the topic, as well as data consistently showing that the middle classes are increasingly dispersed and mixed in French urban space. It confounds spatial differentiation, segregation, inequality and mobility; it conflates so-called poor ghettos with chic ghettos; and it presents as a new and ominous development calling for novel policy intervention the formation of exclusive upperclass areas that have existed for nearly a century.

[31] Due to a rigid application of the rule of hypo-descent, this instrument for the sociodicy of slavery that assigns a black identity to every person with 'one drop of black blood', the category of mulatto or *métis* has no socially recognized existence in American society in spite of the quasi-universal intermixing of the 'black community' (three-quarters of African Americans have nonblack ancestors), a case virtually unique in the world according to F. James Davis (1991).

moved out of public housing projects (Santelli 2001) and by the insistent demand of their siblings trapped in the declining *cités* to be treated by the French state not as 'ethnics' but as full-fledged citizens.

In his *Vermischte Bemerkungen*, Ludwig Wittgenstein recommends that we 'beware of the power that language has to make everything look the same' (Wittgenstein 1977: 14–15). This warning seems to apply with particular pertinence to the term 'ghetto', the main effect of whose uncontrolled usage – scientifically fraudulent and politically irresponsible – in the French debate on the transformation of the city has so far been to obscure the process of decomposition of established working-class territories and to reinforce the spiral of stigmatization that tends to make the *banlieues* over into so many symbolic ghettos.

6

Stigma and Division
From the Core of Chicago to the Margins of Paris

Two closely interwoven trends have reshaped the visage of Western European cities over the past two decades. The first is the unexpected resurgence of multifarious inequalities and the crystallization of novel forms of socioeconomic marginality, which are widely perceived to have a distinctly 'ethnic' component and to feed off processes of spatial segregation and public unrest (which they fuel in return). The second is the irruption and spread of racializing ideologies and xeno-phobic tensions consequent upon the simultaneous increase in per-sistent unemployment and the permanent settlement of immigrant populations hitherto viewed as 'birds of passage' intent on returning to their sending society (Castles 1984; Hadjimichalis and Sadler 1996).

The structures of this 'new poverty' (Marklund 1990) are far from fully elucidated, but their empirical manifestations display a number of clear commonalities across national boundaries. Long-term job-lessness and the proliferation of precarious and low-pay employment, the accumulation of multiple deprivations within the same lower-class households and neighbourhoods, the curtailing of social net-works and slackening of personal ties, and finally the difficulty that established programmes of social insurance and public assistance have in remedying or checking hardship and isolation: all of these phenomena can be observed, to varying degrees, in nearly all advanced societies.[1] At the same time, growing concern has been expressed

[1] For an overview of emerging debates over the 'new poverty' in England, Holland, Italy, France and Germany, respectively, see Townsend et al. (1987), Engbersen (1989), Mingione and Morlicchio (1993), Paugam (1993) and Alisch and Dangschat (1998); for a continental panorama prepared for the European Commission, Room (1990).

throughout the continent about the development of 'European racism', which has stimulated renewed theorizing about its historical or functional linkages with immigration, the crisis of the national order, and various facets of the ongoing post-Fordist economic transition (e.g., Bovenkerk et al. 1990; Balibar 1991; Wieviorka 1993; Musterd et al. 1998).[2]

The coincidence of novel forms of urban exclusion with the apparent rise of ethnoracial segregation and strife has given *prima facie* plausibility to the notion that European poverty was being 'Americanized' – that is, falling in line with a pattern of segregation, destitution and violence (mis)identified with the black ghetto. Hence most European analysts and commentators (though by no means all) have turned to the United States for analytic assistance in their effort to puzzle out the current deterioration of urban conditions and relations in their respective countries. This has translated into the transatlantic diffusion of concepts, models and sometimes ready-made theories from recent (and not-so-recent) American social science.[3] This intellectual importation is especially visible in the worried and confused public debate that developed in France – and several neighbouring countries such as Belgium, Germany and Italy – about the presumed formation of immigrant 'ghettos' in degraded working-class districts harbouring large housing estates destined for low-income families colloquially known as *cités*. It can be detected also in the spread of the notion of 'underclass' in Great Britain and its smuggling into the Netherlands to address the strain put on the national regime of citizenship by the emerging concatenation of joblessness, ethnic discrimination and neighbourhood decline.[4] Such conceptual

[2] An administrative expression of this rising political concern in the European Union was the creation in 1997 of the European Monitoring Centre on Racism and Xenophobia, based in Vienna, entrusted with collecting reliable and comparable data measuring manifestations of racism among its member countries.

[3] For instance, in France the first Chicago School (of the interwar decades) has become quite fashionable in some sectors of the intellectual field as public attention to the city mounted (as attested by the translations of Louis Wirth's *The Ghetto* and of an anthology of writings by the founders of urban ecology), even though this paradigm is largely discredited in the more advanced sectors of urban research in the United States, after the cumulative theoretical critiques of the past two decades (see, e.g., Gottdiener and Feagin 1988, Walton 1990, and Flanagan 1993).

[4] I provided a snapshot of the swirling debate about 'ghettos' in France in the previous chapter and a detailed critique of the myth of the '*cités*-ghettos' in Wacquant (1992b). The discussion about the crystallization of an 'underclass' is mapped out by Dahrendorf (1989) and Westergaard (1992) for Great Britain, and by Engbersen et al. (1993) for the Netherlands (where the term takes on a meaning sharply divergent from the one it conveys in the United States).

borrowings, however, provide but a shaky analytical scaffolding inasmuch as they presume precisely that which needs to be established: that the American conceptual idiom of 'race relations' and its derivatives have purchase on the urban realities of Europe – leaving aside the question of whether conventional US categories (or more recent notions such as the semi-scholarly tale of the 'underclass') pack any analytical power on their own turf to start with.

The 'Americanization' of poverty in the European city?

The best way to answer this question, or at least to reframe it productively, is through a systematic, empirically grounded, cross-national comparison of contemporary forms of urban inequality and marginality. This comparison must be carried out according to a design that (i) does not presuppose that the analytic apparatus forged on one continent should be transposed wholesale on to the other; (ii) is sensitive to the fact that all 'national' conceptual tools have embedded within them specific social, political and moral assumptions reflective of the particular history of classification struggles in each country; (iii) attends consistently to the meanings and lived experience of social immobility and urban dispossession; and (iv) strives to embed individual strategies and collective trajectories in the local social and spatial structure of the metropolis as well as within the broader national frameworks of market and state.

This chapter seeks to contribute to such a comparative sociology of urban marginality through an analysis of the social and mental structures of urban relegation in the US 'Black Belt' and the French 'Red Belt'. As previously indicated, the term 'Black Belt' is used here to designate the remnants of the historic 'dark ghetto' (Clark 1965) of the large cities of the Northeast and Midwest of the United States, i.e., the decaying African-American districts of the metropolitan core that have dominated scientific, policy and popular discussions of racial division and poverty in North America at the close of the twentieth century (Holdt 1985; Wilson 1987; Moore and Pinderhughes 1993).[5] The expression 'Red Belt' refers not simply

---

[5] I leave aside the thorny question of how the segregated neighbourhoods inhabited by the black middle and upper classes located outside the traditional 'Bronzeville' of Chicago relate to the 'hyperghetto' to form a reconfigured, spatially decentred and socially differentiated contraption containing black Americans in the post-Fordist metropolis. It will be tackled in a later study (to be published under the title *The Two Faces of the Ghetto*).

to the towns of the outer ring of Paris that formed the historic strong-hold of the French Communist Party at the apogee of the Fordist era, but, more generally, to the traditional mode of organization of 'workers' cities' in France (Magri and Topalov 1989) as in its main neighbouring nations. This mode was concretized in a well-identified and bounded life-space anchored by high concentrations of industrial male employment, a strong workerist culture and a solidaristic class consciousness, stamped by the civic incorporation of the populations via a dense web of union-based and municipal organizations creating a close integration of work, home and public life. It is in these periph-eral (de)industrial(izing) districts, inside of which working-class families reside and circulate, that urban inequalities and disorders coalesced during the 1980s, making the question of the *banlieue* arguably the single most pressing public issue in France during that decade and since.[6]

Both the black American ghetto and the French working-class *banlieues* are historical constellations, not unchanging archetypes. It is essential, then, to avoid vague generalities that are difficult to either prove or disprove, to anchor our examination firmly in both time and space. In the first part of this book, I mapped out and explained the structural and experiential transformation of the black American ghetto over the quarter-century following the peaking of the Civil Rights movement. In this second part, I articulate and evaluate the thesis of the transatlantic convergence of urban poverty regimes on the pattern of African-American exclusion at the close of the twentieth century. This is emphatically not a matching of America's 'eternal ghetto' and the '*banlieues* of forever' of France. Rather, it is a theoretically guided empirical comparison of the (hyper)ghetto of Chicago and the (postindustrial) working-class periphery of Paris as of the early 1990s.

This cross-national and continental comparison uses data from a wide range of primary and secondary sources and combines observa-tions drawn from censuses, quantitative surveys and field studies of the American ghetto and France's working-class *banlieues* in the era of post-Fordist restructuring. On the American side, the analysis focuses on the South Side ghetto of Chicago where I conducted ethnographic fieldwork in 1988–1991. The South Side is a sprawling

[6] On the historical formation of the Parisian Red Belt, read the monograph on Bobigny by Stovall (1990) and, on its recent decomposition, Bacqué and Fol (1997). Jazouli (1992) recounts the initial rise of the *banlieue* to the forefront of public issues in the 1980s. Breton (1983) offers an insider's account of the distinctively workerist atmosphere of daily life and culture in the exemplary Red Belt town of La Courneuve.

and desolate all-black zone harbouring some 150,000 inhabitants, the vast majority of whom are unemployed and live beneath the federal 'poverty line' under conditions of extreme dispossession and systemic insecurity documented in chapters 2–4. On the French side, it centres on the Red Belt city of La Courneuve and its infamous public housing concentration called Les Quatre mille. La Courneuve is an older, Communist-governed, northeastern suburb of Paris with a population of 36,000 (about one-fifth of them foreigners) situated midway between the national capital and the Roissy-Charles de Gaulle airport, in the midst of a densely urbanized and rapidly declining industrial landscape. The low-income estate of Quatre mille consists of two massive high-rise clusters, the 'Quatre mille south' and the 'Quatre mille north', sprawled over some fifty acres. It counts thirty-two concrete 'slabs' (or *barres* as they are called locally) of sixteen storeys and four towers of twenty-six storeys comprising a total of 3,667 housing units – of which a thousand were renovated in the late 1980s under the state-sponsored Neighbourhood Social Development programme. The main buildings are gigantic blocks of concrete, fourteen or sixteen storeys high and extending nearly 200 yards in length, christened after famous writers, artists and scientists (Verlaine, Renoir, Debussy, Curie, etc.). The *cité* was erected from 1957 to 1964 to help resolve the acute housing shortage plaguing France in the postwar period. For more than two decades, it remained the property of the city of Paris, which used it as a dumping ground for its problem populations and in particular for relieving itself of lower-class households displaced by the urban renewal of the eastern boroughs of the capital. Residents of La Courneuve are keenly aware of this and are quick to point out that 'Chirac [the Mayor of Paris between 1978 and 1995] sent us all the families he wanted to get rid of' (Avery 1987: 28).[7]

I presented in the preceding chapters and related publications a detailed sociography of Chicago's racialized core and the working-class margins of Paris which spotlights a number of parallel morpho-logical traits and trends.[8] In summary, both sites were found (i) to have a rapidly declining population with (ii) a skewed age and class

---

[7] After a bitter and hard-fought battle, the Communist municipality wrested control over the project in 1984. Since then, the management of the Quatre mille and similar large estates in the close ring around the capital has remained a bone of contention and major stake in the political tussle between the left-wing mayors of Red Belt cities and the central government.

[8] See Wacquant (1995a) for a more detailed discussion of the data, comparability of sources, and a number of methodological and theoretical caveats, and chapters 2 and 3 *supra* for a contemporary sociography of Chicago's South Side.

structure characterized by a predominance of youths, manual workers and deskilled service employees, and (iii) to harbour large concentrations of 'minorities' or phenotypically marked populations (North-African immigrants and their offspring on the one side, African Americans on the other) which (iv) exhibit abnormally high levels of unemployment due to deindustrialization and the makeover of the labour market associated with the revamping of national and international capitalism during this period. This comparison also turned up profound structural, functional and ecological differences suggesting that the declining French working-class *banlieues* and the black American ghetto constitute two *different sociospatial formations*, obeying discrepant institutional logics of segregation and aggregation, and spawning significantly higher rates of poverty, isolation and assorted hardships in the dark ghetto. To condense: relegation operates on the basis of ethnoracial membership reinforced by both social class and state in the fin-de-siècle Black Belt, whereas it proceeds principally on the basis of class and is partly *mitigated* by public policy in the Red Belt. As a result, the former is a racially and culturally uniform microcosm characterized by low institutional density and weak penetration of the social state, whereas the latter is mixed in terms of both ethnonational recruitment and class composition with a strong presence of public institutions.

This chapter complements the top-down structural, functional and ecological contrast between the French working-class *banlieues* and the black American ghetto sketched in the preceding chapter by taking the reader inside these two locales at ground level. This bottom-up approach aims to discern key invariants and variations in the social-organizational and cognitive structures of urban relegation by comparing two dimensions of daily life that are salient in both territories, albeit with divergent inflections, degrees of urgency, and sociopolitical dynamics. The first part of the chapter addresses the powerful territorial stigma attached to residence in an area that is not merely situated at the bottom of the hierarchy of places that make up the metropolis but is also publicly recognized as a 'dumping ground' for poor people, downwardly mobile working-class households, and dishonoured categories. Poverty is too often equated with insufficient income or sheer material dispossession. But, aside from being deprived of adequate conditions and means of living, to be poor in a rich society also entails, to varying degree, being assigned to the status of a *social anomaly* and being deprived of control over one's collective representation and identity (Simmel [1908] 1965). The analysis of public taint in the black American ghetto and the

French urban periphery leads us to stress the increasing weight of the *symbolic dispossession* that has turned their inhabitants into veritable urban outcasts at century's end. The second part of the chapter probes the bases and operation of the 'principles of social vision and division' that organize everyday life (Bourdieu [1987] 1989) and serve as frameworks for the contests that cut through stigmatized neighbourhoods of concentrated poverty in France and the United States. Specifying the basis of public taint attached to residence in the Red Belt enables us to identify the main factors accounting for the muted social potency of ethnoracial categorization in the Red Belt in spite of its discursive proliferation in the public sphere since the mid-1980s. The next chapter will complement this sociocognitive analysis by comparing the organizational density and diversity of the Red Belt and the Black Belt and by examining the differential impact of delinquency and street violence on public space and everyday social relations in these two urban settings.

Territorial stigmatization: experience, roots and effects

Any comparative sociology of the novel forms of urban poverty crystallizing in advanced societies at century's turn must begin with the *powerful stigma attached to residence in the bounded and segregated spaces,* the 'neighbourhoods of exile'[9] to which the populations marginalized or condemned to redundancy by the post-Fordist reorganization of the economy and the post-Keynesian reconstruction of the welfare state are increasingly consigned. Not only because it is arguably the single most protrusive feature of the lived experience of those entrapped in these sulfurous zones, but also because this stigma helps explain certain similarities in their strategies of coping and escape, and thereby many of the surface cross-national commonalities that have given plausibility to the thesis of a transatlantic convergence between the 'poverty regimes' of Europe and the United States.

---

[9] To borrow the title of the noted study of France's declining working-class *banlieues* by François Dubet and Didier Lapeyronnie (1992: 114) who write: 'The world of the *cités* is dominated by a feeling of exclusion which manifests itself first of all in the themes of reputation and scorn. The various *cités* are hierarchized on a scale of infamy that affects all of their aspects . . . and each one of their residents. There is a veritable stigma of the *cités*.' Huttman (1991) provides evidence of a similar stigma attached to districts of public housing estate concentrations in England, West Germany, Holland and Sweden. The accentuation of defamation through the 1990s is documented by Wassenberg (2004).

'It's like you got the plague here'

Because they constitute the lowest tier of the nation's public housing stock, have undergone continual material and demographic decline since their erection in the early 1960s, and have received a strong inflow of foreign families from the late 1970s onwards (Barrou 1992), the *cités* of the French urban periphery suffer from a negative public image that instantly associates them with endemic deprivation, immigration and insecurity. So much so that the worst of them are frequently baptized 'little Chicagos', by both their residents and outsiders.[10] Two other labels commonly used to denote the desolation and presumed dangerousness of the public housing estates of France's declining *banlieues* are 'Harlem' and 'Le Bronx'.

The low-income estate of the Quatre mille in La Courneuve initially packed 4,100 units designed to accommodate a population of 17,500 composed mainly of repatriates from formerly French Algeria, displaced residents of the suburban 'shanty-towns' of the 1950s, and later immigrant workers and their families. Much like the public housing projects of Chicago and other major American cities at their inception (Hirsch 1983; Harloe 1985), the *cité* was much desired and admired when it was inaugurated. Its creation was greeted with enthusiasm and accompanied by a vibrant celebration of *grands ensembles* (high-rise projects) supposed to re-create the frugal but warm conviviality of the imaginary working-class suburbs of yesteryear (Bachmann and Basier 1989: 38). A city official reminisced in an interview with the author:

> When I arrived in La Courneuve from [the rural province] of Limousin in 1964, I thought I was in the United States, it was so big, so bright, and so beautiful! I truly marvelled at the sight of the towers.

A short decade later, however, this positive picture of the 'blue estate' had been overlaid by an imagery of anonymity, dissolution and dread as middle-class families moved out, unemployment rose,

---

[10] For instance, Dubet (1987: 75), Laé and Murard (1985: 7–8), Dubet and Lapeyronnie (1992: 115), and Chignier-Riboulon (1999). Bachmann and Basier (1989: 86, 97) open their study of the image of La Courneuve in the public mind with a chapter entitled 'Chicago, Warsaw, New Delhi, La Courneuve'. They mention that, as early as 1971, the former owner of the then only movie theatre in the *cité* created a furor by publicly comparing La Courneuve with Chicago. In 1983, the city police found it necessary explicitly to remind journalists that 'La Courneuve is not Chicago, let's not exaggerate.'

and the *cité* turned into a repository for the most dispossessed residents of La Courneuve. By 1984, 790, or 22 per cent, of 3,603 housing units were occupied by households of foreign origin, and one in five families were behind in payment of their rent. Fully 46 per cent of the residents were under age 20, and the average household size of 3.9 persons was substantially above the city average of 2.9. Together, the loss of jobs, depopulation and bad reputation of the project accounted for the nearly 500 units vacant in 1990. With an official unemployment rate exceeding 30 per cent, the highest of all the neighbourhoods targeted by the state's urban renewal policy in the country according to city documents, more than half of the households in the Quatre mille battled the plague of long-term joblessness. This evolution is typical of the collective fate of large public housing estates in France's urban periphery over the past quarter-century, and it goes a long way toward explaining the taint now widely associated with living in one of them.

To dwell in a Red Belt low-income complex means to be confined to a branded space, to a blemished setting experienced as a 'trap' (Pialoux 1979: 19–20; Bachmann and Basier 1989). Thus, like the media, the inhabitants of the Quatre mille themselves routinely refer to their estate as a 'dumpster', 'the trash can of Paris', or even a 'reservation' (Avery 1987: 13), a far cry from the placid bureaucratic designation of 'sensitive neighbourhood' used by the public officials in charge of the state's urban renewal programme aimed at deprived districts after the late 1980s. By the closing decade of the century, the press of stigmatization had risen sharply due to the explosion of discourses on the alleged formation of '*cités*-ghettos' widely (mis)represented as growing pockets of 'Arab' poverty and disorder symptomatic of the incipient 'ethnicization' of France's urban space. In the case of La Courneuve, this perception was founded in part on the demography of phenotypically distinct populations in the early 1990s: six in ten foreign residents in the city came from North Africa, with 52 per cent from Algeria and another 8 per cent from Morocco and Tunisia, while 12 per cent originated in Spain and Italy, and the remainder in West Africa and Asia. (In the ensuing decade, the share of Algerians decreased substantially as they migrated to better housing in the outer suburbs of Paris, and the weight of Turks, Eastern Europeans, and sub-Saharan and Eastern Africans increased accordingly.)

It should be stressed, however, that the *cité* of the Quatre mille does not exist *as such* in the perceptions of its residents. The folk taxonomies that the latter use to organize their daily round at ground level distinguish numerous sub-units within the sprawling estate, which in effect has only an administrative and symbolic existence – although the consequences of this collective designation are very real. What appears from the outside to be a monolithic entity is experienced by its members as a finely differentiated congeries of 'micro-locales' centred on buildings and even on different stairwells inside the same building. People from the northern cluster of the project, in particular, want nothing to do with their counterparts of the southern cluster, whom they consider to be 'hoodlums' (*racailles* or *cailleras* in the local youth slang), and vice versa. 'For the residents of the Quatre mille, to change building sometimes means to change lives' (Bachmann and Basier 1989: 46; also Dulong and Paperman 1992). Yet it remains the case that *cités*-dwellers share a vivid awareness of being 'exiled' to a degraded space that collectively disqualifies them (Pétonnet 1979: 211; Paugam 1991).

Rachid, a former resident of the Quatre mille, gives virulent expression to this sense of indignity when asked about the eventuality of moving back into the project: 'For us to return there, it would be to be insulted once again. *The Quatre mille is an insult* . . . For many people, the Quatre mille is experienced as a shame.' When the interviewer inquires about the possibility of salvaging the housing project through renovation, the youth's answer is no less blunt:

> To renovate is to partake in shame. If you agree to play this game, then in a way you're endorsing shame. We've reached a point of no return where you got no solution but to raze the whole thing. Besides folks here agree there's only one solution: 'Gotta blow it up'. Go and ask them! . . .
>
> When you don't feel good inside, when you don't feel good outside, you got no job, you got nothing going for you, then you break things, that's how it is. The shit they're doing trying to fix the garbage disposals and the hallway entrances, painting the place up, that's no use: it's gonna get ripped right away. It's dumb. It's the whole thing that's the problem. . . . You gotta raze the whole thing. (Cited in Euvremer and Euvremer 1985: 8–9)

For Sali, another youth of North African descent from the Quatre mille, the project is 'a monstrous universe' experienced by its residents as an instrument of social confinement: 'It's a jail. They [second-generation residents] are in jail, they got tricked real good, so when they get together, they have karate fights against the mailboxes and they bust everything up. It's not hard to understand why' (ibid.: 9; also Bourdieu 1991b: 12–13). The verbal violence of these youths, as well as the vandalism they commit, may be interpreted as a response to the socioeconomic and symbolic violence to which they feel subjected by being thus relegated to a defamed place stripped of life opportunities. Not surprisingly, they show great distrust toward local leaders and bitterness about the inability of political institutions to grasp and rectify their daily difficulties (Aïchoune 1991; Jazouli 1992).

It is hardly possible for residents of the *cité* to disregard the scorn of which they are the object since the social taint of living in a low-income housing project that has become closely associated with poverty, crime and moral degradation in the public mind affects all realms of existence – whether it is searching for employment, pursuing romantic involvements, dealing with public agencies such as the police, the health and social services, or simply talking with acquaintances. Residents of the Quatre mille are quick to impute the ills of their life to the fact of being 'stuck' in a 'rotten' housing project that they come to perceive through a series of homological oppositions (*cité*/city, us/them, inside/outside, closed/open, low/high, dark/bright, savage/civilized) that reproduce and effectively endorse the derogatory judgement of outsiders.

> Why do we get thrown in jail? That's because of the *cité*. You feel inferior to others, you're not like the others: the others, they have buddies in the city, they throw parties, they got a clean house where, if you do something, water doesn't run in, the walls don't crumble on you. You got a reputation right away when you come from the *cité*. As long as the person doesn't know where you're coming from, you're fine, but once you've told her, you feel embarrassed, you dare not speak. (Cited in Pialoux 1979: 23)

When asked where they reside, many of 'those who work in Paris say vaguely that they live in the northern suburbs' (Avery 1987: 22) rather than reveal their address in La Courneuve. Some go so far as to walk to the nearest police station when they call taxicabs to avoid the humiliation of being picked up at the doorstep of their building inside the project's perimeter. Parents forewarn their daughters against going out with 'guys from the Quatre mille'. Inside every working-class *banlieue*, there is a fine hierarchical gradation of disrepute among the various projects whose manipulation calls for skilful stigma management. A youth from a declining *cité* in northern France relates:

> 'And then it's kind of funny when you talk with, say, girls who live in a *cité* that's a little bit cleaner, a little bit more . . . You tell them "I live

at the Roseraie" . . . They split, that's it. That's why, it's no good. Then you got to rap them hard.' His friend adds: 'They think you're a criminal.' (Bourdieu 1991b: 11)

Discrimination based on one's address hampers the job search and contributes to entrenching local unemployment as residents of the Quatre mille encounter additional distrust and reticence among employers as soon as they mention where they live. A janitor of the *cité* relates a typical incident in which he helped new tenants contact local firms by telephone, only to be told that there was no position open as soon as he revealed where he was calling from: 'It's like you got the plague here,' he says in disgust (in Bachmann and Basier 1989: 54).[11] Territorial stigmatization affects interactions not only with employers but also with the police, the courts and street-level bureaucracies such as the state unemployment and welfare offices, all of which are especially prompt to modify their conduct and procedures based on residence in a degraded *cité*. 'All youths recount the change of attitude of policemen when they notice their address during identity checks' (Dubet 1987: 75), for to come from a defamed *cité* triggers among outsiders a reflex suspicion of deviance if not principled guilt. A high-school student tells of being stopped by subway controllers in the Paris métro: 'We took out our identity cards. When they saw that we're from the Quatre mille, I swear to you! They went [he freezes] . . . they turned pale' (in Bachmann and Basier 1989: 65).

'People really look down on you'

In the United States, as we saw in the first part of this book, the dark ghetto stands similarly as the national symbol of urban 'pathology', and its accelerating involution since the racial uprisings of the

[11] This pattern of discrimination is not a phenomenon of the 1990s; it is more or less coextensive with the existence of the *cités*, and the gradual deterioration of their reputation, as noted by Colette Pétonnet (1982: 147) in fieldwork conducted in the early 1970s: 'Shopkeepers and employers display reticence towards a population whose reputation is spreading and is charged with a miserable or vile content. Youths complain: "We can't find any jobs. As soon as we say that we live there, that's it! The boss answers: we'll write you later."' Pialoux (1979: 22) made similar observations in another Red Belt town in the late 1970s: 'We the youths of the *cité, we're kept apart*, it's just like for work: in T., you tell them about the *cité*, they boot you right out the door. Me, I don't say *cité* of C. no more, I say number 70 on S. Avenue. Even in Paris, they know it, the *cité* of C.' What changed over the past decade is the intensity of the stigma and virulence of its negative effects in the context of the mass unemployment and political marginalization plaguing the working class.

mid-1960s is widely regarded as incontrovertible proof of the moral dissolution, cultural depravity and behavioural deficiencies of its inhabitants.[12] Outsiders typically 'view the ghetto as a mysterious and unfathomable place that breeds drugs, crime, prostitution, unwed mothers, ignorance, and mental illness' (Anderson 1990: 167). For residents of the white ethnic neighbourhood of Canarsie in Brooklyn, for instance, the nearby ghetto is an opaque and evil territory to be avoided, a 'jungle infested by dark-skinned "animals" whose wild sexuality and broken families def[y] all ideas of civilized conduct. . . . "They steal, they got no values . . . [I]t's the way they live. They live like animals"' (Rieder 1985: 25, 26). The journalistic reports and academic (pseudo-)theories that have proliferated to account for the putative emergence of a so-called underclass in the racialized urban core in the 1980s have accentuated the *demonization of the black city (sub)proletariat* by symbolically severing it from the 'deserving' working class and by masking the state policies of urban abandonment and punitive containment that are responsible for its downward slide, as shown in chapter 2.

Living in the vestiges of the historic Black Belt of Chicago at century's end carries an automatic presumption of social unworthiness and moral inferiority, which translates into an acute consciousness of the symbolic degradation associated with being confined to a loathed and despised universe.[13] A student from a vocational high school on the city's South Side voices this sense of being cut off from and cast out of the broader society in these words:

> People really look down on you because of where you come from and who you are. People don't want to have anything to do with you. . . . You can tell when you go places, people are looking at you like you are crazy or something. (Cited in Duncan 1987: 63)

A professional boxer from a South Side gym who picked up the gloves after a stint in the US Marines reports this telling anecdote about the reaction of a girl he was courting to learning that he came from an ill-reputed project located at the heart of the ghetto:

---

[12] For euphemized scholarly versions of this vision, see, *inter alia*, Banfield (1970), Jencks and Peterson (1991: e.g., 3, 96, 155–6) and Mead (1992); for a critique of these academic views, Katz (1989) and Reed (1992).

[13] This phenomenon is not unique to Chicago's ghetto, as shown by Wilkinson's (1992: esp. 78–88) perceptive ethnographic account of territorial stigmatization in a mixed black–Puerto Rican public housing project in Roxbury in the heart of Boston.

When I first met [the girl who later became] my wife, she had never been home with me an' stuff an' then, uh, after about three weeks, I tell her I said 'I gotta go home for somethin', 'an' when I drove in the projects, I pulled up in front of the projects, she looked at me, she said (in a shrill voice, mixing disbelief and indignation) *'You liiive heeere?!!!'* an' I said (trying to sound matter of fact, but still apologetic) 'Yeah.' She said (firmly) 'Well you can take me home then.' I was like 'no,' she wouldn't even get out, I was like 'get out for a minute,' I said 'I want you to meet my mother 'an' this an' that. An' then you know she was kinda, *scared at first* an' then after a while, an' she told me, she told me she had *never* been into no projects.

The defamation of the ghetto is inscribed first in the brute facts of its physical dilapidation. It is manifested next by the separateness and blatant inferiority of its institutions, be they public schools, social welfare agencies, municipal services, neighbourhood associations, and the rare financial and shopping outlets that survive inside its perimeter (Orfield 1985; Monroe and Goldman 1988). Lastly, it is constantly reaffirmed by the diffident and contemptuous attitudes of outsiders: banks, insurance companies, taxi drivers, delivery trucks and other commercial services studiously avoid the historic Black Belt or venture into it only gingerly.

Residents of adjacent neighbourhoods learn to fear and shun the ghetto and thus organize their daily round so as never to come near to or inside of its dreaded perimeter. The first piece of advice I received from a university official on the day I landed in Hyde Park as a doctoral student at the University of Chicago was not to cross the fortified boundaries that separate this white wealthy enclave from the South Side districts of Oakland-Kenwood, Washington Park and Woodlawn that border it on three of its four sides. People living outside the collapsing core of the black ghetto are reluctant to visit kith and kin there. An unemployed mother of three who resides in a defamed West Side project intones: 'Friends from other places don't want really to come here. And you yourself, you wouldn't want to invite intelligent people here: there's markings and there's writing on the wall, nasty.' Children and women dwelling in public housing in the hyperghetto report that they find it particularly difficult to develop personal ties with outsiders once the latter learn of their place of residence (Kotlowitz 1991: 52).

Desmond Avery (1987: 29), who lived in both the Cabrini Green project in Chicago and the Quatre mille *cité*, remarks that address-based discrimination is at least as prevalent in the Windy City as it is in the deindustrializing periphery of Paris. Ghetto-dwellers are well aware that living in a stigmatized district of the city penalizes them on the labour market. A 41-year-old nurse from the West Side complains:

> I have been to jobs, and I have friends who have gone to jobs, and they asked them what neighbourhood [they were from]. And as soon as they look at your address, they say (in a frightened voice) '*Wow!* you live in this area!', you know. It's just that a lot of people look at your address. I have a friend right now, [at] his job, they told him they'd rather for him to stay a little north, not in this type of neighbourhood. *Your address, it's impression for jobs.*

Residing at the heart of the South Side, and even more so in a public housing project whose name has become virtually eponymous with 'vice and violence' (such as the gigantic estates of the Robert Taylor Homes, Cabrini Green or Henry Horner, which regularly make the news with gruesome stories of crime and welfare abuse), is yet another hurdle in the arduous quest for employment. A jobless woman who lives in the ill-reputed Cabrini Green housing development remarks:

> It's supposed to be discrimination, but they get away with it, you know. Yes, it's important where you live. Employers notice, they notice addresses, when that application's goin' through personnel, they are lookin' at that address: (in a worried tone) 'Oh, you're from *here*!?'

Over and beyond the scornful gaze of outsiders and the brute reality of exclusion from the regular institutions of the national society, the state of advanced dereliction of the local economy and ecology exerts a pervasive *effect of demoralization* upon ghetto residents. Indeed, the words 'depressing' and 'uninspiring' come up time and again in the description that the latter give of their surroundings – a 31-year-old janitor who lives with his wife and three children in the dark basement of a shabby apartment building in Woodlawn even uses the adjective 'uninspirable' to depict his neighbourhood.[14] We

[14] My fieldnotes from the in-depth interviews conducted in their homes with respondents to the Social Opportunity component of the Urban Family Life Project are littered with personal expressions of depression and despondency at the derelict state of the areas I visited. A report on the ABLA housing project on the city's West Side reads: 'This is a neighbourhood for which the adjectives poor or dilapidated are euphemisms, and where the concept of social isolation might well be replaced by social devastation. . . . I confess to coming out of this interview in a state of shock. The combination of the circumstances, R[espondent]'s discourse, and the glimpses he afforded me into his life and his worldview was too much to take.' In several cases, the experience was saddening to the point where I was emotionally unable to transcribe the taped interview for several days after conducting it.

noted previously that two-thirds of the inhabitants of the South Side and West Side of Chicago expect that their neighbourhood will either stay in the same state of blight or further deteriorate in the future; the only route they see for improvement is to move out, to which nearly all aspire. But the possibility of realizing the primitive accumulation of resources needed for upward mobility is eroded by the predatory cast of relations between residents and by the pressure toward social uniformity which weighs on those who try to rise above the poverty level common to most people in their area: 'They won't let you get ahead. Stealin' from you and robbin' you and all that kinda thing,' laments a 27-year-old machine operator from the far South Side. Given the inordinate prevalence of violent crime (recorded in chapters 2 and 4), living in the hyperghetto also entails significant physical risks and, as a corollary, high levels of psychological stress that tend to 'drag you down' and 'wear you out'. A 31-year-old high-school graduate who gets by on casual and intermittent employment obtained at a day-labour agency and lives with his mother in a dilapidated high rise on the Near West Side reports:

> See, this is a violent neighbourhood. You always hear somebody getting' shot, just about every day or something like every night. . . . I see people are crowded up together, especially in the high rises. I would say it drags you down, because, you know, when people get crazy and everything, it'll drag you down. They gonna robbin' you, you know, tryin' to beat you. They don't wanta work, you know, they rather for you to work and then wait for you, you know, to get your paycheck so they can rob you.

No wonder life in the historic Black Belt is suffused with an abiding sense of gloom and social *fatum* which obstructs the future from view and seems to doom one to a life of continued failure and rejection (Monroe and Goldman 1988: 158–9, 273; Kotlowitz 1991; Wacquant 1998).

From spatial stigmatization to social dissolution

Paradoxically, the experiential burden of territorial stigmatization in the 'wide-awake world' (Schutz 1970) weighs more heavily upon the residents of the declining French working-class *banlieues* than it does on their counterparts in America's dark ghetto, even though the latter is a considerably more desolate and oppressive *oekoumene*. Three factors help account for this apparent disjuncture between objective

conditions and the subjective (in)tolerance of those who are subjected to the conditionings that these conditions determine.

First, the very idea of relegation to a separate space of *institutionalized social inferiority and immobility* stands in blatant violation of the
French ideology of unitarist citizenship and open participation in the
national community. This ideology has been deeply internalized and
is loudly invoked by Red Belt youths – it was a leitmotif of the
children of immigrants come from North Africa during their street
protests and marches of the 1980s (Jazouli 1992). Rejection of a
second-tier status of 'subcitizen' was a core tenet of the phalanx of
immigrant-based *banlieues* organizations that emerged in the wake of
the 'March for Equality and against Racism' of 1983 staged in
response to the electoral breakthrough of Le Pen's National Front,
such as the MIB (Mouvement Immigration Banlieues), Convergence
84, SOS Racisme, France Plus, JALB (Jeunes Arabes de Lyon et
Banlieues) and Agora (Bouamama 1994). This forceful rejection is
due to (i) the swift cultural assimilation of the children of postcolonial migrants into French society in spite of the manifold forms of
prejudice and discrimination they encounter; (ii) the absence of any
credible idiom of ethnicity in the discursive repertoire and lack of
influence of immigrant organizations in the national political field;
and, ultimate irony or revenge of history, (iii) the enduring belief,
inherited from the colonial era, that families recently emigrated from
France's former empire have in the universalistic 'civilizing' capacity
of the school system in the context of the generalization of secondary
schooling and renewed expansion of the university system.[15]

By contrast, the rigid colour line of which the black ghetto is the
physical and institutional concretization is so deeply ingrained in the
makeup of the urban and mental landscape of the United States that
it has become part of the *order of things*. The dichotomous black /
white opposition has been a constitutive framework for the organization of the economy and space of the metropolis as well as the
national society and polity for more than three centuries. Inscribed
in bodies and things, buttressed by the law and routinely enforced
by public bureaucracies (Davis 1991), it is totally taken for granted
by a properly socialized American – including by those who have
paradoxically reaffirmed the principle of racial categorization by
descent by asking for the recognition of persons of 'multiracial' origin

---

[15] This belief was to be severely tested and eroded, leading to the bitter disillusion-
ment and widespread sense of betrayal among the first generation of students of
postcolonial origins to accede to higher education in the 1990s (Beaud 2002).

(Daniel 2001). Several academic theories, beginning with the ecological paradigm of the early Chicago School, relayed by the structural-functionalist current and then by the works of Otis Dudley
Duncan and Amos Hawley, have buttressed this vision by presenting
the formation and persistence of segregated and sharply bounded
ethnoracial neighbourhoods as 'natural areas' mechanically produced
by a 'race relations cycle' and other putatively universal urban dynamics that are in fact highly specific to American society (Castells [1977]
1979). The demand to 'rebuild the inner city' – rather than *dissolve*
it – by progressive politicians and black leaders after every major
urban riot (such as the South Central Los Angeles uprising of May
1992 evoked in chapter 1) reveals the extent to which the racial segmentation of the metropolis is taken as an inexorable given.[16]

Second, lacking a socially potent idiom of collective causation,
residents of America's dark ghetto are much more prone to embrac-
ing an individualistic ideology of achievement – and, correspond-
ingly, failure – than their counterparts of the working-class *cités* of
France. Like the vast majority of Americans (Kluegel and Smith
1986: ch. 3), they subscribe to the social-Darwinist view according
to which the position of each in the social and economic hierarchy
of the country ultimately reflects their moral worth and personal
strivings, so that no one, in the final analysis, can be durably penalized by his or her place of residence. This moral individualism powerfully counters the fuzzy sentiment, assembled piecemeal from the
shards of everyday experience, that race, class and space are inflexible
determinants of one's life chances. The same nurse's aide who complained bitterly about address discrimination above also asserted in
the same interview that 'it's all in a person, what a person wish to
have for themselves. If they choose to, even, in any neighbourhood
or community, I believe they could better themselves. But you must
want yourself, and then you must go out and seek.'

Duncan (1987: 89) similarly relates that youths in the devastated
neighbourhood of North Kenwood assessed their success and failures
almost exclusively in personal terms.[17] Interviews conducted by the

---

[16] These leaders forget James Baldwin's (1962: 65) lucid admonition that 'the people
in Harlem know they are living there because white people do not think they are
good enough to live elsewhere. No amount of "improvement" can sweeten this
fact. . . . A ghetto can be improved in one way only: out of existence.'

[17] One of my informants from Woodlawn gave a hyperbolic formulation to this view:
'Well, everybody can survive in this country. You got so much food around. You
can eat out of garbage cans or go to some restaurant and ask for the left-overs. *If
someone starve in this country, it means that somethin's wrong with him.* He weak and
maybe he don't deserve to survive.'

Urban Family Life Project with a sample of residents of the South Side and West Side revealed that the more marginal their social position, the more they tend to see the social world in terms of individual will and efforts, qualified by 'knowing people in the right places' and chance factors, and the more likely they are to disparage persons just like them for failing to take their fate firmly into their own hands.[18] Asked if she believed that 'America is a land of opportunity for all', a 31-year-old unemployed mother, relying on welfare and intermittent stints as a store cashier for a decade to subsist with her three children in a dilapidated project of North Lawndale, exclaims: 'I would say I agree. Because I've lived here. I think a person can live anywhere.' She concedes that residents of her depressed neighbourhood have fewer chances than others but immediately launches into this deprecatory tirade:

> Well, the few that I probably talk to here, to my recollection, they're lazy. A lot of people are lazy. They don't want to work. I want to work; I do not work but *I want to work*. I don't want to just be on public aid. And I've talked to a lot of them: it doesn't matter to them. They say that they're going to be on aid for the rest of their life, they're never going to have anything.
>
> Like to me, you wouldn't want to live in this place here: you would want a nice place for your children to live. By the ones that I've talked to, it's like they don't care. . . . The people in this neighbourhood, they, they don't wanta do anything. They just wanta sit back and just wait on somebody to give them somethin', instead of, you know, taking a jump on life.

A third and perhaps the most crucial difference between Red Belt and Black Belt relates to the nature of the stigma they carry: this stigma is essentially residential in the former but jointly and inseparably *spatial-cum-racial* in the latter. The French *banlieue* is a territorial entity containing a mixed, multiethnic population; it suffices for the residents of the Quatre mille or any other defamed *cité* of the French urban periphery to hide their address to make this status disappear and 'pass' in the broader society – unless they get spotted by their *'dégaine'* (physical demeanour and dress) and speech patterns. Residential stigma is not linked in a univocal manner to a phenotypical or cultural marker that would automatically catalogue them as members of the Red Belt, and use of simple techniques of

---

[18] Research has shown time and again that 'middle-class misconceptions about the motivation of the poor are often held by the poor themselves' (Williamson 1974: 634).

'impression management' (Goffman 1959) enables them to shed the mark, if only temporarily. Thus adolescents from the working-class outskirts of Paris regularly go 'hang out' in the upscale districts or the shopping centres of the capital to escape the abiding ennui of their neighbourhood and gain a sense of excitement. By traversing spaces that both symbolize and contain the life of higher classes (such as the Champs-Élysées or the Forum des Halles, two perennial favourites), they can live for a few hours a fantasy of social inclusion and participate, albeit by proxy, in the wider society (Calogirou 1989: 64–9). This 'consciousness switch' renders more intolerable the prospect of permanent apartness and the outcast status associated with being consigned to a degraded *cité*.

Residents of the American Black Belt are not granted the luxury of this dual 'awareness context' (Glaser and Strauss 1965). For the ghetto is not simply a spatial entity or a mere aggregation of poor families stuck at the bottom of the class structure: it is a *specifically racial formation* designed to encase a bounded category that has spawned a society-wide web of material and symbolic associations between colour, place and a host of negatively valued social properties (Pettigrew 1971: 91–2, 179–82). The fact that 'race' – or blackness as denegated ethnicity founded on the historic disgrace of slavery – is a marker of collective identity and a principle of social vision and division that is uniformly shared and immediately available for interpretation and use in public space as well as in the interactions that unfold in it (Feagin 1991) makes it nearly impossible for the residents of the racialized core of the US metropolis to shed the stigma attached to ghetto residence. For instance, they cannot casually cross over into adjacent white neighbourhoods, for there 'the sight of a young black man evokes an image of someone dangerous, destructive, or deviant' (Monroe and Goldman 1989: 27; also Anderson 1990: esp. 163–7), so that they will promptly be trailed and stopped by the police.[19]

More generally, unless they offset their low caste status by a competent display of the symbols of middle-class (white) culture, blacks are always *ex definitionis* presumed to be ghetto-dwellers and of low class provenance. As Lewis Killian (1990: 10) writes: 'To most whites, actually accepting blacks as residents of their neighbourhoods seems to mean that drug-ridden welfare recipients from the ghetto

---

[19] My mates from the boxing gym in Woodlawn always refused to wait for me in front of my building, at the edge of the neighbourhood of Hyde Park, only three blocks from the club, because it guaranteed that they would get questioned by the private police force diligently patrolling the enclave of the University of Chicago.

will be on their doorsteps tomorrow.' In contrast with residents of France's declining urban periphery, ghetto blacks in the United States suffer from *conjugated stigmatization*: they cumulate the negative symbolic capital attached to skin colour *and* to consignment to a closed, reserved and inferior territory itself devalued by its double status as racial reservation and warehouse for the human rejects of the lowest strata of society. One understands how, being citizens of a race-divided nation-state in which all spheres of life are thoroughly coded by the dichotomous hierarchy black–white (other ethnic categories being positioned in relation to this founding dualism through a process of symbolic triangulation), and given their exceedingly low objective probability of escaping their originary universe, ghetto youths would make a virtue of necessity and accommodate themselves to living with a stigma that is both illegitimate and intolerable to French youths in the derelict *cités* of the Red Belt.

If territorial stigmatization differs in its foundations and nature, its main *effect* is nonetheless similar on the two sides of the Atlantic: it is to stimulate practices of internal social differentiation and distancing that work to decrease interpersonal trust and undercut local solidarity. To regain a measure of dignity and reaffirm the legitimacy of their own status in the eyes of society, the residents of France's working-class *banlieues* like those of the black American ghetto typically overstress their moral worth as individuals or family members (as a good father, mother, son or daughter). And they join their voices to the dominant chorus of denunciation of deviant and delinquent categories, such as those who unduly 'profit' from public assistance programmes, 'welfare cheats' and *'faux pauvres'* who draw the RMI or unemployment benefits when they should not get them, or hoodlums and *cailleras* (low-grade delinquents). It is as if they could (re)gain value only by devaluing a little more their own neighbours and neighbourhood. Following the same logic, residents of the Black Belt and Red Belt deploy a range of strategies of social distinction and withdrawal which converge to undermine community cohesion. These strategies assume three main forms: mutual avoidance, the reconstitution and elaboration of 'infra-differences' or micro-hierarchies detectable only at ground level, and the diversion of public opprobrium onto scapegoats such as notorious 'problem families' and foreigners, or drug dealers and single mothers.[20]

---

[20] See Paugam (1991: 193–205) for a perceptive discussion of these strategies in a low-income estate at the periphery of Brest (Brittany). Numerous quotes could be adduced here. One will have to suffice: 'In this world of negative social homogeneity,

In the French working-class *cité*, residents commonly insist that they have landed there only 'by accident' and are only 'passing' on their way to another district and a better life. And they eagerly rail about the waste of public resources allocated to those who, 'unlike them', do not need state assistance and city services aimed at deprived households. Similarly, in Chicago's hyperghetto, residents disclaim belonging to the neighbourhood as a network of mutual acquaintance and exchange, and they strive to set themselves off from what they know to be a disgraced place and population. Our nurse from North Lawndale speaks for many of her peers of both Black Belt and Red Belt when she stridently states: '*Hell*, I don't know what people [around here] do! I guess I'm pretty much on my own. I don't associate with people in the neighbourhood . . . I mean I speak to them, but as far as knowing what they're about, I don't know.'

To sum up, residents of the French working-class *banlieues* and of the black American ghetto each in their manner form an *impossible community*, perpetually divided against themselves, whose members cannot but refuse to acknowledge the collective nature of their predicament. They are therefore inclined to develop strategies of material and symbolic distancing – culminating in out-migration – that tend to distend and unravel social ties and thereby validate negative outside perceptions of the neighbourhood. Negative representations and sociofugal practices then become articulated to set off a deadly self-fulfilling prophecy through which public taint and collective dishonour end up *producing* that which they claim merely to *record*: namely, social atomism, community 'disorganization' and cultural anomie.[21]

---

the manipulation of gossip aims at "overclassing" oneself and "downclassing" others. . . . Foreigners are, according to the dominant discourse, responsible for the degradation of the neighbourhood, for crime, for the lack of jobs, . . . and for the devalorization and stigmatization of the *cité*. . . . The fantastical negation of relations of neighbouring becomes a necessity' as does 'the stigmatization of the others for their low education and the exaggeration of one's educational abilities. It is crucial to demonstrate one's adherence to dominant norms' (Calogirou 1989: 17, 21–2, 41). On this point, see also Pétonnet (1979: 220–34), Gwaltney (1981: 121–6), Kotlowitz (1991) and Wilkinson (1992).

[21] To stress the *sociofugal and fissiparous tendency* of social strategies and their *desolidarizing effects* as we have done here does not mean that the French *banlieues* and the American ghetto suffer from 'social disorganization', as this notion has been used by the early Chicago School (e.g., Wirth 1964: 44–9) and adopted by poverty researchers since as the unquestioned premiss of their field of inquiry (for a critique of the theory of social disorganization as applied to the ghetto, see Wacquant 1997a).

Social vision and division in ghetto and *banlieue*

We have shown that the organic nexus between territorial stigmatization, physical insecurity and state abandonment, cemented by the racial isolation inflicted upon blacks in the United States, is highly distinctive in the Black Belt. This isolation finds a cognitive extension in the caste cleavage and consciousness that structure everyday life in the ghetto, where the dichotomous division between blacks and whites insinuates itself into all spheres of existence, to the point where it even colours class differentiation among African Americans. In the Parisian Red Belt, by contrast, the dominant opposition pits, not native French residents and immigrants, as the reigning media and political discourse would have it, but *cité* youths against all others. Although foreigners and especially families of North African origins have grown more visibly concentrated in peripheral Red Belt estates since the shutting off of legal immigration in 1974, the French working-class *banlieues* remain a highly heterogeneous universe in which ethnoracial categories have limited potency.

American apartheid and split racial consciousness

In the historical crucible of two and a half centuries of slavery followed by another century of rigid racial separation subtended by multifarious forms of state-sponsored discrimination and racial violence, many of which persist into the present in attenuated forms, African Americans have carved out a rich expressive culture supplying them with a distinctive set of practices and signs through which to construct themselves and impart meaning to the world about them (Levine 1977; Jones 1985; Abrahams 1970).[22] The United States is also a society unique for having a 'classificatory racial system' in which 'anyone who is not completely white and has the slightest trace of black ancestry is considered black' (Patterson 1972: 28). Strict application of this rule of 'hypo-descent' has prohibited mobility

[22] The fact that African-American culture, blending elements imported from Africa and grown in the United States, has long been 'rendered historically inarticulate by scholars' (Levine 1977: p. ix) and continues to be misunderstood (if not negated) by contemporary analysts wedded to functionalist conceptions of culture as a unitary set of 'shared norms and values' or mechanical 'adaptations' to objective conditions, or to positivist modes of reasoning which reduce culture to a 'variable' (whose 'effect' is to be partialled out and weighed – preferably statistically – against those of 'race' or 'space', also treated as independent and unitary factors) does not obviate its existence and potency.

along a colour gradient and blocked the emergence of a mixed-blood or mulatto category socially recognized as such, in spite of the widespread sexual mixing of African- and European-descended populations, resulting in a rigid dualistic opposition between two fictitiously exclusive communities, 'blacks' and 'whites'.

Thus it is not surprising that 'race', understood as membership in a lineage whose ancestors were submitted (or not) to bondage, forms the hub around which the African-American cultural matrix revolves. The impassable and inflexible symbolic boundary that whites have imposed upon blacks throughout the society, most visible in the enduring spatial disjunction between the 'races' and extraordinarily low interracial marriage rates (fewer than 3 per cent of black women take a partner outside their ethnic group), finds its expression in forms of consciousness anchored in a rigid 'us / them' opposition between blacks and whites mirroring the objective caste relations that have prevailed historically between these two categories (Franklin 1993; Dawson 1994; Moran 2003).

Race is inscribed everywhere in the ghetto: in the objectivity of space and of the separate and inferior institutions that confine its population in the manner of a snare, but also in the subjectivity of categories of perception and judgement that its residents engage in their most routine conduct, thoughts and feelings. Indeed, colour consciousness in the Black Belt is so suffusive as to go without saying – so much so that it can go unnoticed even by careful observers because, precisely, it is embedded deep in what Alfred Schutz (1970) calls the 'natural attitude' of everyday life.[23] In the Black Belt, racialized categories have an immediacy and pervasiveness that make them central cognitive and evaluative tools. For instance, the first characteristic that a person conveys to and seeks from others, if implicitly, in mundane conversations (whether face to face or on the telephone) is whether or not he or she is 'a brother' or 'a sister', as this identification will decisively angle the ensuing sequence of interactions. The fact that most residents of the ghetto have few occasions to engage in ongoing encounters with whites – and, increasingly, with middle- and upper-class blacks – on a one-to-one basis further increases the perceptual potency of colour. Kotlowitz (1991: 161) recounts the

---

[23] The ubiquity of racial consciousness among African Americans is richly documented in the 'self-portrait of black America' assembled by John Langston Gwaltney (1981) and in Steven Gregory's (1998) study of the middle class of a black neighbourhood of Queens in New York. Its omnipresence in American social life more broadly is attested by Terkel (1992).

story of a child living in a housing estate on Chicago's West Side who, upon reaching age 10, 'began to wonder aloud about being black. "Do all black people live in projects?" he asked his mother. "Do all black people be poor?"' I was the only white friend that the young men (all of them black, save for a handful of Latinos) I encountered during my three years of ethnographic fieldwork in the neighbourhood of Woodlawn ever had.

That the residents of the historic Black Belt should take the colour line for granted is not surprising given that their existence is almost entirely contained within the racially uniform world of the hyper-ghetto and, for many of them, within a small section of it: their street, block or 'stomping ground' of the immediate vicinity. The white world 'out there' remains largely unknown, for it is virtually inaccessible, save via stereotypical representations conveyed by the mass media and intermittent contact with agencies of human services and social control.[24] Among the subproletarians of Chicago's South Side,

> The Man, it was said, owned everything worth having and wouldn't let black people get in the door. But they practically never saw a white face except on TV and the innocent suburban lives depicted there . . . were as distant from their own as Mars from Earth. Their cityscape was nearly all black, except for a few bureaucrats, teachers, and cops, and they rarely left it; a trip to the [downtown] Loop, for most, was a major expedition. Thirty-ninth street, that's *your* world. . . . The rest was *they* world, a white world with different codes of speech, dress, and conduct. (Monroe and Goldman 1988: 100)

So powerful is the racial prism through which ghetto residents perceive and construct their everyday world that those of them who manage to climb up the class structure and escape Bronzeville are commonly perceived by those they leave behind as 'traitors' to their community who are trying to 'become white' – notwithstanding the fact that most them end up migrating into all-black neighbourhoods at the margins of the ghetto or into rigidly segregated suburbs (Massey et al. 1994; Pattillo-McCoy 2000). Class differences among blacks thus find themselves couched in the idiom of racial division and colour-coded as an analogue of black / white differences. An unemployed young man from Woodlawn rails against the teachers,

[24] 'For many young men at Horner,' an infamous housing project in the city's West Side ghetto, 'their only contact with the world outside their own immediate environs is the courts' (Kotlowitz 1991: 226).

business people and police officers who fled the area since his teenage
years in these terms:

> Everybody tryin' *be white*, try to git behin' a white person, movin' in a
> white neighbourhood: 'I'm the only black *livin' in my neighbourhood'* –
> (in utter disbelief) they be braggin' about that, I'm serious! (snickering)
> 'I'm the *first black out there.*' I said, boy, you sick here! *Bleachin' they
> skin*, I'm like boy! *Normal seekin' the abnormal*, that's what it is.

As long as the residential and interactional structures of 'American
apartheid' (Massey 1990) persist, the dichotomous opposition existing between whites and blacks in objective reality has every reason
to be replicated in the frameworks of collective consciousness of
urban residents.

'Jeunes des cités' *against the rest of the world*

If there is a dominant antagonism that runs through everyday life in
the Red Belt *cités* and stamps the mind of its inhabitants, it is not,
contrary to prevalent journalistic images and policy discourse, one
that opposes immigrants (especially 'Arabs') and autochthonous
French families, but the cleavage dividing youths (*les jeunes*), *native
and foreign lumped together*, from all the other social categories. Youths
are widely singled out by older residents and by the administrative
and political decision-makers of La Courneuve as the chief source of
disorder, delinquency and ambient insecurity in the city, and they
are publicly held up as responsible for the worsening condition and
lugubrious reputation of the degraded *banlieues*. Avery (1987: 112)
reports:

> the bands of youth that congregate in the stairways [of the Quatre
> mille] are a favourite topic of conversation: 'They smash the lightbulbs
> so we can't see what they're up to,' says one. 'They shoot drugs in
> broad daylight,' 'They sit there, they talk real loud, and smoke reefers
> all night long,' 'They piss in the stairwells,' 'We don't like to encounter
> them at night, we are prisoners in our own apartments.'

Mixing fact with fiction, such accusations find an objective basis
in the fact that youths are demographically predominant in projects
like the Quatre mille and that they typically take over the streets and
the few public spaces available, including building hallways and
porches, which makes adults feel that they are misappropriating a
common good for their particular uses, aside from the nuisances that

this diversion occasions for the collectivity (noise, trash, agitation, traffic and trafficking, etc.).[25] Whether they are well founded or not, these grievances invariably portray young people either as generators of trouble or as themselves troubled. Bachmann and Basier (1989: 100) point out that, in La Courneuve, 'in every incident, youths are both the cause and the victims of violence in the *cité*: they stand way out in the foreground.'

As for the youths from stigmatized Red Belt districts, they feel that they are being subjected to a generalized pattern of anti-youth discrimination that obtains both inside and outside their estates. They complain that public authorities neglect them, reject their demands, and ignore their contribution to the life of the neighbourhood, or that government programmes promise much but deliver next to nothing that concretely improves their daily lot; that the police subject them to unwarranted suspicion and intrusive surveillance; and that adults more generally remain blind to their plight and deaf to their concerns. But, above all, youths from the derelict *banlieues* feel that none of the above accord them the recognition and minimal *respect* they deem themselves entitled to: ' "We don't exist, nobody sees us." "They treat us like rats" ' (Lapeyronnie 1992: 11). The seething rage that many experience at being durably shut out from employment and being denied the individual dignity that normally comes with economic self-sufficiency often finds an outlet in a hyperindividualistic celebration of illegal entrepreneurship or a nihilistic discourse glorifying predation and violence as means of access to the sphere of consumption and which, for want of being able to put a face on the impersonal mechanisms that marginalize them, fastens on the police as the target of hostility (Dubet 1987: 80–9; Jazouli 1992: 148–9).

Because the findings of the researchers who have investigated up close the tensions simmering in the housing projects of the degraded working-class *banlieues* at century's end are strikingly at odds with the vision that has come to dominate the media and political debate, they are worth quoting here at some length. Avery (1987: 21), for instance, 'never observed during [his] years in La Courneuve . . .

---

[25] 'In the end, what is it that people reproach youths for? That they occupy the squares, that they sit on the benches or the steps in front of stores . . . , that they stay there talking, laughing, making a racket.' Youths, on the other hand, perceive 'the street as a mere place of well-being, a neutral ground upon which they can put their mark' (Calogirou 1989: 36–7; also Bourdieu 1991b: 12). See Pinçon (1982) for a broader analysis of how the mixing of populations with diverse origins and disparate interests breeds conflict over the use of collective resources in French low-income estates.

situations of overt racial intolerance, of blatant collective scorn' of
the kind he routinely witnessed on Chicago's West Side or in a
British working-class town where he previously resided. Though 14.5
per cent of the electorate of La Courneuve voted for the National
Front in the 1986 legislative elections, he insists that 'there is no
racist climate here, usually. I find on the contrary a lot of mutual
respect and solidarity in the daily life of the *cité*' (Avery 1987: 21–2).
David Lepoutre confirmed this observation a decade later in his
detailed ethnography of the street culture of teenagers in the Quatre
mille: 'Relations of sociability between adolescents are not determined primarily by ethnic origin. Friendships cross cultural barriers
quite easily' (Lepoutre 1997: 80) because the youths mix together
on a daily basis at school as well as in housing, and teenagers of
foreign origin have largely assimilated the national culture.

In an isolated working-class project in the western suburbs of
Paris, Calogirou turned up notably more 'ethnicized' forms of perception of space: different sections of the estate as well as specific
buildings were identified, and referred to, by the presumed ethnoracial or ethnonational composition of its most visible tenants. Nonetheless, she insists that '[t]olerance is the most commonly developed
attitude', and that 'those who establish national or religious restrictions in their network of friends are far and few' (Calogirou 1989:
144).[26] For the youths from these projects, shared residence in the
estate and assorted personal properties override 'ethnic' membership, as indicated by their frequent use of humour to deflect the
derogatory denotation of racist insults – as when, for instance, they
insert such invectives into joking terms of address in their verbal
contests.

The intermingling of categories, collective trajectories and 'ethnic' tensions

How to explain the muted character of ethnic consciousness in the
working-class estates of the Parisian Red Belt in spite of the growing
density of immigrant families in the most degraded housing
projects of the urban periphery – recall that their share in the

---

[26] Calogirou (1989: 93, 96, 98, 101, 115, 131) goes on to show that these networks
systematically cut across ethnic boundaries and nationality groupings. Pétonnet
(1979: 224) likewise emphasizes that 'there is no ethnic hierarchy in the *cité*. There
are only interpersonal hierarchies.' On the rejection of the 'immigrant/native' dichot-
omy in the everyday practices and representations of youths in a stigmatized *cité* of
Lille in northern France, see Bourdieu (1991b).

population of La Courneuve doubled between 1968 and 1990 to top 25 per cent – and the expanding place accorded the thematics of racism in the public sphere as the 1980s wore on? Three reasons may be adduced here briefly.[27]

First, as we noted above, the *cités* of the Red Belt are highly heterogeneous ensembles in terms of ethnoracial recruitment. No *banlieue* is the exclusive or even predominant 'turf' of a particular group because urban space in France is not organized according to the principle of 'ordered segmentation' prevailing in the American metropolis (Suttles 1968) and is tightly managed by the central state and local government rather than left to the racially skewed forces of the real estate market. As a result, immigrant families are widely distributed across neighbourhoods, with the exception of select towns and districts monopolized by upper-class nationals, from which they are totally absent. The main lesson of the previous chapter bears repeating here: the degraded *cités* of the French urban periphery are not ghettos in the sense of an ethnically uniform sociospatial formation based on the forcible relegation of a negatively typed population to a reserved territory in which it develops institutions specific to it. Their makeup typically brings together a majority of French native families and a motley grouping of households from fifteen to fifty nationalities – this mix itself varying strongly across space and over time. It is a fact that residents of foreign origin are disproportionately represented in the Quatre mille compared to their national or regional weight (around 30 per cent compared to 11 per cent and 7 per cent respectively, with a peak at 40 per cent in the southern cluster of the estate). But this overrepresentation results mainly from their skewed class composition, *not* from the ethnoracial segmentation of the housing market. Much as in Great Britain, Belgium or Germany, what ethnic concentrations show up here and there in the French working-class *banlieues* are mainly a by-product of the notably lower distribution of postcolonial immigrant families in the class structure.

---

[27] These three factors do not provide an exhaustive explanation of the limited social efficacy and intensity of ethnoracial divisions in the French Red Belt (which one must clearly distinguish from their growing *salience*, i.e., the degree to which they jut out in the landscape of everyday perception). They are those that most clearly separate the latter from the American hyperghetto. A fuller analysis would require a historical sociology of the bases and effects of the work of *class-making* (starting with the imposition of class as a principle of social vision and division over rival bases of classification) carried out by trade unions, parties and other Left organizations which have traditionally 'melted' immigrants into French society by incorporating them into a unified, ethnically blind working class (Tripier 1990).

They are accentuated, but not primarily driven, by ethnic discrimination in housing, which is inconsistent and deflected by the predominant role of public authorities in the supply of rental units as well as attenuated by the spatial dispersal of upwardly mobile immigrant households. Conversely, the poorest and most destitute Red Belt neighbourhoods do not overlap closely with the *cités* sporting the largest proportions of foreigners (Tabard 1993; Boëldieu and Thave 2000), as the commonly expressed thesis of 'ghettoization' would imply.

This wide mixing and constant churning of populations according to ethnonational origins is decisive in accounting for the overwhelming similarities in the experiences and strategies of Red Belt youths of native French and North African background, a point made effectively by Dubet (1987: 326; see also Bourdieu 1991b: 8):

> In none of the groups did youths introduce immigration as a fundamental cleavage of relations among themselves in a given neighbourhood. Never, in the *cités* where we went [three of them in the Parisian Red Belt, a fourth in the suburbs of Lyons], did youths talk in terms of 'us,' immigrant youths, and 'them,' French youths, or conversely. Connections and friendship ties are multiethnic. This does not necessarily derive from antiracist beliefs; it springs, rather, from the basic fact that, since their childhood, the youths have had the same experiences in *cités* which are not racial ghettos. These teenagers attend the same schools, have the same leisure activities, and go through the same 'horseplay' and misdeeds. There are no bands or gangs formed along the immigrant versus French cleavage, nothing comparable to the English 'skinheads' or to Chicago's 'Spanish Cobras.'[28]

The composite morphology of the *banlieues* ongoingly deflects at ground level the racialized vision bisecting the world into two antagonistic blocs defined along phenotypical and national lines that some

[28] Recapitulating a decade of research on the topic, Dubet and Lapeyronnie (1992: 128) conclude: 'Young French people and immigrant youths experiencing the *galère* [the pattern of 'drifting' common in lower-class projects plagued by high unemployment] are all equally uprooted; they do not oppose each other in terms of culture and differences. Their common experience is that of a composite, mixed-breed (*métissé*), unstable universe in which local ties are more meaningful than national or ethnic roots.' They frequently refer to the multiethnic ties they develop in their neighbourhood through the language of familial bonding: 'When we're in the street . . . we are all brothers: it's the family spirit.' It is revealing that, unlike their American counterparts, rap bands from the French popular *banlieues* are typically pluri-ethnic or '*Black-Blanc-Beur*' as their members like to say, i.e., mixing teenagers of African, European and Maghrebine descent (Durand 2002).

political entrepreneurs and journalists claim (or would like to see) predominate in the declining urban periphery.[29] Age tends to trump ethnicity in the Red Belt *banlieues* because the latter are the site of a crisis of reproduction of the working class that is felt directly by the younger cohorts and is expressed most acutely in their relationship with the generation of their parents, whatever their ethnonational provenance. The *jeunes des cités* are both chief victims and living revelators of the breakdown of the traditional mode of transmission and collective affirmation of working-class status.

Secondly, notwithstanding the steady electoral ascent of Le Pen's National Front and the correlative diffusion of xenophobic themes in local and national political debates, ethnic differences do not constitute *legitimate* principles of claims-making in the French tradition of nationhood. The historical institutionalization of French citizenship as a territorial community defined by acceptance of the civic ideals incarnated by the Republican state – as opposed to a community of descent expressed in cultural terms, as prevailed in Germany until recently for instance (Brubaker 1990) – has, thus far, prevented ethnoracial categories from functioning as the master organizing framework of social perceptions and relations by blocking their usage as bases of collective mobilization and political claims-making in the public sphere. The timid attempt to conscript the *beurs* (French-born children of 'Arab' immigrants) into a distinct voting pressure group during the 1986 legislative campaign foundered on the shoals of a national party system and electoral regime designed to erase all 'intermediary' affiliations by fostering majority rule in large districts. Similar efforts undertaken since from within the established parties of the Left and Right have failed for the same structural reason as well as due to the weak appeal of such identification among the lower class of recent postcolonial extraction and internal resistance to the promotion of the language of ethnicity.

Thus, after quickly establishing itself as a term of protest asserting the collective dignity of the children of Maghrebine immigrants in the early 1980s (Durmelat 1998), by the last decade of the century the category *beur* itself had become contested by young *banlieues* residents, most of whom do not wish to be ethnically tagged in so far as they view such labelling as an additional obstacle in their quest

[29] This does not prevent the trajectories of youths of European and North African parentage from diverging when they enter the low-wage labour market. But the discrepancy becomes salient only later in the lifecourse: so long as youths predominate in the neighbourhood and are still in school, they share most experiences.

for full citizenship rights. As for religion, it has also failed to provide a common basis for pan-ethnic formation: with some four million believers, Islam has undergone spectacular expansion in French society; yet its expression remains restricted to the private sphere, where it functions essentially as a cultural framework for the protection or reconstruction of personal identity according to modalities broadly compatible with social integration (Kepel 1987).

The third reason is the most decisive: the offspring of immigrant families who came from the Maghreb in the 1960s and 1970s, on whom the 'moral panic' over *intégration* has fastened, are in spite of everything fast assimilating into French society. They have overwhelmingly adopted the mainstream cultural and behavioural patterns of the French and have failed to form a distinct 'community' constituted around their specific cultural heritage (Lapeyronnie 1987; Khellil 1991). Indeed, much like the leaders of their associations, which have flourished over the past two decades, they 'forcefully reject any idiom of [ethnic] specificity and assert that the problems they pose are quintessentially French and social' in nature (Dubet and Lapeyronnie 1992: 143). The populations arrived from North Africa are highly diversified in terms of origins and dispersed in their routes toward national incorporation. Their collective organization is weak and undermined by conflicts of all sorts, between nationalities, generations, religious or political orientations, etc., despite the material and administrative support given by the state with a view to structuring these populations and endowing them with recognized interlocutors. It follows that the pan-ethnic identity that pops up here and there among them remains largely defensive and oriented toward individual adaptation; and it is typically based on appropriated physical space rather than ethnic or national origin.[30]

Not only do most so-called second-generation 'Arabs' rapidly melt into the national cultural pattern; a battery of empirical indicators also reveals an overall improvement in their social position and living conditions, in spite of their much higher unemployment rate and lower income than those of native French households. And, notwithstanding the stupendous swelling of the media and political discourse on segregation, there are no statistical indicators suggesting that the

[30] 'Composed of highly assimilated youths', North African associations are 'rarely homogeneous and are not organized on an ethnic basis. They are first and foremost the expression of a given neighbourhood or *cité*' and 'do not lead to political action' (Dubet and Lapeyronnie 1992: 100, 98). This diagnosis is largely confirmed by the later study of Battegay and Boubeker (2001).

spatial separation of the populations (mis)perceived as Arab has risen since the mid-1970s. On the contrary: the growing presence of North Africans and other postcolonial immigrants in low-income estates in the 1990s[31] represents not a statutory decline of the housing market but a material improvement over a previous situation of genuine segregation into shabby 'guest worker hostels', the horrid 'transit estates' managed by the special housing authority of SONACOTRA and illegal 'shanty-towns' (*bidonvilles*) that were much more isolated and dilapidated than are today's low-income housing projects (Sayad 1975; Barrou 1992; Bernadot 1999).

Studies of employment, family, housing and schooling periodically conducted by INSEE (France's national institute for statistics) and INED (its sister centre for demographic research) show that the profile of the recently immigrated population and their descendants is continuously getting closer to that of the native population in terms of occupational distribution, household size and other key demographic characteristics such as fertility, morbidity and mortality (Tribalat 1995). Sexual partnership rates with autochthons are steadily rising, especially among females of North African origin who have higher upward mobility rates via the education system than their male counterparts. Academic inequality between ethnonational groups in France has likewise decreased since the 1970s with the generalized lengthening of secondary education, and students of foreign origin have increased their representation at all levels of the educational system. What is more, the higher they climb up the school ladder, the better their results compared to those of native French children. In fact, differences in academic achievement between them are negligible once class origins and inherited cultural capital are controlled for (Bastide 1982; Van Zanten 1997).

This is not to minimize the cruel reality of durable exclusion from and abiding discrimination on the labour market that weighs heavily on youths of (North) African origin, nor to gainsay the banalization of venomous expressions of xenophobic enmity toward them that are loudly echoed on the political stage. Nor is it to deny that ethnicity has become a more salient if contested marker in French social life at century's

---

[31] In 1989, 74 per cent of households of North African nationalities had access to public housing compared to 45 per cent a decade earlier (Barrou 1992: 128). Segregation is more pronounced across public housing estates, as foreign families tend to be assigned to the most isolated and decrepit suburban projects (which also have more multi-bedroom apartments suited for larger families) vacated by upwardly mobile French families, as opposed to the better maintained, city-centre estates.

end. It is to suggest first, that ethnic distinctions coalescing in and around the declining *banlieues* are based on ambiguous and noninstitutionalized categories that operate inconsistently across organizational domains, so that the resulting divisions do not map neatly on to each other to generate communal boundaries in the Weberian sense of affiliations determining not only 'the sense of honour and dignity' but also 'differences in the conduct of everyday life' eventually leading to 'joint (mostly political) action' (Weber [1918–20] 1978: 386–8).

It is also to stress that, unlike in the American metropolis, where ethnic hostility and violence have been fed by the *deepening* spatial and social schism between poor blacks and the rest of society (Wilson 1987; Jargowsky 1997), disquiet and unrest in the French urban periphery are fuelled by the increased *mixing* of ethnonational categories – especially in housing and schools – and by the *closing* of the economic, social and cultural distance between postcolonial immigrants and the stagnant or downwardly mobile fractions of the native working class stuck in the deteriorating *banlieues*.[32] It follows that, in sharp contrast to the black (sub)proletariat of the American metropolis, the families of Maghrebine origin in the French urban periphery are not travelling uniformly on a dark journey to the nether region of social space. Contrary to the claims of James Hollifield (1991: 141), they are *not* in the process of forming a distinct 'Muslim underclass' – whatever the meaning given to this murky expression. Far from presaging the crystallization of properly ethnic cleavages in the French city, the seemingly 'racial' animosity and simmering tension flaring up in the deindustrializing *banlieues* over the past two decades are expressive of a deepening *social* crisis brought about by persistent un(der)employment and the spatial conjugation of educational exclusion, housing blight and material deprivation in districts where native and immigrant working-class families compete over diminishing collective resources in the context of the breakdown of the perennial mechanisms that used to translate such conflicts into class demands in the political sphere at the level of firm, city and state.

---

[32] The same applies to rioters who shook up the cities of Oldham, Burnley and Bradford in England in 2001, as an echo of the disturbances of the early 1980s analysed in chapter 1: 'The riots should be read in terms of the mature claim of a section of British society for recognition as fully-fledged citizens of a multiethnic and multicultural society, rather than as claims of ethnic recognition alone' (Amin 2003: 462).

Conclusion: the mental structures of marginality

The purpose of this chapter has been to uncover some of the similarities and differences between the 'new urban poverty' in France and in the United States as it is locally structured and experienced by those whom the term (or its equivalents) has come to designate in these two countries. Rather than compare national aggregate statistics on income, standards of living, or consumption patterns, which measure little more than properties of the survey bureaucracies and survey protocols which generate them and take insufficient account of the specificity of welfare states and of the proximate sociospatial environments within which individuals and categories evolve in each society, I have proceeded by way of a contextualized examination of two master aspects of daily life in a neighbourhood of relegation: territorial indignity and its corrosive consequences upon the fabric and form of local social relations, and the principal cleavages that organize the consciousness and interactions of their inhabitants among themselves.

Dissecting the organizational and cognitive makeup of ordinary existence in the Parisian Red Belt and in Chicago's Black Belt, the manner in which the residents of these symbolically spoiled zones negotiate and experience social immobility and ostracization in 'the ghetto' – as media myth in the French case and enduring historic reality in the American case – confirms the correspondence, postulated long ago by Emile Durkheim and Marcel Mauss ([1903] 1967) and recently elaborated by Pierre Bourdieu ([1989] 1996), between social structures and mental structures, the objective divisions that pattern social space and the subjective visions that people acquire of their position and extant possibilities in it. It also underscores the distinctively racial dimension of urban poverty in the United States and points to the uncertainty in the process of collective identity formation in the postindustrial Red Belt caused by the demise of traditional agencies of working-class formation and representation in France (Masclet 2003). Whether France and America converge or continue to differ in the future with regard to the social and spatial patterning of inequality in the city,[33] there can be little doubt that

---

[33] The Durkheimian–Bourdieuan principle of the correspondence of social and symbolic structures supplies a guiding hypothesis for studying the evolution of the American hyperghetto and the French working-class *banlieues* after the 1990s: to the degree that their respective social morphologies changed, we can expect the collective representations effective in and about them to evolve accordingly, and thereby to create fresh possibilities for the emergence of new collective identities and strategies of group-making.

racial separation, where it prevails, *radicalizes* the objective and subjective reality of urban exclusion. And that state support of (or tolerance for) segregation and official recognition of ethnoracial divisions cannot but intensify the cumulation of urban dispossession and exacerbate the destructive consequences of marginality, not only for those submitted to its nefarious tropism and their reserved neighbourhoods, but also for the broader society.

7

Dangerous Places
Violence, Isolation and the State

A major limitation of the animated debate on racial division, class inequality and marginality in the American metropolis that resurged in the mid-1980s is the striking absence of any comparative perspective.[1] One searches in vain through the scholarly and policy literature for a study that would methodically contrast how the United States has handled this tricky triad with how it plays out in the cities of other advanced societies. Discussions of the condition and fate of the urban poor triggered by the 'discovery' (or, to be more accurate, the reinvention) of an 'underclass' have remained remarkably Americanocentric in terms of the categories deployed as well as the issues posed – or carefully avoided. They have proceeded, by and large, through the unconscious and uncontrolled universalization of the established US pattern of linkages among state, economy and city. And they have belaboured 'paradoxes', such as that of the inexorable rise of poverty at the heart of the metropolis after the 'War on Poverty' of the 1960s (Peterson 1991), that would seem odd, even absurd, from the standpoint of other postindustrial countries, in so

---

[1] Two other severe shortcomings are its lack of historical depth and sensitivity and its disconnection from contemporary streams of social and urban theory. Michael Katz (1993) sketches an archaeology of this debate and Jacqueline Jones (1992) draws a fine-grained historical panorama of changing forms of dispossession in America. Put together, these two books invalidate the central premises of the 1980s speculation over the 'underclass', but they were studiously ignored by the protagonists in this debate, which continued unabated until the 'welfare reform' of 1996 effectively effaced the question by thrusting the move 'from welfare to work' to the top of the policy and scholarly agenda. A rare and suggestive attempt to set the problem in theoretical and comparative perspective is Heisler (1991).

far as the said paradoxes reflect the fixations of national ideology
more than the fluctuations of urban reality.[2]

Considerable energy has been dissipated over the question of
'welfare dependency' (a term overloaded with negative moral connotations in a society that sacralizes individual autonomy) and extensive research devoted to detecting the presumed deleterious effects
of public aid receipt on family formation and wage-labour participation in the inner city, when the most elementary international comparison demonstrates that (i) the United States has yet to develop a
welfare state worthy of the name when it comes to support of the
poor; and (ii) that other postindustrial countries with considerably
broader social citizenship rights and more generous systems of protection against the risks of the work life (unemployment, retirement,
illness) sport lower rates of poverty, higher proportions of 'intact'
households among the lower class, and none of the extreme dispossession and blight that ravage the heart of America's large cities
(McFate et al. 1995). Only in the United States, where, true paradox,
it is particularly stingy, is public assistance *presumed* to cause rather
than alleviate urban ills, due to the confluence of the stigmata of
'race', place and 'dependency' that besets ghetto residents.[3] This
pronounced *lack of interest* in comparison is all the more stunning at
a time when most countries in Western Europe are caught in a moral
panic about the 'ghettoization' of postcolonial immigrants in their
urban periphery that has them scrutinizing American models and
policies in an effort to check the mounting dualisms.

Comparing urban trenches

The absence of a cross-national benchmark against which to gauge
the trajectory of America's 'inner city' after the culmination of the

---

[2] There is nothing paradoxical about the fiasco of the 1960s policy of reduction of
urban poverty as the federal government limited itself to *announcing* a 'War on
Poverty' that it never waged for two reasons: the Vietnam War diverted public expenditures from the domestic to the international front; after the ghetto riots of 1964–8,
whites frontally opposed the social policies needed to bridge racial inequalities until
they overturned them (Quadagno 1994).

[3] The real (i.e., political) aim of this apparently neutral 'research question' is, of
course, quite other: as in previous epochs of rapid social and economic restructuring
(Piven and Cloward 1971), it is to devise ways to reduce the claims of the poor, and
particularly the minority poor, on the state so as better to impose upon them the
discipline of the new wave of precarious, low-pay, wage labour.

Civil Rights revolution has not only severely restricted the terms and scope of research, and by the same token hampered the elaboration of rigorous theoretical models. It has also encouraged analysts to take for granted the highly peculiar configuration of America's 'urban trenches' (Katznelson 1981). This, in turn, has led them to gloss over one of the more glaring features of poverty in the US metropolis: namely, that it is pre-eminently a *racialized poverty*, inflicted upon blacks (and other 'minorities' occupying neighbouring locations in symbolic space) by virtue of the subordinate position they occupy in the structure of ethnic and class relations of the country, as attested by their enduring stigmatization, abiding segregation, negligible rates of mixed marriages, and truncated access to the core instruments of social reproduction and mobility.[4] Enduring poverty among urban African Americans is rooted in this historically specific mechanism of *exclusionary closure* that is the *ghetto*, a unique sociospatial means of ethnoracial control whose persistence through the manifold structural transformations that have stamped the twentieth century testifies to the historical resilience of the caste regime of the United States (as I demonstrated in the first part of this book).

This chapter aims to widen the study of the links between racial division, class inequality and the state in urban space by means of a comparison of the economic, sociopolitical and mental structures of neighbourhoods of relegation in France and the United States. In the previous chapter, I used an empirical contrast between Chicago's South Side and a declining working-class town of the Parisian industrial ring to probe the logics of spatial stigmatization and trace the mental structuring of marginality in these two sites. Here I highlight two traits that further distinguish the black American ghetto from urban districts of concentrated poverty in other advanced societies: the pandemic violence which, combined with acute material deprivation and symbolic taint, accounts for the oppressive tenor of everyday life in the historic Black Belt; and the systematic debasement of public institutions that underpins the organizational debilitation and social isolation of the residents of the hyperghetto. The first dimension addressed below, pertaining to crime and insecurity, is critical not only as a major determinant of the quality of life in poor neighbourhoods but also because it feeds the spiral of territorial

---

[4] A signal exception to this pattern of intellectual myopia is the master-book by Douglas Massey and Nancy Denton (1993), which demonstrates the pivotal role that rigid segregation plays in the dynamics of pauperization of the dark ghetto in the postindustrial era, but at the cost of conflating segregation and ghettoization.

stigmatization and thwarts local housing and economic development. The second dimension, organizational density and diversity, concerns the 'provisioning' of the material, social and cultural needs of residents (Hannerz 1980: 103–4), and directly influences their degree and sense of inclusion within the broader society. These two dimensions are closely intricated: the organizational ecology and capacity of a poor district helps determine the types and levels of objective and subjective insecurity; street violence, real or perceived, in turn affects the viability of local institutions and thence the life chances of those who rely upon them.

The *banlieue*, this 'sociologically amorphous space' spanning the periphery of the French city which has served as 'dumping ground' for the lower fractions of the working class since the 1960s (Pétonnet 1979), is a particularly apposite counterpoint for comparison. Like the African-American ghetto, it is a distinct and defamed district located at the bottom of the stratified system of places that makes up the spatial order of the metropolis. Working-class *banlieues* and dark ghetto are also, to varying degrees, 'institutionally incomplete' and heteronomous formations within which 'the pursuit of exchange values is almost totally in the hands of outsiders' (Logan and Molotch 1989: 132). Due to national differences in the social construction and appropriation of space (i.e., summarily put, divergent modes of state regulation of urban development combined with discrepant sequencing and trajectories of class and state formation reinforced by different cultural conceptions of the city), the United States and continental Europe have developed opposite and symmetrical spatial configurations. In America, the suburbs have, since their importation and adaptation from Great Britain at the beginning of the twentieth century, functioned as the near-exclusive haven of the white middle and upper classes (Fishman 1987) while the slum areas of the urban core served as 'container' for blacks and other stigmatized categories (Ward 1989). In France and in most other Continental countries on the other side of the Atlantic, by contrast, the central city has traditionally been monopolized by the elites while workers and marginal categories were pushed out to the outskirts (Préteceille 1973). Hence, although they are situated at opposite poles of the urban spatial system, the French working-class *banlieues* are indeed the structural counterpart of the 'inner city' in the United States.

Finally, like the American ghetto before them, the degraded neighbourhoods of France's popular periphery such as the historic Red Belt of Paris (Stovall 1990) have become virtually identified with social dislocation, ethnonational tension and violence over the past quarter-century. After a decade of periodic outbreaks of collective unrest, the *banlieues* came to be 'perceived as the conjunction of geographic disorder and social disorder' (Mayol 1992: 66), and, like the dark ghetto across the Atlantic, they have been the focal point of a tumultuous debate on the intersection of joblessness, segregation and neighbourhood deterioration.[5] In short, the French Red Belt and the remnants of America's historic Black Belt have, each in its own national order, become emblematic incarnations of 'urban danger' at century's close, in the sense of social decay and physical insecurity as well as in the more politically charged sense that they threaten to unravel the fabric of urban society *in toto*.

The portrait of Chicago's ghetto that follows draws on surveys, face-to-face interviews, and field observations conducted under the aegis of the Urban Family Life Project at the University of Chicago in 1987–90, and in-depth data on the neighbourhood of Woodlawn produced in the course of a three-year ethnography of a boxing gym and its relation to the culture and economy of the street. For the French case, I rely on recent monographs on the decline of Red Belt neighbourhoods as well as on a range of primary and secondary data on the city of La Courneuve, an older industrial centre of the northern inner suburbs of Paris where I conducted field observation in the autumn of 1990 and the spring of 1991. This proud blue-collar municipality of 32,000 ruled by the Communist Party since World War II has suffered direly from the shift to a post-Fordist production regime centred on services and from the plant shutdowns resulting from industrial reconversion. Between 1975 and 1990, its population decreased by one-fifth, the percentage of youths (under age 20) and foreigners increased to reach one-third and one-fifth respectively; in 1990 the official unemployment rate exceeded 17 per cent for the city – one of the highest in the country. Within La Courneuve, I focus on the low-income estate (*cité*) of the Quatre mille, a massive public housing project which cumulates the social and urban ills typifying the 'crisis' of the French working-class *banlieues*.

Recall that, while the Black Belt of Chicago and the Red Belt of Paris occupy homological *positions* in their respective metropolitan order,[6] they differ markedly in terms of the morphological makeup

---

[5] Thus the 1980s in France were simultaneously dubbed the 'decade of new poverty' (LePuill and LePuill 1990) and the 'decade of the *banlieues*' (Jazouli 1992).

[6] It is this homology that provides the theoretical rationale for the comparison, in spite of the functional and compositional differences highlighted in the preceding two chapters. On the theoretical logic of case selection in comparative research, see the useful remarks of Archer (1978).

and social *condition* of their respective populations (see chapters 5 and 6 *supra* and Wacquant 1995a for a more detailed demonstration). First, owing to the extensive social protection afforded by the French welfare state and firmer political regulation of the labour and housing markets,[7] levels of poverty, joblessness and material hardship in the worst Red Belt *banlieues* stand well below the average level of those observed in the black American ghetto. Despite the relentless rise of unemployment, two-thirds of all adults in La Courneuve were gainfully employed in the early 1990s, while 70 per cent of their counterparts on Chicago's South Side had been pushed out of the wage-labour sphere. A large majority of households on the South Side (between two-thirds and three-quarters) had to resort to welfare as their chief means of survival, whereas only a minority of families in La Courneuve received public aid (as distinct from universal social benefits). Second, the rigid racial segmentation that consigns blacks to separate and cloistered areas of the city in the United States is unknown in France (and in other European countries; cf. Musterd et al. 1998), where such limited residential concentrations of immigrants as exist are mainly the by-product of class differences in access to housing. The result is that the American hyperghetto has a monochromic racial makeup as well as an increasingly uniform class recruitment, while the population of Red Belt *banlieues* is extremely diverse in both social and ethnoracial composition. Thus, although the Quatre mille is widely seen from the outside as an 'Arab ghetto', its residents comprise more than twenty-five nationalities and a majority of (employed) native 'whites'. We shall now see that these morphological differences extend to the plane of rates and forms of street violence as well as to the organizational ecology of the two territories.

Delinquency, street violence and the shrinking of public space

The declining French working-class *banlieues* and the black American ghetto have in common that they are commonly regarded in their society as dangerous places where vice and criminality are out of control, where the rule of law is routinely flouted, and which one is

---

[7] These protections include universal health care for wage-earners, family allowances given to all households with children, and generous housing assistance, job (re)training and public jobs for youths as well as close administrative oversight of the use of part-time employment, temporary labour and mass layoffs. They are complemented by a means-tested national guaranteed minimum income plan (RMI) which mandates job search assistance.

well advised to shun. Yet, while their public images are similar, these two urban constellations diverge sharply in the intensity, frequency, degree of social embeddedness, and nature of the illegal or criminal activities they harbour, as well as in the impact that these forms of street violence have on the configuration and flow of daily routines. To anticipate: in La Courneuve's infamous *cité*, the main problem is a feeling of insecurity rooted in the ecology and demography of the neighbourhood and fuelled by petty youth delinquency; on Chicago's South Side, acute physical danger floods everyday life and creates an oppressive climate of terror that has caused the near-complete disappearance of public space.

Youth delinquency and the feeling of insecurity in Red Belt cités

Following a string of highly publicized incidents, like many of its cousins in the formerly industrial periphery of Paris, Marseilles and Toulouse, the *cité* of the Quatre mille in La Courneuve has earned the reputation of being a 'no-go area' despoiled by pandemic crime, where bands of lawless youths and hardened hoodlums impose their rule. Outsiders readily identify the drab estate as an urban purgatory into which one enters at great risk. Rumour has it that the police dare not come into it. Some older tenants of the projects themselves insist that theirs is a tough and risky environment (*'Ça craint'*). This familiar media image, however, bears but a tenuous relation to the quotidian reality of the estate.[8]

It is true that young men from the project commonly engage in vandalism and street fights; that scuffles are frequent and relations with the authorities tense; and that resort to physical violence is notably more frequent in social intercourse internal to the *cité* than in the sociability typical of the middle classes.[9] Nonetheless, it is quite

[8] See Bachmann and Basier (1989) for a fuller analysis of the journalistic construction of the image of the *cité* of the Quatre mille and Dulong and Paperman (1992) for an examination of the production and effects of the 'discourses of insecurity' swirling around the degraded working-class *banlieues*.

[9] Mauger and Fossé-Poliak (1983) have shown that patterns of collective conduct based on an open assertion of 'rough' masculinity (displayed through public drinking, the ostentatious use of foul language, and street fighting) are expressive of the values and public sociability of the working class, but that these behaviours are often misinterpreted as dangerous and delinquent by outside (middle-class) observers. The same sociocultural patterns among black Americans have often been presented as 'ghetto-specific' (e.g., Hannerz 1969 and Wilson 1987), even though they prevail also among white and Latino working-class adolescents in England and in the United States (Willis 1981; Foley 1990; MacLeod 1995) as well as figuring two decades earlier in the registry of traits composing Oscar Lewis's (1961) 'culture of poverty'.

safe to walk about in the Quatre mille, including after nightfall, where one can go about freely in and around buildings as they attract and harbour much public life. In the regional park immediately adjacent to the estate (a three-mile by one-mile expanse of grass, shrubbery and flower beds), one can spot families out for picnics in springtime, joggers and cyclists in action, teenagers playing a game of pick-up soccer on a makeshift field, children flying kites, and couples walking their dogs in the early evening.[10] People who work in the vicinity routinely cross the project grounds to reach the adjacent regional transit station, which is packed with commuters going to and from Paris at rush hours. Those holding jobs inside the Quatre mille express exasperation and disbelief at the idea that their place of employment would put them in any kind of jeopardy. This is because the estate is in constant exchange with the surrounding urban land-scape, as the great majority of its tenants work, shop and entertain themselves outside its perimeter. The permanent presence of resi-dents and especially the young in the squares, play areas and streets that connect the slabs to one another helps to reassure the visitor.

Thefts from parked cars, burglaries and car and motorcycle theft, minor rackets and petty drug dealing are the most common detect-able offences in La Courneuve. In a typical year, there is not a single homicide in the entire city. For instance, in 1983 and 1984, the most serious incidents were eighteen robberies, none of which resulted in serious injury or death. The city has a total police force of only 150, because the rates for various criminal infractions are barely above the national average. For most categories of offences, they compare favourably with those of more upscale cities: for instance, the figure of 10.8 burglaries per 1,000 inhabitants lags well behind that for Paris (25.6). Residents queried on the topic in October 1991 men-tioned no major incident of ethnic or racist violence since the death of little Toufik Ouanès in July 1983, still in everyone's memories – the very fact that this tragic incident rose to the rank of a national event and still stands out in the collective memory is indicative of its anomalous character.[11] The practice of *dépouille* (the stealing of

[10] The data gathered by Amart (1987) on the users of this park turn up no major difference between the Quatre mille and other public parks in neighbouring municipalities.

[11] On the evening of 14 July (Bastille Day), an insomniac tenant infuriated by the racket being made by children outside picked up his hunting rifle and fired towards a group of youths, unintentionally killing 9-year-old Toufik, the son of a North African immigrant. The incident made headlines in the national media and prompted Presi-dent Mitterrand to visit the Quatre mille within days to dramatize public condemna-tion of the slaying and announce a speeding up of state policies of urban renewal.

jackets, shoes and 'Walkmen' under threat of force) has become more common over the past decade, but it occurs mainly between local adolescents and very seldom involves the use of arms. The same is true of collective clashes between *cité* youths, which are highly ritualized and regulated by the complex web of mutual acquaintanceship and exchange between those involved.[12]

Tension between the police and young men from the *cité* is immediately perceptible when they find themselves in physical co-presence, and fights routinely break out during public balls and other outdoor events. But such incidents occur in working-class districts throughout the country at popular celebrations such as the 14th of July or the Saint John Feast. 'They don't escalate into mayhem because the neighbourhood associations are well represented here, they handle that pretty well,' avers a city official who works inside the Quatre mille. The episodic eruptions of violence that attract disproportionate attention from the national media are typically well circumscribed and precisely targeted: they single out certain police and the private security guards of local stores by way of retaliation for what estate youths consider unfair, brutal or disrespectful treatment on the latter's part.

Yet there reigns, among residents of this large declining estate, as in many other *cités* of the French urban periphery, a dull and deeply entrenched *feeling* of insecurity and distrust (Avery 1987: 110; Dulong and Paperman 1992: 58) generated mainly by increasing petty delinquency and by the depressed and depersonalizing setting of this closed milieu in which heterogeneous and vulnerable populations come into daily contact.[13] This sentiment drives many residents of La Courneuve to equip their homes, cars and shops with reinforced doors and other alarm systems; some elderly residents even carry gas canisters for self-defence (though they appear to be a minority). From the standpoint of the authorities, petty drug dealing – and not violence – is viewed as the number one item on the agenda of public

---

[12] Lepoutre (1997: 195–228) underlines the social and cultural embeddedness of street fights in the Quatre Mille by showing that they follow a set of precise rules stipulating time, place and motive and the double imperative of publicity (among peers) and clandestinity (*vis-à-vis* the authorities).

[13] This is a distinctive characteristic of isolated public housing estates in France: 'Petty delinquency is a component of the feeling of insecurity: fear of being broken into or of having one's car stolen, fear of being mugged on the street, in parking lots, in the metro. The lumping of youths and criminals as well as immigrants and criminals is widespread' (Calogirou 1989: 39). This point is also stressed by Pinçon (1982), Bachmann and Basier (1989) and Dubet and Lapeyronnie (1992).

safety in the Quatre mille. The basement 'cellars' of most buildings have been condemned to prevent youths from hiding in them to consume illegal substances, and it is not hard to spot dealers when they work the vicinity of the local supermarket. But the drug trade in La Courneuve pales in intensity, volume and sophistication when compared to its counterpart in Chicago. Street-level distribution is intermittent and involves primarily opiates and marijuana rather than 'hard' drugs such as heroin or derivatives of cocaine (though the latter are in circulation). This is because youths from the popular *banlieues* of Paris make a sharp differentiation between 'grass', which they view as a non-addictive kind of recreational intoxicant similar to alcohol, and 'powder', considered highly addictive, destructive and a symbol of pathology. Athough it has risen noticeably in recent years with the increase in persistent unemployment among neigh- bourhood residents, drug trafficking remains a marginal activity which attracts mainly jobless school dropouts who are often them- selves substance (ab)users and whose main motivation is to generate the income needed to support their own consumption or the petty cash to cover minor daily expenses (cigarettes, gas for the car, etc.).

Its recent expansion notwithstanding, the narcotics trade in La Courneuve is nowhere close to evolving into the highly differentiated, self-sustaining economy generating cash flows in the tens of millions of dollars and allowing for durable careers outside the regular labour market that grew in the black American ghetto during the 1980s. Due to its limited volume, it has not spawned a specific 'culture' or distinct web of loose-knit but extensive networks of users and traders linked to each other (Williams 1992), and even less so organized enterprises whose structure, staff and sales are akin to those of main- line commercial firms.[14] In the Quatre mille, drugs are synonymous with social withdrawal, not with the individual pursuit of sensuous gratification and economic opportunity. The kind of 'open-air' drug supermarket scene described by Bourgois ([1992] 1998) in East Harlem is unthinkable in the French context, as is the conspicuous trade of cocaine, amphetamines, Angel Dust and Karachi on street corners that I was able to observe in many sections of Chicago's South Side. Petty theft, drug use, the resale of stolen goods, vandal- ism and alcoholism are the most common forms of visible delin-

---

[14] Adler (1995) tracks how the Chambers brothers built a 'crack empire' in the ghetto of Detroit that generated annual sales estimated by the authorities (during their trial for homicide and racketeering in 1991) at 55 million dollars at its peak, which made it the city's leading business.

quency in the degraded *cités* of the Red Belt. Much of this delinquency is opportunistic and displays a strong ludic or expressive dimension: its main purpose is to generate not so much money as 'action', or to vent the rage felt at being encaged in a social universe perceived as devoid of opening or hope of palpable improvement.

The favourite delinquent activities of teenagers include riding the train to Paris without paying, sneaking into cinemas for free, stealing from stores (Calogirou 1989: 120) or from schools and other public buildings, street larceny (motorcycles are a favourite target), or acts of minor vandalism such as 'tagging' or destroying post boxes and other building equipment. In more extreme cases, cars are set on fire in parking lots in a sort of inverted *potlatch* whereby local youths incinerate the instrument of the geographic and social mobility which is denied to them. Such delinquency has more to do with 'getting a good laugh', challenging authorities, and expressing one's anger than with entering into a criminal career (Dubet and Lapeyronnie 1992: 135–6). Remarkably, residents of the Quatre mille make a distinction between pilfering committed inside the estate and theft (*fauche* or *resquille*) committed outside its perimeter. Thieves who prey on 'their own', that is, on neighbours and occupants of the buildings close by, are openly reprimanded or excluded from networks of reciprocity.[15] Similarly, in the projects studied by Dubet (1987), residents did not tolerate stealing inside the *cité*. This is in sharp contrast with criminal practices in the black hyperghetto, where, as we saw in chapters 2 and 4, internal predation is endemic and takes on distinctively more virulent and destructive forms that informal mechanisms of social control are powerless to rein in.

Street violence and the shrivelling of public space on Chicago's South Side

The physical insecurity that plagues the historic Black Belt in the American metropolis is incomparable with that of the *cités* of the

---

[15] In Blanchard, a 'transitional housing' *cité* in Rouen studied by Laé and Murard (1985: 15–16), premature death (from disease and assorted ill health) is banal and 'takes the appearance of a fate. . . . The perspective of early passing jumbles all phases of life. . . . The paucity of jobs, experienced as cruel, coincides with this vision of a life cycle deployed over twenty years at most.' But, there again, violent death is extremely rare, and the most serious crimes involve robbery, not homicide. Larceny and car theft are the prototypal delinquent acts at Blanchard, and both are condoned so long as they are committed outside the estate: such petty crime brings into the *cité* additional resources which immediately enter local networks of exchange.

French urban periphery, the British inner cities or the districts of relegation of other cities in continental Europe. If the impact of delinquency on daily life in La Courneuve is felt mainly at the level of representations and collective sentiments, violence in its most brutal forms – including assault and battery, shootings, rape and homicide – is so intense and prevalent inside the hyperghetto that it has forced a complete reorganization of the fabric of daily life.[16]

Epidemiological surveys conducted by the Center for Disease Control in Atlanta reveal that, at the beginning of the 1990s homicide had become the leading cause of mortality among younger ghetto residents. Thus an overwhelming majority of the 849 homicides recorded in the city of Chicago in 1990 (compared to 1,355 *for the whole of France* that year) occurred inside the ghetto: according to the annual crime report compiled by the Federal Bureau of Investigation, 'the typical 1990 murder victim was a black male, under 30, killed by gunfire in the poorest neighbourhoods' of a big city (*Chicago Tribune*, 1991). In the Wentworth police district which comprises the historic Black Belt of the South Side, ninety-six homicides were reported that year for a staggering rate approaching 100 per 100,000 residents, twenty times the rate for the city's white bourgeois neighbourhood of Lincoln Park or Lake View. A tactical officer in the district laments: 'We have murders on a daily basis that never make the news. No one really knows or cares.'[17] Police also complain that young criminals routinely employ high-powered weapons such as submachine and automatic guns: 'Kids used to have bats and knives. Now they're equipped with better guns than we have' (ibid. 14).

Dubrow and Garbarino (1989: 5) compare the vicinity of public housing projects on Chicago's South Side to 'a war zone complete with noncombatants fleeing the front lines'. The most serious dangers cited by mothers living there are shootings, gangs and darkness in descending order, whereas mothers living in a demographically com-

[16] For a fuller portrait of criminal violence and analyses of its impact on daily life in the ghetto at century's close, see Sullivan (1989), Anderson (1990), Bourgois (1995), Adler (1995), Pinderhughes (1997) and McCord (1997), as well as chapter 4 *supra*.

[17] According to several informants, an unknown but not negligible number of homicides committed in the ghetto are not reported, even to the police, because the bodies do not turn up there or because residents fail to inform authorities of these deaths for fear of reprisal or judicial complications. A young man from South Shore (near Woodlawn) whom I interviewed on the topic summed up his reaction to witnessing shootings thus: 'I just turn my head and don't look.'

parable neighbourhood in the near suburbs mention the fear of kid-
napping, traffic accidents and drugs. In Woodlawn, as in most other
districts of the city's historic Black Belt, residents commonly barri-
cade their homes and apartments behind wrought-iron bars and
gates; they tailor their daily round so as to minimize forays outside
and to avoid public places and facilities; and they hurry inside at
nightfall: 'I never go to Washington Park at night or without my gun.
Why? If one of them punks jump on me, they gonna get some of my
piece,' intones an elderly informant. During the summer of 1991,
the Mayor of Chicago, called upon by indignant South Side residents
to account for the fact that one cannot walk safely across public parks
even in broad daylight, inadvertently conceded that gangs and drug
dealers, not local government, controlled this section of the city
when, out of exasperation, he compared it with Bogota – this was at
the time when the Medellín cartel was terrorizing the Columbian
capital with fire-bombings and spectacular daylight assassinations. In
many areas of the South Side, public phones have been disconnected
to prevent their use by drug dealers, and stations of the elevated train
line are closed to entry in a last-ditch attempt to limit crime on the
public transport system.

Owing to the widespread circulation of handguns and narcotics,
the street itself has mutated into a grotesque theatre of aggressive
masculinity on whose stage violent confrontation serves as the currency of honour and where the slightest pretext – an involuntary
bump, a side glance, a cap turned the wrong side or the wrong-colour
jacket – can tip a banal impersonal encounter into a lethal pageant
of brutality. 'Everybody in d'ghetto frustrated,' explains a 28-year-
old former gang member from Woodlawn, 'so when you bump into
a guy, (in an exaggerated, angry snarl) "Nigga, I'mma kill ya!" *I'm
serious*, tha's frustration.' And he continues:

> You gotta be strong an' learn how to survive. When you out there on
> d'street, some crazy guy might wanna jump on you and bust your head
> for no reason. You gotta know how t'protect yourself, how to survive.
> I always watch my back and I would kill to protect myself and my right
> to live. You gotta be a man, tha's the only way. Shiiit! sometime, I
> think *I was better off in jail*: it's worse out there now.[18]

[18] Kotlowitz (1991: 236) describes how a mother of four living in a West Side
housing project 'couldn't stop thinking in [her son] Terrence [who had just been
sentenced to eight years in prison]. She tried to rationalize his imprisonment. It would
be good for him to get off the streets, to get away from the drugs and the shootings.
If he were out there, he might just get in more serious trouble.'

Violent death is so much part of everyday life that the mere fact of reaching adulthood is considered an accomplishment worthy of public acknowledgement. When young men from the hyperghetto are asked what has become of their childhood friends, the most frequent answers they give revolve around the macabre triptych: in jail, involved in drugs (as dealer or addict), dead and buried (most often as a result of a shooting). A janitor at a Woodlawn McDonald's puts it this way: 'I seen people shot. I seen people killed. I seen a person *shot, killed* that was standin' right next to me an' I felt that it coulda been me an' hum, the best thing that I need to do was change my acquaintances.'

In the neighbourhood of Kenwood, about two miles north on the shore of Lake Michigan, homicides were so frequent in the mid-1980s that teenagers interviewed by Duncan (1987) started 'a serious discussion as to whether it was possible to live past thirty'. Of a group of friends raised together at the heart of the historic Black Belt, Monroe and Goldman (1988: 269) write: 'They were all successes in their way, *victors by the mere fact of being alive* with some change in their pockets and a smile for a new day' (emphasis added). The harshness of living conditions, the banality of sudden death, and the astronomical rates of incarceration – nearly half the city's black men aged 18–35 are under criminal justice supervision – explains why prison is perceived as an annexe to the ghetto and penal confinement as a variant on everyday life in the Black Belt.[19]

Anthropologist Philippe Bourgois, who conducted five years of fieldwork on the crack trade in New York's East Harlem, suggests that the streets of the hyperghetto have become the crucible of a veritable *culture of terror* that grows in a functional relationship with the illegal street-level drug trafficking that dominates the booming underground economy of the urban core. In this commerce, regular displays of violence are 'essential for maintaining credibility and for preventing rip-offs by colleagues, customers and intruders'. Reinterpreted in the logic of the criminal economy, such violence is a 'judicious case of public relations, advertising, rapport building, and long-term investment in one's "human capital develop-

[19] 'Doing time didn't scare Honk; it wasn't much worse than living in the projects, and in the joint, unlike the street, they fed you free. . . . The ghetto and the Graybar Hotel [i.e., the prison], his new address, were otherwise pretty much the same' (Monroe and Goldman 1988: 123, 154). See also Kotlowitz (1991: 112, 236) and Adler (1995: *passim*).

ment" '. The need to cultivate this culture of terror – to generate income, intimidate rivals, or merely to preserve some degree of individual autonomy and physical integrity – extends well beyond those who partake directly in the drug trade, with the result that it 'poisons interpersonal relationships throughout much of the community by legitimizing violence and mandating distrust' (Bourgois 1989: 631–2, 635).

In the French working-class *cité*, delinquency is a source of nagging annoyance rather than ubiquitous danger. Violence in public space is sharply limited and remains embedded in the fabric of local networks of exchange and status: it is a 'form of regulation applied to intensive social practices, a moment of sociability in which physical force is asserted . . . as the foundation of repute' (Laé et Murard 1988: 20). In the American hyperghetto, criminality is more economic than ludic; violence is pandemic because of the dominance of the informal economy over the wage-labour sector and the breakdown of both public and private institutions. And violent crime is largely divorced from local social relations, save those that pertain to the microcosm of the gang as a quasi-institutionalized social predator or informal entrepreneur (Sánchez-Jankowski 1991; Venkatesh 1997). These sharply divergent types and levels of violence, in turn, point to the different organizational frameworks of the French working-class *banlieues* and the black American ghetto, as well as to the different types and levels of social control that these two urban constellations anchor.

Institutional isolation versus organizational desertification

A major characteristic of the defamed enclaves of persistent poverty to which the urban outcasts of century's close are relegated is the extent to which they harbour the institutions intended to fulfil the basic needs of their residents and to incorporate them into the surrounding society. Here again, at the level of lived experience, Red Belt and Black Belt turn out to be rather germane: both are perceived as organizationally deficient, and the populations who dwell in each deplore the dearth of institutions needed to contribute to the functioning and well-being of the neighbourhood. But objective comparison yields another striking transatlantic contrast: the working-class *cités* of the French periphery are home to a plethora of grass-roots organizations and public services due in good measure to renewed state intervention,[20] whereas the black American ghetto has undergone an accelerating process of organizational desertification which I argued in chapter 2 was directly induced by the abdication of the state. To be more precise, the large low-income estates of La Courneuve and similar Red Belt cities suffer from an *overpenetration* of public-sector agencies which tend to atomize and isolate their users, whereas the South Side has weathered the sudden *withdrawal and near-collapse* of public institutions.

Organizational density and institutional isolation in the Quatre mille

In the eyes of its residents (as well as in the perception of municipal managers), the Quatre mille is a 'void' where basic amenities and public services are grievously lacking. Yet dominant institutions are far from absent from the *cité*. Of the ten public kindergardens and thirteen primary schools that the city counts, twelve are located right on the project grounds, and two of La Courneuve's six high schools sit not far from it. Medical and social services are also well represented within the housing complex; major facilities such as the public health centre, the local office for welfare services, and six nurseries financed by the regional district of Seine-Saint-Denis are right at the tenants' doors. Additionally, eight major administrative offices are located inside the estate, including the regional 'Social Security' administration (covering health, welfare and family assistance), a state taxation outlet, a Centre for Information on Women's Rights, and the headquarters of the local HLM (low-income housing) authority.

The list of cultural facilities located in the Quatre mille is no less impressive.[21] It comprises the Houdremont Cultural Centre (inaugurated in 1977), which houses the National Conservatory of the Region as well as music and popular dance workshops; the Centre for the Dramatic Arts and its acting school, with an 800-seat auditorium; a House for Youth (*Maison des jeunes*) and a public library; a youth club offering sporting, crafts, cultural and academic pro-

---

[20] Also, voluntary organizations have grown throughout French society more generally in the 1980s (Mendras and Cooke [1989] 1991), and immigrants' associations in particular have proliferated after legal restrictions on their creation and activities were lifted by the Socialist government in 1981.

[21] This partial census is based on administrative documents supplied by the city as well as on field observations conducted in October–November 1990 and May–June 1991. A fuller list of the organizations active in the Quatre mille as of the mid-1980s is in Avery (1987: 52–6).

grammes; a government-sponsored Computer Training Centre (with more than 120 members and 30 personal computers as of 1991) and a city-run crime prevention association. Several 'leisure centres' keep some 2,500 pupils busy on Wednesdays when school is out, as well as in the evenings and during school holidays. Finally, three religious facilities – a Catholic church, a Protestant church and a synagogue – are located inside the project, where a small Jehovah's Witness group is also busy looking for recruits.[22] As Avery (1987: 31) notes, 'social structures of communication are plentiful.' Aside from the numerous associations and clubs, there are posters on most walls as well as graffiti, and inscriptions scribbled in *verlan* (the slang of *banlieues* youths) cover many buildings.

Yet the sentiment of institutional abandonment and lack prevalent among residents of the Quatre mille should not be dismissed as misperception. It is founded, first, on the personal experience and collective memory of an earlier state of the *cité*, corresponding to the full bloom of the Red Belt, when the Communist Party and its antennae, work-based organizations and civic associations, wove a tight net of shared cultural categories, overlapping relations and rolling activities that created an abiding sense of collectivity and dignity (Bacqué and Fol 1997).[23] With the steep decline of factory-based employment and sapping of the Communist apparatus, these political, trade and neighbourhood-based institutions have wilted and been gradually superseded by the bureaucracies of the social state and local third-sector outfits whose capacity to encompass and organize social life is comparatively reduced.

Second, the estate suffers greatly from a paucity of sporting and recreational facilities relative to the large teenage population – remember that nearly half of *cité* dwellers are under 20 years old – and to the 30-per-cent-plus unemployment rate, which excludes many households from access to commercial forms of entertainment. Local teenagers have no set place to congregate and hang out together. The sole cinema of the project closed down in 1973 because it was losing

[22] In 1987, a makeshift mosque, which had opened in 1982, was attended by thirty believers a day on average (other informal, private places of congregation for Muslims have developed since). The Catholic church had 50 regulars at mass and around 160 children in religious school. As for the synagogue, it welcomed an average of 60 worshippers daily, out of 1,200 Jews estimated to reside in the Quatre mille. The Jehovah's Witnesses numbered around 120 (Avery 1987: 53).
[23] Topalov (2003) warns against exaggerating the unity and homogeneity of the 'traditional working-class neighborhood' in his critical excavation of the overlapping emergence of this category in American, British and French sociology.

too much money and being constantly subjected to minor degradation. Numerous stores, including the estate's only fast-food outlet and the Yuro theatre, went out of business in the early 1980s, due to nagging petty crime and vandalism which raised insurance costs. The commercial decline of the Quatre mille is also explained by neighbourhood depopulation, which reduced its aggregate consumption capacity, and the habit developed by the remaining tenants of going shopping in larger, better stocked supermarkets located in the nearby towns. Only a couple of bars remain inside the Quatre mille, and they make sure to close early at night to avoid trouble. The commercial strip of the main tower, which services the southern cluster of the *cité*, featured twenty-seven shops in 1986, but only seventeen of them were still in operation five years later. Apart from the bakery, the newspaper and tobacco shop and the pharmacy, sales among local businesses are stagnant or diminishing. The atmosphere of the Viniprix, the last food mart in operation in the Quatre mille, is stamped by a feeling of monotonous anxiety characteristic of the *cité*, and its managers are downright depressed about the commercial prospects of the neighbourhood.

Notwithstanding the high density of formal organizations in the Quatre mille, local and state officials worry openly about the inefficiency and indifference of public institutions in large housing estates. This perceived shortcoming of public services is due in part to the stigma that weighs upon those assigned to work in a Red Belt city and its loathed *cités*. A high-ranking state manager from the local Préfecture confessed straight out in an interview: 'There's no glory in being appointed to Seine-Saint-Denis: for a civil servant, to be sent there is like *punishment*, it's like you're being cast aside.' Moreover, the organizations that operate in these estates are better adapted to the middle-class aspirations and values of those who administer them than to the needs of the (sub)proletarian publics they are supposed to serve. And, on many fronts, they come woefully short of meeting pent-up demand because of the high concentration of socially and economically vulnerable families in search of multiple forms of assistance (Simon 1992).[24] This disjunction finds an expression in the perennial congestion of public services, which causes residents of the Quatre mille to waste considerable time waiting in lines and manoeuvring the intricacies of the local street-level bureaucracies.

---

[24] Likewise, the distribution of public infrastructure and amenities in greater Paris closely mirrors the pronounced pattern of class segregation in this region (Pinçon-Charlot et al. 1986).

This, in turn, makes the project over into what Avery (1987: 176) describes as

> a zone of impossibility where everything becomes strangely burden-some and complicated, even in state agencies or commercial services that ordinarily have nothing to do with social problems: a post office, a bank, a supermarket where people stand in line sombrely, where everything seems to operate as if in slow motion, where employees and customers alike display a vaguely martyrized expression. What is at first merely a specific problem turns into a generalized atmosphere.

The lack of efficiency and coordination between the myriad public and semi-public organizations implanted in and about the Quatre mille is compounded by the notion that many of their long-term users eventually develop that one is 'owed' assistance and services, a notion that can inspire passivity and apathy among the most marginalized.[25] Ultimately, the structural inability of these programmes of distribution of public goods, and especially of the local schools, to offset the breakdown of the traditional mode of social reproduction and political representation of the working class and to deliver what matters most to the residents of the *cité* – a secure job and the stability of life and extended temporal horizon that come with it – breeds discontent and turns these programmes into additional mechanisms of marginalization in the eyes of the locals (Balazs and Sayad 1991). *Dependency upon and dissatisfaction with state institutions get locked into a vicious cycle* wherein each reinforces the other. The prevalence of public-sector organizations, and especially of welfare agencies, also accentuates the negative image of the estate, fuelling the spiral of stigmatization and sociofugal strategies that sap social cohesion and aggravate internal dissension – so much so that several large French cities, such as Montpellier in the south, refused to participate in the state-run Neighbourhood Social Development plan just to

[25] 'The long duration and permanence of public aid leads ["target populations"] to consider them as an endless flow, as something that is owed to them' (Laé and Murard 1985: 61). See also Jazouli (1992: 121–2) on similar effects of job assistance for youths and Paugam (1991: 107–16) on the moral career of long-term recipients of public aid. This process of 'settlement' is thwarted in the black American ghetto, where no welfare recipient is secure in her status due to the Malthusian organization of the public aid bureaucracy and the routine implementation of punitive procedures expressly designed to deny or reduce claimants' access to public resources (e.g., Kotlowitz 1991: 80, 103). Not to mention that welfare benefits are so meagre in the United States as to be woefully inadequate even for mere subsistence (Edin 1991).

avoid having their worst districts publicly labelled 'sensitive neighbourhoods'.[26]

Paradoxically, then, the overrepresentation of public agencies and facilities in the Red Belt *cité* relative to other formal organizations, and their insufficient carrying capacity relative to local needs, contribute to further defaming the neighbourhood and intensify the sentiment of discontent and isolation prevalent among its residents. Yet, even as they complain about the ubiquitous interference of the state in their life, *banlieue* dwellers constantly demand more government action in the form of crime control (including tougher repression of delinquents) and expanded social programmes and public aid (Dubet 1987: 249, 260–6). The French state thus finds itself in a catch-22 situation where the more it intervenes to stem public disorders in the declining periphery on the social front, the more glaring its inability to remedy the underlying economic marginalization of its residents and the more its managers are called upon to provide social compensation, which can only feed the cycle of claims-making and recrimination.

Public-sector dereliction and the organizational desertification of the ghetto

Since the 1970s, the ghettos of Chicago and other major cities across the United States have been sapped by the sharp rise in joblessness and poverty associated with the postindustrial restructuring of central-city economies (Wilson 1987). In marked contrast with France's poor *banlieues*, they have also absorbed the frontal shock of the wide retrenchment of the social sector of the state. Deep cuts in federal funds for urban and community development, the continual reduction of welfare payments, the constant shrinkage of unemployment insurance and medical coverage, regressive tax reforms, and state and city policies of 'planned shrinkage' (detailed in chapter 2) have combined to unravel the web of programmes that had sustained inner-city residents since the days of Lyndon Johnson's 'Great Society'. The rollback of the state resulted in a spectacular deterioration of the remaining public facilities and in the accelerating decomposition

---

[26] For two evaluations of the 'perverse effects' of the main planks of the 'city policy' rolled out by the Socialist government at the close of the 1980s, see Jazouli (1992: 115–35) and Bonetti et al. (1991). For a suggestive analysis of the 'institutional bad faith' framing the bureaucratic intervention of the French state in declining estates, read Bourdieu et al. ([1993] 1999: 205–6).

of the organizational fabric of the ghetto, already debilitated by its loss of an economic function. What is more, the city's own development efforts were harnessed to supporting private investment, expanding and enriching corporate services downtown, and attracting (or retaining) white upper-class households in the centre and north side of town, at the cost of abandoning the ghettos of the West Side and South Side to continuing decay.[27]

Due to grievous shortages in the budgets and staff allocated to the ghetto, public authority can offer neither minimal physical security nor effective legal protection there; and it cannot procure the elementary municipal services that residents of neighbourhoods outside the Black Belt take for granted. On Chicago's South Side, the police cannot fulfil their basic mission of law enforcement for want of the means to heed all requests for intervention. Patrol officers in the Wentworth district answer emergency calls without interruption from the moment they begin their workday to the end of their shift. Yet the district routinely runs out of cars and must 'simulcast' what are called 'in-progress calls' on the radio frequency of other districts in the hope that a detective team from an adjacent area will be available to respond.[28] The justice system is similarly engorged and overwhelmed by the staggering growth of criminal cases generated by the aggressive deployment of the police to stem the social disorders generated by the economic involution of the hyperghetto. Prosecutions brought before the Cook County court jumped from 13,000 in 1982 to 21,000 in 1990, forcing the county to divert the overflow of cases to four suburban courts. With more than 12,000 inmates, the city's jail system was so overcrowded that, in 1988 alone, more than 25,000 arrestees had to be released on their own recognizance and let walk after charges were dropped or reduced for lack of room to detain them. No wonder so many ghetto residents have lost all trust in the state's capacity to enforce the law and choose instead to take justice into their own hands (Kotlowitz 1991: 47, 225, 233, and Anderson 1990).

[27] 'Commercial districts, housing, and infrastructure [located in poor neighbourhoods] away from the center of Chicago have suffered from long-standing neglect, whose magnitude serves to justify continued inattention' (Squires et al. 1987: 168).

[28] Kenneth Clark's (1965: 86) observation forty years ago about Harlem remains apposite today: 'The unstated and sometimes stated acceptance of crime and violence as normal for a ghetto community is associated with a lowering of police vigilance and efficiency when the victims are also lower-status people. This is another example of the denial of a governmental service – the right of adequate protection – which is endured by the powerless ghetto.'

The same goes with public health, as previously indicated in chapter 2. Most of the community health facilities of the South Side closed down during the 1980s. Like half a dozen similar establishments, the Woodlawn Community Hospital, located on 61st Street near Cottage Grove Avenue, fell into bankruptcy in 1987 due to lagging and insufficient Medicaid reimbursements and the inadequate (or nonexistent) health care coverage of its usual clientele. It was then razed to make room for a public housing complex for the elderly, exclusively African Americans, which thus imported more poor black residents into the neighbourhood. After the University of Chicago hospitals pulled out of the city's emergency care network in 1990 to boost their profitability, victims of serious injury and trauma who cannot supply proof of enrolment in a health insurance plan have to be ambulanced for nearly ten miles, all the way to the decrepit and overburdened Cook County hospital. In 1991, the South Side had not a single health facility providing prenatal health services to uninsured expectant mothers and no drug rehabilitation programme readily accessible to those without the means to pay for it out of their own pockets.

The calamitous state of housing – not to mention streets, bridges, train tracks and sewers – in the Black Belt speaks volumes about the state of abandonment in which it has been left since the riots of the late 1960s. Whereas in La Courneuve and other Red Belt projects, city and state have joined to conduct a sweeping urban rehabilitation programme designed to improve living conditions and to stop the retreat of public services in large housing estates, the historic South Side is blighted by thousands of abandoned buildings, burnt-out or boarded-up stores, while thousands more dwellings are run down, improperly heated and structurally unsound – they would be declared unfit for habitation if the city gave itself the means to enforce its own housing code. In the neighbourhood of Woodlawn, there was virtually no new construction or renovation between 1950 and 1995, even though close to half of the initial housing stock was destroyed by arson and dereliction during this period (Wacquant 1995a). Most churches, which dotted the landscape and formed the organizational backbone of Chicago's 'Bronzeville' in its heyday (Drake and Cayton [1945] 1993), have long since closed their doors. Those that have survived are typically small and fragile congregations with a handful of members and decrepit facilities, when they are not ramshackle 'storefront' operations whose very existence hinges on the tireless activity of their individual founders. Churches endeavour to compensate as best they can for the glaring penury of government services, by organizing pantries and soup kitchens to feed the hungry, setting up shelters for the growing ranks of homeless, and running drug counselling programmes, job banks, literacy campaigns, and community clean-ups or social gatherings. But their most pressing mission at century's close is simply to survive day to day in the face of dwindling attendance and sagging resources.[29]

No institution is more emblematic of the organizational debilitation and political abandonment suffered by Chicago's hyperghetto than public schools (Kozol 1991: 40–82; *Chicago Tribune* 1992). First, as pointed out in chapter 2, the public education system has become a veritable *academic reservation* for poor minorities as whites as well as middle- and upper-class families of all ethnic provenances have fled into the private sector or outside the city altogether: over seven in ten of its pupils come from households living below the federal poverty line, and nearly nine in ten are black or Hispanic. Second, children in the fin-de-siècle Black Belt are schooled in ageing and overcrowded facilities, by undertrained and underpaid teachers, and with outdated and grossly insufficient supplies. Most secondary establishments on the South Side and West Side lack staff, classrooms, desks and chairs, black boards and books, and even adequate toilet facilities. They typically have no library, no working photocopying machine, no science lab and no chemical supplies to run experiments with; the textbooks they use, for those lucky to have enough of them, are frequently outdated rejects from suburban schools. One illustration: in 1991, students in a contemporary history course at Martin Luther King High School were using a book in which Richard Nixon was still the country's sitting President.

There is virtually no academic counselling – the DuSable High School, lodged at the heart of the South Side, has one counsellor for 420 students, compared to one for 25 on average in the public schools of affluent suburbs – and no programme to ease the transition from school to work. It is difficult for teenagers in the ghetto to envisage going to university, given that most of the secondary schools they attend do not offer college preparatory classes and that students are massively channelled onto vocational tracks anyway. Finally,

---

[29] One example: Christmas mass at the Church of Santa Clara in Woodlawn in 1989 recorded an attendance of fewer than two dozen (counting out-of-town guests and a handful of foreign visitors such as myself and my companion), less than one-tenth of the average attendance at its weekly 'soup kitchen'. In the nearby neighbourhood of Kenwood, a house of worship attracting twenty to thirty parishioners on Sunday was considered successful (Duncan 1987: 8). The decline of the role of religious institutions was just as glaring on Chicago's West Side (Kotlowitz 1991: 143).

much of the energy of the staff must be diverted to tasks that have little to do with teaching and learning. At the Fiske Elementary School in Woodlawn, only two blocks away from the University of Chicago's business school (but outside the perimeter of operation of its lavishly staffed private police force), the priorities of the daily round are, first, to feed children when they arrive so that they do not fall asleep or act aggressively during classes because they are hungry and, second, to provide physical security for the pupils and staff by means of a militia of parent volunteers that patrols the school grounds throughout the day armed with baseball bats. To complete this picture, Woodlawn has no high school, no museum, no cinema or other cultural facility of any sort, and the sole surviving public library in the neighbourhood is both grossly under-equipped and under-utilized, limping along with a miserly budget that does not allow it to reach out to residents.

It is *as if public policies were designed to devalorize public institutions so as to encourage exit into the private sector* by all those who can still leave the sinking ship of the hyperghetto and its *separate and unequal facilities*. Thus, in the early 1990s, city and state leaders joined with business organizations to consistently oppose – even actively lobby against – the tax increases needed to improve the public education system. Reagan's Secretary of Education famously denounced Chicago's public schools as 'the worst in America' but then dismissed demands for more federal funding for urban schooling and social services.[30] As a result of the erosion of its tax base, the city's public school system receives $90,000 less per pupil over his or her academic career than the public school system of the rich white suburbs of northern Chicago. Officials keep maintaining that funding is not the issue, but then they furiously resist sharing resources across jurisdictions. When asked to justify the refusal of his administration to funnel additional monies to Chicago's decaying public schools to correct this egregious inequity, Governor Thompson responded in 1988, with an expression laden with racial overtones: 'We can't keep throwing money into a black hole.' Remarkably, not one of the city's last five mayors sent his or her children to a public school, and only about one-third of the system's teachers enrol their offspring in it (and when they do so, it is generally in privileged establishments such as 'magnet schools'). As one alderman put it with disconcerting

[30] The erosion of federal funding and glaring inequities in the local financing of urban public schools and their effects on the academic chances of poor minorities are discussed in Kantor and Brenzel (1993) and Walters (1993: 586–9).

candour: 'Nobody in their right mind would send [their] kids to public school' in Chicago (Kozol 1991: 53).

The policy of social retrenchment pursued by the federal and local state authorities in the ghetto is at once a central component and a major determinant of a wider process of *organizational desertification* that has virtually emptied the Black Belt of its formal institutions. We noted in chapter 2 that the number of businesses operating in Woodlawn has plummeted from 700 in 1950 to about 100 in 1990. Whereas, until the 1960s, the neighbourhood harboured banks, stylish hotels, department stores, night clubs and cinemas, and light manufacturing, by the early 1990s it contained mostly liquor stores and dingy lounges, small laundromats and beauty parlours, fast-food and family-owned eateries, a smattering of currency exchanges, and an assortment of thrift stores, cheap clothing shops and furniture outlets, most of which are operated by marginal Asian or Middle Eastern entrepreneurs and their kin. It is no exaggeration to say that, in broad swathes of the historic Black Belt, the regular wage-labour economy has been superseded by the irregular and illegal street economy as primary source of employment and income. This conjoint withdrawal of the social state and the market accounts for the acute material destitution and atmosphere of dull tension that pervade the hyperghetto, similar to those that stamp daily life in a country ravaged by civil war. For they have undermined the proximate means of formal and informal social control through which most criminal behaviour is ordinarily checked (Sullivan 1989) and which, backed up by the presence of public agencies, usually help to hold 'urban disorder' in abeyance (Skogan 1988).

In the manner of a magnifying glass, the comparison between Red Belt and Black Belt reveals the role of state structures and public policies in fashioning the institutional articulation of 'race', class and space on the two sides of the Atlantic. In the French working-class *banlieues*, highly conspicuous public institutions weave a vital socio-economic safety net and contribute significantly to increasing social control. But bureaucratic imbroglio and cacophony also induce apathy and stoke collective frustration among the population. The responsiveness of the political system in the short term of electoral cycles even encourages movements of urban protest – including the periodic outbursts of collective violence that have become a regular feature of life in the declining *banlieues*. By contrast, in the Black Belt of the American metropolis, the collapse of public institutions is the leading cause of systemic physical and social insecurity and of the far-reaching decomposition of the organizational fabric of neighbourhoods after the ebbing of the Civil Rights movement. This decomposition, in turn, collapses the structure of opportunities, shrinks the set of viable life strategies, and stimulates individual strategies of internal predation or out-migration that further accelerate the involutive decline of the ghetto.

Conclusion: reaffirming the obligations of the state

From schools and welfare to housing, justice, health care and physical infrastructure, the public institutions of the American hyperghetto have been abandoned to a spiral of deterioration to a degree such that, far from enhancing the life chances and fostering the integration of its residents into national life, they further accentuate their stigmatization and deepen their marginalization. Social isolation in the racialized urban core, understood as the slackening or severing of ties to the central institutional nodes of society, is not a state rooted in the individual behaviour or moral constitution of those relegated to it, any more than it is a property of their culture or social networks – *pace* William Julius Wilson (1991). Rather, the isolation of America's urban outcasts is the *product of an active process of institutional detachment* and segregation (in the etymological sense of 'setting apart') fostered by the decomposition of the public sector. It follows that its sources are not simply economic, located in the ongoing post-Fordist restructuring of the metropolitan labour market; they are also and above all *properly political*, rooted in the abandonment of the ghetto by the state permitted by the marginalization of poor urban blacks in the local and national political fields.

The contraction and dereliction of an already miserly public sector are key to the deadly effect of the spread of economic redundancy inside the ghetto. As Simon (1992: 64) points out in the case of the French working-class *banlieues* and Dangschat (1994) about the German inner city, so long as public institutions have the capacity to adequately service them and form an organizational buffer against exclusion, the concentration of the poor in isolated urban districts need not necessarily translate into an aggravation of their situation. On the contrary, it can facilitate the accumulation of social capital and the meshing of networks of sociability and reciprocity that are essential supports of (sub)proletarian life strategies.[31] It is not the

---

[31] The monographs by Michael Young and Peter Willmott (1954, 1986), Ida Susser (1982) and Mercedes González de la Rocha (1994) demonstrate this in the case,

concentration of poverty *per se*, but its *concentration in the very peculiar US context conjugating segregation, stigmatization and political abandonment*, which accounts for the brutal deterioration of the ghetto and the untold suffering it exacts of its residents.

As the institutional concretization of multiple forms of material and symbolic duress exerted against Americans of African ancestry, the ghetto has always been a place saturated with danger and whirling with violence.[32] Since its birth at the beginning of the twentieth century, when 'Negroes' were forced to reside inside their reserved perimeter, denied access to industrial employment and marginalized in the political field, it has of necessity harboured in its midst a disproportionately large sector of illegal activities conducive to high crime rates (Light 1977; Lane 1986). Yet one cannot grasp the routinization of violence that has shredded the fabric of daily life in the racialized urban core of the American metropolis at century's close if one construes it only as a means and offshoot of novel forms of entrepreneurialism in the informal economy. It is also *in part* the grossly distorted expression of a *lumpen* protest, by its perpetrators, against an institutional order which casts them out of the broader society, a response to the unprecedented violence visited upon them by the impersonal machineries of the neoliberal state and the deregulated market, which would assume a more political form in a different context such as the centralized Jacobin framework of France (as argued in chapter 1). A former high-ranking member of the Black Gangster Disciples who now rents himself out at day-labour agencies hints at this when commenting on the tragically inward-turning, self-destructive nature of criminality in the hyperghetto:

'Cause, see, the Man downtown who pullin' the string, they cain't get to him. So they take they frustrations on the guy next door to them, the guy across the street from them. Instead of bein' *wise* and goin' to see Mayor Daley or Governor Edwards or somethin'. Go take out your frustration on *them: go see Bush* [the father], *go see Ronald Reagan!* Don't bother *me, 'cuz I ain't did nuttin' to you.* A lotta guys, it's the frustration: *they frustrated, man, with they lives.*

---

respectively, of Cockney workers of the East End of London during the 1950s, residents of the multiethnic working-class neighbourhood of Greenpoint (Brooklyn) in New York during the 1970s, and the families living in a dispossessed neighbourhood of Guadalajara, Mexico, between 1982 and 1988.

[32] It suffices, to realize this, to read the first sociological survey of the urban Black Belt, carried out by W. E. B. Du Bois ([1899] 1996) at the birth of the Philadelphia ghetto in 1899.

In the safe and distant observatories of their cushy offices in private universities and conservative think tanks, perched high above the imploding ghetto, advocates of state paternalism – such as political scientist Lawrence Mead (1992) – have called for the punitive disciplining of poor blacks so that they be forcibly made to fulfil those 'obligations of citizenship' supposedly asked of all Americans.[33] It remains to be seen whether these righteous entrepreneurs in public morality will display the same zeal when it comes to demanding that the state be held equally accountable for providing the basic public goods and for ensuring the fundamental citizenship rights that the vast majority of Americans take for given even as they are denied daily to those imprisoned in the permanent insecurity and incivility of the hyperghetto.

[33] For Mead (1986), the 'crisis of the welfare state' afflicting the advanced societies is moral rather than fiscal or political. The cardinal defect of public assistance programmes in the United States is their 'permissiveness': they canonize the 'entitlements' of the poor rather than the wholesome assertion of their 'obligations' toward the collectivity, and *primus inter pares* the obligation to submit to precarious wage labour in order to taste the moralizing virtues of work. Mead curiously fails to cover the obligations of the middle and upper classes, who are the major beneficiaries of the largesse of social spending in the United States through regressive fiscality, and the obligations of big business, which is massively subsidized by the federal government. According to the economists and tax experts of the Cato Institute (a far Right-wing think tank that can hardly be suspected of exaggeration), Washington handed out $85 billion of 'corporate welfare' in 1995, equal to four times the budget allotted to the main public aid programme (AFDC) that year (Moore and Stansel 1995).

Part III

Looking Ahead: Urban Marginality in the Twenty-First Century

8

The Rise of Advanced Marginality
Specifications and Implications

I noted in the opening chapter of this book how, over the past two decades, the self-image that advanced capitalist societies had forged of themselves in the postwar period as increasingly pacified, homogeneous and cohesive collectivities – 'democratic' in Tocqueville's sense of the term, 'civilized' in Norbert Elias's lexicon – was shattered by the virulent outbreaks of public disorder that accompanied the palpable resurgence of inequality and marginality in the Western metropolis. Two parallel debates thus developed in the United States and the European Union about the intersection of poverty, racial division or postcolonial immigration, and urban decline as persistent joblessness, social deprivation and ethnic tension (real or perceived as such) punctuated by outbreaks of collective violence rose in unison in big cities on both sides of the Atlantic after the dismantling of the Fordist–Keynesian social compact.

'Underclass' and 'banlieue': the faces of advanced marginality

With the accelerating dislocation and degradation of the segregated metropolitan core, US social scientists and public policy experts grew alarmed about the alleged emergence and consolidation of a black 'underclass', characterized as entrapped in decaying inner cities, prone to antisocial behaviours, and increasingly isolated from the broader society.[1] Meanwhile in France, as in a number of neighbour-

[1] The more notable studies on the topic include Glasgow (1981), Wilson (1987 and 1993), Jencks and Peterson (1991), Massey and Denton (1993), Moore and Pinder-hughes (1993), and Katz (1993). For a dissection of the invention of the scholarly

ing countries, a veritable moral panic broke out over the rise of exclusion and segregation in the '*banlieue*', incarnated by the consolidation of '*cités*-ghettos' believed to pose a mortal threat to the republic's 'integration model' and public order, as established working-class boroughs of the urban periphery were caught in a tailspin of deterioration just as former 'guest workers' and their children became a growing and permanent component of their population.[2] On both sides of the Atlantic, the theme of the dualization – or polarization – of the city took centre stage in the most advanced sectors of urban theory and research, as the extremes of high society and dark ghetto, luxurious wealth and utter destitution, cosmopolitan bourgeoisie and urban outcasts, flourished and decayed side by side.[3]

Taken together, these trends would seem to partake of an epochal turn marked by the transatlantic convergence of patterns of urban marginality and the ethnicization of the European city on the American model. 'With the Americanization of western Europe . . . the questions concerning democracy, race, culture and social solidarity that Gunnar Myrdal raised in An American Dilemma half a century ago are re-emerging in new forms as demanding moral-political questions not only for the US but for the EU, which aspires to be the United States of Europe' (Schierup 1995: 359–60).[4] But close analysis of the ecology, structural location, social composition and organizational makeup of long-standing or newly emerging territories of relegation in the Old and New Worlds proposed in this book suggests that European regimes of urban poverty *are not being 'Americanized'*. Contrary to the superficial accounts given of them by the media and by intellectuals eager to put a scholarly gloss on the prefabricated problematics of political discussion, the profound transformations

---

myth of the 'underclass' and its functions in the US intellectual and political-journalistic fields, cf. Wacquant (1996a); for a homegrown discussion of the analytic limitations and policy liabilities of this notion, see respectively Marks (1991) and Gans (1991).

[2] See, among many books published in the same brief period, Paugam (1991), Jazouli (1992), Dubet and Lapeyronnie (1992), Wihtol de Wenden and Daoud (1994) and Vieillard-Baron (1994). The diffusion of the alarmist discourse on '*cités*-ghettos' in France was recapitulated in chapter 5. For parallels in the German debate, see Alisch and Dangschat (1998).

[3] The thesis of urban dualization is elaborated or challenged by Castells (1989), Mollenkopf and Castells (1991), Sassen (1991b), Fainstein et al. (1992), Martinotti (1993), Waldinger (1996), Mingione (1996), Friedrichs and O'Loughlin (1996) and Häußermann (1998). Marcuse (1993) warns against the risk of exaggerating the novelty of contemporary urban divisions.

[4] A similar view is formulated in the French debate by Godard (1993) and in the American discussion by Hollifield (1991) and Hein (1993).

undergone by the popular boroughs of the Continent's big cities do not amount to a process of ghettoization. They have not triggered or resulted in the formation of ethnically homogeneous enclosed spaces wherein a 'negatively privileged' category (to speak like Max Weber) is forced to develop its own institutions in response to rejection by the dominant society – as was the case for African Americans during the decades of industrial consolidation in the twentieth century.

The paired comparison between neighbourhoods of relegation in Chicago's Black Belt and in the Parisian Red Belt laid out in chapters 5–7 has enabled us to demonstrate that, despite similar morphological tendencies and kindred lived experiences, the French working-class periphery and the African-American ghetto remain two sharply *distinct sociospatial constellations*. And for good reasons: they are the legacies of different urban histories and modes of 'sorting' of population; and they remain embedded in divergent articulations of welfare state, market and appropriated physical space – all of which result in levels of poverty, isolation and distress in the remnants of the US ghetto that have no equivalent in European cities.

To put it briefly – since we shall return to this question in the next and closing chapter – sociospatial relegation in the American Black Belt results from 'exclusionary closure' (as conceptualized by Max Weber and Frank Parkin (1978: 44–73) after him) operating on an ethnoracial basis anchored by an encompassing dichotomous opposition between 'blacks' and 'whites'.[5] This closure has been bolstered at the material and symbolic levels by the structure and policies of the state, and redoubled by class divisions after the acme of the Civil Rights movement – that is, since the collapse of the communal ghetto of the Fordist–Keynesian era and its replacement by a hyperghetto founded on a double 'rejection on the basis of class and race' (Clark 1965: 21). Not so in the French Red Belt: in France, relegation to a degraded *banlieue* operates first on grounds of class position; it is then exacerbated by (post)colonial origin (itself closely correlated with class profile) but also partially alleviated by the protective and compensatory action of the (central and local) state, without which an even broader fraction of the urban proletariat would be

---

[5] This dualistic opposition, established by the strict application of the principle of 'hypo-descent' to resolve symbolically the historic contradiction between slavery and democracy, admits of no mediating term and is virtually unique on earth for its rigidity and persistence (Davis 1991). The black/white division constitutes the binary framework within which the position of the other officially recognized ethnic categories (Hispanics, Asians, Native Americans, persons of mixed descent, etc.) is defined, whether they are racialized or not.

marginalized. A cross-sectional sociography of these two urban forms confirms the discrepancy between the two dynamics that have produced and reproduced them: the fin-de-siècle hyperghetto of the United States is a closed, racially monotone and culturally unified cosmos characterized by low organizational density and limited as well as receding penetration by the welfare state, whereas its structural counterpart on the French side is fundamentally heterogeneous in its ethnonational and even social recruitment, open to its surrounding milieu, and backed by a comparatively strong presence of public institutions.

This differential coupling of class, place and (ethnic or national) origin on the two sides of the Atlantic does not, however, obviate the possibility that the recent transformations of the US ghetto and the French working-class *banlieues*, as well as the deteriorating inner cities or urban peripheries of the United Kingdom, Germany, Belgium and Italy, herald the crystallization of a novel, still inchoate yet *distinctive regime of urban poverty* that diverges both from America's traditional ghetto and from the European 'workers' space' of the long twentieth century (Willmott 1963; Verret 1979; Bagnasco 1986). Viewed from this angle, the 'return of the repressed' realities of economic penury and social destitution, ethnoracial division and public violence, and their accumulation in the same distressed urban areas, suggests that First World cities are henceforth confronted with what one may call *advanced marginality*. These new forms of exclusionary closure translating into expulsion to the margins and crevices of social and physical space have arisen – or intensified – in the post-Fordist metropolis, not as a result of economic mismatches or backwardness but, on the contrary, as an effect of the uneven, disarticulating mutations of the *most advanced sectors* of Western economies, as these bear on the lower fractions of the recomposing working class and subordinate ethnic categories, as well as on the territories they occupy in the dualizing city (Sassen 1991b; Mingione 1991; Castells 1998).

The qualifier 'advanced' is meant here to indicate that these forms of marginality are not *behind* us: they are not residual, cyclical or transitional; and they are not being gradually resorbed by the expansion of the 'free market', i.e., by the further commodification of social life, starting with essential public goods and services, or by the (protective or disciplinary) action of the welfare state. Rather, they stand *ahead of us*: they are etched on the horizon of the becoming of contemporary societies. It is therefore urgent to diagnose them, to give ourselves the means to elaborate new paths of public intervention capable of checking or redirecting the structural forces that generate them, among which polarized economic growth and the fragmentation of wage labour, the casualization of employment and the autonomization of the street economy in degraded urban areas, mass joblessness amounting to outright deproletarianization for the more vulnerable segments of the working class (especially youths shorn of institutionalized cultural capital), and, last but not least, state policies of social retrenchment and urban abandonment. If new mechanisms of social and political incorporation are not put in place to reintegrate the populations cast out in these territories of perdition, one can expect that urban marginality will continue to rise and spread and, along with it, the street violence, civic alienation, organizational desertification and economic informalization that increasingly plague the redoubts of relegation in the metropolis of advanced society.

Six distinctive properties of the rising regime of marginality

An ideal-typical characterization of this new marginality *in statu nascendi* may be provisionally sketched by contrasting it with a selective tableau of the features of urban poverty in the postwar era of Fordist growth and prosperity (1945–75). An ideal type, one must recall with Max Weber (1949: 86–92), is not a purely 'synthetic construct' offered for purposes of analysis, but a sociohistorical abstraction from real instances of a phenomenon. Ideal-typical concepts assist us in formulating hypotheses and then confronting them with empirical reality; they offer us a baseline for identifying significant variations and their possible causes. As heuristic devices, however, they are not covered by criteria of truth or falsehood: simply, they turn out to be fruitful or not for research.[6]

The compact characterization of 'advanced marginality' that follows is offered with reservation, knowing full well that, as Ludwig Wittgenstein once warned (1977: 55), 'concepts may alleviate mischief or they may make it worse; foster it or check it'. Binary oppositions of the kind fostered by such conceptual exercise are well suited to exaggerating differences, confounding description and prescrip-

---

[6] To assess the value of the 'mental picture' (*Gedankenbild*) that the ideal-type constitutes, 'there is no other criterion than that of the efficacy of the knowledge of the relations between the concrete phenomena of culture, for their causal conditionality and meaning' (Weber 1949: 92).

tion, and setting up overburdened dualisms that erase continuities, underplay contingency, and overestimate the internal coherence of social forms. With these caveats in mind, one may single out six distinctive features of advanced marginality for further scrutiny.[7] The synchronic and cross-sectional characterization of advanced marginality sketched here will then be amplified and further elaborated from a diachronic and dynamic perspective in the next and closing chapter.

1   Wage labour as vector of social instability and life insecurity

Whereas in the decades of Fordist expansion or at the apogee of 'organized capitalism' (Lash and Urry 1987; Crouch and Streeck 1997), the wage–labour relation offered an efficient solution to the dilemmas of urban marginality, it is manifest that under the ascending new regime, it must be considered (also) as part of the problem.

By becoming 'internally' unstable and heterogeneous, differentiated and differentiating, wage work has turned from fount of homogeneity, solidarity and security into a source of social fragmentation and precariousness for those confined to the border zones of the employment sphere (Lebaude 1994; Osterman 1999; Vosko 2000; Barbier and Nadel 2002).[8] Witness, among other indicators, the proliferation of part-time, 'flexible', variable-schedule positions; fixed-term contracts with reduced (or non-existent) social and medical coverage whose extension and eligibility conditions are negotiable (or based on a fee); pay scales modulated according to performance and date of first employment (as opposed to length of employment); the reduction of the average job tenure and the cor-

[7] It is by design that we mix among these features trends, processes and outcomes as well as proximate causes and propitiating factors. It would be premature at this early stage to try to separate these out. As Robert Merton (1983) was fond of saying, one must 'specify the phenomenon' before attempting to explain it.

[8] And for a growing number of wage-earners closer to the core: 'Since 1985', notes Paul Hirsch (1993: 144–5, 154–5), internal labour markets based on 'long-term reciprocal commitments, careers within companies, attractive wages, and job security' have 'come under attack from opinion leaders in both academe and the business press.' With the decline of these internal markets due to corporate 'downsizing' (lately christened 'rightsizing'), even the employment environment of 'the managerial class begins to look much more like [that of] labour'. And 'as the management class begins to see itself as more and more like labour and less like capital, the polarization of society may increase'.

relative increase in staff turnover; the spread of subcontracting and related tactics used by businesses to make their employees bear the risks of vagaries in economic activity and evade the homogenizing effects of state regulation of wage work (e.g., the manipulation of weekly hours to avoid paying benefits, the multiplication of subsidized employment in France, or that country's aborted attempt to create a sub-minimum wage for unskilled youths, under the Balladur government in the spring of 1995 and again under Galouzeau de Villepin in the spring of 2006). The resurgence of sweatshops redolent of the nineteenth century, the return of piecework and homework, the development of telework and two-tier wage scales, the outsourcing of employees and the individualization of remuneration and promotion grids, the institutionalization of 'permanently temporary' work, the swelling of state-sponsored work contracts, not to mention the multiplication of 'make-work' or forced-work formulas (baptized 'workfare' in the United States and government-funded 'public utility work' and traineeships in France) imposed as a condition of receipt of public assistance: all point to the rampant *desocialization of wage labour*. The fading of labour law and the splintering of social legislation endorse this uneven diversification of the statutory and juridical traits of employment.[9]

In addition to the erosion of the integrative capacity of the wage–labour relation, each of the elements of security stipulated under the Fordist–Keynesian social contract (Standing 1993) has been eroded and is either forsaken or under frontal attack: labour market security (via state efforts to ensure full employment), income security (through social provision, jobless benefits and incorporation into unions), and employment security (by means of the reduction of capitalist command over terms of hiring and firing). All in all, the structural roots of economic uncertainty and social precariousness have ramified and extended in breadth as well as depth. With national inflections depending on the country, they have everywhere disproportionately struck lower-class families and youths, unskilled women and stigmatized ethnic categories. And it is only logical that, at the spatial level, the destabilizing effects of the diversification and degradation of the condition of workers have accumulated in the

---

[9] On the 'disorganization' of wage labour, see Boyer (1988), Burtless (1990), Freeman and Katz (1994) and Regini (1995). MacLeod (1995) draws a vivid, ground-level, ethnographic portrait of the structural disorientation and dereliction affecting working-class youths in the new low-wage labour market in a northeastern American city; see also MacDonald (1997) on England and Roulleau-Berger and Gautier (2002) on France.

urban zones where the unstable fractions of the new postindustrial proletariat are concentrated.[10]

2 Functional disconnection from macroeconomic trends

Advanced marginality is increasingly disconnected from cyclical fluctuations and global trends in the economy, so that expansionary phases in aggregate employment and income have little beneficial effect upon it. Social conditions and life chances in neighbourhoods of relegation in Europe and the United States changed very little, if at all, during the boom years of the 1980s and the second half of the 1990s, but they worsened noticeably during phases of slowdown and recession (Wilson 1996; Kesteloot 2000).

Thus youth joblessness, which strikes with particular force the children of the working class (especially those issued from postcolonial immigration), has kept rising for two decades in France's dispossessed *banlieues* under every government, of the Right and Left alike, even those of Michel Rocard and Lionel Jospin during which a strong growth surge caused a temporary let-up in unemployment at the national level. Between 1990 and 1999, the unemployment rate among those aged 15 to 24 increased from 20 per cent to 26 per cent in the country, but for youths living in the 750 'sensitive urban zones' earmarked by the 1996 Pact for the Renewal of Urban Policy, these percentages stood at 20 per cent and 40 per cent respectively. Moreover, the ranks of precarious wage-earners in the country – tallying those on fixed-term contracts, temporary work, subsidized jobs and training programmes – swelled from 1.98 million (corresponding to one worker in eleven) in 1990 to 3.3 million (one in seven) in 1999. But among the 4.7 million residents of the 'sensitive zones' the rate of precarious employees leapt from 13 per cent to 20 per cent, so that by the end of the decade fully 60 per cent of youths there were jobless or in insecure posts (Le Toqueux and Moreau 2000), despite the resurging economic expansion and the government programme of mass creation of targeted 'youth jobs'. In Chicago, as was pointed out in chapter 3, 80 per cent of ghetto residents reported a deterioration in their financial situation after four consecutive years of buoyant

[10] 'In some locations, all the problems that are the effect of the degradation of the wage-earner's condition are crystallized in a particularly dramatic fashion: high unemployment rate, establishment of permanent insecurity, rupture of class solidarities and the bankruptcy of family, educational and cultural modes of transmission, the absence of prospects and plans for coping with the future, etc.' (Castel 1995: 427).

economic growth during Ronald Reagan's presidency, and most expected their neighbourhood to continue to deteriorate, a prediction that was largely verified, since poverty levels in the dispossessed zones of US cities barely budged over the ensuing decade.

Considering this asymmetric relation between national and even regional aggregate unemployment and labour market trends, on the one hand, and neighbourhood conditions, on the other, and given the current slope of productivity gains and emerging forms of 'jobless growth' (Dunkerley 1996), it would take miraculous rates of economic expansion to hope to absorb back into the employment pool those who have been durably expelled from it. In 1994, the European Commission predicted in its White Book on competitiveness, growth and employment that it would add 15 million jobs before 2000, for an employment growth of 2 per cent per annum and a real GDP growth rate of 3.5 per cent. Instead, it achieved a yearly growth rate of 2.3 per cent and expanded overall employment by only 0.7 per cent for an added 5 million jobs.[11] This implies that, short of sharing available work or guaranteeing an income decoupled from wage labour, policies aimed at expanding the sphere of gainful employment have every chance of being both costly and inefficient, since their benefits will 'trickle down' to the new urban outcasts last, only after every other underprivileged category has benefited from this extension.

3   Territorial fixation and stigmatization

Rather than being disseminated throughout working-class areas, advanced marginality tends to be concentrated in isolated and bounded territories increasingly perceived by both outsiders and insiders as social purgatories, leprous badlands at the heart of the postindustrial metropolis where only the refuse of society would agree to dwell.

When these 'penalized spaces' (Pétonnet 1982) are, or threaten to become, permanent fixtures of the urban landscape, discourses of vilification proliferate and agglomerate about them, 'from below', in the ordinary interactions of daily life, as well as 'from above', in the

---

[11] We are, moreover, concerned here not with fluctuations in aggregate employment intensity (as measured by the 'Okun coefficient' linking real output and the unemployment rate, as discussed by Padalino and Vivarelli (1997)) but with the contents of growth in jobs situated in the skills bracket and geographical zones accessible to the urban poor.

journalistic, political and bureaucratic (and even scientific) fields.[12]
A *taint of place* is thus superimposed on the already existing stigmata
traditionally associated with poverty and ethnic origin or postcolonial
immigrant status, to which it is closely linked but not reducible. It
is remarkable that Erving Goffman (1963) does not mention place
of residence as one of the 'disabilities' that can 'disqualify the individual' and deprive him or her of 'full acceptance by others'. Yet
territorial infamy displays properties analogous to those of bodily,
moral and tribal stigmata, and it poses dilemmas of information
management, identity formation and social relations quite similar to
these, even as it also sports distinctive properties of its own. Of the
three main types of stigma catalogued by Goffman (1963: 4–5) –
'abominations of the body', 'blemishes of the character', and marks
of 'race, nation and religion' – it is to the third that territorial stigma
is akin, since, like the latter, it 'can be transmitted through lineages
and equally contaminate all members of a family'. But, unlike these
other stamps of dishonour, it can be easily dissimulated and attenuated – even annulled – through geographic mobility and minimal
cultural disguising.

In every metropolis of the First World, one or more towns, districts
or clumps of public housing are publicly known and recognized as
those urban hellholes in which violence, vice and dereliction are the
order of things. Some even acquire the status of national eponym for
all the evils and dangers now believed to afflict the dualized city:[13]
Les Minguettes and La Courneuve or the Mirail housing complex
in Toulouse for France; South Central Los Angeles, the Bronx and
the project of Cabrini Green in Chicago for the United States; Duis-
berg-Marxloh and Berlin-Neukölln for Germany; the districts of
Toxteth in Liverpool, Saint Paul in Bristol, or the Meadow Well
estate in Newcastle for England; and Bijlmer and Westlijke Tuinst-
eden in Amsterdam for the case of Holland. Even the societies that
have best resisted the rise of advanced marginality, like the Scandinavian countries, are affected by this phenomenon of territorial stig-

[12] Social scientists have added significantly to the burden of urban infamy by con-
cocting pseudo-scholarly notions that dress up ordinary class and racial prejudices
in an analytic-sounding language. Such is the case, e.g., with the asinine category of
underclass area put forth by Erol Ricketts and Isabel Sawhill (1988) to characterize
(in perfectly circular fashion) neighbourhoods inhabited by the 'underclass', defined
by a quantified battery of spatially measured behavioural 'pathologies'.

[13] Some 'hotbeds' of urban perdition, such as the Bronx for example, achieve a
similar status on the international level, as Auyero points out (1999) in his study of
a shanty-town in Greater Buenos Aires.

matization linked to the emergence of zones reserved for the urban outcasts:

> It doesn't matter where I travel [through the provinces of Sweden], everywhere I get the same questions when the people I meet hear where I come from: 'Do you live in Tensta? How can you live there? How can you manage to live in a ghetto?' (Pred 2000: 129)[14]

Whether or not these areas are in fact dilapidated and dangerous, and their population composed essentially of poor people, minorities and foreigners, matters little in the end: when it becomes widely shared and diffused, the prejudicial belief that they are suffices to set off socially noxious consequences.

This is true at the level of the structure and texture of everyday social relations. I stressed in chapter 6 how much living in a (sub)proletarian housing project on the periphery of Paris creates a 'muted sentiment of guilt and shame whose unacknowledged weight warps human contact' (Pétonnet 1982: 148). People there commonly hide their address, avoid having family and friends visit them at home, and feel compelled to make excuses for residing in an infamous locale that stains the image they have of themselves. 'I'm not from the *cité*, me myself,' insists a young woman from Vitry-sur-Seine, 'I live here because I have problems right now but I'm not from here, I have nothing to do with all those people over here' (Pétonnet 1982: 149). One of her neighbours invites the anthropologist not to confuse the *cité* with a neighbourhood, 'because in a neighbourhood you have everybody . . . whereas here you have only shit' (Pétonnet 1982: 14). Similarly, we have seen that inhabitants of Chicago's hyperghetto commonly deny belonging to the microsociety of the neighbourhood and strive to distance themselves from a place and population that they know are universally sullied, and of which the media and certain scholarly discourse never stop giving a debased image.

The acute sense of social indignity that enshrouds neighbourhoods of relegation can be attenuated only by thrusting the stigma onto a

---

[14] Tensta is a neighbourhood in the northern suburbs of Stockholm which houses high concentrations of unemployed and immigrants. In turn-of-the-century Sweden, 'problem neighbourhoods' (*problemområde*) like Rinkebÿ in Stockholm and Rosengård in Malmö, are commonly and openly designated by the quasi-synonym of 'neighbourhoods of high immigrant density' (*invandrartätomrade*). A fairly similar doublet is used to point to zones of urban relegation in Holland: '*achterstandswijken*' and '*concentratiebuurten*' (Uitermark 2003).

faceless, demonized other – the downstairs neighbours, the immigrant family dwelling in an adjacent building, the youths from across the street who 'do drugs' or engage in street 'hustling', or yet the residents over on the next block whom one suspects of illegally drawing unemployment or welfare support. This logic of *lateral denigration and mutual distanciation*, which tends to further unravel the already weakened collectives of deprived urban zones, is difficult to check inasmuch as

> the stigmatized neighbourhood symbolically degrades those who live in it and degrade it symbolically in return, since, being deprived of all the assets necessary to participate in the various social games, their common lot consists only of their common excommunication. Assembling in one place a population homogeneous in its dispossession also has the effect of accentuating dispossession. (Bourdieu [1993] 1999: 129, my translation)

The effects of territorial stigmatization are also felt at the level of public policies. Once a place is publicly labelled as a 'lawless zone' or an 'outlaw estate', outside the common norm,[15] it is easy for the authorities to justify special measures, deviating from both law and custom, which can have for effect – if not for intention – to destabilize and further marginalize their occupants, and to submit them to the dictates of the deregulated labour market, render them invisible, or drive them out of a coveted space.[16] Thus, in the wake of a series of

---

[15] I could cite here countless books on the *banlieues* that have flooded French bookstores over the past several years, in which class racism rivals fantasies about the foreign peril. I shall mention just one, whose title aptly sums up its outlook: *Outlaw Estates: Another World, a Youth that Imposes its own Laws* (*Cités hors-la-loi. Un autre monde, une jeunesse qui impose ses lois*) (Henni et Marinet 2002; Marinet is one of the journalists from the national television channel France 2 who originated the media myth of the explosion of '*tournantes*' ('gang rapes') in the dispossessed *banlieues*). Under cover of analysis and sounding a civic alarm, these books partake of the discourse of vilification of neighbourhoods of exile and help effect the symbolic deportation of their residents.

[16] One would need, in this perspective, to examine how the demonic legend of the 'underclass' (paradoxically promoted also by progressive academics) helped to legitimize, on the one hand, the 'reform' of welfare leading to the establishment of 'workfare' in the United States with the Personal Responsibility and Work Opportunity Act of 1996 and, on the other, the policy of massive destruction of large housing projects in the ghetto under the pretext of the alleged benefits of spatial dispersion for the poor, officialized by the 1998 Quality Housing and Work Responsibility Act (Crump 2003). The similarity in the labelling of these two laws is revealing of their converging purpose: to enforce low-wage work.

sensationalistic reports on television, the neighbourhood of São João de Deus, a 'slummified' sector of northern Porto with a strong and conspicuous presence of Gypsies and Cape Verdean descendants, is nowadays known throughout Portugal as the infernal incarnation of the *'bairro social degradado'*. The municipality of Porto took advantage of its squalid reputation as a *'hipermercado das drogas'* to launch a sweeping 'urban renewal' operation which, thanks to a series of muscular police raids, aims essentially at expelling and scattering the local addicts, squatters, unemployed and other human detritus to insert the neighbourhood back into the city's real estate circuit – without worrying in the slightest way over the fate of the thousands of residents thus displaced.[17]

4 Spatial alienation and the dissolution of 'place'

The obverse side of this process of territorial stigmatization is the dissolution of 'place': that is, the loss of a humanized, culturally familiar and socially filtered locale with which marginalized urban populations identify and in which they feel 'at home' and in relative security. Theories of post-Fordism intimate that the current reconfiguration of capitalism involves not only a vast reshuffling of firms and economic flows, jobs and people *in space* but also a sea-change in the organization and experience *of space* itself (see especially Harvey 1989; Soja 1989; and Shields 1991). These theories are consistent with the radical makeover of both the black American ghetto and the working-class *banlieues* of France since the close of the 1970s, as these have been gradually reduced from communal 'places' bathed in shared emotions and joint meanings, supported by practices and institutions of mutuality, to indifferent 'spaces' of mere survival and relentless contest.

The distinction between these two conceptions or modes of appropriation of the extant environment may be formulated thus: ' "Places" are "full" and "fixed," stable arenas', whereas ' "spaces" are "potential voids," "possible threats," areas that have to be feared, secured or fled' (Smith 1987: 297). The shift from a politics of place to a

---

[17] I am indebted to Luis Fernandes (of the University of Porto) for this information, and I refer the reader to his analysis of the spatial stigmatization attached to the 'psychotropic territories' of the Portuguese city (Fernandes 1998: 68–79, 151–4 and 169–74). Fraser (1996) shows similarly how the process whereby the degraded inner-city district of Moss Side in Manchester 'acquired an iconic status nationally as the symbol of "dangerous Britain"' after the 1981 riots decisively angled the policy approach taken to 'fixing [it] as a national problem'.

politics of space, adds sociologist Dennis Smith, is encouraged by the weakening of bonds founded upon a territorial community inside the city. It is also fostered by the tendency of individuals to retreat into the privatized sphere of the household, the strengthening of feelings of vulnerability arising in the course of the pursuit of economic security, and the generalized weakening of social collectives.[18] One must be careful here not to romanticize conditions in the proletarian neighbourhoods and segregated enclaves of yesteryear: there never was a 'golden age' when life in the American ghetto and the French popular *banlieues* was sweet and social relations therein harmonious and fulfilling. Yet it remains that the experience of urban relegation has, on this plane, changed in ways that make it distinctively more burdensome and alienating today.

To illustrate briefly: until the 1960s, the black American ghetto was still a 'place', a collective *oekoumene*, a humanized urban landscape with which blacks felt a strong positive identification – even as it was the product of brutal and inflexive racial oppression – as expressed in the rhetoric of 'soul' (Hannerz 1968), and over which they desired to establish collective control – such was the priority goal of the Black Power movement (Van DeBurg 1992). Today's hyperghetto is a 'space', and this denuded space is no longer a shared resource that African Americans can mobilize and deploy to shelter themselves from white domination and where they hope to find collective support for their strategies of mobility. On the contrary: it has become a vector of intra-communal division and an instrument for the virtual imprisonment of the black urban subproletariat, a dreaded and detested territory from which, as one informant from Chicago's South Side abruptly put it, 'everybody's tryin' to get out'.[19]

Far from providing a protective shield from the insecurities and pressures of the outside world, as we have seen in chapters 2–4, the space of the hyperghetto is akin to an entropic and perilous battlefield upon which a four-corner contest is endlessly waged between (i)

[18] For a painstaking analysis of the 'defensive and withdrawn privatism' of the traditional working-class and its accentuation against the backdrop of group decomposition in a northern mining town of France, see Schwartz (1990). For a description of the unravelling of forms of neighbourhood sociability and solidarity inside the West Side and South Side ghettos of Chicago under the pressure of extreme deprivation and endemic violence, read the narrative accounts of Kotlowitz (1991) and Jones and Newman (1997).

[19] The (partially unsuccessful) efforts of the black middle class of the South Side of Chicago to distance itself spatially and socially from the crumbling core of the ghetto and the threats it contains are skilfully studied by Pattillo-McCoy (1999).

independent and organized street predators (hustlers and gangs) who seek to plunder what meagre riches still circulate in it; (ii) local residents and their grass-roots organizations (such as MAD, 'Mothers Against Drugs', on the West Side of Chicago, or block clubs and merchants' associations where they have survived) who strive to preserve the use- and exchange-value of their neighbourhood; (iii) state agencies of surveillance and social control entrusted with containing violence and disorder within the perimeter of the racialized metropolitan core, including social workers, teachers, the police, the courts, probation and parole agents, etc.; and (iv) outside institutional predators (realtors in particular) for whom converting fringe sections of the Black Belt for the uses of the middle and upper classes coming back into the city can yield phenomenal profits.[20]

5   Loss of hinterland

Adding to the erosion of place is the disappearance of a viable hinterland. In previous phases of modern capitalist crisis and restructuring, workers temporarily rejected from the labour market could fall back upon the social economy of their community of provenance, be it a functioning working-class borough, the communal ghetto, or a rural village in the back country or in their country of emigration (Young and Willmott 1954, 1986; Kornblum 1974; Piore 1979; Sayad 1991).[21]

When they were dismissed from the factories and foundries, mills and car shops of Chicago where they toiled on account of a cyclical downturn in the industrial economy, the residents of mid-twentieth-century Bronzeville could rely on the support of kin, clique and church. Most inhabitants in their district remained wage-earners and a densely knit web of neighbourhood-based organizations helped

---

[20] See Venkatesh (2000) for a contextualized account of the struggles of the 1990s between the tenants of the Robert Taylor Homes, the local gangs, the Chicago Housing Administration, and various other city agencies; and Abu-Lughod et al. (1994) and Mele (1999) on the battles over the 'gentrification' of working-class districts reinvested in by the (petty) bourgeoisie in New York City in the 1990s.

[21] On this topic, one would benefit from a critical rereading of the classic analysis of Larissa Lomnitz ([1975] 1977) on the 'substitute social security system' composed of friends and neighbours in the shanty-towns of Mexico and the monograph by Carol Stack (1974) on women's networks of mutual help in a black ghetto of the Midwest. The collapse of the rural hinterland in the case of Algerian immigrants in France is gravely and bravely dissected in Rabah Ameur-Zaïmeche's award-winning picture *Bled Number One* (2006).

cushion the blow of economic hardship. Moreover, the 'shady enterprises' of the criminal and street economies, which ramified across the entire black class structure, supplied precious stopgap employment (Drake and Cayton [1945] 1993: 524–5). By contrast, a majority of the residents of the South Side in 1990 were jobless; the heart of the Black Belt has been virtually emptied of its means of collective sustenance; and bridges to wage work outside have been drastically narrowed if not cut off by the outright deproletari-anization of large segments of the local population: brothers and sisters, uncles and friends, are hard pressed to help one find employ-ment when they have themselves long been jobless (Sullivan 1989; Wilson 1996).

Nowadays, individuals durably excluded from paid employment in neighbourhoods of relegation cannot readily rely on collective informal support while they wait for new work which, moreover, may well never come or come only in the guise of insecure and inter-mittent sub-employment. To survive, they must resort to individ-ual strategies of 'self-provisioning', 'shadow work' and unreported employment, underground commerce, criminal activities and quasi-institutionalized 'hustling' (Gershuny 1983; Pahl 1987; Engbersen 1996; Wacquant 1998), which do little to reduce precariousness, since 'the distributional consequences of the pattern of informal work in industrial societies is to reinforce, rather than to reduce or to reflect, contemporary patterns of inequality' (Pahl 1989: 714). The character of the informal economy has also changed in large cities. It is more and more disjoined from the regular wage-labour sector, when it is not directly dominated by criminal trades (Barthélémy et al. 1990; Leonard 1998). It follows that its parallel circuits offer fewer and fewer entry points into the 'legit' occupational world so that youths who engage in underground work often have every chance of being durably marginalized (Bourgois 1995). If the poor neigh-bourhoods of the Fordist era were 'inner-city slums of hope', their descendants of the age of deregulated capitalism are more akin to the 'shanty-towns of despair' of the South American urban periphery – to borrow the apt expression of Susan Eckstein (1990).

6 Social fragmentation and symbolic splintering, or the unfinished genesis of the 'precariat'

Advanced marginality also differs from previous forms of urban poverty, in that it develops in the broader context of class decomposi-tion (Azémar 1992; Dudley 1994) rather than class consolidation, under the pressure of a double tendency toward precarization and *de-proletarianization* rather than toward proletarian unification and homogenization (Kronauer et al. 1993; Wilson 1996). Those who are subjected to its tropism and caught in its swirl therefore find themselves disconnected from the traditional instruments of mobilization and representation of constituted groups and, as a consequence, deprived of a *language*, a repertoire of shared images and signs through which to conceive a collective destiny and to project possible alternative futures (Stedman Jones 1983).

Ageing industrial labourers and lower-level clerks reduced to being operatives on a white-collar assembly line or made expendable by technological innovations and the spatial redistribution of productive activities; precarious and temporary workers in the deregulated service sectors; apprentices, trainees and holders of fixed-time job contracts; the unemployed running out of rights and participants in 'social minima' programmes; long-term recipients of public aid and the chronically 'homeless'; beggars, delinquents and hustlers living off the booty economy of the street; human rejects of the social and medical services and regular customers of the criminal justice system; the disenchanted offspring of the declining fractions of the autochthonous working class facing the unexpected competition of youths from ethnically stigmatized communities and of new immigrant inflows on the markets for jobs, affordable housing and credentials: how to forge a sense of a common condition and purpose when economic emergency and social necessity are so diversely configured? How are we to unify categories that, while they may occupy, briefly or durably, close positions in the structure of social and urban space in synchronic cross-section, follow divergent trajectories or embody dissimilar dispositions and orientations towards the future? And how, beyond these neighbouring solidarities, to establish tangible and efficient links with the range of unskilled employees destabilized by the desocialization of labour at all levels of the socio-occupational hierarchy (Perrin 2004)?

The very proliferation of labels used to designate the dispersed and disparate populations caught in the pincer of social and spatial marginalization – 'new poor', '*zonards*', 'the excluded', 'underclass', '*banlieues* youth', '*racailles*' or 'yobs', and the trinity of '*sans*' recently anointed in the French political debate (the job-*less*, home-*less* and paper-*less* migrants) – speaks volumes on the state of *symbolic derangement* afflicting the fringes and fissures of the recomposed social and urban structure. The absence of a common idiom around and by which to unify themselves accentuates the objective fragmentation of today's urban poor. The perennial organizational instrument of collective voice and claims-making of the urban proletariat – namely, manual trade unions and their public-sector offshoots – is proving strikingly ill-suited to tackle issues that arise and spill beyond the conventional sphere of regulated wage work, and their defensive tactics often only aggravate the dilemmas they face and deepen the multiple cleavages that separate them from the new (sub)proletarians of the margins.[22] The nascent organizations of the dispossessed of all stripes, such as unions of the jobless, homeless and paperless immigrant defence groups, and grass-roots associations battling on the multiple fronts of 'exclusion', where they have emerged, are too fragile and have yet to earn official recognition on the political stage to hope to exert more than intermittent and pointed pressure (Siméant 1998; Demazière and Pignoni 1999).

As for the Left-wing parties, to whom the task of representing the categories deprived of economic or cultural capital in the political field traditionally falls, they are much too preoccupied with their internecine struggles and entrapped in party-machine logics and media coups – when they have not openly reoriented themselves towards the educated middle classes like the Socialist Party in France and Germany – to understand the nature and scale of the upheavals refashioning neighbourhoods of relegation, on the one hand, and to envisage and engage the bold public policies necessary to stem the spiral of advanced marginalization, on the other.[23]

The very difficulty of naming the fragments, scoria and splinters of the dualized market society that collect in the dispossessed zones of the metropolis attests to the fact that the 'precariat' – if one may name thus the insecure fringes of the new proletariat – has not yet even acceded to the status of an 'object class' (Bourdieu 1977), 'compelled to form its subjectivity out of its objectification' by others. It remains in the state of a simple composite conglomerate, *collectio personarium plurium*, made up of heterogeneous individuals and categories *negatively defined* by social privation, material need and

---

[22] This is the case when unions relinquish hard-won collective rights to ward off mass layoffs or plant relocations, or when they accept the establishment of two-tier pay and benefit systems as a means of curtailing the erosion of their membership (as is the case in a number of key sectors in the United States, such as the automobile industry, telephone services and air transport).

[23] Olivier Masclet (2003) shows, based on an in-depth study of a Communist municipality in the close suburban ring of Paris, how social and spatial marginalization was accompanied by the marginalization of 'cité activists' in the local political field.

symbolic deficit. Only an immense, specifically political work of aggregation and re-presentation (in a triple cognitive, iconographic and dramaturgical sense) can hope to enable this conglomerate to accede to collective existence and thus to collective action. But this work stumbles over an unavoidable and insuperable contradiction, springing as it does from the fissiparous tendencies that are constitutive of it: the 'precariat' is a sort of *stillborn group*, whose gestation is necessarily unfinished since one can work to consolidate it only to help its members flee from it, either by finding a haven in stable wage labour or by escaping from the world of work altogether (through social redistribution and state protection). Contrary to the proletariat in the Marxist vision of history, which is called upon to abolish itself in the long term by uniting and universalizing itself, the 'precariat' can only make itself to immediately unmake itself.[24]

Implications for urban theory and research

If a form of marginality of a 'third kind', coterminous with, but different from, established forms embodied by the historic Black Belt of the United States and the traditional Red Belt of France, is indeed incubating in the neighbourhoods of relegation of the postindustrial metropolis, two challenges arise, the one intellectual and the other political, that call for a radical *revamping of inherited modes of social analysis* and political action when it comes to issues of urban inequality at century's dawn.

For social science research, each of the ideal-typical features of advanced marginality specified in the preceding section supplies a topic for empirical investigation.[25] To what extent has the texture of the wage–labour relation changed, and what are the ramifying effects, in the short and long run, of these changes upon the life strategies of various categories of wage-earners and wage-seekers trapped at the bottom of the spatial order (Castel 1995; Shulman

---

[24] For a collection of texts, documents and calls for the European mobilization of the 'precariat' (a term launched by Droits Devants, see 'Globalisation du précariat, mondialisation des résistances', *EcoRev*, May 2005), consult the multilingual site <http://republicart.net/disc/precariat/index.htm>. For an analysis of the rise of instability in the labour market and the new forms of mobilization it has generated on the margins of regular wage labour, see Perrin (2004).

[25] The selective references that follow are inserted to point to existing works that provide possible models, materials or pathways toward further analysis, or clues for comparison and critique.

2003)? What processes link the erosion of the figure of the 'collective worker' to the internal diversification of the categories shorn of credentials and skills and to the distribution of socioeconomic redundancy across groups and urban areas (Cross 1992; Uwe 2003)? How do aggregate trends in employment, flexibility, productivity, wages and social benefits concretely reshape the labour market(s) faced by the residents of dispossessed districts (Roulleau-Berger and Gautier 2002; Munger 2002). Is it the case that economic growth is now largely without repercussions in neighbourhoods of relegation and that the tightening of the labour market, when it does occur, does not 're-proletarianize' their residents (Osterman 1991; Engbersen et al. 1993)?

Is territorial stigmatization only a subtle modality of ethnic discrimination in disguise, or can one muster data demonstrating that it exerts real – and deleterious – effects independently of, and in addition to, invidious ethnoracial or ethnonational distinctions, including *within* the same group (Auyero 1999; Waley 2000; Tilly et al. 2001)? Why does spatial defamation affect public housing with special virulence, and what policies can be designed to counter the lingering negative image of such estates when they undergo urban renewal (von Hoffman 1996; Wassenberg 2004)? Is the loss of a lived sense of place in territories of urban deportation an artefact of distant observation and the nostalgic gaze of informants or a deeply felt everyday reality? And, if so, how does it differ from the experience of deracination characteristic of previous eras of working-class formation and transformation (Thrift and Williams 1987; Jones 1992; Sayad and Dupuy 1995)? What languages do the new (sub)proletarians of the polarized city borrow from or forge anew to make sense of their situation and (re)articulate a collective identity: an idiom that reconnects them to yesteryear's working class from which they issue, stresses ethnic heritage and cultural differences, pits them against the state as so many street rebels, or incites them to turn on one another, nay against themselves (Bourdieu et al. 1999; Young 2004)? And how do state structures, public policies and hegemonic ideologies *inside* the dominant class impact the social, spatial and symbolic transformation of which neighbourhoods of relegation are the precipitate?

One of the main tasks of ongoing and future research on advanced marginality is to establish how each of its six properties specifies itself differently in different countries and/or types of urban environment as a function of the social and political history of which the city and its divisions are the theatre and product.[26] Let me stress here that these questions have immediate relevance for public action, in that it is difficult to tackle this or that concrete manifestation of the new marginality unless one first elaborates an empirical assessment of its distinctive features and elucidates analytically how these features may facilitate or hinder conventional modes of policy remediation, to the point of rendering them inoperative if not counterproductive (Engbersen 2001). In this regard, it is worthwhile to pay particular attention to the discourses and categories developed by professionals in the representation of the social world – politicians, journalists, state managers, experts in both public and private sectors, civil and religious leaders, academics, activists, etc. – and the *reality effects* they wield (Bourdieu 1982) whenever they succeed in imposing their vision of the city and in defining with authority the 'problems' that accumulate in dispossessed districts as referring to some specific register: economic (unemployment, precariousness, poverty), social (inequality, disaffiliation, exclusion), ethnic (discrimination, segregation, ghettoization), cultural (individualism and 'multiculturalism'), moral (individual responsibility and work ethic), spatial (housing deterioration and ecological enclosure), criminal (delinquency and violence), or specifically political (state responsibility, solidarity, citizenship).[27]

For social scientists intending to (re)construct a general theory of contemporary societies, the urban dualisms coalescing on the threshold of the twenty-first century constitute a crucial test and raise in a pointed manner the question of the adequacy of the conceptual frameworks and analytical approaches inherited from an era of capitalist organization that is now bygone. Should one consider the categories amalgamated under the woolly and spongy terms of 'the

---

[26] This is what Janet Perlman does in a forthcoming book on the transformation of the *favelas* of Rio de Janeiro between 1969 and 2005, entitled *Marginality: From Myth to Reality*, which revisits her classic work *The Myth of Marginality* (Perlman 1976) thirty years later.

[27] It is particularly important to reconstruct the folk theories that the high state nobility and city elites develop to describe, explain and manage urban relegation and those who suffer its burden (Bourdieu et al. [1993] 1999: 219–47, 261–9, 927–39). Recent studies on marginality produced by the two dominant strands of quantitative empiricism and urban ethnography are of no help in this regard, since they focus almost exclusively on the poor themselves. The work of Sylvie Tissot (2005) on the fabrication of the problematic of 'exclusion in the *banlieues*' at the intersection of the French academic, bureaucratic and journalistic fields is a signal exception here.

excluded' in Europe and 'the underclass' in the United States – whose empirical referents are both unstable and incoherent[28] – as part of a popular class or 'working class' when that class itself is agonizing – indeed fast disappearing *in the particular historical form* in which we have known it for much of the past century (Mann 1995)? Do they stand at the fringe of the deregulated service proletariat in an entirely new class constellation? Or are the residents of districts of relegation located 'outside' the class structure altogether, having fallen into a zone of enduring social liminality wherein a specific tropism operates that would effectively isolate them from neighbouring categories (Wilson 1987; Morris 1994)?

Stigmatized territories of urban dereliction provide a propitious terrain for reformulating 'from below' in empirical terms the debate opposing the proponents of the recomposition of the class structure and the partisans of the 'death of class' (Marshall 1997; Wright 1997; Pakulski and Waters 1996). Short of entering fully into that debate, I would underline that the comparison of emerging forms of marginality in the black American ghetto and in the French urban periphery set forth in this book suggests that we need to *revise – but not renounce – class analysis* to take account of the desocialization of wage labour and to better attend to the mutually structuring relations between class, space and that rival principle of vision and division that is ethnicity (denegated as 'race' or not). In so far as the experience of long-term unemployment and persistent underemployment has become a central feature of life among unskilled workers, it is no longer possible to continue to analyse the class dynamics of the advanced societies simply in terms of occupational position, as if being 'in the paid labour force' was a homogeneous and stable status (Wright 1997). It becomes urgent to consider how mass joblessness and casual wage work, especially when they are spatially concentrated, affect the lower end of the class structure and undermine the morphological and mental consolidation of the working class from below.[29]

---

[28] These semi-scholarly notions are what Kenneth Burke calls 'terministic screens': they hide more than they reveal and constitute yet another obstacle to an adequate grasp of the reconfiguring of marginality in the post-Fordist city.

[29] Erik Wright (1997: 103) discusses joblessness briefly to check that varying rates of unemployment do not skew his measurements of the evolution of the size of the working class. His extended consideration of theories of proletarianization is not matched by a similar treatment of *de*proletarianization, which he construes only as entailing an 'upward' climb into 'the expert and expert-manager class location', thus missing the corresponding 'downward' slide into casual labour and the informal

Similarly, have the categories of 'race', 'minority', and 'immigrant', which play a determinative role in the social genesis and political treatment of districts of dereliction, not been rendered analytically problematic, nay obsolete *in their habitual conformation,* by the fact that their empirical contents have become strongly internally differentiated, unstable and dispersed, referring to widely disparate classification grids, social trajectories and lived experiences inside of the same society (Koser and Lutz 1999; Rumbaut and Portes 2001) as well as across societies and eras? Lest the reader (mis)take these remarks for some 'postmodernist' call to cast off the indispensable instruments of a critical and 'concrete science of empirical reality' (to borrow the words of Max Weber), and with them the *least imperfect* intellectual weapons we have at our disposal in our effort to understand and eventually change the world, let me stress that recognizing that the concepts of class and race should be re-examined and modified, perhaps even overhauled, *so as to increase their theoretical potency,* does not come down to saying (i) that they are devoid of analytic and political value; (ii) that objective class divisions and ethnoracial cleavages have suddenly vanished into thin air; or (iii) that they exist only in the form of local, transient, infinitely malleable and forever fugitive 'discursive' accomplishments, as some radically constructivist (or deconstructionist) approaches would have it.

Finally, if (national or postnational) *citizenship* is, along with class, ethnic affiliation (racialized or not), gender and age, a central pivot of 'exclusionary closure' and entitlement to goods and services distributed in the name of the collectivity at the margins of the city, then it is urgent that we develop a refined sociological theory of this institution central to capitalist modernity yet still peripheral to the study of urban transformations, in spite of the explosion of citizenship studies over the past decade (but see Holston 1999 and Bloemraad 2002). Models of the new sociospatial order of the polarized metropolis would benefit from drawing and building on recent studies of citizenship that have laboured to revise the overly evolutionary, progressivist and consensual model inherited from T. H. Marshall, and to take into account the multiple fractures of citizenship, its

---

economy. Only in a footnote at the very end of his book *Class Counts* does Wright (1997: 531) concede that he has not addressed 'the expansion of the so-called "underclass" – the part of the population that is economically oppressed but marginalized from the process of capitalist exploitation. It is certainly plausible that one of the ramifications of the relative decline of the working class in the labour force is the expansion of the "relative surplus population," the part of the population that cannot find a place within capitalist class relations.'

increasing disconnection from the national and its variegated 'pluralization', including in and through urban space.[30] In turn, rethinking the mechanisms that link group membership and advanced marginality will require examining up close what 'mediating institutions' (Lamphere 1992) need to be bolstered or invented to 'resolidarize' the city and beget through the agency of public institutions the social integration that previously resulted from incorporation into a compact class or ethnoracial community. All of this points to the pressing need to go beyond the rudimentary paradigm centred on the 'state-and-market' duet that implicitly undergirds most current thinking in social science and public policy, without for that matter falling into the conceptual morass of 'civil society' (this inchoate notion that, all too often, stops analysis precisely where it should get started).

Towards a revolution in public policy

At the political level, the onset and spread of advanced marginality pose formidable dilemmas and demand a radical questioning of traditional modes of state intervention. It is a delusion to think that bringing people back into the labour market will durably reduce poverty in the city – this much is clearly demonstrated by the continuous swelling of the ranks of the 'working poor' in the United States and their appearance in Western Europe as overall employment has expanded to record levels along with substandard job slots. This is because the wage-labour relation itself has become a source of built-in economic insecurity and social instability at the bottom of the revamped class structure. In the face of the diffusion of desocialized work and its fixation in neighbourhoods of relegation, standard Keynesian or 'social democratic' modes of state intervention are doomed to stall, disappoint and eventually discredit themselves, paving the way for a further expansion of market rule. As for conservative policies of *laissez-faire et laissez-passer*, they need not detain us here since *causes* of advanced marginality can hardly be counted upon to provide *remedies* for it. Comparative analysis shows that these policies have everywhere produced more poverty and life

[30] Among the works partaking of the remarkable flowering of citizenship studies oriented toward the question of urban inequalities, one can note Bouamama (1992), Morris (1994), Soysal (1994), Roche and Van Berkel (1997) and Crouch et al. (2001).

instability along with higher socioeconomic inequality (Esping-Andersen and Regini 2000).

If it is true that the functional linkages between economic growth and employment, and between employment and individual or household subsistence strategies via the 'family wage', have been loosened, nay severed, then social policies aimed at combating advanced marginality will have to *reach 'beyond employment' and extend outside of the market paradigm* that upholds it to generate efficacious solutions (Offe and Heinze 1992). Owing to the ever-tighter constraints induced by regional and global interdependencies, generalized 'reflation' of the economy now appears to be beyond the means of any one country, and limited public job creation schemes are clearly insufficient to make a sizable dent in structural and disguised unemployment (this much the French experience of the end of the 1980s and 1990s has taught us). The route of the prolific development of low-pay precarious service job pursued by the United States, symbolized by the meteoric rise of Wal-Mart to the rank of first employer in the land (see box), promises only to spread poverty around and to generalize insecurity (Freeman 1994; Osterman 1999), as does the state retraction and labour flexibility option favoured by employers the world over for all-too-obvious reasons.

The social cul-de-sac of the Wal-Mart route

With a staff of 1.2 million of whom 30 per cent are part-timers, Wal-Mart pays its 'sales associates' (the most common position) an average of $8.23 an hour, coming to a maximum of $13,861 per year, or nearly a thousand dollars under the federal 'poverty line' for a family of three (meanwhile, its CEO Lee Scott received a compensation package worth 23 million dollars in 2004, on global revenues approaching $300 billion). One-half of its employees are not covered by its medical plan; its two pension plans fail to guarantee a fixed income to retirees, and most of the company's retirement assets are invested in its own stock (as was the case with Enron). As a result, tends of thousands of Wal-Mart staff in many states have to resort to welfare, Medicaid, housing assistance, and other government support to sustain themselves even as they work.

The retail giant has a policy of pushing out older employees with more seniority to keep a younger, healthier, and lower-wage workforce that thereby remains largely ineligible for its meagre (and costly) benefit plans. Its rule of 'open availability' requires that 'associates' be open to flexible scheduling 24 hours a day 7 days a week (nearly half of its 4,000 stores are open around the clock), which greatly facilitates dumping older staff. Wal-Mart has also adopted 'wage caps' that limit the maximum amount an employee can earn in a given job, irrespective of seniority and companywide pay increases. Finally, it has repeatedly been found to violate labour laws by employing illegal immigrants and underage youths, and by forcing its associates to work overtime and during lunch breaks for free, under fear of being dismissed or seeing their weekly hours abruptly reduced at the whim of supervisors to levels that would force them to starve or resign.

This despotic labour regime is made possible by Wal-Mart's ferocious campaigns against unionization and lavish donations to the coffers of politicians from both ruling parties. Wal-Mart labour policy is enthusiastically supported by Wall Street investment houses, which see it as a model of efficient management of labour (treated as an adjustment variable and disposable resource) resolutely turned toward maximizing shareholder value.

Only one viable solution seems to remain: in the short run, to reestablish and/or expand state services so as to guarantee a minimally equitable provision of basic public goods across all urban areas and immediately alleviate the dire hardship created by the *social disinvestment* entailed in the retrenchment – partial (in Continental Europe) or wholesale (in the United States) – of public institutions in territories of relegation over the past two decades; and, over the longer run, to relax the obligation of participation in wage work and enlarge social redistribution so as (i) to reduce labour supply and (ii) to restabilize and restructure the system of strategies of reproduction and mobility of the households trapped at the bottom of the dualizing hierarchy of classes and places.

It is high time for us to forsake the untenable assumption that a large majority of the adults of advanced society can or will see their basic needs met by lifelong formal employment (or by the permanent employment of members of their households) in the commodified economy. This is to say that public policies designed to counter advanced marginality must go against the grain of the recent slide or drift towards 'workfare' designed to make the obligation of low-wage (sub)employment a norm of citizenship. They must facilitate and smooth out the severance of subsistence from work, income from paid labour, and social participation from participation in wage employment. They must, that is, fully recognize and institutionalize the 'right to life' which Karl Polanyi (1944) counterposed to the dictatorship of the unfettered market and which has already been *de facto* introduced in a blind, partial and selective mode by evolving state programmes and civic standards. As the noted ILO economist Guy Standing writes:

> If the labour market cannot generate income security, as presumed in the creation of the postwar social consensus, then, to allow the 'labour market' to operate efficiently, social policy should *decouple income security from the labour market*. (Standing 1993: 57)

This decoupling can be effected at once by instituting a guaranteed minimum income or 'basic income' plan, that is, by granting unconditionally to all members of a given society on an individual basis, without means test or work requirement, adequate means of subsistence and social participation. Thanks to their stupendous wealth and continually increasing economic productivity, the rich capitalist societies of the twenty-first century have the means for this; it only remains for them to develop the political will and collective intelligence to do it.[31]

Whether it is done incrementally by piecemeal expansion of the reach of currently existing income support programmes, or through the 'big-bang' creation *ex nihilo* of brand new sets of protective and redistributive measures, the institution of a 'citizen's wage' is a tall order that requires a thorough revision of our accepted conceptions of work, money, time, utility, collective welfare and social justice. Philippe Van Parijs (1993: 7) rightly sees in it 'a profound reform that belongs in the same league as the abolition of slavery or the introduction of universal suffrage'. Yet, however utopian or unpalatable, costly or unrealistic, it might appear to us today, one thing is certain: as persistent and acute marginality of the kind that has plagued American and European cities over the past two decades

---

[31] The excellent collection of essays by Van Parijs (1993) argues the case for (and against) basic income on grounds of liberty, equality, economic efficiency and community. See also Brittan and Webb (1990), Fitzpatrick (1997) and Van Parijs (2001), as well as the research and evaluations of policy experiments amassed by the BIEN (Basic Income European Network, on line at <www.etes.ucl.ac.be/BIEN>) in Europe and the BIG network (Basic Income Guarantee, <www.usbig.net>) in North America.

continues to mount, strategies for the 'government of misery' (Procacci 1993) will have to be reorganized in ways so drastic that they can hardly be foretold today.

Before the French Revolution, the very idea of overturning the monarchy was properly unthinkable: how indeed was a child-people to live and prosper without the protection and guidance of their fatherly king (Hunt 1992)? Yet 1789 came, and came by storm. The institutionalization of the citizenship right to subsistence and well-being outside the yoke of the market could well be the Bastille of the new millennium.

9

Logics of Urban Polarization
from Below

All social phenomena are, to some degree, the work of collective
will, and collective will implies choice between different possible
options. . . . The realm of the social is the realm of modality.
Marcel Mauss, 'Les civilisations. Éléments et formes' (1929)

By way of conclusion, this chapter deepens the analysis of the major
modalities of emergence and diffusion of new forms of urban inequality and marginality in the advanced societies of the capitalist West at
the turn of the century. These forms are fuelling what can be syn-
thetically described as a process of *polarization 'from below'* in that
they multiply unstable social positions and ensnare vulnerable
populations at an increasing remove from the middle and upper tiers
of the structure of classes and places. A complementary process of
polarization 'from above' operates at the other end of social and physical space, which tends to concentrate and unify (within a city or
country as well as across national borders) the powers held by the
owners and managers of large corporations, top professionals in law
and culture, members of the high state nobility and the officials and
experts working for international organizations that compose the
new transnational ruling class (Sklair 2001; Dezalay and Garth 2002;
Bourdieu [1989] 1996). Although analytically distinct, these two
processes are closely linked empirically, and they combine to redraw
the social and spatial structure of the big cities, which will be
approached here through its lower pole. The argument unfolds in
two steps.[1]

[1] A more detailed analysis than can be given here would gain from differentiating
between three modalities of urban polarization: (1) the deepening of the objective
gap between opposed sets of positions, as measured by the social and spatial distance

First, I further elaborate a compact characterization of what I take to be a *new regime of urban marginality*. This regime has been ascendant for the past three decades or so, that is, since the close of the Fordist era defined by standardized industrial production, mass consumption, the patriarchal nuclear family, and a Keynesian social contract binding them together under the tutelage of the social welfare state (Amin 1994; Boyer and Durand 1998). Yet, as I indicated in the preceding chapter, the full impact of this regime lies ahead of us, because its advent is tied to the development of the most advanced sectors of capitalist economies – this is why I give it the designation of *advanced* marginality. It is not a residue from the past or a transitional phenomenon, as theories of deindustrialization and the skills or spatial mismatch hypothesis would have it, any more than it is the result of a 'lack of entrepreneurial spirit' in poor neighbourhoods (Teitz and Chapple 1998), but a harbinger of the future. Identifying the distinctive properties of this emerging regime of urban marginality and the forces that drive its consolidation as part of the ascendant mode of capitalist growth helps us to pinpoint what exactly is new about the 'new poverty' of which the city is the site and fount. It also enables us better to discern why established policy remedies, based on accelerating economic growth and extending the wage work sphere, whether it be by deregulating the lower segments of the labour market, subsidizing low-pay jobs, lowering the real cost of unskilled labour or instituting 'workfare'-style programmes to force people into existing employment slots (Peck 2001), are fundamentally unsuited to correcting it.

I then turn to the question that has implicitly informed or explicitly guided European debates on the resurgence of destitution, division and tension in the transforming metropolis over the past dozen years: namely, are we witnessing an *epochal convergence of urban poverty regimes across the Atlantic* on the US pattern? Backed by the methodical comparison of the black American ghetto of Chicago and a working-class estate of the deindustrializing periphery of Paris presented in the second part of the book, I argue that, contrary to widespread journalistic portrayals and the hasty pronouncements of scholars inspired by the political mood of the day more than by solid empirical investigation, such is not the case: although it is fuelled by

---

that separates them (architecture); (2) the growth of inequality in *access* to dominant and dominated positions (mobility); (3) variations in the *number* of agents occupying them (morphology). A given metropolitan structure can become polarized along one or another of these axes or, indeed, through any combination of them.

common structural forces, urban relegation follows different social and spatial dynamics on the two continents that correspond to the distinct state configurations, paths for civic incorporation, and urban legacies of the Old and New Worlds.

Lumping these variegated dynamics under the catch-all term 'Americanization' – or one of its derivatives, such as ethnicization, ghettoization or multiculturalism, as a number of commentators of the urban scene have been wont to do – is neither empirically illuminating nor analytically correct. The combined resurgence of inequality and regained hegemony of US-rooted concepts across the globe (Bourdieu and Wacquant [1998] 1999) must not blind us to the persistent divergences in the ways whereby societies produce, organize and categorize marginality as well as react to urban polarization, *even as its structural sources are similar* across nations. The *decomposition of working-class territories* as the physical and social space for the assembly and deployment of strategies of reproduction of the urban proletariat, on one side, and the *implosion of the black ghetto* as mechanism for the economic exploitation and social ostracization of a dishonoured ethnic group, on the other, are not homologous processes, even when they produce similar symptoms (material deprivation, family instability, degradation of housing, street crime, etc.) and parallel perceptions (such as the lived experience of indignity, the stigma of place, and the everyday climate of anguish and fear). But the persistence of historically anchored differences between US and European neighbourhoods of relegation is itself a historical phenomenon, and therefore it is *historically reversible*. This implies that the state elites of European countries must beware of pursuing public policies inspired by neoliberalism that reinforce the blind force of market sanctions and discriminatory biases in the allocation of space, jobs, public goods and people. By contributing to destabilizing and isolating definite urban zones, these policies encourage their populations to pursue divergent and even oppositional life strategies that can set off self-reinforcing cycles of social involution and cultural closure akin to those that underlie the hyperghetto in the United States.[2]

---

[2] The recent importation and wide diffusion across Europe of the language of 'diversity' in government and corporate circles, for the ostensive purpose of soothing festering ethnoracial divisions, is the cultural counterpart and policy complement to the programmes of economic deregulation, state withdrawal and workfare modelled on the United States, along with punitive policies targeted at the disruptive fractions of the urban proletariat.

This last chapter, then, is an effort to diagnose the social forces and forms with which our present urban predicament is pregnant and that promise to fashion the metropolis of tomorrow – unless we exercise our 'collective will', as Marcel Mauss (1929) urged us, and act to check mechanisms and steer current trends in a different direction. It stresses that, for all the talk of urban rebirth and renewed prosperity that accompanied the millenarist celebration of 2000, for those trapped in the lower reaches of the dualizing class structure and for the declining lower-class neighbourhoods of formerly industrial cities to which they find themselves consigned, the prosperity of the 'new economy' has yet to come and the rosy promise of the 'information age' remains a bitter fairy tale.[3]

Symptoms of advanced marginality in the city

The close of the twentieth century has witnessed a momentous makeover of the roots, makeup and consequences of urban poverty in Western society. The latest wave of 'modernization' of advanced economies, that is, the acceleration of the process of capitalist rationalization triggered by the planetary restructuring of the system of commodity production and distribution under the aegis of the 'shareholder value', the crystallization of a new international division of labour (fostered by the frantic velocity of financial flows and increased mobility of the labour factor across porous national boundaries), and the growth of novel knowledge-intensive industries based on information technologies and spawning a dual occupational structure (Castells 1989; Fligstein 1997), has been accompanied by what one might call the *modernization of misery*: the ascent of a new regime of urban marginality that contrasts sharply with that which prevailed during the three decades after World War II (as specified in the previous chapter).[4]

[3] Manuel Castells (1998: 128–52) saw well that the emergence of a globalized 'informational mode of production' has for its corollary the creation of vast 'black holes', not only at the international level but also at the core and on the peripheries of First World cities.

[4] One can see a validation of this analysis based on international comparison in the fact that Robert Castel (1995: 402) arrives at a similar diagnosis through a historical approach: his reconstruction of the genesis of the 'wage-earning society' leads him to conclude that 'the casualization of labour and unemployment are built into the present dynamic of modernization. They are the inevitable consequences of new modes of organizing employment, the long shadow thrown by industrial restructuring and the struggle for competitiveness.'

Whereas in the Fordist age poverty in the Western metropolis used to be mainly residual or cyclical, embedded in working-class communities, geographically diffuse and considered remediable by means of the continued expansion of the commodity form, it now appears to be increasingly persistent if not permanent, disconnected from macroeconomic fluctuations, and fixated upon neighbourhoods of relegation enshrouded in a sulfurous aura, within which social isolation and alienation feed upon each other as the chasm between those consigned there and the broader society deepens. The consolidation of this new regime of urban marginality is treading diverse routes and taking different concrete forms in the various countries of the First World, in keeping with the variety of national modalities of organization of capitalism (Crouch and Streeck 1997). In the United States and the United Kingdom, it has been greatly facilitated by the aggressive campaign of deunionization conducted by employers and by the policy of wholesale state retrenchment and marketization of public goods pursued over the past two decades by conservative parties as well as by the traditionally progressive parties (the New Democrats and New Labour) after their neoliberal *aggiornamento*. The American pattern is also highly peculiar, in that the rigid and stubborn sociospatial ostracization imposed upon blacks in the major urban centres has powerfully inflected, concentrated and exacerbated the rise of marginality (Massey and Denton 1993). In other nations endowed with robust welfare states, whether of the corporatist, Catholic or social-democratic type, and far less segregated cities (Domburg-de Rooij and Musterd 2002), such as northern Europe and Scandinavia, the onset of advanced marginality has been partly contained but not wholly prevented. And it has gradually become embroiled with the burning question of the 'integration' of postcolonial migrants and Third World refugees, as reflected in the public anguish over the crystallization of immigrant 'ghettos' gripping the continent from Malmö to Marseilles and Madrid to Munich (see, e.g., Martiniello 1995; Hadjimichalis and Sadler 1995; Pred 1997).

Whatever the label used to designate it – 'underclass' in America and Great Britain, 'new poverty' in the Netherlands, Germany and northern Italy, 'exclusion' in France, Belgium, Spain and certain Nordic countries – the telltale signs of advanced marginality are immediately familiar to even the casual observer of the Western metropolis: homeless men and families vainly scrambling about for shelter and the means to regain control over lives cast adrift; beggars on public transportation playing music or spinning heart-rending tales of personal disaster and dereliction, or kneeling on the sidewalk, prostrated, to plead for petty cash, clutching a cardboard sign laconically broadcasting 'I am hungry'; soup kitchens teeming not only with drifters and assorted human wreckage but also with wage-earners in situations of chronic underemployment;[5] the continuous undertow of low-grade predatory crime and the insolent prosperity of the parallel economies of the street spearheaded by the retail sale of drugs; the proliferation of marginal trades of street scavenging and foraging redolent of Third World cities; the mingling despondency and rage of youths shut out from gainful employment who cannot move out of their parents' house and get their own life and family started; and the bitterness of older workers made obsolete by dein-dustrialization and technological upgrading, or by firm strategies of 'externalization' of the workforce favouring younger and fresher employees; the sense of retrogression, indignity and insecurity that pervades dispossessed neighbourhoods locked in a seemingly unstop-pable and bottomless spiral of deterioration; and, lastly, the rise of public violence, overt xenophobia and hostility towards and amongst the poor, which translates, for instance, into the proliferation of penal measures and police tactics aimed at cleaning up the street by repress-ing loitering, panhandling and assorted 'sub-criminal behaviours' propelled by a 'criminology of intolerance' (Young 1999: 121–40).

Everywhere state elites, public policy experts and city managers have become acutely concerned with and eager to prevent or contain the 'disorders' brewing within and around expanding enclaves of urban perdition. Thus the sprouting of research on urban decline and the unravelling of lower-class neighbourhoods supported by various national and transnational bodies, such as the European Commission (with its Targeted Socio-Economic Programme on exclusion and integration, among others), the OECD, and even NATO on the European side, and major philanthropic and research foundations (Ford, Rockefeller, MacArthur, Social Science Research Council, Urban Institute, etc.) on American shores.

Four structural logics fuel the new urban poverty

But the distinctive structural properties of 'modernized misery' in the city are much less evident than its concrete manifestations. In

[5] For a kaleidoscopic portrait from below of the life of the social rejects driven onto the streets in France and North America, and a sample of their tactics for material survival and mutual recognition, read Laé and Murard (1995), Snow and Anderson (1993), Lanzarini (2000) and Hagan and McCarthy (1997).

the preceding chapter, we took a cross-sectional view to uncover six distinctive properties of the emerging regime of marginality which can be observed in nearly all of the advanced countries, with diverse national inflections (corresponding broadly to national constellations of market, state and family).[6] Put in longitudinal perspective, these six properties can be grasped as the product of four logics that jointly reshape the features of urban poverty in rich societies and foster the multiplication of positions situated at or near the bottom of the social and spatial hierarchy. These logics of the fin de siècle stand in stark contrast to those that commanded the composition and distribution of poverty in the era of Fordist expansion from the close of World War II to the middle of the 1970s (and, in an attenuated form, for most of the long century of the apogee of industrial capitalism from 1880 to 1980). They are the resurgence of social inequality under the press of occupational dualization; the fragmentation of the wage–labour form; the retraction of the social welfare state; and spatial concentration and territorial denigration.

1   Macrosocial dynamic: occupational dualization and the resurgence of inequality

The new urban marginality results not from economic backwardness, sluggishness or decline but from *rising inequality in the context of rapid economic advancement* and overall prosperity. Perhaps the most enigmatic attribute of the new marginality, indeed, is that it has spread and hardened in an era of capricious but sturdy growth that has brought about a generalized upgrading of standards of living and spectacular material betterment for the more privileged members of First World societies.

Notwithstanding the ritualized talk of 'crisis' among the political personnel through the past two decades, the leading capitalist countries have all seen their collective wealth expand significantly since the 'oil shocks' of the mid-1970s. In constant currency, the Gross Domestic Product of the United States grew by 130 per cent between

---

[6] Esping-Andersen (1999) offers a sustained argument stressing postindustrial diversity: the transformation of social space in advanced countries is not dictated by homogenizing global trends such as tertiarization, digital technologies and international economic alignments, but is decisively shaped also by varied combinations of household economies, national welfare regimes and institutional frameworks channelling market forces. The same diversity can be expected to obtain at the bottom of the social and spatial order and to shape multiple profiles of urban poverty within the parameters of advanced marginality set out in the previous chapter.

1975 and 2000, and those of France, the United Kingdom and Germany by 75–80 per cent. But along with average enrichment came the deepening of disparities: opulence and indigence, luxury and penury, copiousness and impecuniousness have flourished right alongside each other. Thus the city of Hamburg, by some measurements the richest in Europe, sports both the highest proportion of millionaires and the highest incidence of public assistance receipt in Germany (Dangschat 1994), while New York City and Los Angeles are home to the largest colonies of the upper class on the planet, but also to the greatest armies of the homeless and indigent in the Western hemisphere (Mollenkopf and Castells 1991; Scott and Soja 1996).

The two phenomena, though apparently contradictory, are in point of fact closely linked. For the novel paths for productivity- and profit-seeking in the 'high-tech', degraded manufacturing, and business and financial service sectors that drive turn-of-the-century capitalism tend to split the workforce and to polarize access to, and especially rewards from, durable employment. Postindustrial modernization translates, on the one hand, into the multiplication of highly skilled and highly remunerated positions for university-trained professional and technical staff and, on the other, into the deskilling and outright elimination of millions of jobs as well as the swelling of casual employment slots for uneducated workers (Sassen 1991b; Carnoy et al. 1993; Gregory et al. 2000; Dangschat 2002). The growing concentration of wealth, in the form of income, financial assets and property, at the top of the class structure has even spawned a vigorous demand for a postindustrial brand of personal chefs, high-priced butlers and urban domestics, the latter supplied mostly by cheap female immigrant labour that caters to the full gamut of household needs of the new corporate nobility: driving their children to and from school and assorted cultural activities, walking and tending pets, cooking, cleaning, as well as provisioning the home and providing for personal security. What is more, today jobless production and growth in many economic sectors are not dystopian possibilities but a bittersweet reality (Rifkin 1995). Witness the virtual emptying of the harbour of Rotterdam, perhaps the most modern in the world and a major contributor to the rise of unemployment in this Dutch city above the 20 per cent mark in the middle of the 1990s.

The more the revamped capitalist economy advances, the wider and deeper the imprint of the new marginality, and the more plentiful the ranks of those thrown into the throes of material misery and social insecurity with little respite or recourse, even as official unemployment drops and national income increases in the country. In September 1994, the US Census Bureau reported that the American poverty rate had risen to a ten-year high of 15.1 per cent (corresponding to a total of 40 million poor people in the richest society on the planet) even though America had just experienced two years of robust economic expansion. Five years later, the poverty rate in large cities had barely budged in spite of the sturdiest phase of economic growth in national history and the lowest official employment rate sported in three decades (in 2004, there were still 37 million poor for a rate of 13 per cent, even as the economy was supposed to be near 'full employment'). Meanwhile the European Union (with fifteen members) officially tallied a record 52 million poor, 17 million unemployed and 3 million homeless – and counting – even though the continent had regained economic growth and improved its global competitiveness. As major multinational firms such as Renault, Michelin and Total in France were turning unprecedented profits and seeing the value of their stock zoom up, they also expanded the use of subcontracting and 'turned out' workers by the thousands.

In addition to being rooted deep in the very structure of the new capitalism, advanced marginality has been 'decoupled' from cyclical fluctuations in the national and international economy. The consequence is that upswings in aggregate income and employment have at best modest effects upon living conditions and life chances in the neighbourhoods of relegation of Europe and the United States, whereas downswings cause further deterioration and distress in them. Unless this disconnection is remedied by social and fiscal policies reducing the scale of inequalities and redistributing resources downward, further economic growth promises to produce more urban dislocation and demoralization among those thrust and trapped at the bottom of the emerging urban order.

2   Economic dynamic: the desocialization of wage labour

The new urban marginality is the by-product of a double transformation of the sphere of work filtered, as it were, through the spatial, cultural and political structures that mould the working class. The first is *quantitative* and entails the disappearance of millions of low-skilled jobs under the concomitant pressure of automation, competition from cheap labour overseas, and the displacement of the economic centre of gravity towards personal and business services.

The other is *qualitative*, involving the deterioration and dispersion of basic conditions of employment, remuneration and social insurance for all wage-earners save those in the most protected sectors. These two transformations have combined to destabilize the working class, render its traditional mode of reproduction obsolete, and feed the process of polarization from below.

From the time when Friedrich Engels ([1845] 1987) wrote his classic exposé on the condition of the working class in Manchester's factories to the crisis of the great industrial heartlands of Euro-American capitalism a century and a half later, one could rightly assume that expanding wage labour supplied a viable and efficacious solution to the problem of urban poverty. Under the new economic regime, this presupposition is at best dubious and at worst plain wrong – and in both cases it turns out to be very costly in social terms. First, a significant *fraction of the working class has been made redundant* and constitutes an 'absolute surplus population' that will likely never find stable work again. This is particularly true of older industrial workers laid off due to plant shutdowns and relocation: they are unlikely to have (or to be in a position to acquire) the skills and contacts needed to reconvert themselves into flexible service workers, even during prosperous phases (Dudley 1994). This is also the case with youths who exited the school system at an early age, who are without qualifications or experience in the world of the firm, and who find themselves pushed to the tail end of the 'queue' of job applicants, due to discrimination based on their physical appearance (skin colour), manner of speaking or demeanour, or residence in a stigmatized estate (Petersen and Mortimer 1994; MacDonald 1997; Richard 2000). At any rate, given the loosening of the functional linkage between macroeconomic activity and social conditions in the deprived enclaves of the First World metropolis, and considering the productivity increases permitted by automation, computerization and the strategies of labour externalization of large firms, even miraculous rates of growth would not suffice to absorb back into the workforce all those who have been *deproletarianized* – that is, durably and forcibly expelled from the wage-labour market to be replaced by a mix of machines, cheap part-time labour, or immigrant and foreign workers (Rifkin 1995).

Second, and more crucially, it is the character of the wage–labour relation itself that has changed over the past two decades in a manner such that it no longer grants foolproof protection against the menace of poverty even to those who enter it. With the expansion of 'contingent' labour, part-time and 'flexitime', and temporary work and short-term contracts that carry fewer or no benefits,[7] the erosion of union protection, the diffusion of two-tier pay scales, the resurgence of sweatshops, piece rates and famine wages, and the growing privatization of social goods such as health coverage, *the wage-labour contract itself has become a source of fragmentation and precariousness* rather than social homogeneity and security for those consigned to the peripheral segments of the employment sphere (see Mabit and Boissonnat 1995; MacDonald and Sirianni 1996; Leonard 1998).

During the golden age of Fordism, wage labour tended to homogenize the workforce by creating a community of fate along a linear lifecourse pegged on the '40–50–60' schema: 40 hours of employment per week for about 50 weeks of the year until one retires at age 60 (to average standards roughly across countries for the second half of the twentieth century). With the onset of *desocialized wage labour*, employment no longer supplies a common temporal and social framework because the terms of the labour contract are increasingly volatile and individualized, job tenures are shorter and unstable, and a growing number of positions do not entail a collective mechanism of protection against material deprivation, illness or joblessness, not to mention adequate retirement (Barker and Christensen 1998; Osterman 1999). In short, whereas economic growth and the correlative expansion of the wage sector used to provide a universal cure for poverty, today they are part and parcel of the problem for those at the foot of the occupational ladder.

3   Political dynamic: the recoiling of the social state

The dualization and desocialization of labour are not the only factors fuelling the rise of the new urban poverty. For, alongside market forces, welfare states are major producers and shapers of urban inequality and marginality. States not only deploy programmes

---

[7] Recall that, in the United States, labour legislation imposes no obligations on employers in matters of social and medical insurance, and fails to mandate paid (or unpaid) holidays and dismissal procedures (most low-skilled staff can be fired without motive, forewarning or compensation). The existence of 'benefits' – i.e., the 'social advantages' granted by firms to their employees on a case-by-case basis – goes hand in hand with the level of qualification required for the job and/or the presence of unions (a portion of these benefits is sometimes paid to the union, which then functions in the manner of a pension fund at the level of the firm or local industry). The vast majority of unskilled jobs are thus not only insecure and underpaid, but they also have no attached pension or insurance rights: in 1995, 65 per cent of wage-earners without a high-school diploma had no health coverage and 79 per cent had no retirement programme to contribute to (Freeman 1998).

and policies designed to 'mop up' the most glaring consequences of economic transformations and to cushion (or not) their social and spatial impact downstream. They also act upstream by helping to determine who gets relegated, how, where and for how long. States are major engines of stratification in their own right (Esping-Andersen 1990 and 1999), and nowhere more so than at the bottom of the sociospatial order: they provide or preclude access to adequate schooling and job training; they set conditions for labour market entry and exit via administrative rules for hiring, firing and retirement; they stipulate basic employment conditions and minimal standards of consumption; they distribute (or fail to distribute) basic public goods, such as housing and health care, and provide supplementary income through the mediation of public aid, social transfers and public services; they actively support or hinder certain household configurations and family arrangements; and they co-determine both the material intensity and the geographic exclusivity and density of misery through a welter of administrative and fiscal schemes governing the uses of space (Newman and Thornley 1996; Cullingworth 1997).

The *retraction and disarticulation of the social welfare state* are two major causes of the material deterioration and social denudement agglomerating in the neighbourhoods of relegation of the metropolis of advanced societies. This is particularly obvious in the United States, where the population covered by social insurance schemes has shrunk steadily for three decades (fewer than one-third of laid-off wage-earners are covered by unemployment benefits), while means-tested programmes targeted at the poor were cut and gradually turned into instruments of surveillance and control. The 'welfare reform' concocted by the Republican Congress and signed into law by President Clinton in the summer of 1996 is emblematic of this logic (Wacquant 1997b). It has replaced the entitlement to public aid with the obligation to work, if necessary at insecure and flexible jobs for substandard wages, imposed on all able-bodied persons, including young mothers caring for infants. It has amputated funding for assistance and established a lifetime cap on public support. Lastly, it has transferred administrative responsibility from the federal government to the fifty states and their 3,000-odd counties, thus aggravating existing inequalities in access to welfare and accelerating the incipient privatization of social policy (Katz 1986, 1996: 312–21).

A similar logic of curtailment and decentralized delegation ('devolution' in US political lingo) has presided over the wholesale or piecemeal makeover of social protection and transfer systems in the United Kingdom, Germany, Italy and France. Even the Netherlands and the Scandinavian countries have implemented measures designed to reduce access to public support, to curb the growth of social budgets, and to 'activate' labour market participation (Leibfried and Pierson 1995). Everywhere the litany of 'globalization' and the budgetary strictures imposed by the Maastricht Treaty (and successor treaties of the same ilk) have served to justify these measures and excuse social disinvestment in formerly working-class areas highly dependent on state provision of public goods. The growing and glaring shortcomings of national welfare schemes have spurred regional and municipal authorities to institute their own stopgap support programmes in response to extreme distress (especially to cushion the local consequences of the swelling of the ranks of the long-term unemployed and homeless), which in turn has increased the administrative complexity, heterogeneity and disparities of social provision (Bagnasco and Le Galès 1997).

Now, the singsong on the obsolescence, and therefore irrelevance, of the 'national state' has become a commonplace of intellectual conversation and policy nostrums the world over. It is fashionable nowadays among ruling circles (of the Right and Left indifferently) to bemoan the incapacity of central political institutions to check the mounting social dislocations consequent upon global capitalist restructuring. But significant and persistent discrepancies in the rates and flows of upward and downward mobility, the incidence and persistence of poverty, and the degree of social isolation of the unemployed and poor urban residents in different countries suggest that news of the death of the welfare state has been greatly exaggerated (Therborn 1996; Gallie and Paugam 2000; Pierson 2001). Thus, at the beginning of the 1990s, tax and social transfer programmes lifted a majority of poor households to near the median national income level in the Netherlands (62 per cent) and France (52 per cent); in West Germany only one-third of poor families (i.e., with an income less than one-half of the national median figure) escaped poverty thanks to government support, and in the United States *virtually none*. Destitution has been eliminated among children in Scandinavian countries, while it plagues one child in six (and every other black child) in the United States (McFate et al. 1995). Likewise, the type of social protection (universalist, work-centred or liberal) has a decisive impact on the situation of the unemployed in European countries: around 1995, 67 per cent of the unemployed in Denmark lived below the poverty line before receiving social transfers, but only 7 per cent did so *after* the transfers; the corresponding percentages were 61 per cent and 51 per cent in the United Kingdom and 49 per cent and 23 per cent in France. In other words, state programmes were 'rescuing' 83 per cent of unemployed Danes from poverty, but only 38 per cent of their French equivalents and fewer than 10 per cent of their British cousins (Nolan et al. 2000: 92–5). Another major political source of variation among advanced societies is the degree and kind of action their central and local governments undertake on the housing front in terms of the building, rental, siting and upkeep of abodes accessible to the lower class. Here again, public housing policies remain distinctively national programmes (Oxley and Smith 1996) that powerfully impact the fate and shape of the new urban (sub)proletariat everywhere.

In sum, national states and their local extensions have long exerted, and continue to exert, a decisive influence over the nature and scale of inequalities and the sociospatial distribution of poverty – and they remain perfectly capable of ensuring high levels of wages and social protection, while thwarting the accumulation of hardships among the same populations and territories, so long as those who steer them have the political will to do so (Alisch and Dangschat 1998; Gregory et al. 2000; Huber and Stephens 2001). Consequently, it is imperative to bring the state back to the epicentre of the comparative sociology of urban marginality as a *generative* and not merely as a *remedial* institution, a force that not only can cure but paradoxically co-produces (and can therefore better pre-empt) the very problems of which neighbourhoods of relegation are at once receptacle, crucible and emblem.

4   Spatial dynamic: concentration and defamation

In the postwar decades of industrial expansion, poverty in the metropolis was broadly distributed throughout working-class districts and tended to affect a cross-section of manual and unskilled labourers, as well as a significant swathe of the lower-middle class living in public housing estates. By contrast, advanced marginality displays a distinct tendency to conglomerate in and coalesce around 'hard core', 'no-go' areas that are clearly identified – by their own residents no less than by outsiders – as urban infernos rife with deprivation, immorality, illegality and violence, where only the discards of society would brook living.

The South Side of Chicago and the South Bronx in New York City, Moss Side in Manchester and Brixton in London, Regents Park in Toronto and São João de Deus in Porto, Gutleutviertel in Hamburg and Niewe Westen in Rotterdam, Rinkebÿ on the outskirts of

Stockholm and Porta Palazzo at the heart of Turin, Vénissieux in the suburbs of Lyon and Bobigny or Bondy at the edge of Paris: these entrenched quarters of misery have 'made a name' for themselves as repositories for all the urban ills of the age, places to be avoided, feared and deprecated. It matters little that the discourses of demonization that have mushroomed about them often have only tenuous connections to the reality of everyday life in them. A *suffusive territorial stigma* is firmly affixed to the residents of such zones of socioeconomic and symbolic exile that adds its own burden to the disrepute of poverty and the resurging prejudice against ethnoracial minorities and immigrants.[8]

Along with territorial stigmatization comes a sharp diminution of identification and attachment to a community of fate that used to characterize older working-class towns and districts – except among youths, for which identification with one's place of residence can assume exacerbated forms that reflect the closure of the lived universe (Lepoutre 1997). Now the neighbourhood no longer offers a shield against the insecurities and pressures of the outside world; it is no longer this familiar landscape, unified by a shared culture, which reassured and reaffirmed the residents in their collective meanings and forms of mutuality. It has mutated into an empty space of competition and conflict, a danger-filled battleground for the daily contest for subsistence, scarce collective resources (such as the use of public spaces and amenities) and, above all, for finding the means to escape. This weakening of territorially based communal bonds, nay their inversion into *negative social and symbolic capital*, in turn fuels a retreat into the sphere of privatized consumption and stimulates strategies of mutual distancing and denigration ('I am not one of them') that further undermine local solidarities and confirm deprecatory perceptions of the neighbourhood.[9]

Now, this dynamic of spatial concentration could turn out to be a transitional (or cyclical) phenomenon eventually leading to the dissemination of marginality across the city. But everything indicates that the territorial stigma now firmly affixed to these districts of urban

[8] Seán Damer (1989) offers a compact analysis of this process of public defamation in the case of Glasgow, Alietti (1998) for central Milan, and Pred (2000) for the 'suburbs' of Stockholm and Malmö with dense immigrant populations.

[9] Olivier Schwartz (1990) retraces this process of withdrawal into the family and private sphere in the case of workers in a mining town in Nord-Pas-de-Calais. Charlesworth (2000) describes the effacing of working-class culture and the collapse of local solidarities in the case of casualized proletarians in a small town of Yorkshire, in England.

perdition would survive past the hypothetical scattering of dispossessed and tainted populations (Wassenberg 2004). And for those presently consigned to the bottom of the hierarchical system of places that compose the new spatial order of the city, the future is right now. Lastly, it must be stressed again that these widely despised zones of relegation are first and foremost creatures of state policies in matters of housing, urban development and regional planning. In the final analysis, their possible dispersion or rebuilding, just like their emergence and consolidation, is an eminently political question.

The spectre of transatlantic convergence exorcized

One question is at the back of everyone's mind when it comes to the deterioration of social conditions and life chances in the disreputable districts of the First World metropolis: does the rise of this new marginality signal a structural *rapprochement* between Europe and the United States on the model of the latter (see, e.g., Cross 1992; Musterd 1994; Van Kempen and Özüekren 1998). Framed in such simplistic and binary terms, the question hardly admits of an analytically rigorous answer. For regimes of urban marginality are complex and capricious creatures; they are composed of imperfectly articulated ensembles of categories of perception and institutional mechanisms tying together economy, state, place and society (conceived as a historical mesh of material and symbolic relations) that do not evolve in step and, moreover, differ significantly from country to country with national conceptions and institutions of citizenship. It is therefore necessary first to rephrase this query before one can hope to give it a reasoned and empirically founded answer. One may accordingly give it three different meanings, from the pure to the diluted.

1. If by convergence, one means the wholesale 'Americanization' of urban patterns of exclusion in the European city leading down the path of *ghettoization* of the kind imposed upon African Americans since they joined industrial cities at the beginning of the twentieth century (i.e., entailing the constitution of a segmented, parallel, sociospatial formation serving the dual function of economic extraction and social ostracization of a defamed category), then the answer is clearly negative. Contrary to first impressions and to superficial accounts nourished by their concerted backing by political leaders,

journalists and media-oriented intellectuals, the changeover of the social and spatial structures of the continental metropolis has not triggered a process of ghettoization. We showed it in the second part of this book in the case of the Red Belt of Paris: the transformation of the working-class towns or neighbourhoods of the European city is not spawning ethnically uniform sociospatial ensembles based on the forcible relegation of stigmatized populations into enclaves where these populations evolve group- and place-specific organizations that substitute for and duplicate the institutional framework of the broader society (albeit at an inferior and incomplete level), and lead them to forge a shared cultural identity enabling them to act as such on the historical stage.

The demonstration for the Parisian periphery applies equally to the deindustrializing districts of the other cities of Europe: there is no Turkish ghetto in Berlin, any more than there is an Arab ghetto in Marseilles, a Surinamese ghetto in Amsterdam, or a Caribbean ghetto in Liverpool. Residential and/or commercial clusters founded primarily on ethnic affinity and economic constraint do exist in all these cities. Prejudice, discrimination based on phenotype and patronym, as well as episodic violence against immigrants (or persons supposed to be such) are also brute and brutal facts of life in all major urban centres of Europe (Wrench and Solomos 1993; Witte 1996; Pred 1997). Combined with their much lower class distribution and higher rates of joblessness, on the one hand, and state policies that have facilitated the exit of the middle class and the established working class to single-home tracts and the abandonment of large estates (Bachmann and Le Guennec 1996), on the other hand, this discrimination explains the disproportionate representation of foreign-origin populations in urban territories of exile.

But discrimination and segregation must not be confounded with ghettoization. These are three forms of ethnoracial domination which, even as they are closely nested in the manner of Russian dolls – discrimination produces segregation, which, in turn, serves as *possible* anchor for ghettoization as encapsulation in a parallel institutional network – are nonetheless distinct and irreducible one to the other (Wacquant 1997c). Such immigrant concentrations as flare up here and there in Europe are not the product of the organizational enclosure of a bounded group founded on rigid spatial confinement – as evidenced, among other indicators, by very moderate rates of segregation, rising rates of intermarriage, and the spatial diffusion of immigrants when their educational and class position improve (Huttman 1991; Tribalat 1995; Petsimeris 1998). Indeed, if anything characterizes the neighbourhoods of relegation that have sprouted across the European continent as mechanisms of reproduction of the Fordist working class and its territories floundered and then broke down, it is their *extreme ethnic heterogeneity* as well as their institutional *incapacity* to satisfy the basic needs and encompass the daily round of their inhabitants and their *failure* to produce a unified cultural identity – three properties among others that make them more akin to *anti-ghettos* (Wacquant 2005).

2. If by convergence between Europe and the United States, one implies that *self-reinforcing cycles of ecological disrepair, social deprivation and violence*, eventually leading to spatial emptying and institutional abandonment, are now operative on the Continent, then again the answer is negative. This is because European zones of urban exile which constitute the lower nodes of polarization, as it were, remain – with few exceptions such as some southern Italian cities and with reservations about the British case – deeply penetrated by the state. The kind of 'triage' and purposive desertion of urban areas to 'economize' on public services that remade the visage of the American metropolis after 1970 is unimaginable in the European political context, in which the bureaucratic monitoring of the national territory remains fine-grained and far-reaching (Häußermann 1998; Hall 2002: chs 6 and 7), and where the state remains the guarantor of mandatory minimum support to marginal categories.[10]

At the same time, there can be no question that the capacity of European states to govern the territories of relegation that they have themselves fashioned, at the point of confluence of their economic, social and urban policies, is being severely tested and could prove unequal to the task if recent trends toward the spatial concentration of persistent joblessness continue unabated (Engbersen 1997). But

---

[10] A radical reorientation of the actions of the central and local welfare state aimed at improving the economic attractiveness of cities at the expense of the services offered to vulnerable social categories, of the kind implemented in the United States in the 1970s, is simply not politically viable on the European Continent. With the exception of Great Britain, which has aligned itself with the United States by importing from across the Atlantic central elements of its economic, social and penal policies, the 'sombre prognosis' of a transatlantic convergence of urban policies 'does not seem to suit the European cities, which are anxious to protect their populations from the rigours of economic competition and to maintain as far as possible the level of support linked to the welfare state, especially at the national level. In this sense, the cities often work in association with the state, and not in opposition to it' (Le Galès 1996: 563).

this is a matter of political will and state strategy, and not an inexorable tendency inscribed in the necessity of some transcontintental convergence.

3. But the notion of 'Americanization' could be invoked here, more modestly, to spotlight the *growing salience of ethnoracial divisions and tensions* in the European metropolis. In such case, the answer might be a qualified and provisional yes were it not for the following three strong counters that dilute the notion of 'Americanization' to the point where it becomes inchoate if not empty. First, the pertinence of ethnicity in urban experience does not automatically imply that an objective process of segmentation of space along ethnoracial lines is under way, or that the societies of the Old World are witnessing the formation of 'minorities' in the sense of ethnic communities mobilized and recognized as such in the public sphere (Musterd et al. 1998). Indeed, such a process of ethnogenesis pertains primarily not to urban dynamics but to the struggles internal to the political field: it is not neighbourhoods which secrete 'minorities' but the state, through its work of official nomination and efficient classification, and the forces which clash in the bureaucratic field to inflect its action according to their material and symbolic interests (Nagel 1986; Bourdieu [1993] 1994; Weiß 2001).[11]

Next, ethnoracial conflicts are not a novel phenomenon in the European city: they have ebbed and flowed throughout the twentieth century as a function of (i) struggles between the central state and regional cultures, as exemplified today by the deep divisions between the Flemish and Walloons in Belgium, the festering Corsican question in France, or the continuing push for greater autonomy of the Catalans in Spain; (ii) internal and external currents of migration channelled by market forces and state policies; (iii) cycles of class mobilization during periods of rapid social and economic restructuring (Noiriel 1992; Macdonald 1993).[12] This means that there is little that is distinctively 'American' about such pattern.

Lastly, and contrary to the US scenario, divisions and tensions with an ethnic or racialized tenor in the Old World metropolis are

---

[11] At this level, one cannot give a generic response for Europe as a whole, since the countries of the Union diverge considerably in their juridical and political treatment of marks of origins and cultural differences, whether national, regional, linguistic or issuing from the colonial past.

[12] The overlap of ethnoregional and ethnoracial dynamics in the construction of French identity is well illustrated in the comparative case study by Lawrence et al. (2001) of Moselle, Flanders and the Alpes maritimes between the two World Wars.

generally fuelled not by the widening of the gap separating (postco-lonial) immigrants and natives (of European descent) but by their growing *propinquity* in social and physical space. Ethnonational exclu-sivism is a nativist reaction to the individual and collective downward mobility experienced by families of the autochthonous working class made all the more intolerable by the concurrent advances of rival populations of postcolonial origins, before it expresses a profound ideological switch to a racialist register that would mark a historic rupture in the process of collectivity formation on the Continent. Notwithstanding faddish blanket proclamations about the 'globaliza-tion of race' (Winant 1994: ch. 8), which blithely confound the planetary diffusion of US discourse on racial division with the uni-versal revelation of this cleavage in the objectivity of social and mental structures, the increased salience and weight of ethnicity in European public discourse as in everyday life across the Continent pertains more to a 'chauvinistic' politics of class than to a politics of identity (Patterson 1977).

Coping with advanced marginality: the turn to the penal state

In their effort to tackle emergent forms of urban relegation, if only to contain their disruptive social effects and negative political reper-cussions, nation-states face a policy choice with a three-pronged alternative. Which branch of this alternative becomes the dominant path followed by the members of the European Union will largely determine the kind of supranational society they are to become.

The first option, representing a sort of immobile middle ground, consists in *patching up and redeploying the existing programmes of the welfare state* aimed at supporting or re-arming marginalized popula-tions. This can be done, for instance, by extending medical coverage, reinforcing emergency programmes such as the *SAMU social* (France's 'crisis social work' teams for street derelicts patterned after medical emergency squads), by 'activating' assistance programmes to make them over into springboards towards training and employment, or by authorizing recipients of public aid packages to combine work and aid for a preset period (to close 'poverty traps'), not to mention mobilizing the networks of the nonprofit sector. It is clear that this is not getting the job done, or the problems posed by advanced mar-ginality would not be so pressing today, and their accumulation in the dispossessed redoubts of the city would have been thwarted if not inverted. One might even argue that, shorn of a clear philosophy and operating increasingly on the subnational scale (at the level of the region, municipality or neighbourhood) and in part subcontracted to the nonprofit sector, these piecemeal, short-term responses to the recurrent disruptions caused by urban polarization from below can contribute to perpetuating them in so far as they increase the bureaucratic cacophony and inefficiency of the state, which cannot but sap the legitimacy of the social treatment of poverty in the long run.

The second, regressive and repressive, solution is to *criminalize poverty via the punitive containment of the poor* in the increasingly isolated and stigmatized neighbourhoods in which they are confined, on the one hand, and in jails and prisons which operate as their spillway, on the other. This is the route taken by the United States in the aftermath of the ghetto uprisings of the 1960s and in reaction to the generalization of social insecurity over the ensuing two decades (Tonry 1995; Wacquant 2004/2008). It is not by happenstance that the stupendous expansion of the carceral sector of the American state – the population behind bars has quadrupled in twenty-five years, and departments of correction have risen to the rank of third largest employer in the country, even as crime levels remained *grosso modo* constant and then declined sharply over that period – was started just when unemployment and casual (under)employment were spreading, public assistance was fast shrinking before being 'reformed' into a system of forced employment (called 'workfare'), and when the ghetto was imploding as the result of the combined pressure of black mobilization, deindustrialization and public policies of urban abandonment. Indeed, the atrophy of the social state and the hypertrophy of the penal state in the United States are two correlative and complementary transformations that partake of the institution of a new government of misery, whose function is precisely to impose desocialized wage labour as a norm of citizenship for the lower class while providing a functional substitute for the ghetto as a mechanism of racial control.

Although the United States is truly exceptional for the zeal with which it has embraced this 'solution' to social polarization and for the scale on which it has implemented it,[13] the temptation to rely on

[13] With 710 inmates per 100,000 residents in 2000, the United States has become world leader in incarceration. It confines five to twelve times as many people proportionately as the EU countries (when the EU had fifteen members), although the latter sport levels of crime (aside from homicide) similar to those of the United States.

the police, judicial and carceral institutions to stem the effects of social insecurity generated by the spread of precarious work and the retrenchment of social welfare is present throughout Europe. This can be seen by noting four deep-seated features of penal evolution on the continent:

1 The spectacular rise of incarceration rates among most member countries of the European Union over the past two decades:[14] between 1983 and 2000, this rate jumped from 70 to 95 inmates per 100,000 in France, from 73 to 93 in Italy, from 87 to 124 in England, from 28 to 90 in the Netherlands, and from 37 to 114 in Spain.

2 The massive overrepresentation, within the carceral population, of non-European immigrants and of persons of colour, as well as of drug retailers and users, the homeless, the mentally ill and other rejects from the labour market. Thus, in 1997, foreigners comprised more than one-third of the population under lock in Germany, Belgium and Holland, and nearly one-quarter in France, Italy and Austria (although they only made up between 2 and 8 per cent of the population of those countries).

3 The overcrowding of custodial establishments, which reduces detention to its raw function of warehousing undesirable categories. In 1997, over one-third of the jails and prisons of France and Belgium and one-half of the prisons of Italy and Spain were in a situation of 'critical overcrowding' (with an inmate count exceeding capacity by 20 per cent). The congestion of confinement facilities translates into a shrinkage of living and private space, the deterioration of sanitary standards and medical conditions, the rise of violence and suicide, and penury in exercise as well as programmes for education, training and preparation for returning to society.

4 The generalized hardening of penal policies, more openly turned towards incapacitation at the expense of rehabilitation, and tacitly guided by the principle of 'less eligibility',[15] even when it grossly contravenes efforts to reduce recidivism after release.

[14] The statistics that follow are drawn from the editions of the *Statistique pénale annuelle du Conseil de l'Europe* published by the Council of Europe in Strasbourg for the years covered.

[15] Applied to the penal realm, the Benthamite criterion of 'less eligibility' (initially formulated in 1796 and introduced during the Irish famine of 1840 for individuals asking for welfare support) stipulates that the situation of the most favoured inmate should always be less desirable than that of the least favoured 'free' worker, so that wage-earners are not incited to commit crimes to improve their condition by getting themselves imprisoned.

Recent shifts in public discourse on urban disorder reveal a similar drift towards the penal treatment of poverty and the dislocations which, paradoxically, arise from having truncated the social and economic capacities of the state. One is thus impelled to predict that a 'downward' convergence of Europe on the social front, entailing further deregulation of the labour market and the continued reduction of the collective safety net, will ineluctably result in an 'upward' harmonization on the penal front feeding a new burst of carceral inflation throughout the Continent (Wacquant 1999).

Despite the colossal social and financial costs of the mass confinement of poor and disruptive populations, imprisonment remains a seductive diversion and tempting stopgap counter to mounting urban dislocations even in the most tolerant and egalitarian societies such as the Nordic countries (Christie 1998). But, aside from the powerful political and cultural obstacles that stand in the way of the wholesale carceralization of misery embedded in the makeup of social-democratic or Christian-democratic states of Europe as well as in the civic ethos of their population, punitive containment leaves untouched the root causes of the new marginality. This is to say that its implementation is bound to fail in the long run and eventually point to a third, progressive response to urban polarization from below: the *offensive reconstruction of the social state* that would put its structure and policies in accord with the emerging economic conditions, the transformation of family forms and the remaking of gender relations as well as with new social aspirations to participation in collective life (Esping-Andersen 2002).

Radical innovations, such as the institution of a 'citizen's wage' (or basic income grant provided to all without restrictions) that would decouple subsistence from work, free education and job training through the lifecourse, and an effective guarantee of universal access to the three essential public goods of housing, health and transportation, are needed to expand the sphere of social rights and check the deleterious effects of the fragmentation of wage labour (Van Parijs 1995; Standing 2004). In the end, this third option is the only viable response to the historic challenge that advanced marginality poses to democratic societies as they cross the threshold of the new millennium.

Postscript: Theory, History and Politics in Urban Analysis

This book takes stock of a decade of research in the comparative sociology of urban marginality in the United States and Western Europe (1987–97). It originates in a triple jolt. The first was the shock, inseparably emotional and intellectual, felt upon discovering the quasi-lunar vestiges of the black ghetto spread out right under my apartment window on 61st Street, on the edge of the University of Chicago campus where I had come to pursue a doctorate in sociology (which was set to tackle the making and crumbling of the colonial system in New Caledonia, where I had spent the previous two years). Dwelling on the socioracial line of fracture that haunts America and having to learn firsthand the practical techniques whereby (poor) blacks and (rich) whites attempt to disentangle and deny on a daily basis the Gordian knot of class, race and space in the metropolis, it was impossible for me not to take as object of study so outlandish an urban constellation that questioned me rudely every day.

The second jolt was my encounter with William Julius Wilson: it proved just as difficult not to be swept away by the irrepressible *passio sciendi* of this exceptional scholar for the fate of the black American ghetto and its residents, and not to pounce on his invitation to collaborate with him in the analysis of the contemporary transformations on that South Side of Chicago which had become my adopted turf and field of investigation.[1] The third shock was the explosion

---

[1] Even when I differ from Wilson's approach and diverge from his conclusions, my analyses remain indebted to him. Ludwig Wittgenstein remarks in *On Certainty* that 'the *questions* that we raise and our *doubts* rest on this: some propositions are substracted from doubt, as the hinges upon which these questions and these doubts turn'. Wilson's *œuvre*, and especially his master book *The Declining Significance of Race* (Wilson 1980), has supplied the hinges upon which turns all research on the intersection of racial division and class inequality in the United States.

and diffusion, in France and neighbouring countries, of a panic discourse on the sudden proliferation of 'immigrant ghettos', the so-called crisis of 'integration' and the supposed 'Americanization' of the European city. This discourse, which has inflated without let-up since the early 1990s, demanded a double response from me, in that it kept referring without rhyme or reason to the black American ghetto – and, singularly, to that of Chicago – and it seemed to me to reiterate, nay aggravate, a number of analytical blunders and policy errors made in the US debate on poverty, economy and state that was then resurging. So much to say that the comparative study of the varied social positions, strategies and experiences of the destabilized and stigmatized strata of the new urban proletariat in formation in the advanced societies on the two sides of the Atlantic after the dismantling of the Fordist–Keynesian social compact gradually imposed itself upon me as a kind of duty at once scientific and civic.

A revised and enlarged version of a collection of articles originally prepared at the behest of South American colleagues (in Argentina and Brazil), the present text deepens, clarifies and refines the analyses formulated between 1989 and 1997, but without fundamentally altering their tenor or tonality,[2] for two reasons. The first is a point of method: every sociological analysis is necessarily *dated and situated*, inasmuch as it is empirically grounded. That offered here deals with the declining US ghetto and French working-class *banlieues* at the outset of the last decade of the twentieth century. It stresses that these neighbourhoods of relegation are *historical entities* that must not be artificially frozen in static typologies, not be treated as self-sustaining constellations existing outside of the confluence of market, state, class and ethnic factors that in fact ongoingly fabricate them by writing themselves onto physical space. It presents an inventory of urban marginality and a balance sheet of the forces that mould it that contribute to a historical sociology of the present, and offers a conceptual and empirical basis for deciphering this or that evolution observed or conjectured since – such as the efforts of the state to break up the physical core of the hyperghetto by destroying large public housing concentrations on the US side and the growing attention accorded to spatial inequality and ethnic discrimination in the public sphere on the French side.

---

[2] An effort was made to minimize repetitions while preserving the integrity and autonomy of each chapter, so that the reader may navigate them individually or in the order that best suits her interests.

For the reader who would regret not being provided with a more 'newsy' picture (responding directly to the November 2005 riots in particular), I will recall that the pace of research is not that of media commentary or public action, and also that the task of social science is not to surf the wave of current events, but to bring to light the durable and invisible mechanisms that produce them. The endlessly rising discursive velocity of journalism and politics, rooted in their ever-closer mutual interconnection and facilitated by their correlative disconnection from social reality, tends to create the illusion that urban practices and representations fluctuate and renew themselves continuously. In truth, the social and mental structures characteristic of a society, city or type of neighbourhood in a given period are not fleeting effusions that appear, mutate and disappear over a few months or years following the irruption of such-and-such 'event', however spectacular it may be and even as it gets instantly converted into a *'fait de société'* or official 'social problem' by the presentist and doxosophic lens of journalism. In point of fact, if there is one striking feature of public debate about the urban poor of our time, it is the permanence of the gaze that exoticizes them[3] and of the propensity to proclaim as radically new long-term trends, cyclical phenomena or eminently banal facts that appear unprecedented and unfathomable only because they are grasped from afar and from above (as with the theme, as hollow as it is lurid, of the *'ultraviolence'* of youths from the working-class *banlieues* which has recently invaded the French press).

The second reason supporting the decision to substantially revise, but not to substantively amend, the texts on which this book is based is that the decade that has elapsed since the completion of this research programme has largely *confirmed its main findings and validated the analytical blueprint of the new regime of marginality* with which it culminated. To begin with the perennial return of collective

---

[3] Proof is the astonishing resurgence of modes of expression and action issued straight from the colonial era among the French political and intellectual elites in reaction to the wave of riots of November 2005, ranging from the exhumation of a law dating from the Algerian War to proclaim a state of emergency that effectively assimilated the revolting *banlieues* youths to 'natives' in a state of insurrection, to the racist delirium of one cabinet minister and member of the Académie française over African polygamy as the source of the disorders to the nauseating ruminations of one magazine philosopher on the 'anti-republican pogrom' with an 'ethnic and religious' basis, fed by the 'hatred' for the West of 'the blacks and Arabs' of France.

violence: the diagnosis put forth in 1993, which saw the eruptions in outlying housing estates that rocked France in the late 1980s as 'mixed riots' in terms of both composition and motivations, was verified by the wave of unrest that swept the country's urban periphery in November 2005. The same causes – deproletarianization, relegation and stigmatization – produced the same effects, but on a wider geographic scale and at an accelerated tempo due to the intervention of three aggravating factors: the deepening of work precariousness and social insecurity in urban zones left fallow over the past fifteen years; the state policy of police encirclement of dispossessed neighbourhoods, launched by Jean-Pierre Chevènement under the Jospin government in 1997 and subsequently amplified by Nicolas Sarkozy under the Raffarin and Galouzeau de Villepin governments; the astounding blindness of state decision-makers and the persistent autism of the top political personnel regarding the *social* realities and demands of the residents of districts of dereliction, exacerbated by the fierce competition, at the top of a discredited executive branch, between a Prime Minister desperate to position himself as a viable candidate for the 2007 presidential race and a Minister of the Interior obsessed with polishing his image as a manly man of action.[4]

To continue, the thesis that the post-civil rights trajectory of the ghetto was economically underdetermined and politically overdetermined has been corroborated by the unexpected conjunction of the sudden vanishing of the problematics of the 'underclass' caused by the so-called welfare reform of 1996 and the spectacular physical overhaul of the inner city by the policy of poverty 'deconcentration' via massive public housing demolition (O'Connor 2000; Galster and Zober 1997; Crump 2002). These converging ecological and intellectual changes have demonstrated with special clarity the degree to which the makeup of the racialized urban core and the research agenda accreting about it in the United States are spawns of state actions and imperatives. They reinforce my contention that the comparative sociology of class, ethnicity and marginality in the metropolis must urgently *(re)politicize its models*, not in the naive sense of injecting partisan political judgement into scholarship, but by bringing the multisided roles of the state in articulating this triad to the

---

[4] For an in-depth diagnosis of the November 2005 disorders that deploys the analytical framework developed in this book, see Loïc Wacquant, 'Burn Baby Burn, French Style? Roots of the Riots in the French City' (forthcoming, available in oral form as a 'webcast' at <http://sociology.berkeley.edu/faculty/wacquant/>).

analytic centre.[5] Such an approach offers a powerful empirical critique and theoretical alternative to the ecological thematics of 'neighbourhood effects' that conveys a falsely depoliticized vision of urban inequality, in which spatial processes appear self-evident, self-generated, or left unexplained when in reality they track the extent to which the state works or fails to equalize basic life conditions and strategies across places. It is not by coincidence that the study of the 'contextual effects' and 'social capital' of neighbourhoods of relegation became a major intellectual industry after the mid-1990s in the United States, and with a few years' lag in Western Europe (Sampson et al. 2002; Marpsat 1999; Friedrichs et al. 2003; Brännström 2004), that is, after the state had renounced its traditional missions of economic regulation and social protection, thus creating the conditions under which scholars could (mis)attribute to space, disparities generated by the uneven retraction of public policies of provision.

The past decade has also confirmed that the dissolution of the working-class territories of Europe does not lead to the crystallization of American-style ghettos but, rather, to motley and dependent entities that are more akin to *anti-ghettos*. Neighbourhoods of relegation in France (Germany, Italy, Belgium, Holland, etc.) are characterized by their low to moderate levels of segregation and lack of demographic coherence and cultural unity, the very weak encompassing and structuring capacity of the organizations specific to them, and, for this very reason, the absence of institutional parallelism. They are not incubators of homogeneous ethnic 'communities' clamouring for recognition as such in the public sphere. On the contrary, the demands of their residents are fundamentally social, having to do not with difference or 'diversity' (the latest buzzword in the worldly sectors of the intellectual field) but *equality* in treatment by or access to the police, the school system, housing, health care and, above all, employment. They pertain to the *sphere of citizenship and not that of ethnicity* (whether defined on a national, linguistic or confessional basis).

Those bent on finding parallels between US patterns of urban marginality and the trajectory of postcolonial migrants in the French urban periphery – and in the European metropolis more generally – would gain more empirical traction and theoretical leverage by com-

[5] I say re-politicize because earlier studies of the responses of postindustrial cities to economic decline gave pride of place to the material and regulatory roles of the state, showing that 'those who hold and use state power *can* allow the fate of cities to be determined mainly in the private economy, but that is a matter of public choice rather than iron necessity' (Gurr and King 1987: 4).

paring the 'visible minorities' of the Continent not with African Americans, but with contemporary Mexican Americans or earlier streams of newcomers to America from the Old World.[6] Much as the cross-Mediterranean journey of North African labourers and their families was determined by the colonial penetration of the Maghreb by France, the similarly rural and working-class migration of Mexicans into the United States was triggered by American economic and political domination of their country. This migration has been both supported and periodically denounced by the US state, which complains about the 'burden' of the undocumented denizens whose very entry it has organized, much as the French state does about its Maghrebine population. Mexicans and Mexican Americans are the target of widespread if low-grade prejudice in US society; they are commonly stigmatized in schools, discriminated against in the labour market, and somewhat concentrated spatially. But they have never been ghettoized in the manner of African Americans (Massey and Denton 1993; Moore and Pinderhughes 1993). Because they did not bear the indelible stain of enslavement, they were never immured in an exclusive space and forcibly encased in parallel institutions designed to keep them forever separated from white society. As a result, their ethnic neighbourhoods have a diverse composition and porous boundaries, and they tend to function as springboards towards the broader society. For Mexican Americans, class mobility is more difficult to achieve than for Anglo Americans, but it does translate into spatial mobility, cultural assimilation and marital mixing – so many characteristics that make them close analogues to French citizens of North African origins, who sport a germane pattern of segmented and conflictual incorporation into the national body (Santelli 2001).

Likewise, the evolution of the social and spatial structures of the segregated core of the US metropolis and of the outskirts of the European city since its initial formulation (in 1993) seems to me to have validated the conceptual schema of 'advanced marginality' put forward in the third part of the book. And it has sharpened the political alternative posed by the consolidation of this new regime of poverty between the penalization of misery and the proactive (re)construction of a social state capable of severing the umbilical

---

[6] For starters, on the comparison with Mexican Americans, see Portes and Bach (1985), and Pitti (2003) on structural determinants of migration and historical paths of incorporation, Dohan (2003) on lower-class strategies to manage marginality at ground level, and Alba (2005) for cross-national mapping.

cord between subsistence and wage work inherited from the industrial era. In all the advanced societies, the dazzling growth of corporate benefits now goes hand in hand with the fragmentation of wage work. It is no accident that, in the spring of 2006, the benefits amassed by the firms listed on the CAC 40 (the French stock market index) beat all records to date (with 87 billion euros in a year), while the ranks of those earning the legal minimum wage and receiving the RMI (*Revenu minimum d'insertion*, the national minimum income grant given to those falling through through the cracks of employment and welfare programmes) reached unprecedented peaks (with 2.5 million workers earning the base hourly pay, amounting to 17 per cent of the active population, excluding temporary posts and the agricultural sector, nearly half of whom work part-time, and 1.2 million receiving the RMI), at the very moment when the last government headed by Jacques Chirac was attempting to normalize job precariousness among youth by forcefully imposing the CPE (*Contrat Première Embauche*, a special employment contract for those under 26 allowing employers to fire them without motive or penalty for up to two years). Everywhere, the functional disconnection between the evolution of the national and global capitalist economy and that of the neighbourhoods of relegation has become glaring. Everywhere, the spatial stigmatization and alienation of the vulnerable fractions of the urban proletariat have deepened, and with them the sense of collective downfall and the symbolic quarantining of the categories that compose it.

Finally, the methodical comparison of the implosion of the black American ghetto with the decomposition of the working-class territories of France and Western Europe at the close of the past century reveals the pivotal role played by the state in the social and mental structuring of urban marginality. The fatalist discourse endlessly rehashed by the economic and political leaders of the advanced countries since the middle of the 1970s (the refrain of the 'crisis of the welfare state' having been replaced by the mantric invocation of 'globalization'), intended to give credibility to the notion that national states no longer have the capacity to act, is directly belied by the persistence, over the past decade, of very pronounced differences in the fate of the 'precariat' in the different postindustrial societies according to the type of state and to the social, fiscal and economic policies that it has implemented.[7]

[7] On this point, see Gallie (2004), Alesina and Glaeser (2004) and Paugam (2005). Linda Weiss (1998) has similarly shown in *The Myth of the Powerless State* that successful integration into the globalized economy depends directly on the capacities and policies of the national state.

Sociological analysis here opens onto, not a finding of impotence leading to a smug or resigned submission to the forces of the world, but a reasoned reaffirmation of the *primacy of the political* as the capacity to articulate and engage collective choices made with full knowledge of causes and consequences. Coming on the heels of the popular rejection of a market-friendly constitution for the European Union, the simultaneous intensification of public 'disorders' in the *banlieues* and of popular mobilizations against work precariousness of which France was the theatre between November 2005 and April 2006 opens original prospects in this regard. By tearing the ideological veil of the spatial, ethnic and law-and-order thematics, it has brought to light the causal connection between the fate of the urban outcasts and the social question of the new century, namely, the desocialization of wage labour and its reverberations at the lower end of the structure of classes and places. It behoves us to make the best possible use of this clarification in analysis and in action.

Acknowledgements and Sources

It would take a supplemental chapter to thank adequately all the colleagues, students, officials, friends and kin who have contributed to facilitating, correcting and enriching the inquiries of which this book offers a synthesis with their queries, criticisms and support of manifold kinds over the years.

Pierre Bourdieu and Bill Wilson deserve special mention because they have been at once incomparable mentors and living models of scientific rigour and civic engagement. In the United States, my gratitude goes to Janet Abu-Lughod, Javier Auyero, Philippe Bourgois, Rogers Brubaker, Craig Calhoun, Alex Portes, Saskia Sassen and Eric Wanner, as well as to my Berkeley colleagues, Manuel Castells, Claude Fischer, Mártin Sánchez-Jankowski, Nancy Scheper-Hughes and Allan Pred. My mates from the boxing gym at the Woodlawn Boys Club and our coach DeeDee Armour offered me, collectively, the best seminar of initiation to the prosaic realities of the ghetto that a young sociologist could ever have dreamed of.

On the European side, I am particularly thankful to the members of the Centre de sociologie européenne and the Centre de sociologie urbaine, especially Yvette Delsaut, Remi Lenoir, Monique Pinçon-Charlot and Michel Pinçon, Louis Pinto, Franck Poupeau and the much-missed Abdelmalek Sayad, as well as to Rosemary Crompton (Leicester), Godfried Engbersen (Leiden, then Rotterdam), Enzo Mingione (Milan), and Hartmut Häußermann (Berlin). For the field study of the Quatre mille estate and of urban policy in Seine-Saint-Denis, I am indebted to the staff of the city of La Courneuve (especially Mme Delahaye and the Service de documentation municipal), Nicole Tabard (INSEE), Claire Guignard (Haut commissariat à l'intégration), Nicole Smadja (Préfecture of the Île-de-France region), M. Galibourg (Direction départementale de l'Équipement in Bobigny) and Sonia Serkoff (Commissariat au Plan).

The investigations whose results are reported herein and their publication were made possible by material support from the Urban Family Life Project at the University of Chicago, the Joint Center for Political and Economic Studies, the Russell Sage Foundation, the Center on Institutions and Governance at the University of California-Berkeley, the Maison des Sciences de l'Homme and the Collège de France. They were facilitated by a Century Fellowship from the University of Chicago, a Tocqueville Fellowship from the Franco-American Foundation and a Lavoisier Fellowship from the French Ministry of Foreign Affairs, and later by Harvard University's Society of Fellows. The administrative assistance of Angie Perez in Chicago, Diana Morse at Harvard, and Rosine Christin and Marie-Christine Rivière in Paris was precious, as was the hospitality of the Maison Suger and of my Uncle André and Aunt Odile during my sojourns in Paris.

The final revision of the text owes much to the judicious criticisms and suggestions, both theoretical and stylistic, of Sébastien Chauvin, Etienne Ollion and Gretchen Purser, and to the efficiency of Molly Ward and the patience of John Thompson and Megan Comfort.

The chapters in this book are based on working texts published at different stages in the advancement of the research. The original references are:

Chapter 1: 'O Retorno do recalcado: violência urbana, "raça" e dualização em três sociedades avançadas', *Revista Brasileira de Ciências sociais* 24 (February 1995): 16–30 (plenary lecture presented at the seventeenth annual meetings of ANPOCS in Caxambu, Brazil, 24 October 1993), and 'The Return of the Repressed: Violence, 'Race', and Dualization in Three Advanced Societies', *RSF Working Papers*, no. 24 (New York: Russell Sage Foundation, 1993).

Chapter 2: 'The New Urban Color Line: The State and Fate of the Ghetto in Postfordist America', in Craig J. Calhoun (ed.), *Social Theory and the Politics of Identity* (Cambridge, MA: Basil Blackwell, 1994), pp. 231–76 (presented under the title 'Caste, classe et État: éléments de sociologie du ghetto noir américain', Centre de sociologie urbaine, CNRS, Paris, 3 February 1993, and as a Globus lecture, City University of New York, Baruch College, New York, 20 April 1993).

Chapter 3 draws on an article co-authored with William Julius Wilson: 'The Cost of Racial and Class Exclusion in the Inner City', *The Annals of the American Academy of Political and Social Science* 501 (January 1989): 8–25.

Chapter 4: 'West Side Story à Chicago', *Projet*, 238 (Spring 1994), (special issue on 'Les Frontières de l'insécurité'): 53–61.

Chapter 5: 'Banlieues françaises et ghetto noir américain: de l'amalgame à la comparaison', *French Politics and Society* 10/4 (Fall 1992): 81–103.

Chapter 6: 'Urban Outcasts: Stigma and Division in the Black American Ghetto and the French Urban Periphery', *International Journal of Urban and Regional Research* 17/3 (September 1993): 366–83 (based on a paper presented at the conference of the International Sociological Association on 'Comparative Trends in Urban Inequality', University of California, Los Angeles, 17 April 1992).

Chapter 7 was originally drafted for an edited volume by the Urban Family Life Project in Chicago that never saw print. A portion was incorporated in 'Fascia Rossa, Fascia Nera: colori, classi i luoghi dei ghetti di Chicago e della periferia parigina', *Inchiesta* (Milan) 97–8 (December 1992): 17–29, at the behest of Enzo Mingione.

Chapter 8 is based on a report commissioned by the Organization for Economic Cooperation and Development and presented at the Meeting of Experts on Distressed Urban Areas, OECD, Paris, 21–2 March 1994, and published in part under the title 'The Rise of Advanced Marginality: Notes on its Nature and Implications', *Acta sociologica* 39/2 (1996): 121–39.

Chapter 9 is an expanded version of the plenary lecture delivered to the Meetings of the Nordic Sociological Association on 15 June 1997 and published in Danish under the title 'Marginalitet i Storbyerne i det Kommende Årtusind', *Social Kritik* 52–3 (November 1997) (special issue on 'Globalization, Civil Society and Democracy'): 40–9, and in English as 'Urban Marginality in the New Millennium', *Urban Studies* 36/10 (September 1999): 1639–47.

Image credits

Page 13, Prologue: police officer protecting stores damaged in the riots, Los Angeles, April 1992. © Peter Turnley/CORBIS.

Page 41, Part 1 – From Communal Ghetto to Hyperghetto: Homeless man pushing his cart in North Lawndale on Chicago's West Side, 1988. © Camilo Vergara.

Page 133, Part 2 – Black Belt, Red Belt: Man walking under the "El" on 63rd Street on Chicago's South Side, 1990. © Loïc Wacquant. A typical building in the Quatre mille estate, La Courneuve, 2006. © Loïc Wacquant.

Page 227, Part 3 – Looking Ahead: Urban Marginality in the 21st Century: Two men walking down a street in Alfortville, a southern working-class *banlieue* of Paris, 2004. © Aubert/aubertolivier.org.

References

Abercrombie, Nicolas and John Urry. 1983. *Capital, Labour and the Middle Classes*. London: George Allen and Unwin.

Abrahams, Roger D. 1970. *Positively Black*. Englewood Cliffs, NJ: Prentice-Hall.

Abu-Lughod, Janet L. 1999. *New York, Chicago, Los Angeles: America's Global Cities*. Minneapolis: University of Minnesota Press.

Abu-Lughod, Janet L. et al. 1994. *From Urban Village to East Village: The Battle for New York's Lower East Side*. Oxford and Cambridge, MA: Basil Blackwell.

Adler, William M. 1995. *Land of Opportunity: One Family's Quest for the American Dream in the Age of Crack*. New York: The Atlantic Monthly Press.

ADRI (Agence pour le Développement des Relations Interculturelles). 1992. *L'Intégration des minorités immigrées en Europe*, 2 vols. Paris: Éditions du Centre national de la fonction publique territoriale.

Agier, Michel. 1999. *L'Invention de la ville. Banlieues, townships, invasions et favelas*. Paris: Archives Contemporaines.

Aïchoune, Farid. 1991. *Nés en banlieue*. Paris: Editions Ramsay.

Alba, Richard. 2005. 'Bright vs. Blurred Boundaries: Second-generation Assimilation and Exclusion in France, Germany, and the United States.' *Ethnic and Racial Studies* 28/1 (January): 20–49.

Alesina, Alberto and Edward L. Glaeser. 2004. *Fighting Poverty in the US and Europe: A World of Difference*. New York: Oxford University Press.

Alietti, Alfredo. 1998. *La convivenza difficile: Coabitazione interetnica in un quartiere di Milano*. Turin: L'Harmattan Italia.

Alisch, Monika and Jens S. Dangschat. 1998. *Armut und soziale Integration*. Leverkusen: Leske & Budrich.

Allen, Sheila and Marie Macey. 1990. 'Race and Ethnicity in the European Context.' *British Journal of Sociology* 41/3 (September): 375–93.

Allmendinger, Philip and Mark Tewdwr-Jones. 2000. 'New Labour, New Planning? The Trajectory of Planning in Blair's Britain.' *Urban Studies* 37/8 (July): 1379–1402.

Amart, Laure. 1987. *La Fréquentation du parc de La Courneuve*. Paris: Laboratoire d'économétrie de l'École Polytechnique, mimeographed.

Amin, Ash (ed.). 1994. *Post-Fordism: A Reader*. Malden, MA: Basil Blackwell.

Amin, Ash. 2003. 'Unruly Strangers? The 2001 Urban Riots in Britain.' *International Journal of Urban and Regional Research* 27/2 (June): 460–3.

Amnesty International USA. 1992. *Police Brutality in Los Angeles, California, United States of America*. London: Amnesty International.

Anderson, David C. 1995. *Crime and the Politics of Hysteria: How the Willie Horton Story Changed American Justice*. New York: Times Books.

Anderson, Elijah. 1978. *A Place on the Corner*. Chicago: University of Chicago Press.

Anderson, Elijah. 1990. *Streetwise: Race, Class, and Change in an Urban Community*. Chicago: University of Chicago Press.

Archer, Margaret S. 1978. 'The Theoretical and the Comparative Analysis of Social Structure.' In Margaret Archer and Salvador Giner (eds), *Contemporary Europe: Social Structures and Cultural Patterns* (London: Routledge and Kegan Paul), pp. 11–27.

Aschenbrenner, Joyce. 1975. *Lifelines: Black Families in Chicago*. Prospect Heights, IL: Waveland Press.

Auletta, Ken. 1982. *The Underclass*. New York: Vintage Books.

Auyero, Javier. 1999. ' "This is Like the Bronx, Isn't It?" Lived Experiences of Slum-dwellers in Argentina.' *International Journal of Urban and Regional Research* 23/1 (March): 45–69.

Auyero, Javier. 2000. *Poor People's Politics: Peronist Survival Networks and the Legacy of Evita*. Durham, NC: Duke University Press.

Avery, Desmond. 1987. *Images brisées d'une cité. Civilisations de La Courneuve*. Paris: L'Harmattan.

Axinn, June and Mark J. Stern. 1988. *Poverty and Dependency: Old Problems in a New World*. Lexington, MA: Lexington Books.

Azémar, Guy-Patrick (ed.). 1992. *Ouvriers, ouvrières. Un continent morcelé et silencieux*. Paris: Éditions Autrement.

Bachmann, Christian and Luc Basier. 1989. *Mise en images d'une banlieue ordinaire. Stigmatisations urbaines et stratégies de communication*. Paris: Syros-Alternatives.

Bachmann, Christian and Nicole Le Guennec. 1996. *Violences urbaines. Ascension et chute des classes moyennes à travers cinquante ans de politique de la ville*. Paris: Albin Michel.

Bacqué, Marie-Hélène and Françoise Fol. 1997. *Le Devenir des banlieues rouges*. Paris: L'Harmattan.

Bagnasco, Arnaldo. 1986. *Torino. Un profilo sociologico*. Turin: Einaudi.

Bagnasco, Arnaldo and Patrick Le Galès (eds). 1997. *Villes en Europe*. Paris: La Découverte.

Bailey, Thomas and Roger Waldinger. 1991. 'The Changing Ethnic/Racial Division of Labor.' In John H. Mollenkopf and Manuel Castells (eds),

Dual City: Restructuring New York (New York: Russell Sage Foundation), pp. 43–78.

Balazs, Gabrielle and Abdelmalek Sayad. 1991. 'La violence de l'institution: entretien avec le principal d'un collège de Vaulx-en-Velin.' *Actes de la recherche en sciences sociales* 90 (December): 53–63.

Baldassare, Mark (ed.). 1994. *The Los Angeles Riots: Lessons for the Urban Future*. Boulder, CO: Westview Press.

Baldwin, James. 1962. *Nobody Knows My Name*. New York: Delta Books.

Balibar, Etienne. 1991. 'Es Gibt Keinen Staat in Europa: Racism and Politics in Europe Today.' *New Left Review* 186 (March): 5–19.

Banfield, Edward C. 1970. *The Unheavenly City: The Nature and Future of our Urban Crisis*. Boston: Little, Brown.

Barbier, Jean-Claude and Henri Nadel. 2002. *La Flexibilité du travail et de l'emploi*. Paris: Flammarion.

Barker, Kathleen and Kathleen Christensen (eds). 1998. *Contingent Work: American Employment Relations in Transition*. Ithaca, NY: Cornell University Press.

Barrou, Jacques. 1992. *La Place du pauvre. Histoire et géographie sociale de l'habitat HLM*. Paris: L'Harmattan.

Barthélémy, Philippe et al. 1990. *Underground Economy and Irregular Forms of Employment (travail au noir): Final Synthesis Report*. Brussels: European Economic Community, mimeographed.

Bastide, Henri. 1982. *Les Enfant d'immigrés et l'enseignement français. Enquête dans les établissements du premier et second degré*. Travaux et documents, no. 97. Paris: INED and Presses Universitaires de France.

Battegay, Alain and Ahmed Boubeker. 2001. 'L'action associative des jeunes maghrébins: entre affirmation d'un droit de cité et pratiques urbaines.' *Annales de la recherche urbaine* 89: 95–101.

Beaud, Stéphane. 2002. *80% au bac . . . et après? Les enfants de la démocratisation scolaire*. Paris: La Découverte.

Beauregard, Robert A. 1993. *Voices of Decline: The Postwar Fate of U.S. Cities*. Cambridge, MA: Blackwell.

Beeghley, Leonard. 1984. 'Illusion and Reality in the Measurement of Poverty.' *Social Problems* 31/1 (February): 322–33.

Bell, Daniel. 1960. *The End of Ideology*. Glencoe, IL: The Free Press.

Benyon, John (ed.). 1984. *Scarman and After*. Oxford: Pergamon Press.

Bernardot, Marc. 1999. 'Chronique d'une institution: la Sonacotra (1956–1976).' *Sociétés contemporaines* 33–4 (April): 39–57.

Berry, Brian J. L. 1979. *The Open Housing Question: Race and Housing in Chicago, 1966–1976*. Cambridge, MA: Ballinger.

Best, Joel (ed.). 1989. *Images of Issues: Typifying Contemporary Social Problems*. New York: Aldine de Gruyter.

Best, Joel. 1990. *Threatened Children: Rhetoric and Concern About Child-Victims*. Chicago: University of Chicago Press.

Binder, Alberto. 2004. *Policías y Ladrones. La Inseguridad en Cuestión*. Buenos Aires: Capital Intelectual.

Blank, Rebecca M. and Maria J. Hanratty. 1991. 'Responding to Need: A Comparison of Social Safety Nets in the United States and Canada.' Working Paper no. 34. Evanston, IL: Center for Urban Affairs and Policy Research, Northwestern University.

Blauner, Robert. 1972. *Racial Oppression in America*. New York: Harper & Row.

Blauner, Robert. 1989. *Black Lives, White Lives: Three Decades of Race Relations in America*. Berkeley: University of California Press.

Block, Fred. 1987. *Revising State Theory: Essays on Politics and Postindustrialism*. Philadelphia: Temple University Press.

Bloemraad, Irene. 2002. 'Citizenship and Immigration: A Current Review.' *Journal of International Migration and Integration* 1/1: 9–37.

Bluestone, Barry and Bennett Harrison. 1988. *The Great U-Turn: Corporate Restructuring and the Polarizing of America*. New York: Basic Books.

Boëldieu, Julien and Suzanne Thave. 2000. 'Le logement des immigrés en 1996.' *INSEE Première* 730 (August).

Bonelli, Laurent. 2001. 'Les Renseignements généraux et les violences urbaines.' *Actes de la Recherche en Sciences Sociales* 136–7 (March): 95–103.

Bonetti, Michel, Michel Conan and Barbara Allen. 1991. *Développement social urbain. Stratégies et méthodes*. Paris: L'Harmattan.

Boskin, Joseph. 1970. 'The Revolt of the Urban Ghettos, 1964–1967.' In Richard P. Young (ed.), *Roots of Rebellion: The Evolution of Black Politics and Protest since World War II* (New York: Harper & Row), pp. 309–27.

Bouamama, Saïd. 1992. *De la galère à la citoyenneté. Les jeunes, la cité, la société*. Paris: Desclée de Brouwer.

Bouamama, Saïd. 1994. *Dix ans de marche des Beurs. Chronique d'un mouvement avorté*. Paris: Desclée de Brouwer.

Bourdieu, Pierre. 1975. 'Structures sociales et structures de perception du monde social.' *Actes de la recherche en sciences sociales* 2 (March): 18–20.

Bourdieu, Pierre. 1977. 'Une classe objet.' *Actes de la recherche en sciences sociales* 17–18 (May): 2–5.

Bourdieu, Pierre. 1980. *Le Sens pratique*. Paris: Editions de Minuit. Tr. as *The Logic of Practice* (Cambridge: Polity, 1990).

Bourdieu, Pierre. 1982. *Ce que parler veut dire. L'économie des échanges linguistiques*. Paris: Fayard. Tr. as *Language and Symbolic Power* (Cambridge: Polity, 1991).

Bourdieu, Pierre. 1986. 'The Forms of Capital.' In John G. Richardson (ed.), *Handbook of Theory and Research for the Sociology of Education* (Westport, CT: Greenwood Press), pp. 241–58.

Bourdieu, Pierre. [1987] 1989. 'Social Space and Symbolic Power.' *Sociological Theory* 7/1 (Spring): 14–25. Repr. in *In Other Words: Essays Toward a Reflexive Sociology* (Cambridge: Polity, rev. edn 1994).

Bourdieu, Pierre. [1989] 1996. *The State Nobility: Elite Schools in the Field of Power*. Cambridge: Polity.

Bourdieu, Pierre. 1991a. 'Une mission impossible: entretien avec Pascale Rémond, chef de projet dans le nord de la France.' *Actes de la recherche en sciences sociales* 90 (December): 84–94. Tr. in abridged form as 'An Impossible Mission,' in Pierre Bourdieu et al., *The Weight of the World* (Cambridge: Polity, 1999), pp. 189–202.

Bourdieu, Pierre. 1991b. 'L'ordre des choses: entretien avec deux jeunes gens du Nord de la France.' *Actes de la recherche en sciences sociales* 90 (December): 7–19. Tr. in abridged form as 'The Order of Things,' in Pierre Bourdieu et al., *The Weight of the World* (Cambridge: Polity, 1999), pp. 60–76.

Bourdieu, Pierre. [1993] 1994. 'Rethinking the State: On the Genesis and Structure of the Bureaucratic Field.' *Sociological Theory* 12/1 (March): 1–19.

Bourdieu, Pierre. [1993] 1999. 'Effects of Place.' In Pierre Bourdieu et al., *The Weight of the World* (Cambridge: Polity), pp. 123–8.

Bourdieu, Pierre et al. [1993] 1999. *The Weight of the World: Social Suffering in Contemporary Society.* Cambridge: Polity.

Bourdieu, Pierre and Loïc Wacquant. [1998] 1999. 'The Cunning of Imperialist Reason.' *Theory, Culture, and Society* 16/1 (February): 41–57.

Bourgois, Philippe. 1989. 'In Search of Horatio Alger: Culture and Ideology in the Crack Economy.' *Contemporary Drug Problems* 13 (Winter): 619–49.

Bourgois, Philippe. [1992] 1998. 'Just Another Night in a Shooting Gallery.' *Theory, Culture, and Society* 15/2 (May): 37–66.

Bourgois, Philippe. 1995. *In Search of Respect: Selling Crack in El Barrio.* New York: Cambridge University Press.

Bovenkerk, Frank, Robert Miles and Gilles Verbunt. 1990. 'Comparative Studies of Migration and Exclusion on the Grounds of "Race" and Ethnic Background in Western Europe: A Critical Appraisal.' *International Sociology* 5/4 (December): 475–90.

Boyer, Jean-Claude. 2000. *Les Banlieues en France. Territoires et sociétés.* Paris: Armand Colin.

Boyer, Paul. 1978. *Urban Masses and Moral Order in America, 1820–1920.* Cambridge, MA: Harvard University Press.

Boyer, Robert (ed.). 1988. *The Search for Labour Market Flexibility: The European Economies in Transition.* Oxford: Clarendon Press.

Boyer, Robert and Jean-Pierre Durand. 1998. *L'Après-fordisme,* new expanded edition. Paris: Syros.

Bradbury, Katharine L. and Lynn E. Brown. 1986. 'Black Men in the Labor Market.' *New England Economic Review* 26/1 (March-April): 32–42.

Brännström, Lars. 2004. 'Poor Places, Poor Prospects? Counterfactual Models of Neighbourhood Effects on Social Exclusion in Stockholm, Sweden.' *Urban Studies* 41/13 (December): 2515–37.

Breton, Emile. 1983. *Rencontres à La Courneuve.* Paris: Messidor/Temps Actuel.

Brewer, Rose M. 1987. 'Black Women in Poverty: Some Comments on Female-Headed Families.' *Signs: Journal of Women in Culture and Society* 13/2 (Winter): 331–9.

Brint, Steven and Jerome Karabel. 1989. *The Diverted Dream: Community Colleges and the Promise of Educational Opportunity in America, 1900–1985*. New York: Oxford University Press.

Brittan, Samuel and Steven Webb. 1990. *Beyond the Welfare State: An Examination of Basic Incomes in a Market Economy*. Aberdeen: Aberdeen University Press.

Brubaker, William Rogers. 1990. 'Immigration, Citizenship, and the Nation-State in France and Germany: A Comparative Historical Analysis.' *International Sociology* 5/4 (December): 379–407.

Brubaker, Rogers. 1992. *Citizenship and Nationhood in France and Germany*. Cambridge, MA: Harvard University Press.

Brune, Tom and Eduardo Camacho. 1983. *Race and Poverty in Chicago: A Special Report: Analysis and Data Reflecting Race and Poverty in Chicago based on the 1980 U.S. Census*. Chicago: Center for Community Research and Assistance.

Bureau of the Census. 1985. *Current Population Reports*. Series P-60, no. 146. Washington, DC: Government Printing Office.

Burtless, Gary (ed.). 1990. *A Future of Lousy Jobs?: The Changing Structure of U.S. Wages*. Washington: Brookings Institution.

Calogirou, Claire. 1989. *Sauver son honneur. Rapports sociaux en milieu urbain défavorisé*. Paris: L'Harmattan.

Cameron, Stuart and John Doling. 1994. 'Housing Neighbourhoods and Urban Regeneration.' *Urban Studies* 31/7 (August): 1211–23.

Caplovitz, David. 1967. *The Poor Pay More: Consumer Practices of Low-Income Families*. Glencoe, IL: Free Press.

Cappelli, Peter, Laurie Bassi, Harry Katz, David Knoke, Paul Osterman and Michael Useem. 1997. *Change at Work*. New York: Oxford University Press.

Caraley, Demetrios. 1992. 'Washington Abandons the Cities.' *Political Science Quarterly* 107/1 (Spring): 1–30.

Cardoso, Fernando Enrique and Enzo Faletto. 1979. *Dependency and Development in Latin America*. Berkeley: University of California Press.

Carnoy, Martin et al. 1993. *The New Global Economy in the Information Age: Reflections on Our Changing World*. University Park, PA: Pennsylvania State University Press.

Cashmore, Ellis and Eugene McLaughlin (eds). 1992. *Out of Order: Policing Black People*. London: Routledge.

Caskey, John P. 1994. *Fringe Banking: Check-Cashing Outlets, Pawnshops and the Poor*. New York: Russell Sage Foundation.

Castel, Robert. 1978. 'La "guerre à la pauvreté" et le statut de la misère dans une société d'abondance.' *Actes de la recherche en sciences sociales* 19 (January): 47–60.

Castel, Robert. 1995. *Les Métamorphoses de la question sociale. Une chronique du salariat*. Paris: Fayard.

Castells, Manuel. [1977] 1979. *The Urban Question: A Marxist Approach*. Cambridge, MA: MIT Press.

Castells, Manuel. 1989. *The Informational City: Information Technology, Economic Restructuring, and the Urban-Regional Process*. Cambridge, MA: Basil Blackwell.

Castells, Manuel. 1998. *The Age of Information*, vol. 3: *End of Millennium*. Malden, MA: Basil Blackwell.

Castles, Stephen. 1984. *Here for Good: Western Europe's New Ethnic Minorities*. London: Pluto Press.

Castles, Stephen. 1993. *The Age of Migration: International Population Movements in the Modern World*. New York: Guilford.

CERC (Centre d'études des revenus and des coûts). 1989. *Les Français et leurs revenus. Le tournant des années 1980*. Paris: La Documentation française.

CERC (Centre d'études des revenus and des coûts). 1997. *Les Inégalités d'emploi et de revenu. Mise en perspective et nouveaux défis*. Paris: La Découverte.

Champagne, Patrick. [1993] 1999. 'The Journalistic Vision.' In Pierre Bourdieu et al., *The Weight of the World* (Cambridge: Polity), pp. 46–59.

Charlesworth, Simon J. 2000. *A Phenomenology of Working Class Experience*. Cambridge: Cambridge University Press.

Chevigny, Paul. 1995. *Edge of the Knife: Police Violence in the Americas*. New York: New Press.

Chicago Fact Book Consortium. 1995. *Local Community Fact Book: Chicago Metropolitan Area, 1990*. Chicago: Academy Chicago Publishers.

Chicago Tribune (Staff of). 1986. *The American Millstone: An Examination of the Nation's Permanent Underclass*. Chicago: Contemporary Books.

Chicago Tribune. 1989. 'High-risk pregnancies dumped on County Hospital, study finds.' 24 January.

Chicago Tribune. 1990. 'School lets out, fear rushes in: gangs terrorize area after classes.' 24 January.

Chicago Tribune. 1991. '849 homicides places 1990 in a sad record book.' *Chicago Tribune*, 2 January.

Chicago Tribune (Staff of). 1992. *The Worst Schools in America*. Chicago: Contemporary Press.

Chignier-Riboulon, Franck, 1999. *L'Intégration des Franco-Maghrébins. L'exemple de l'Est Lyonnais*. Paris: L'Harmattan.

Chitwood, Dale D., James E. Rivers and James A. Inciardi (eds). 1995. *The American Pipe Dream: Crack, Cocaine, and the Inner City*. Fort Worth, TX: Wadsworth.

Christie, Nils. 1998. 'Eléments de géographie pénale.' *Actes de la recherche en sciences sociales* 124 (September): 68–74.

Christopher, Warren. 1991. *Report of the Independent Commission on the Los Angeles Police Department*. Los Angeles: Diane Publishing Co.

Clark, Kenneth B. 1965. *Dark Ghetto: Dilemmas of Social Power*. New York: Harper & Row.

Cohen, Stanley. 1972. *Folk Devils and Moral Panics: The Creation of Mods and Rockers*. London: McGibbon and Kee. New expanded edn. London: Routledge, 2002.

Collins, Sharon M. 1983. 'The Making of the Black Middle Class.' *Social Problems* 30/4 (April): 369–82.

Committee on Ways and Means. 1997. *1996 Green Book*. Washington, DC: Government Printing Office.

Conseil de l'Europe. 2002. *Statistique pénale annuelle du Conseil de l'Europe, Enquête 2000*. Strasbourg: Conseil de l'Europe.

Cook, Thomas J. 1970. 'Benign Neglect: Minimum Feasible Understanding.' *Social Problems* 18/2 (Fall): 145–52.

Cross, John C. 1998. *Informal Politics: Street Vendors and the State in Mexico City*. Stanford, CA: Stanford University Press.

Cross, Malcolm (ed.). 1992. *Ethnic Minorities and Industrial Change in Europe and North America*. Cambridge: Cambridge University Press.

Cross, Malcolm and Michael Keith (eds). 1993. *Racism, the City and the State*. London: Unwin Hyman.

Crouch, Colin and Wolfgang Streeck (eds). 1997. *Political Economy of Modern Capitalism: Mapping Convergence and Diversity*. London: Sage.

Crouch, Colin, Klaus Eder and Damian Tambini. 2001. *Citizenship, Markets, and the State*. New York: Oxford University Press.

Crowley, John. 1992. 'Minorités ethniques et ghettos aux États-Unis: modèle ou anti-modèle pour la France?' *Esprit* 182 (June): 78–94.

Crump, Jeff. 2002. 'Deconcentration by Demolition: Public Housing, Poverty, and Urban Policy.' *Environment and Planning D: Society and Space* 20/5: 581–96.

Crump, Jeff. 2003. 'The End of Public Housing as We Know It: Public Housing Policy, Labor Regulation and the US City.' *International Journal of Urban and Regional Research* 27/1 (March): 179–87.

Cullingworth, Barry. 1997. *Planning in the USA: Policies, Issues and Processes*. New York: Routledge.

Cultures et Conflits. 1992. Thematic issue on 'Emeutes urbaines: le retour du politique' (no. 5, Spring). Paris: L'Harmattan.

Curtis, Lynn A. 1985. *American Violence and Public Policy: An Update of the National Commission on the Causes and Prevention of Violence*. New Haven, CT: Yale University Press.

Dahrendorf, Ralf. 1989. *The Underclass and the Future of Britain*. Windsor: St George's House, Tenth Annual Lecture.

Damer, Seán. 1989. *From Moorepark to 'Wine Alley': The Rise and Fall of a Glasgow Housing Scheme*. Edinburgh: Edinburgh University Press.

Damon, Julien (ed.). 2004. *Quartiers sensibles et cohésion sociale*. Paris: La Documentation française.

Dangschat, Jens S. 1994. 'Concentration of Poverty in the Landscapes of "Boomtown" Hamburg: The Creation of a New Urban Underclass?' *Urban Studies* 31/7 (August): 1133–47.

Dangschat, Jens S. 2002. *Modernisierte Stadt, gespaltene Gesellschaft. Ursachen von Armut und sozialer Ausgrenzung.* Berlin: VSA Verlag.

Daniel, G. Reginald. 2001. *More Than Black? Multiracial Identity and the New Racial Order.* Philadelphia: Temple University Press.

Danzinger, Sheldon and Peter Gottschalk (eds). 1993. *Uneven Tides: Rising Inequality in America.* New York: Russell Sage Foundation.

Danzinger, Sheldon H. and Daniel H. Weinberg (eds). 1986. *Fighting Poverty: What Works, What Doesn't.* Cambridge, MA: Harvard University Press.

Darden, J. T. and S. M. Kamel. 2000. 'Black Residential Segregation in the City and Suburbs of Detroit: Does Socioeconomic Status Matter?' *Journal of Urban Affairs* 22/1 (January): 1–13.

Davis, F. James. 1991. *Who Is Black? One Nation's Definition.* University Park, PA: Pennsylvania State University Press.

Davis, Mike. 1992. 'L.A. Intifada: An Interview with Mike Davis.' *Social Text* 33 (December): 19–33.

Dawson, Michael C. 1994. *Behind the Mule: Race and Class in African-American Politics.* Princeton: Princeton University Press.

Demazière, Didier and Maria-Teresa Pignoni. 1999. *Chômeurs, du silence à la révolte. Sociologie d'une action collective.* Paris: Hachette.

Dezalay, Yves and Bryant G. Garth. 2002. *The Internationalization of Palace Wars: Lawyers, Economists, and the Contest to Transform Latin American States.* Chicago: University of Chicago Press.

Dohan, Daniel. 2003. *The Price of Poverty: Money, Work, and Culture in the Mexican American Barrio.* Berkeley: University of California Press.

Domburg-de Rooij, T. and Sako Musterd. 2002. 'Ethnic Segregation and the Welfare State.' In I. Schnell and V. Ostendorf (eds), *Studies in Segregation and Desegregation* (Aldershot: Ashgate), pp. 107–31.

Drake, St. Clair and Horace R. Cayton. [1945, 1962] 1993. *Black Metropolis: A Study of Negro Life in a Northern City.* Chicago: University of Chicago Press.

Dubet, François. 1987. *La Galère. Jeunes en survie.* Paris: Fayard.

Dubet, François and Didier Lapeyronnie. 1992. *Les Quartiers d'exil.* Paris: Seuil.

Dubois, Vincent. 1999. *La Vie au guichet. Relation administrative et traitement de la misère.* Paris: Économica.

Du Bois, W. E. B. [1899] 1996. *The Philadelphia Negro: A Social Study.* Philadelphia: University of Pennsylvania Press.

Dubrow, Nancy F. and James Garbarino. 1989. 'Living in the War Zone: Mothers and Young Children in a Public Housing Development.' *Child Welfare* 68/1 (January): 3–20.

Dudley, Kathryn Marie. 1994. *The End of the Line: Lost Jobs, New Lives in Postindustrial America.* Chicago: University of Chicago Press.

Dulong, Renaud and Patricia Paperman. 1992. *La Réputation des cités HLM. Enquête sur le langage de l'insécurité.* Paris: L'Harmattan.

Duncan, Arne. 1987. 'The Values, Aspirations, and Opportunities of the Urban Underclass.' Unpublished Honors thesis, Harvard University.

Dunford, Michael. 1995. 'Metropolitan Polarisation, the North–South Divide and Socio-Spatial Inequality in Britain.' *European Urban and Regional Studies* 2: 145–70.

Dunford, Michael and Diane Perrons. 1994. 'Regional Inequality, Regimes of Accumulation and Economic Development in Contemporary Europe.' *Transactions of the Institute of British Geographers* 19/2 (June): 163–82.

Dunkerley, Michael. 1996. *The Jobless Economy? Computer Technology in the World of Work*. Cambridge: Polity.

Durand, Alain-Philippe (ed.). 2002. *Black, Blanc, Beur: Rap Music and Hip-Hop Culture in the Francophone World*. Lanham, MD: Scarecrow Press.

Durkheim, Emile and Marcel Mauss. [1903] 1967. *Primitive Classification*. Tr. with introduction by Rodney Needham. Chicago: University of Chicago Press.

Durmelat, Sylvie. 1998. 'Petite histoire du mot beur: ou comment prendre la parole quand on vous la prête.' *French Cultural Studies* 26: 191–207.

Eckstein, Susan. 1990. 'Urbanization Revisited: Inner-City Slums of Hope and Squatter Settlements.' *World Development* 18/2 (February): 165–81.

Edin, Kathryn. 1991. 'Surviving the Welfare System: How AFDC Recipients Make Ends Meet in Chicago.' *Social Problems* 38/4 (November): 462–74.

Edin, Kathryn. 2000. 'What Do Low-Income Single Mothers Say about Marriage?' *Social Problems* 47/1 (January): 112–33.

Edsall, Thomas Byrne and Mary D. Edsall. 1991. *Chain Reaction: The Impact of Race, Rights, and Taxes on American Politics*. New York: Norton.

Eitzen, D. S. and K. E. Smith. 2003. *Experiencing Poverty: Voices from the Bottom*. Belmont, CA: Wadsworth.

Elias, Norbert. [1937] 1978. *The Civilizing Process*. Oxford: Basil Blackwell.

Elliott, James R. and Mario Sims. 2001. 'Ghettos and Barrios: The Impact of Neighborhood Poverty and Race on Job Matching among Blacks and Latinos.' *Social Problems* 48/3 (September): 341–61.

Emigh, Rebecca Jean and Iván Szelényi (eds). 2001. *Poverty, Ethnicity and Gender in Eastern Europe During the Market Transition*. Westport, CT: Praeger.

Engbersen, Godfried. 1989. 'Cultures of Long-Term Unemployment in the New West.' *The Netherlands Journal of Social Sciences* 25/2 (October): 75–96.

Engbersen, Godfried. 1996. 'The Unknown City.' *Berkeley Journal of Sociology* 40: 87–112.

Engbersen, Godfried. 1997. *In de schaduw van morgen. Stedelijke marginaliteit in Nederland*. Amsterdam: Boom.

Engbersen, Godfried. 2001. 'The Urban Palimpsest: Urban Marginality in an Advanced Society.' *Focaal. Tijdschrift voor antropologie* 38/2 (Spring): 125–38.

Engbersen, Godfried, Kees Schuyt, Jaap Timmer and Frans Van Waarden. 1993. *Cultures of Unemployment: A Comparative Look at Long-Term Unemployment and Urban Poverty*. Boulder, CO: Westview Press.

Engels, Friedrich. [1845] 1987. *The Condition of the Working Class in England*. Preface by Victor Kiernan. London: Penguin.

Erder, Sema. 1997. *Kentsel gerilim* [Urban Tension]. Ankara: Umag.

Esping-Andersen, Gøsta. 1990. *The Three Worlds of Welfare Capitalism*. Princeton: Princeton University Press.

Esping-Andersen, Gøsta. 1999. *Social Foundations of Postindustrial Economies*. Oxford: Oxford University Press.

Esping-Andersen, Gøsta (ed.). 2002. *Why We Need a New Welfare State*. Oxford: Oxford University Press.

Esping-Andersen, Gøsta and Marino Regini (eds). 2000. *Why Deregulate Labour Markets?* Oxford: Oxford University Press.

Euvremer, Luc and Yves Euvremer. 1985. 'La honte.' *Archivari* (July): 6–10.

Fainstein, Norman. 1987. 'The Underclass/Mismatch Hypothesis as an Explanation for Black Economic Deprivation.' *Politics and Society* 15/4 (Winter): 403–52.

Fainstein, Susan S. and Norman I. Fainstein. 1989. 'The Racial Dimension in Urban Political Economy.' *Urban Affairs Quarterly* 25/2 (December): 187–99.

Fainstein, Susan S., Ian Gordon and Michael Harloe (eds). 1992. *Divided Cities: New York and London in the Contemporary World*. Oxford: Basil Blackwell.

Farley, Reynolds. 1996. *The New American Reality: Who We Are, How We Got There, Where We Are Going*. New York: Russell Sage Foundation.

Farley, Reynolds and Walter R. Allen. 1987. *The Color Line and the Quality of Life in America*. New York: Russell Sage Foundation.

Farley, Reynolds, Howard Schuman, Suzanne Bianchi, Diane Cosalanto and Shirley Hatchett. 1978. '"Chocolate City, Vanilla Suburbs": Will the Trend Toward Racially Separate Communities Continue?' *Social Science Research* 7/4 (December): 319–44.

Fassmann, Heinz and Rainer Münz. 1996. *Migration in Europa. Historische Entwicklung, aktuelle Trends, politische Reaktionen*. Frankfurt: Campus Verlag.

Fauset, Arthur. 1944. *Black Gods of the Metropolis: Negro Religious Cults of the Urban North*. Philadelphia: University of Pennsylvania Press, reissued 1971.

Feagin, Joe R. 1991. 'The Continuing Significance of Race: Antiblack Discrimination in Public Places.' *American Sociological Review* 56/1 (February): 101–16.

Fernandes, Florestan. 1978. *A Integração do Negro na Sociedade de Classes*, 2 vols. São Paulo: Editora Ática.

Fernandes, Luis. 1998. *O sítio das drogas. Etnografia das drogas numa periferia urbana*. Lisboa: Editorial Notícias.

Fields, Barbara Jeanne. 1990. 'Slavery, Race, and Ideology in the United States of America.' *New Left Review* 181 (May–June): 95–118.

Fischer, Claude S. 1982. *To Dwell Among Friends: Personal Networks in Town and City*. Chicago: University of Chicago Press.

Fishman, Robert. 1987. *Bourgeois Utopias: The Rise and Fall of Suburbia*. New York: Basic Books.

Fitzpatrick, Tony. 1999. *Freedom and Security: An Introduction to the Basic Income Debate*. London: Palgrave Macmillan.

Flanagan, William G. 1993. *Contemporary Urban Sociology*. Cambridge: Cambridge University Press.

Fligstein, Neil. 1997. *Markets, Politics, and Globalization*. Uppsala: Uppsala University Press.

Fogelson, Robert M. (ed.). 1971. *Violence as Protest: A Study of Riots and Ghettos*. Garden City, NY: Doubleday.

Foley, Donald. 1973. 'Institutional and Contextual Factors Affecting the Housing Choices of Minority Residents.' In Amos H. Hawley and Vincent P. Rock (eds), *Segregation in Residential Areas* (Washington, DC: National Academy of Sciences), pp. 185–247.

Foley, Douglas. 1990. *Learning Capitalist Culture: Deep in the Heart of Tejas*. Philadelphia: University of Pennsylvania Press.

Franklin, John Hope. 1980. *From Slavery to Freedom: A History of Negro Americans*, 5th edn. New York: Knopf.

Franklin, John Hope. 1993. *The Color Line: Legacy for the Twenty-First Century*. Columbia, MO: University of Missouri Press.

Franklin, Raymond. 1991. *Shadows of Race and Class*. Minneapolis: University of Minnesota Press.

Fraser, Penny. 1996. 'Social and Spatial Relationships and the "Problem" Inner City: Moss-Side in Manchester.' *Critical Social Policy* 49: 43–65.

Freeman, Richard B. (ed.). 1994. *Working Under Different Rules*. New York: Russell Sage Foundation.

Freeman, Richard B. 1998. 'Le modèle économique américain à l'épreuve de la comparaison.' *Actes de la recherche en sciences sociales* 124 (September): 36–48.

Freeman, Richard B. and Lawrence F. Katz (eds). 1994. *Differences and Changes in Wage Structures*. Chicago: University of Chicago Press.

Freyre, Gilberto. [1938] 1946. *The Masters and the Slaves: A Study in the Development of Brazilian Civilization*. New York: Knopf.

Friedrichs, Jürgen and John O'Loughlin (eds). 1996. *Social Polarization in Post-Industrial Metropolises*. New York: Walter de Gruyter.

Friedrichs, Jürgen, George Galster and Sako Musterd. 2003. 'Neighbourhood Effects on Social Opportunities: The European and American Research and Policy Context.' *Housing Studies* 18/6 (November): 797–806.

Galbraith, John Kenneth. 1958. *The Affluent Society*. Boston: Houghton Mifflin.

Gallie, Duncan (ed.). 2004. *Resisting Marginalization: Unemployment Experience and Social Policy in the European Union*. Oxford: Oxford University Press.

Gallie, Duncan and Serge Paugam (eds). 2000. *Welfare Regimes and the Experience of Unemployment in Europe*. Oxford: Oxford University Press.

Galster, George and Anne Zober. 1997. 'Will Dispersed Housing Programmes Reduce Social Problems in the US?' *Housing Studies* 13/5: 605–22.

Gans, Herbert J. 1991. 'The Dangers of the Underclass: Its Harmfulness as a Planning Concept.' In *People, Plans and Policies: Essays on Poverty, Racism, and Other National Urban Problems* (New York: Columbia University Press), pp. 328–43.

Gans, Herbert J. 1994. 'Positive Functions of the Undeserving Poor: Uses of the Underclass in America.' *Politics and Society* 22/3 (September): 269–83.

Garbarino, James, Kathleen Kostelny and Nancy Dubrow. 1991. *No Place to be a Child: Growing Up in a War Zone*. Lexington, MA: Lexington Books.

Gephart, Martha A. and Robert W. Pearson. 1988. 'Contemporary Research on the Urban Underclass: A Selected Review of the Research that Underlies a New Council Program.' *Items: Social Science Research Council* 42/1–2 (June): 1–10.

Gershuny, Jonathan I. 1983. *Social Innovation and the Division of Labour*. Oxford: Oxford University Press.

Gervais-Lambony, Philippe, Sylvie Jaglin and Alan Mabin. 1999. *La Question urbaine en Afrique Australe*. Paris: Karthala.

Gittleman, Maury B. and David R. Howell. 1995. 'Changes in the Structure and Quality of Jobs in the United States: Effects by Race and Gender, 1973–1990.' *Industrial and Labor Relations Review* 48/3 (April): 420–40.

Glaser, Barney G. and Anselm L. Strauss. 1965. *Awareness of Dying*. New York: Aldine de Gruyter; new edn. 2005.

Glasgow, Douglas. 1981. *The Black Underclass: Poverty, Unemployment, and Entrapment of Ghetto Youth*. New York: Vintage.

Godard, Francis. 1993. 'La ville américaine: futur de nos villes?' *PIR-Villes* 2: 4–10.

Goffman, Erving. 1959. *The Presentation of Self in Everyday Life*. Garden City, NY: Doubleday.

Goffman, Erving. 1963. *Stigma: Notes on the Management of Spoiled Identity*. New York: Simon & Schuster.

Goldberger, Marie-Françoise, Philippe Choffel and Jean-Luc Le Toqueux. 1998. 'Les zones urbaines sensibles.' *Insee Première* 573 (April).

Goldstein, Donna M. 2003. *Laughter Out of Place: Race, Class, Violence, and Sexuality in a Rio Shantytown*. Berkeley: University of California Press.

González de la Rocha, Mercedes. 1994. *The Resources of Poverty: Women and Survival in a Mexican City*. Cambridge, MA: Blackwell Publishers.

González de la Rocha, Mercedes, Elizabeth Jelín, Janice Perlman, Bryan R. Roberts, Helen Safa and Peter M. Ward. 2004. 'From the Marginality of the 1960s to the "New Poverty" of Today: A LARR Research Forum.' *Latin American Research Review* 39/1 (January): 183–203.

Goode, Erich and Nachman Ben-Yehuda. 1994. 'Moral Panics: Culture, Politics, and Social Construction.' *Annual Review of Sociology* 20: 149–71.

Gooding-Williams, Robert (ed.). 1993. *Reading Rodney King, Reading Urban Uprising.* New York: Routledge.

Gordon, Linda (ed.). 1990. *Women, the State, and Welfare.* Madison: University of Wisconsin Press.

Gordon, Milton. 1961. 'Assimilation in America: Theory and Reality.' *Daedalus* 90/2 (Spring): 263–85.

Gottdiener, Mark and Joe R. Feagin. 1988. 'The Paradigm Shift in Urban Sociology.' *Urban Affairs Quarterly* 24/2 (December): 163–87.

Gregory, Mary, Wiemer Salverda and Stephen Bazen. 2000. *Labour Market Inequalities: Problems and Policies of Low-Wage Employment in International Perspective.* Oxford: Oxford University Press.

Gregory, Steven. 1998. *Black Corona: Race and the Politics of Place in an Urban Community.* Princeton: Princeton University Press.

Guest, M., D. Avery, Gunnar Almgren and Jon M. Mussey. 1998. 'The Ecology of Race and Socioeconomic Distress: Infant and Working-Age Mortality in Chicago.' *Demography* 35/1 (February): 24–34.

Gurr, Ted Robert and Desmond S. King. 1987. *The State and the City.* Chicago: University of Chicago Press.

Gusfield, Joseph. 1981. *The Culture of Public Problems: Drinking-Driving and the Symbolic Order.* Chicago: University of Chicago Press.

Gwaltney, John Langston. 1981. *Drylongso: A Self-Portrait of Black America.* New York: Vintage.

Habermas, Jürgen. [1981] 1984. *The Theory of Communicative Action*, vol. 1: *Reason and the Rationalization of Society.* Boston: Beacon Press.

Hadjimichalis, Costis and David Sadler (eds). 1995. *Europe at the Margins: New Mosaics of Inequality.* New York: John Wiley.

Hagan, John and Bill McCarthy. 1997. *Mean Streets: Youth Crime and Homelessness.* Cambridge: Cambridge University Press.

Hagan, John, Paul Hirschfield and Carla Shedd. 2002. 'First and Last Words: Apprehending the Social and Legal Facts of an Urban High School Shooting.' *Sociological Methods and Research* 31/2 (November): 218–54.

Hall, Peter. 2002. *Urban and Regional Planning.* London: Routledge.

Handler, A., D. Rosenberg, M. Driscol, M. Cohen, E. Swift, P. Garcia and J. Cohn. 1991. 'Regional Perinatal Care in Crisis: A Case Study of an Urban Public Hospital.' *Journal of Public Health Policy* 12/2 (Summer): 184–98.

Hannerz, Ulf. 1968. 'The Rhetoric of Soul: Identification in Negro Society.' *Race* 9/4 (Winter): 453–65.

Hannerz, Ulf. 1969. *Soulside: Inquiries into Ghetto Culture and Community.* New York: Columbia University Press.

Hannerz, Ulf. 1980. *Exploring the City: Inquiries Toward an Urban Anthropology.* New York: Columbia University Press.

Harloe, David. 1985. *Private Rented Housing in the United States.* London: Croom Helm.

Harrell, Adele V. and George E. Peterson (eds). 1992. *Drugs, Crime, and Social Isolation: Barriers to Urban Opportunity.* Washington, DC: Urban Institute Press.

Harris, Fred and Roger W. Wilkins (eds). 1988. *Quiet Riots: Race and Poverty in the United States (The Kerner Report, Twenty Years Later).* New York: Pantheon.

Harrison, Bennett. 1994. *Lean and Mean: The Changing Landscape of Corporate Power in the Age of Flexibility.* New York: Basic Books.

Hartner, Susan (ed.). 1998. *Illinois Statistical Abstract.* Urbana: University of Illinois Press.

Harvey, David. 1989. *The Condition of Postmodernity: An Inquiry into the Origins of Cultural Change.* Oxford: Basil Blackwell.

Häußermann, Hartmut (ed.). 1998. *Großstadt. Soziologische Stichworte.* Opladen: Leske & Budrich.

Hazen, Don (ed.). 1992. *Inside the LA Riots: What Really Happened and Why it Will Happen Again.* New York: Independent Publishers Group.

Hazzard-Gordon, Katherine. 1991. *Jookin': The Rise of Social Dance Formations in African-American Culture.* Philadelphia: Temple University Press.

Hein, Jeremy. 1993. 'Ethnic Pluralism and the Disunited States of North America and Western Europe.' *Sociological Forum* 8/3 (September): 507–16.

Heisler, Barbara Schmitter. 1991. 'A Comparative Perspective on the Underclass: Questions of Urban Poverty, Race, and Citizenship.' *Theory and Society* 20/4 (August): 455–83.

Henni, Amar and Gilles Marinet. 2002. *Cités hors-la-loi. Un autre monde, une jeunesse qui impose ses lois.* Paris: Ramsay.

Herbert, Steve. 1997. *Policing Space: Territoriality and the Los Angeles Police Department.* Minneapolis: University of Minnesota Press.

Hicks, Donald A. 1985. *Advanced Industrial Development: Restructuring, Relocation, and Renewal.* Boston: Oelgeschlager, Gun & Hain.

Hilgartner, Stephen and Charles S. Bosk. 1988. 'The Rise and Fall of Social Problems: A Public Arenas Model.' *American Journal of Sociology* 94/1 (July): 53–78.

Himmelfarb, Gertrude. 1994. *The De-moralization of Society: From Victorian Virtues to Modern Values.* New York: Vintage Books.

Hirsch, Arnold R. 1983. *Making the Second Ghetto: Race and Housing in Chicago, 1940–1960.* Cambridge: Cambridge University Press.

Hirsch, Paul M. 1993. 'Undoing the Managerial Revolution? Needed Research on the Decline of Middle Management and Internal Labor

Markets.' In Richard Swedberg (dir.), *Explorations in Economic Sociology* (New York: Russell Sage Foundation), pp. 145–57.

Hirschman, Charles. 1983. 'America's Melting Pot Reconsidered.' *Annual Review of Sociology* 9: 397–423.

Hochschild, Jennifer L. 1995. *Facing Up to the American Dream.* Princeton: Princeton University Press.

Holdt, Jacob. 1985. *American Pictures: A Personal Journey Through America's Underclass.* New York: Farrar, Straus, Giroux.

Hollifield, James F. 1991. 'Immigration and Modernization.' In James F. Hollifield and George Ross (eds), *Searching for the New France* (New York: Routledge), pp. 113–50.

Holston, James (ed.). 1999. *Cities and Citizenship.* Durham, NC: Duke University Press.

Holzner, Lutz. 1993. 'Minority Relations and Conflict in the Emerging European Community, Specifically Germany, France and Great Britain.' *Humboldt Journal of Social Relations* 19/2 (Spring): 157–92.

hooks, bell. 1992. 'Loving Blackness as Political Resistance.' In *Black Looks: Race and Representation* (Boston: South End Press), pp. 9–20.

Horsman, Reginald. 1986. *Race and Manifest Destiny: Origins of American Racial Anglo-Saxonism.* Cambridge, MA: Harvard University Press.

Huber, Evelyne and John D. Stephens. 2001. *Development and Crisis of the Welfare State: Parties and Policies in Global Markets.* Chicago: University of Chicago Press.

Hudson, Michael (ed.). 1996. *Merchants of Misery: How Corporate America Profits from Poverty.* Monroe, ME: Common Courage Press.

Hunt, Lynn. 1992. *The Family Romance of the French Revolution.* Berkeley: University of California Press.

Husbands, Christopher T. 1991. 'The Support for the "Front National": Analyses and Findings.' *Ethnic and Racial Studies* 14/3 (July): 382–416.

Huttman, Elizabeth H. 1991. 'Subsidized Housing in Western Europe: Stigma and Segregation.' In Elizabeth H. Huttman, Wim Blauw and Juliet Saltman (eds), *Urban Housing Segregation of Minorities in Western Europe and the United States* (Durham, NC: Duke University Press), pp. 215–35.

Jackson, Kenneth T. 1985. *Crabgrass Frontier: The Suburbanization of the United States.* New York: Oxford University Press.

Jacquier, Claude. 1991. *Voyage dans six quartiers européens en crise.* Paris: L'Harmattan.

Jargowsky, Paul A. 1997. *Poverty and Place: Ghettos, Barrios, and the American City.* New York: Russell Sage Foundation.

Jargowsky, Paul A. and Mary Jo Bane. 1991. 'Ghetto Poverty in the United States, 1970–1980.' In Christopher Jencks and Paul E. Peterson (eds), *The Urban Underclass* (Washington, DC: The Brookings Institution), pp. 235–73.

Jazouli, Adil. 1992. *Les Années banlieues.* Paris: Seuil.

Jencks, Christopher and Paul E. Peterson (eds). 1991. *The Urban Underclass.* Washington, DC: The Brookings Institution.

Jobard, Fabien. 2002. *Bavures policières? La force publique et ses usages.* Paris: La Découverte.

Johnson, Bruce, Terry Williams, Kojo A. Dei and Harry Sanabria. 1990. 'Drug Abuse in the Inner City: Impact on Hard-Drug Users and the Community.' In Michael Tonry and James Q. Wilson (eds), *Drugs and Crime* (Chicago: University of Chicago Press), pp. 9–67.

Johnson, James H., Cloyzelle K. Jones, Walter C. Farrell, Jr., and Melvin L. Oliver. 1992. 'The Los Angeles Rebellion: A Retrospective View.' *Economic Development Quarterly* 6/4 (November): 356–72.

Johnson, James H., Walter C. Farrell and Melvin L. Oliver. 1993. 'Seeds of the Los Angeles Rebellion of 1992.' *International Journal of Urban and Regional Research* 17/1 (March): 115–19.

Jones, Jacqueline. 1985. *Labor of Love, Labor of Sorrow: Black Women, Work, and the Family from Slavery to the Present.* New York: Vintage.

Jones, Jacqueline. 1992. *The Dispossessed: America's Underclasses from the Civil War to the Present.* New York: Basic Books.

Jones, LeAlan and Lloyd Newman. 1997. *Our America: Life and Death on the South Side of Chicago.* New York: Washington Square Press.

Jones, Yvonne V. 1988. 'Street Peddlers as Entrepreneurs: Economic Adaptation to an Urban Area.' *Urban Anthropology* 17/2–3 (Summer–Fall): 143–70.

Kantor, Harvey and Barbara Brenzel. 1993. 'Urban Education and the "Truly Disadvantaged": The Historical Roots of the Contemporary Crisis.' In Michael B. Katz (ed.), *The 'Underclass' Debate: Views from History* (Princeton: Princeton University Press), pp. 366–404.

Kasarda, John D. 1989. 'Urban Industrial Transition and the Underclass.' *Annals of the American Academy of Political and Social Science* 501 (January): 26–47.

Katz, Michael B. [1986] 1996. *In the Shadow of the Poorhouse: A Social History of Welfare in America,* new expanded edn. New York: Basic Books.

Katz, Michael B. 1989. *The Undeserving Poor: From the War on Poverty to the War on Welfare.* New York: Pantheon.

Katz, Michael B. (ed.). 1993. *The 'Underclass' Debate: Views from History.* Princeton: Princeton University Press.

Katznelson, Ira. 1981. *Urban Trenches: Urban Politics and the Patterning of Class in the United States.* New York: Pantheon.

Keil, Charles. 1966. *Urban Blues.* Chicago: University of Chicago Press.

Keiser, R. Lincoln. 1969. *The Vice Lords: Warriors of the Streets.* New York: Holt.

Kepel, Gilles. 1987. *Les Banlieues de l'Islam. Naissance d'une religion en France.* Paris: Seuil.

Kerner Commission. [1968] 1988. *The Kerner Report: The 1968 Report of the National Advisory Commission on Civil Disorders.* New York: Pantheon Books.

Kesteloot, Christian. 2000. 'Post-Fordist Polarization in a Fordist Spatial Canvas.' In Peter Marcuse and Ronald Van Kempen (eds), *Globalizing Cities: A New Spatial Order?* (Oxford: Blackwell), pp. 186–210.

Keyder, Caglar. 2005. 'Globalization and Social Exclusion in Istanbul.' *International Journal of Urban and Regional Research* 29/1 (March): 124–34.

Khellil, Mohand. 1991. *L'Intégration des Maghrébins en France*. Paris: Presses Universitaires de France.

Killian, Lewis M. 1990. 'Race Relations and the Nineties: Where are the Dreams of the Sixties?' *Social Forces* 69/1 (September): 1–13.

Kluegel, James R. and Eliot R. Smith. 1986. *Beliefs about Inequality: Americans' Views of What Is and What Ought to Be*. New York: Aldine de Gruyter.

Knotterus, J. David. 1987. 'Status Attainment Research and Its Image of Society.' *American Sociological Review* 52/2 (March): 113–21.

Kornblum, William. 1974. *Blue-Collar Community*. Chicago: University of Chicago Press.

Kornblum, William. 1984. 'Lumping the Poor: What *is* the "Underclass"?' *Dissent* 64/3 (Summer): 295–302.

Koser, Khalid and Helma Lutz (eds). 1999. *The New Migration in Europe: Social Constructions and Social Realities*. London: Palgrave Macmillan.

Kotlowitz, Alex. 1991. *There Are No Children Here: The Story of Two Boys Growing Up in the Other America*. New York: Doubleday.

Kozol, Jonathan. 1991. *Savage Inequalities: Children in America's Schools*. New York: Crown Publishing.

Kronauer, Martin, Berthold Vogel and Frank Gerlach. 1993. *Im Schatten der Arbeitsgesellschaft. Arbeitslose und die Dynamik sozialer Ausgrenzung*. Berlin: Campus Verlag.

Kumar, Krishan. 1995. *From Post-Industrial to Post-Modern Society: New Theories of the Contemporary World*. Oxford: Basil Blackwell.

Kusmer, Kenneth L. 1976. *A Ghetto Takes Shape: Black Cleveland, 1870–1930*. Urbana: University of Illinois Press.

Kusmer, Kenneth L. 1986. 'The Black Urban Experience in American History.' In Darlene Clark Hine (ed.), *The State of Afro-American History: Past, Present, and Future* (Baton Rouge: Louisiana State University Press), pp. 91–135.

Ladányi, János and Iván Szelényi. 2002. 'Ciganyok es szegenyek Magyarorszagon, Romaniaban es Bulgariaban' [The Nature and Determinants of Poverty among the Roma: A Comparative Study of Hungary, Romania, and Bulgaria]. *Szociologiai Szemle* 4: 72–94.

Laé, Jean-François and Numa Murard. 1985. *L'Argent des pauvres. La vie quotidienne en cité de transit*. Paris: Seuil.

Laé, Jean-François and Numa Murard. 1988. 'Protection et violence.' *Cahiers internationaux de sociologie* 35/84 (January–June): 19–39.

Laé, Jean-François and Numa Murard. 1995. *Les Récits du malheur*. Paris: Descartes & Cie.

Lago, Luciana Corrêa do. 2005. *Desigualdades e segregação na metrópole. O Rio de Janeiro em tempo de crise*. Rio de Janeiro: Revan.

Lamphere, Louise (ed.). 1992. *Structuring Diversity: Ethnographic Perspectives on the New Immigration*. Chicago: University of Chicago Press.

Landry, Bart. 1987. *The New Black Middle Class*. Berkeley: University of California Press.

Lane, Roger. 1986. *Roots of Violence in Black Philadelphia, 1860–1900*. Cambridge, MA: Harvard University Press.

Lanzarini, Corinne. 2000. *Survivre dans le monde sous-prolétaire*. Paris: Presses Universitaires de France.

Lapeyronnie, Didier. 1987. 'Les jeunes Maghrébins nés en France: assimilation, mobilisation et action.' *Revue française de sociologie* 28/2 (June): 287–318.

Lapeyronnie, Didier. 1992. 'L'exclusion et le mépris.' *Les Temps modernes* (December): 2–17.

Lapeyronnie, Didier and Marcin Frybes. 1990. *L'Intégration des minorités immigrées. Étude comparative France-Grande-Bretagne*. Issy-les-Moulineaux: ADRI.

Lash, Scott and John Urry. 1987. *The End of Organized Capitalism*. Madison: University of Wisconsin Press.

Lauritzen, Janet and Robert J. Sampson. 1998. 'Minorities, Crime, and Criminal Justice.' In Michael Tonry (ed.), *The Handbook of Crime and Punishment* (New York: Oxford University Press), pp. 58–84.

La Vigne, Nancy G., Cynthia A. Mamalian, Jeremy Travis and Christy Visher. 2003. *A Portrait of Prisoner Reentry in Illinois*. Washington, DC: Urban Institute.

Lawrence, Paul, Timothy Baycroft and Carolyn Grohmann. 2001. ' "Degrees of Foreignness" and the Construction of Identity in French Border Regions during the Inter-war Period.' *Contemporary European History* 10/1 (January): 51–71.

Lebaude, Alain. 1994. *L'Emploi en miettes*. Paris: Hachette.

Le Bras, Hervé. 1989. 'Le spectre des ghettos: et si l'Europe tombait dans le piège américain?' *Le Nouvel Observateur: L'Europe multiraciale* 4 (January–February).

Le Galès, Patrick. 1996. 'L'Exclusion et la politique urbaine.' In Serge Paugam (ed.), *L'Exclusion: l'état des savoirs* (Paris: La Découverte), pp. 376–85.

Le Galès, Patrick and Michael Parkinson. 1993. '*Inner city policy* en Grande-Bretagne: origine et principaux programmes.' *Revue française d'administration publique* 74: 483–98.

Leibfried, Stefan and Paul Pierson (eds). 1995. *European Social Policy Between Fragmentation and Integration*. Washington, DC: The Brookings Institution.

Le Monde. 1991. 'La Ville et ses banlieues.' *Le Monde: Dossiers et documents* 185 (February).

Lenoir, Noëlle, Claire Guignard-Hamon and Nicole Smadja. 1989. *Bilan et perspectives des contrats de plan de développement social des quartiers*. Paris: Commissariat général au plan/La Documentation française.

Leonard, Madeleine. 1998. *Invisible Work, Invisible Workers: The Informal Economy in Europe and the US*. Basingstoke: Palgrave Macmillan.

Lepoutre, David. 1997. *Cœur de banlieue. Codes, rites et languages*. Paris: Odile Jacob.

Le Puill, Gérard and Stéphane Le Puill. 1990. *La Décennie des nouveaux pauvres*. Paris: Messidor/Editions sociales.

Leray, Rudy. 1989. 'Les quartiers sensibles en Ile-de-France.' In *Données sociales Ile-de-France 1989*. Paris: INSEE.

Lerner, Daniel. 1958. *The Passing of Traditional Society: Modernizing the Middle East*. Glencoe, IL: Free Press.

Le Toqueux, Jean-Luc and Jacques Moreau. 2000. 'Les zones urbaines sensibles: forte progression du chômage entre 1990 et 1999.' *INSEE Première*, no. 334 (October).

Levine, Lawrence. 1977. *Black Culture and Black Consciousness: Afro-American Folk Thought from Slavery to Freedom*. New York: Oxford University Press.

Lewis, David Levering. 1970. *King: A Critical Biography*. New York: Praeger.

Lewis, Oscar. 1961. *The Children of Sanchez: Autobiography of a Mexican Family*. New York: Vintage.

Lewis, Sydney. 1995. *Hospital: An Oral History of Cook County Hospital*. New York: New Press.

Lieberson, Stanley. 1985. *Making it Count: The Improvement of Social Theory and Social Research*. Berkeley: University of California Press.

Liebow, Elliot. 1967. *Tally's Corner: A Study of Negro Streetcorner Men*. Boston: Little, Brown and Co.

Light, Ivan. 1977. 'The Ethnic Vice Industry, 1880–1944.' *American Sociological Review* 42/3 (June): 464–79.

Lipsitz, George. 1988. *A Life in the Struggle: Ivory Perry and the Culture of Opposition*. Philadelphia: Temple University Press.

Lipsky, Michael J. 1980. *Street Level Bureaucracy: Dilemmas of the Individual in Public Services*. New York: Russell Sage Foundation.

Loewenstein, Gaither. 1985. 'The New Underclass: A Contemporary Sociological Dilemma.' *Sociological Quarterly* 26/1 (Spring): 35–48.

Logan, John R. and Harvey L. Molotch. 1989. *Urban Fortunes: The Political Economy of Place*. Berkeley: University of California Press.

Lomnitz, Larissa. [1975] 1977. *Networks and Marginality: Life in a Mexican Shantytown*. New York: Academic Press.

Mabit, René and Jean Boissonnat (eds). 1995. *Le Travail dans vingt ans*. Paris: Odile Jacob.

MacDonald, Cameron Lynn and Carmen Sirianni (eds). 1996. *Working in the Service Society*. Philadelphia: Temple University Press.

MacDonald, Robert (ed.). 1997. *Youth, the 'Underclass' and Social Exclusion*. London: Routledge.

Macdonald, Sharon (ed.). 1993. *Inside European Identities: Ethnography in Western Europe*. New York: Berg.

Mackert, Jürgen (ed.). 2004. *Die Theorie sozialer Schließung. Tradition, Analysen, Perspektiven*. Wiesbaden: VS Verlag für Sozialwissenschaften.

MacLeod, Jay. 1995. *Ain't No Makin' It: Aspirations and Attainment in a Low-Income Neighborhood*, 2nd expanded ed. Boulder, CO: Westview Press.

Macpherson, Crawford Brough. 1964. *The Political Theory of Possessive Individualism: Hobbes to Locke*. Oxford: Oxford University Press.

Magri, Susanna and Christian Topalov (eds). 1989. *Villes ouvrières, 1900–1950*. Paris: L'Harmattan.

Mann, Michael. 1995. 'Sources and Variations of Working Class Movements in Twentieth Century Europe.' *New Left Review* 22: 14–54.

Marcuse, Peter. 1989. ' "Dual City": A Muddy Metaphor for a Quartered City.' *International Journal of Urban and Regional Research* 13/4 (December): 697–708.

Marcuse, Peter. 1993. 'What's So New about Divided Cities?' *International Journal of Urban and Regional Research* 17/3 (September): 355–65.

Marcuse, Peter and Ronald van Kempen (eds). 2002. *Of States and Cities: The Partitioning of Urban Space*. New York: Oxford University Press.

Marcuse, Peter, Peter Medoff and Andrea Pereira. 1982. 'Triage as Urban Policy.' *Social Policy* 12/3 (Winter): 33–7.

Marklund, Stephan. 1990. 'Structures of Modern Poverty.' *Acta Sociologica* 33/2 (May): 125–40.

Marks, Carole. 1991. 'The Urban Underclass.' *Annual Review of Sociology* 17: 445–66.

Marpsat, Maryse. 1999. 'La Modélisation des "effets de quartier" aux États-Unis: une revue des travaux récents.' *Population* 54/2 (March–April): 303–30.

Marshall, Gordon. 1997. *Repositioning Class: Social Inequality in Industrial Societies*. London: Sage.

Marshall, T. H. [1949] 1964. *Class, Citizenship, and Social Development*. New York: Doubleday.

Martiniello, Marco. 1995. *Migration, Citizenship, and Ethno-National Identities in the European Union*. London: Avebury.

Martinotti, Guido. 1993. *Metropoli. La nuova morfologia sociale della città*. Bologna: Il Mulino.

Masclet, Olivier. 2003. *La Gauche et les cités. Enquête sur un rendez-vous manqué*. Paris: La Dispute.

Maspéro, François. 1990. *Les Passagers du Roissy-Express*. Paris: Seuil.

Massey, Douglas S. 1990. 'American Apartheid: Segregation and the Making of the Underclass.' *American Journal of Sociology* 96/2 (September): 329–57.

Massey, Douglas S. and Nancy A. Denton. 1987. 'Trends in Residential Segregation of Blacks, Hispanics, and Asians.' *American Sociological Review* 52/6 (December): 802–25.

Massey, Douglas S. and Nancy A. Denton. 1989. 'Hypersegregation in U.S. Metropolitan Areas: Black and Hispanic Segregation Along Five Dimensions.' *Demography* 26/3 (August): 373–91.

Massey, Douglas S. and Nancy A. Denton. 1993. *American Apartheid: Segregation and the Making of the Underclass*. Cambridge, MA: Harvard University Press.

Massey, Douglas S. and Mary Fischer. 1999. 'Does Rising Income Bring Integration? New Results for Blacks, Hispanics, and Asians in 1990.' *Social Science Research* 28/3 (September): 316–26.

Massey, Douglas S. and Andrew B. Gross. 1991. 'Explaining Trends in Residential Segregation, 1970–80.' *Urban Affairs Quarterly* 27: 13–35.

Massey, Douglas and Brendan Mullan. 1984. 'Processes of Hispanic and Black Spatial Assimilation.' *American Journal of Sociology* 89/4 (January): 836–73.

Massey, Douglas, Andrew Ross and Kumiko Shibuya. 1994. 'Migration, Segregation, and the Concentration of Poverty.' *American Sociological Review* 59/3 (May): 425–45.

Massey, Douglas S., Gretchen A. Condram, and Nancy Denton. 1987. 'The Effect of Residential Segregation on Black Social and Economic Well-Being.' *Social Forces* 66/1 (September): 29–56.

Mauger, Gérard and Claude Fossé-Polliak. 1983. 'Les loubards.' *Actes de la recherche en sciences sociales* 50: 49–57.

Maurin, Éric. 2004. *Le Ghetto français*. Paris: Seuil.

Mauss, Marcel. 1929. 'Les civilisations. Éléments et formes.' Repr. in *Œuvres*. vol. 2: *Représentations collectives et diversité des civilisations* (Paris: Minuit, 1974), pp. 456–79.

Mayol, Pierre. 1992. 'Radiographie des banlieues.' *Esprit* 182 (June): 65–77.

McAdam, Doug. 1981. *Political Process and the Development of Black Insurgency*. Chicago: University of Chicago Press.

McCord, C. and H. Freeman. 1990. 'Excess Mortality in Harlem.' *New England Journal of Medicine* 322/3: 173–7.

McCord, Joan (ed.). 1997. *Violence and Childhood in the Inner City*. Cambridge: Cambridge University Press.

McFate, Katherine, Roger Lawson and William Julius Wilson (eds). 1995. *Poverty, Inequality, and the Future of Social Policy: Western States in the New World Order*. New York: Russell Sage Foundation.

McRoberts, Omar M. 2003. *Streets of Glory: Church and Community in a Black Urban Neighborhood*. Chicago: University of Chicago Press.

Mead, Lawrence. 1986. *Beyond Entitlements: The Social Obligations of Citizenship*. New York: Free Press.

Mead, Lawrence. 1989. 'The Logic of Workfare: The Underclass and Work Policy.' *Annals of the American Academy of Political and Social Science* 501 (January): 156–69.

Mead, Lawrence. 1992. *The New Politics of Poverty*. New York: Basic Books.

Mele, Christopher. 1999. *Selling the Lower East Side: Culture, Real Estate, and Resistance in New York City*. Minneapolis: University of Minnesota Press.

Mendras, Henri with Alistair Cooke. [1989] 1991. *Social Change in Modern France: Towards a Cultural Anthropology of the Fifth Republic*. Cambridge: Cambridge University Press.

Merton, Robert K. 1983. 'Three Fragments from a Sociologist's Notebook.' *Annual Review of Sociology* 13: 1–28.

Meyer, Stephen. 2000. *As Long As They Don't Move Next Door: Segregation and Racial Conflict in American Neighborhoods*. Lanham, MD: Rowman and Littlefield.

Miles, Robert. 1992. 'Le racisme européen dans son contexte historique: réflexions sur l'articulation du racisme et du nationalisme.' *Genèses* 8 (June): 108–31.

Miller, Eleanor. 1987. *Street Woman*. Philadelphia: Temple University Press.

Mingione, Enzo. 1991. *Fragmented Societies: A Sociology of Economic Life Beyond the Market Paradigm*. Oxford: Basil Blackwell.

Mingione, Enzo (ed.). 1993. Special issue on 'The New Urban Poverty and the Underclass.' *International Journal of Urban and Regional Research* 17/3 (September): 324–428.

Mingione, Enzo (ed.). 1996. *Urban Poverty and the 'Underclass'*. Malden, MA: Blackwell Publishers.

Mingione, Enzo and Enrica Morlicchio. 1993. 'New Forms of Urban Poverty in Italy: Risk Path Models in the North and South.' *International Journal of Urban and Regional Research* 17/3 (September): 413–27.

Mithun, Jacqueline S. 1973. 'Cooperation and Solidarity as Survival Necessities in a Black Urban Community.' *Urban Anthropology* 2/1 (Spring): 25–34.

Mollenkopf, John H. and Manuel Castells (eds). 1991. *Dual City: Restructuring New York*. New York: Russell Sage Foundation.

Monroe, Sylvester and Peter Goldman. 1988. *Brothers: Black and Poor – A True Story of Courage and Survival*. New York: William Morrow.

Moore, Joan and Raquel Pinderhughes (eds). 1993. *In the Barrio: Latinos and the Underclass Debate*. New York: Russell Sage Foundation.

Moore, Stephen and Dean Stansel. 1995. *Ending Corporate Welfare as We Know It*. Washington, DC: Cato Institute.

Moran, Rachel. 2003. *Interracial Intimacy: The Regulation of Race and Romance*. Chicago: University of Chicago Press.

Morenoff, Jeffrey D. and Robert J. Sampson. 1997. 'Violent Crime and the Spatial Dynamics of Neighbourhood Transition: Chicago, 1970–1990.' *Social Forces* 76/1 (September): 31–64.

Morris, Aldon. 1984. *The Origins of the Civil Rights Movement: Black Communities Organizing for Change*. New York: Free Press.

Morris, Lydia. 1994. *Dangerous Classes: The Underclass and Social Citizenship*. London: Routledge.

Moynihan, Daniel Patrick. 1969. 'Toward a National Urban Policy.' *The Public Interest* (Fall): 8–9.

Munger, Frank (ed.). 2002. *Laboring Below the Line: The New Ethnography of Poverty, Low-Wage Work, and Survival in the Global Economy*. New York: Russell Sage Foundation.

Murray, Charles. 1984. *Losing Ground: American Social Policy, 1950–1980*. New York: Basic Books.

Murty, Komanduri, Julian B. Roebuck and Gloria R. Amstrong. 1994. 'The Black Community's Reactions to the 1992 Los Angeles Riot.' *Deviant Behavior* 15/1 (January): 85–104.

Musterd, Sako (ed.). 1994. Special issue on 'A Rising European Under-class?' *Built Environment* 20/3 (Fall).

Musterd, Sako. 2005. 'Social and Ethnic Segregation in Europe: Levels, Causes, and Effect.' *Journal of Urban Affairs* 27/3 (August): 311-48.

Musterd, Sako, Wim Ostendorf and Matthijs Breebaart (eds). 1998. *Multi-Ethnic Metropolis: Patterns and Policies*. Dordrecht: Kluwer.

Myrdal, Gunnar. 1944. *An American Dilemma: The Negro Problem and Modern Democracy*. New York: Harper.

Nagel, Joanne. 1986. 'The Political Construction of Ethnicity.' In Susan Olzak and Joanne Nagel (eds), *Competitive Ethnic Relations* (Orlando, FL: Academic Press), pp. 93–112.

Nathan, Richard P. 1987. 'Will the Underclass Always be with Us?' *Society* 24/3 (March): 57–62.

Newman, Katherine. 1988. *Falling from Grace: Downward Mobility in the Age of Affluence*. New York: Free Press.

Newman, Peter and Andy Thornley. 1996. *Urban Planning in Europe: International Competition, National Systems, and Planning Projects*. London: Routledge.

Noiriel, Gérard. 1988. *Le Creuset français. Histoire de l'immigration, XIXe–XXe siècles*. Paris: Seuil. Tr. as *The French Melting Pot: Immigration, Citizenship, and National Identity* (Minneapolis: University of Minnesota Press, 1996).

Noiriel, Gérard. 1992. *Population, immigration et identité nationale en France: XIXe–XXe siècles*. Paris: Hachette.

Nolan, Brian, Richard Hauser and Jean-Paul Zoyem. 2000. 'The Changing Effects of Social Protection on Poverty.' In Duncan Gallie and Serge Paugam (eds), *Welfare Regimes and the Experience of Unemployment in Europe* (Oxford: Oxford University Press), pp. 87–106.

O'Connor, Alice. 2000. 'Poverty Research and Policy for the Post-Welfare Era.' *Annual Review of Sociology* 26: 547–62.

O'Connor, Alice, Chris Tilly and Lawrence D. Bobo (eds). 2001. *Urban Inequality: Evidence from Four Cities*. New York: Russell Sage Foundation.

Offe, Claus. 1985. *Disorganized Capitalism: Contemporary Transformations of Work and Politics*, ed. John Keane. Cambridge, MA: MIT Press.

Offe, Claus and Rolf G. Heinze. 1992. *Beyond Employment: Time, Work, and the Informal Economy*. Philadelphia: Temple University Press.

Oliver, Melvin. 1988. 'The Urban Black Community as Network: Toward a Social Network Perspective.' *Sociological Quarterly* 29/4: 623–45.

Orfield, Gary. 1985. 'Ghettoization and Its Alternatives.' In Paul Peterson (ed.), *The New Urban Reality* (Washington, DC: The Brookings Institution), pp. 161–93.

Osofsky, Gilbert. 1968. 'The Enduring Ghetto.' *Journal of American History* 55/2 (September): 243–55.

Osterman, Paul. 1991. 'Gains from Growth? The Impact of Full Employment on Poverty in Boston.' In Christopher Jencks and Paul E. Peterson (eds), *The Urban Underclass* (Washington, DC: The Brookings Institution), pp. 122–43.

Osterman, Paul. 1999. *Securing Prosperity: The American Labor Market: How it has Changed and What to Do about It*. Princeton: Princeton University Press.

Oxley, Michael and Jacqueline Smith. 1996. *Housing Policy and Rented Housing in Europe*. London: Chapman and Hall.

Padalino, Samanta and Marco Vivarelli. 1997. 'The Employment Intensity of Economic Growth in the G-7 Countries.' *International Labour Review* 136/2: 199–213.

Padilla, Felix. 1987. *Puerto Rican Chicago*. Notre Dame, IN: University of Notre Dame Press.

Padilla, Felix. 1992. *The Gang as an American Entreprise*. New Brunswick, NJ: Rutgers University Press.

Pahl, Raymond E. 1987. 'Does Jobless Mean Workless? Unemployment and Informal Work.' *Annals of the American Academy of Political and Social Science* 493 (September): 36–46.

Pahl, Raymond E. 1989. 'Is the Emperor Naked? Some Questions on the Adequacy of Sociological Theory in Urban and Regional Research.' *International Journal of Urban and Regional Research* 13/4 (December): 709–20.

Pakulski, Jan and Malcolm Waters. 1996. *The Death of Class*. London: Sage.

Palidda, Salvatore. 2000. *Polizia Postmoderna. Etnografia del nuovo controllo sociale*. Milan: Feltrinelli.

Pamuk, Ayse and Paulo Fernando Cavallieri. 1998. 'Alleviating Urban Poverty in a Global City: New Trends in Upgrading Rio de Janeiro's Favelas.' *Habitat International* 22/4 (December): 449–62.

Parker, Karen F. and Patricia L. McCall. 1999. 'Structural Conditions and Racial Homicide Patterns: A Look at the Multiple Disadvantages in Urban Areas.' *Criminology* 37/3 (August): 447–77.

Parkin, Frank. 1978. *Marxism and Class Theory: A Bourgeois Critique*. New York: Columbia University Press.

Parsons, Talcott. 1971. *The System of Modern Societies*. Englewood Cliffs, NJ: Prentice-Hall.

Pastor, Manuel. 1995. 'Economic Inequality, Latino Poverty, and the Civil Unrest in Los Angeles.' *Economic Development Quarterly* 9/3 (August): 238–58.

Patterson, Orlando. 1972. 'Toward a Future That Has No Past: Reflections on the Fate of Blacks in the Americas.' *The Public Interest* 27 (Spring): 25–62.

Patterson, Orlando. 1977. *Ethnic Chauvinism: The Reactionary Impulse.* London: Stein and Day.

Patterson, Orlando. 1998. *Rituals of Blood: Consequences of Slavery in Two American Centuries.* New York: Civitas Books.

Pattillo-McCoy, Mary. 1999. *Black Picket Fences: Privilege and Peril Among the Black Middle Class.* Chicago: University of Chicago Press.

Pattillo-McCoy, Mary. 2000. 'The Limits of Out-Migration for the Black Middle Class.' *Journal of Urban Affairs* 22/3 (Fall): 225–41.

Paugam, Serge. 1991. *La Disqualification sociale. Essai sur la nouvelle pauvreté.* Paris: Presses Universitaires de France.

Paugam, Serge. 1993. *La Société française et ses pauvres.* Paris: Presses Universitaires de France.

Paugam, Serge. 2005. *Les Formes élémentaire de la pauvreté.* Paris: Presses Universitaires de France.

Peattie, Lisa. 1968. *The View from the Barrio.* Ann Arbor: University of Michigan Press.

Peck, Jamie. 2001. *Workfare States.* New York: Guilford.

Pereira, Virgílio Borges. 2005. *Classes e culturas de classe das famílias portuenses.* Porto: Affrontamento.

Perlman, Janet. 1976. *The Myth of Marginality: Urban Poverty and Politics in Rio de Janeiro.* Berkeley: University of California Press.

Perrin, Évelyne. 2004. *Chômeurs et précaires au coeur de la question sociale.* Paris: La Dispute.

Petersen, Anne C. and Jeylan T. Mortimer (eds). 1994. *Youth Unemployment and Society.* Cambridge: Cambridge University Press.

Petersilia, Joan. 1993. 'Crime and Punishment in California: Full Cells, Empty Pockets, and Questionable Benefits.' *California Policy Seminar Brief* 5/11 (May): 1–12.

Peterson, Paul. 1991. 'The Urban Underclass and the Poverty Paradox.' In Christopher Jencks and Paul E. Peterson (eds), *The Urban Underclass* (Washington, DC: The Brookings Institution), pp. 3–27.

Pétonnet, Colette. 1979. *On est tous dans le brouillard. Ethnologie des banlieues.* Paris: Galilée.

Pétonnet, Colette. 1982. *Espace habités. Ethnologie des banlieues.* Paris: Galilée.

Pétonnet, Colette. 1985. 'La pâleur noire: couleur et culture aux États-Unis.' *L'Homme* 97–8 (January–June): 171–87.

Petsimeris, P. 1998. 'Urban Decline and the New Social and Ethnic Divisions in the Core Cities of the Italian Industrial Triangle.' *Urban Studies* 35/3: 449–65.

Pettigrew, Thomas F. 1971. *Racially Separate or Together?* New York: McGraw-Hill.

Pettiway, Leon E. 1985. 'The Internal Structure of the Ghetto and the Criminal Commute.' *Journal of Black Studies* 16/2 (December): 189–211.

Philpott, Thomas Lee. 1978. *The Slum and the Ghetto: Neighborhood Deterioration and Middle-Class Reform, Chicago 1880–1930.* New York: Oxford University Press.

Pialoux, Michel. 1979. 'Jeunesse sans avenir et travail intérimaire.' *Actes de la recherche en sciences sociale* 26–7 (April): 19–47.

Pierson, Paul (ed.). 2001. *The New Politics of the Welfare State.* New York: Oxford University Press.

Pinçon, Michel. 1982. *Cohabiter. Groupes sociaux et modes de vie dans une cité HLM.* Paris: Ministère de l'urbanisme et du logement, Plan Construction, Collection 'Recherches'.

Pinçon-Charlot, Monique, Edmond Préteceille and Paul Rendu. 1986. *Ségrégation urbaine. Classes sociales et équipements collectifs en région parisienne.* Paris: Éditions Anthropos.

Pinderhughes, Howard. 1997. *Race in the 'Hood: Conflict and Violence Among Urban Youth.* Minneapolis: University of Minnesota Press.

Pino, Julio César. 1997. *Family and Favela: The Reproduction of Poverty in Rio de Janeiro.* Westport, CT: Praeger.

Piore, Michael J. 1979. *Birds of Passage: Migrant Labour and Industrial Societies.* Cambridge: Cambridge University Press.

Piore, Michael J. and Charles F. Sabel. 1984. *The Second Industrial Divide: Possibilities for Prosperity.* New York: Basic Books.

Pitti, Stephen J. 2003. *The Devil in Silicon Valley: Northern California, Race, and Mexican Americans.* Princeton: Princeton University Press.

Piven, Frances Fox and Richard A. Cloward. 1971. *Regulating the Poor: The Functions of Public Welfare.* New York: Vintage.

Piven, Frances Fox and Richard A. Cloward. 1977. *Poor People's Movements: Why They Succeed, How They Fail.* New York: Vintage.

Polanyi, Karl. 1944. *The Great Transformation: The Political and Economic Origins of Our Time.* Boston: Beacon Press.

Porter, Bruce and Marvin Dunn. 1984. *The Miami Riot of 1980: Crossing the Bounds.* Lexington, MA: Lexington Books.

Portes, Alejandro. 1972. 'The Rationality of the Slum: An Essay on Interpretive Sociology.' *Comparative Studies in Society and History* 14/3 (June): 268–86.

Portes, Alejandro. 1999. 'La mondialisation par le bas: l'émergence des communautés transnationales.' *Actes de la recherche en sciences sociales* 129 (September): 15–25.

Portes, Alejandro and Robert L. Bach. 1985. *Latin Journey: Cuban and Mexican Immigrants in the United States.* Berkeley: University of California Press.

Portes, Alejandro and Ruben G. Rumbaut. 1990. *Immigrant America: A Portrait.* Berkeley: University of California Press.

Portes, Alejandro and Saskia Sassen-Koob. 1987. 'Making It Underground: Comparative Material on the Informal Sector in Western Market Economies.' *American Journal of Sociology* 93/1 (July): 30–61.

Pred, Allan Richard. 1997. 'Somebody Else, Somewhere Else: Racisms, Racialized Spaces and the Popular Geographical Imagination in Sweden.' *Antipode* 29/4 (October): 383–416.

Pred, Allan Richard. 2000. *Even in Sweden: Racisms, Racialized Spaces, and the Popular Geographical Imagination*. Berkeley: University of California Press.

Préteceille, Edmond. 1973. *La Production des grands ensembles*. Paris: Mouton.

Procacci, Giovanna. 1993. *Gouverner la misère. La question sociale en France, 1789–1848*. Paris: Seuil.

Quadagno, Jill. 1994. *The Color of Welfare: How Racism Undermined the War on Poverty*. New York: Oxford University Press.

Rainwater, Lee. 1970. *Behind Ghetto Walls: Black Family Life in a Federal Slum*. New York: Aldine.

Rank, Mark Robert. 1994. *Living on the Edge: The Realities of Welfare in America*. New York: Columbia University Press.

Ranney, David C. 1993. 'Transnational Investment and Job Loss in Chicago.' In Dick Simpson (ed.), *Chicago's Future in a Time of Change* (Chicago: Stipes Publishing Company), pp. 88–98.

Ratner, Mitchell S. (ed.). 1992. *Crack Pipe as Pimp: An Ethnographic Investigation of Sex-For-Crack Exchanges*. Lexington, MA: Lexington Books.

Reed, Adolph, Jr. 1992. 'The Underclass as Myth and Symbol: The Poverty of Discourse About Poverty.' *Radical America* (January): 21–40.

Regini, Marino. 1995. *Uncertain Boundaries: The Social and Political Construction of European Economies*. Cambridge: Cambridge University Press.

Reiner, Robert. 1997. 'The Police and Policing.' In Mike Maguire, Rod Morgan and Robert Reiner (eds), *The Oxford Handbook of Criminology* (Oxford: Oxford University Press), pp. 997–1050.

Reinerman, Craig and Harry Levine. 1997. 'The Crack Attack: Politics and Media in the Crack Scare.' In Craig Reinerman (ed.), *Crack in America: Demon Drugs and Social Justice* (Berkeley: University of California Press), pp. 18–51.

Ribeiro, Luiz César de Queiroz. 1996. 'Rio de Janeiro: exemplo de metropole partida e sem rumo?' *Novos Estudos CEBRAP* 45 (July): 167–82.

Richard, Jean-Luc. 2000. 'Une approche de la discrimination sur le marché du travail: les jeunes adultes issus de l'immigration étrangère en France.' *Revue européenne des migrations internationales* 16/3: 53–83.

Ricketts, Erol R. and Isabel V. Sawhill. 1988. 'Defining and Measuring the Underclass.' *Journal of Policy Analysis and Management* 7 (Winter): 316–25.

Rieder, Jonathan. 1985. *Canarsie: The Jews and Italians of Brooklyn Against Liberalism*. Cambridge, MA: Harvard University Press.

Rifkin, Jeremy. 1995. *The End of Work: The Decline of the Global Work Force and the Dawn of the Post-Market Era*. New York: G. P. Putnam's Sons.

Robinson, Jennifer. 1996. *The Power of Apartheid: State, Power and Space in South African Cities*. Boston: Butterworth Heinemann.

Roche, Maurice and Rik Van Berkel (eds). 1997. *European Citizenship and Social Exclusion*. Avebury: Ashgate.

Roebuck, Julian B. and Wolfgang Frese. 1977. *The Rendezvous: A Case Study of an After-Hours Club*. New York: Free Press.

Room, Graham. 1990. *New Poverty in the European Union*. London: Macmillan.

Rosenberg, Sam. 1983. 'Reagan Social Policy and Labour Force Restructuring.' *Cambridge Journal of Economics* 7/2 (June): 179–96.

Rostow, Walt W. 1960. *Stages of Economic Growth: A Non-Communist Manifesto*. Cambridge: Cambridge University Press.

Roulleau-Berger, Laurence and Madeleine Gautier (eds). 2002. *Les Jeunes et l'emploi dans les villes d'Europe et d'Amérique du Nord*. Lyons: Editions de l'Aube.

Rumbaut, Ruben G. and Alejandro Portes (eds). 2001. *Ethnicities: Children of Immigrants in America*. Berkeley: University of California Press.

Sampson, Robert J., Jeffrey D. Morenoff and Thomas Gannon-Rowley. 2002. 'Assessing "Neighborhood Effects": Social Processes and New Directions in Research.' *Annual Review of Sociology* 28: 443–78.

Sánchez-Jankowski, Martín. 1991. *Islands in the Street: Gangs in Urban American Society*. Berkeley: University of California Press.

Sánchez-Jankowski, Martín. 1994. 'Les gangs et la presse: la production d'un mythe national.' *Actes de la recherche en sciences sociales* 101–2 (March): 101–18.

Santelli, Emmanuelle. 2001. *La Mobilité sociale dans l'immigration. Itinéraires de réussite des enfants d'origine algérienne*. Toulouse: Presses Universitaires du Mirail.

Sassen, Saskia. 1989a. *The Mobility of Labor and Capital: A Study in International Investment and Labor*. Cambridge: Cambridge University Press.

Sassen, Saskia. 1989b. 'America's "Immigration Problem."' *World Policy Journal* 6/4 (Fall): 811–32.

Sassen, Saskia. 1991a. 'Internationalization, Informalization, and Economic Polarization in New York City's Economy.' In John H. Mollenkopf and Manuel Castells (eds), *Dual City: Restructuring New York* (New York: Russell Sage Foundation), pp. 79–102.

Sassen, Saskia. 1991b. *The Global City: New York, London, Tokyo*. Princeton: Princeton University Press. Revised and expanded edition, 2001.

Sawhill, Isabel V. 1989. 'The Underclass: An Overview.' *The Public Interest* 96 (Summer): 3–15.

Sayad, Adbelmalek. 1975. 'Le foyer des sans-famille.' *Actes de la recherche en sciences sociales* 32–3 (June): 89–104.

Sayad, Abdelmalek. 1991. *L'Immigration ou les paradoxes de l'altérité*. Brussels: De Boeck Université.

Sayad, Abdelmalek, with Éliane Dupuy. 1995. *Un Nanterre algérien, terre de bidonvilles*. Paris: Editions Autrement.

Scharf, Jagna Wojcika. 1987. 'The Underground Economy of a Poor Neighborhood.' In Leith Mullings (ed.), *Cities of the United States: Studies in Urban Anthropology* (New York: Columbia University Press), pp. 19–50.

Schierup, Carl-Ulrik. 1995. 'A European Dilemma: Myrdal, the American Creed, and EU Europe.' *International Sociology* 10/4 (December): 347–67.

Schlay, Anne B. 1987. 'Credit on Color: Segregation, Racial Transition, and Housing-Credit Flows.' In *Fair Housing in Metropolitan Chicago: Perspectives after Two Decades: A Report to the Chicago Area Fair Housing Alliance* (Chicago: The Chicago Area Fair Housing Alliance), pp. 109–88.

Schutz, Alfred. 1970. *On Phenomenology and Social Relations: Selected Writings*. Chicago: University of Chicago Press.

Schwartz, Olivier. 1990. *Le Monde privé des ouvriers. Hommes et femmes du Nord*. Paris: Presses Universitaires de France.

Scott, Allen J. and Edward W. Soja (eds). 1996. *The City: Los Angeles and Urban Theory at the End of the Twentieth Century*. Berkeley: University of California Press.

Scott, Allen J. and Michael Storper (eds). 1986. *Production, Work, Territory: The Geographical Anatomy of Industrial Capitalism*. Boston: Allen & Unwin.

Seligman, Amanda I. 2005. *Block by Block: Neighborhoods and Public Policy on Chicago's West Side*. Chicago: University of Chicago Press.

Sheppard, Harold L. 1966. *The Job Hunt: Job Seeking Behavior of Unemployed Workers in a Local Economy*. Baltimore: Johns Hopkins University Press.

Shields, Rob. 1991. *Places on the Margin: Alternative Geographies of Modernity*. London: Routledge.

Shulman, Beth. 2003. *The Betrayal of Work*. New York: New Press.

Silver, Hilary. 1993. 'National Conceptions of the New Urban Poverty: Social Structural Change in Britain, France, and the United States.' *International Journal of Urban and Regional Research* 17/3 (September): 336–54.

Silverman, Maxim. 1990. 'The Racialization of Immigration: Aspects of Discourse from 1968 to 1981.' *French Cultural Studies* 1/2 (March): 111–28.

Siméant, Johanna. 1998. *La Cause des sans-papiers*. Paris: Presses de Sciences Po.

Simmel, Georg. [1908] 1965. 'The Poor.' *Social Problems* 13/2 (Fall): 118–40.

Simon, Patrick. 1992. 'Banlieues: de la concentration au ghetto.' *Esprit* 182 (June): 58–64.

Sinfield, Andrew. 1980. 'Poverty and Inequality in France.' In Victor George and Roger Lawson (eds), *Poverty and Inequality in Common Market Countries* (London: Routledge and Kegan Paul).

Sklair, Leslie. 2001. *The Transnational Capitalist Class*. Oxford: Basil Blackwell.

Skogan, Wesley G. 1988. 'Community Organization and Crime.' *Crime and Justice: An Annual Review of Research* 5: 39–78.

Slessarev, Helene. 1997. *The Betrayal of the Urban Poor*. Philadelphia: Temple University Press.

Small, Mario. 2004. *Villa Victoria: The Transformation of Social Capital in a Boston Barrio*. Chicago: University of Chicago Press.

Smith, Dennis. 1987. 'Knowing your Place: Class, Politics, and Ethnicity in Chicago and Birmingham, 1890–1983.' In Nigel Thrift and Peter Williams (eds), *Class and Space: The Making of Urban Society* (London: Routledge and Kegan Paul), pp. 277–305.

Snow, David A. and Leon Anderson. 1993. *Down on Their Luck: A Study of Homeless Street People*. Berkeley: University of California Press.

Snow, David A. and Leon Anderson. 1994. 'L'industrie du plasma.' *Actes de la recherche en sciences sociales* 104 (September): 25–33.

Soja, Edward W. 1989. *Postmodern Geographies: The Reassertion of Space in Critical Social Theory*. London: Verso.

Solomos, John. 1988. *Black Youth, Racism, and the State*. Cambridge: Cambridge University Press.

Somers, Margaret R. 1993. 'Citizenship and the Place of the Public Sphere: Law, Community and Political Culture in the Transition to Democracy.' *American Sociological Review* 58/5 (October): 587–620.

Son, In Soo, Suzanne W. Model and Gene A. Fisher. 1989. 'Polarization and Progress in the Black Community: Earnings and Status Gains for Young Black Males in the Era of Affirmative Action.' *Sociological Forum* 4/3 (September): 309–27.

Soulignac, Françoise. 1993. *La Banlieue parisienne. Cent cinquante ans de transformations*. Paris: La Documentation française.

Soysal, Yasemin Nuhoglu. 1994. *Limits of Citizenship: Migrants and Postnational Membership in Europe*. Chicago: University of Chicago Press.

Spear, Allan H. 1968. *Black Chicago: The Making of a Negro Ghetto, 1890–1920*. Chicago: University of Chicago Press.

Spector, Malcolm and John I. Kitsuse. 1987. *Constructing Social Problems*. New York: Aldine de Gruyter.

Squires, Gregory D., Larry Bennett, Kathleen McCourt and Philip Nyden. 1987. *Chicago: Race, Class, and the Response to Urban Decline*. Philadelphia: Temple University Press.

Stack, Carol. 1970. 'The Kindred of Viola Jackson: Residence and Family Organization of an Urban Black American Family.' In Norman E. Whitten and John F. Szwed (eds), *Afro-American Anthropology: Contemporary Perspectives* (New York: Free Press), pp. 303–11.

Stack, Carol. 1974. *All Our Kin: Strategies for Survival in a Black Community*. New York: Harper & Row.

Standing, Guy. 1993. 'The Need for a New Social Consensus.' In Philippe Van Parijs (ed.), *Arguing for Basic Income: Ethical Foundations for a Radical Reform* (London: Verso), pp. 47–60.

Standing, Guy (ed.). 2004. *Promoting Income as a Right: Europe and North America*. London: Anthem Press.

Starr, Roger. 1976. 'Making New York Smaller.' *New York Times Magazine*, 14 November.

Stearns, Linda Brewster and Charlotte Wilkinson Coleman. 1990. 'Industrial and Local Labor Market Structures and Black Male Employment in the Manufacturing Sector.' *Social Science Quarterly* 71/2 (June): 285–98.

Stedman Jones, Gareth. 1983. *Languages of Class: Studies in English Working Class History 1832–1982*. Cambridge: Cambridge University Press.

Stoléru, Lionel. 1974. *Vaincre la pauvreté dans les pays riches*. Paris: Flammarion.

Stovall, Tyler. 1990. *The Rise of the Paris Red Belt*. Berkeley: University of California Press.

Streitweiser, Mary and John Goodman, Jr. 1983. 'A Survey of Recent Research on Race and Residential Location.' *Population Research and Policy Review* 2: 253–83.

Sullivan, Mercer L. 1989. *'Getting Paid': Youth Crime and Work in the Inner City*. Ithaca, NY: Cornell University Press.

Susser, Ida. 1982. *Norman Street: Poverty and Politics in an Urban Neighborhood*. New York: Oxford University Press.

Susser, Ida and John Kreniske. 1987. 'The Welfare Trap: A Public Policy for Deprivation.' In Leith Mullings (ed.), *Cities of the United States: Studies in Urban Anthropology* (New York: Columbia University Press), pp. 51–68.

Suttles, Gerald. 1968. *The Social Order of the Slum: Ethnicity and Territory in the Inner City*. Chicago: University of Chicago Press.

Tabard, Nicole. 1993. 'Des quartiers pauvres aux banlieues aisées: une représentation sociale du territoire.' *Économie et statistique* 270: 5–22.

Tarrius, Alain. 1992. *Les fourmis d'Europe. Migrants riches, migrants pauvres et nouvelles villes internationales*. Paris: L'Harmattan.

Taylor, Carl. 1989. *Dangerous Society*. East Lansing: Michigan State University Press.

Teitz, Michael B. and Karen Chapple. 1998. 'The Causes of Inner City Poverty: Eight Hypotheses in Search of Research.' *Cityscape: A Journal of Policy Development and Research* 3/3: 33–70.

Terkel, Studs. 1992. *Race: How Blacks and Whites Think and Feel About the American Obsession*. New York: Anchor Books.

Therborn, Göran. 1996. *European Modernity and Beyond: The Trajectory of European Societies, 1945–2005*. London: Sage.

Thrift, Nigel. 1993. 'An Urban Impasse?' *Theory, Culture, and Society* 10/2 (May): 229–38.

Thrift, Nigel and Peter Williams (eds). 1987. *Class and Space: The Making of Urban Society*. London: Routledge and Kegan Paul.

Thurow, Lester. 1987. 'A Surge in Inequality.' *Scientific American* 256/5 (May): 30–7.

Tilly, Chris, Phillip Moss, Joleen Kirschenman and Ivy Kennelly. 2001. 'Space as Signal: How Employers Perceive Neighborhoods in Four Metropolitan Labor Markets.' In Alice O'Connor et al. (eds), *Urban Inequality: Evidence from Four Cities* (New York: Russell Sage Foundation), pp. 304–38.

Tissot, Sylvie. 2005. 'Les sociologues et la banlieue: la construction savante du problème des "quartiers sensibles".' *Genèses* 60 (September): 57–75.

Tobin, Gary A. 1987. *Divided Neighborhoods: Changing Patterns of Racial Segregation*. Newbury Park, CA: Sage Publications.

Tomaskovic-Devey, Donald. 1993. *Gender and Racial Inequality at Work: The Sources and Consequences of Job Segregation*. Ithaca, NY: Cornell University Press.

Tonry, Michael. 1994. 'Racial Politics, Racial Disparities, and the War on Crime.' *Crime & Delinquency* 40/4: 475–94.

Tonry, Michael. 1995. *Malign Neglect: Race, Class, and Punishment in America*. New York: Oxford University Press.

Topalov, Christian. 2003. ' "Traditional Working-Class Neighborhoods": An Inquiry into the Emergence of a Sociological Model in the 1950s and 1960s.' *Osiris* 18: 213–33.

Touraine, Alain. 1990. 'Le syndrome américain.' *Le Figaro*, 9 October.

Touraine, Alain. 1991a. 'La France perd-elle la tête?' *Le Monde*, 17 July.

Touraine, Alain. 1991b. 'Rencontre avec Alain Touraine: diagnostic sur l'état de la sociologie and de la société française.' *Sciences humaines* 3: 12–14.

Townsend, Peter. 1993. 'Underclass and Overclass: The Widening Gulf between Social Classes in Great Britain in the 1980s.' In Geoff Payne and Malcolm Cross (eds), *Sociology in Action* (London: Macmillan), pp. 137–54.

Townsend, Peter, Paul Corrigan and Uwe Kowarzick. 1987. *Poverty and Labour in London*. London: Low Pay Unit.

Tribalat, Michèle. 1995. *Faire France. Une grande enquête sur les immigrés et leurs enfants*. Paris: La Découverte.

Tripier, Maryse. 1990. *L'Immigration dans la classe ouvrière en France*. Paris: L'Harmattan.

Turner, Bryan S. 1986. *Citizenship and Capitalism: The Debate over Reformism*. London: Methuen.

Turner, Bryan S. (ed.). 1992. *Citizenship and Social Theory*. Newbury Park, CA: Sage.

Uitermark, Justus. 2003. ' "Social Mixing" and the Management of Disadvantaged Neighbourhoods: The Dutch Policy of Urban Restructuring Revisited.' *Urban Studies* 40/3 (March): 531–49.

Unsworth, Clive. 1982. 'The Riots of 1981: Popular Violence and the Politics of Law and Order.' *Journal of Law and Society* 9/1 (Summer): 63–85.

Uwe, Hans-Otto (ed.). 2003. *Territorializierung der Sozialen Welt*. Opladen: Leske and Budrich.

Van DeBurg, William L. 1992. *New Day in Babylon: The Black Power Movement and American Culture, 1965–1975*. Chicago: University of Chicago Press.

Van Kempen, Robert and A. O. Özüekren. 1998. 'Ethnic Segregation in Cities: New Forms and Explanations in a Dynamic World.' *Urban Studies* 35: 1631–56.

Van Parijs. Philippe (ed.). 1993. *Arguing for Basic Income: Ethical Foundations for a Radical Reform*. London: Verso.

Van Parijs, Philippe. 1995. *Real Freedom for All: What (if Anything) can Justify Capitalism?* New York: Oxford University Press.

Van Parijs, Philippe. 2001. *What's Wrong with a Free Lunch?* Boston: Beacon Press.

Van Zanten, Agnès. 1997. 'Schooling Immigrants in France in the 1990s: Success or Failure of the Republican Model of Integration?' *Anthropology & Education Quarterly* 28/3 (September): 351–74.

Vanneman, Reeve and Lynn Cannon Weber. 1987. *The American Perception of Class*. Philadelphia: Temple University Press.

Vélez-Ibañez, Carlos G. 1983. *Rituals of Marginality: Politics, Process, and Culture Change in Central Urban Mexico, 1969–1974*. Berkeley: University of California Press.

Venkatesh, Sudhir Alladi. 1997. 'The Social Organization of Street Gang Activity in an Urban Ghetto.' *American Journal of Sociology* 103/1 (July): 82–111.

Venkatesh, Sudhir. 2000. *American Project: The Rise and Fall of a Modern Ghetto*. Cambridge, MA: Harvard University Press.

Vergara, Camilo José. 1995. *The New American Ghetto*. New Brunswick, NJ: Rutgers University Press.

Verret, Michel. 1979. *L'Espace ouvrier*. Paris: Armand Colin.

Vieillard-Baron, Hervé. 1994. *Les Banlieues françaises ou le ghetto impossible*. Paris: Editions de l'Aube.

Vigil, James Diego. 1988. *Barrio Gangs: Street Life and Identity in Southern California*. Austin: University of Texas Press.

von Hoffman, Alexander. 1996. 'High Ambitions: The Past and Future of American Low-Income Housing Policy.' *Housing Policy Debate* 7/3: 423–46.

Vosko, Leah F. 2000. *Temporary Work: The Gendered Rise of a Precarious Employment Relationship*. Toronto: University of Toronto Press.

Wacquant, Loïc. 1989. 'The Ghetto, the State, and the New Capitalist Economy.' *Dissent* (Fall): 508–20.

Wacquant, Loïc. 1991. 'What Makes A Ghetto? Notes Toward a Comparative Analysis of Modes of Urban Exclusion.' Paper presented at the Russell Sage Foundation Conference on 'Poverty, Immigration, and Urban Marginality in Advanced Societies', Paris, Maison Suger, 10–11 May.

Wacquant, Loïc. 1992a. 'Décivilisation and démonisation: la mutation du ghetto noir américain.' In Christine Fauré and Tom Bishop (eds), *L'Amérique des français* (Paris: Editions François Bourin), pp. 103–25. Tr. in expanded version as 'Decivilizing and Demonizing: The Remaking of the Black American Ghetto', in Steven Loyal and Stephen Quilley (eds), *The Sociology of Norbert Elias* (Cambridge: Cambridge University Press, 2004), pp. 95–121.

Wacquant, Loïc. 1992b. 'Pour en finir avec le mythe des "cités-ghettos": les différences entre la France and les Etats-Unis.' *Annales de la recherche urbaine* 52 (September): 20–30.

Wacquant, Loïc. 1993. 'Désordre dans la ville.' *Actes de la recherche en sciences sociales* 99 (September): 79–82.

Wacquant, Loïc. 1994. 'Le gang comme prédateur collectif.' *Actes de la recherche en sciences sociales* 101–2 (March): 88–100.

Wacquant, Loïc. 1995a. 'The Comparative Structure and Experience of Urban Exclusion: "Race", Class, and Space in Paris and Chicago.' In Katherine McFate et al. (eds), *Poverty, Inequality, and the Future of Social Policy* (New York: Russell Sage Foundation), pp. 543–70.

Wacquant, Loïc. 1995b. 'Pour comprendre la "crise" des banlieues.' *French Politics and Society* 13/4 (Fall): 68–81.

Wacquant, Loïc. 1996a. 'L' "underclass" urbaine dans l'imaginaire social et scientifique américain.' In Serge Paugam (ed.), *L'Exclusion: l'état des savoirs* (Paris: La Découverte), pp. 248–62.

Wacquant, Loïc. 1996b. 'La généralisation de l'insécurité salariale en Amérique: restructurations d'entreprises and crise de reproduction sociale.' *Actes de la recherche en sciences sociales* 115 (December): 65–79.

Wacquant, Loïc. 1997a. 'Three Pernicious Premises in the Study of the American Ghetto.' *International Journal of Urban and Regional Research* 20/3 (June): 341–53.

Wacquant, Loïc. 1997b. 'Les pauvres en pâture: la nouvelle politique de la misère en Amérique.' *Hérodote* 85 (Spring): 21–33.

Wacquant, Loïc. 1997c. 'For an Analytic of Racial Domination.' *Political Power and Social Theory* 11 (Symposium on 'Rethinking Race' with Ann Laura Stoler, Patricia Dominguez, David Roediger and Uday Singh Mehta): 221–34.

Wacquant, Loic. 1998. 'Inside the Zone: The Social Art of the Hustler in the Black American Ghetto.' *Theory, Culture, and Society*, 15/2 (May): 1–36.

Wacquant, Loïc. 1999. *Les Prisons de la misère*. Paris: Raisons d'agir Éditions. Rev. and expanded edn tr. as *Prisons of Poverty* (Minneapolis: University of Minnesota Press, 2009).

Wacquant, Loïc. 2001. 'Deadly Symbiosis: When Ghetto and Prison Meet and Mesh.' *Punishment & Society* 3/1 (Winter): 95–133.

Wacquant, Loïc. 2002a. 'Scrutinizing the Street: Poverty, Morality, and the Pitfalls of Urban Ethnography.' *American Journal of Sociology* 107/6 (May): 1468–532.

Wacquant, Loïc. 2002b. 'Gutting the Ghetto: Political Censorship and Conceptual Retrenchment in the American Debate on Urban Destitution.' In Malcolm Cross and Robert Moore (eds), *Globalisation and the New City* (Basingstoke and New York: Palgrave), pp. 32–49.

Wacquant, Loïc. 2004. *Punir les pauvres. Le nouveau gouvernement de l'insécurité sociale*. Paris: Editions Dupuytren. Tr. as *Punishing the Poor: The New Government of Social Insecurity* (Durham, NC, and London: Duke University Press, 2008).

Wacquant, Loïc. 2005. 'Les deux visages du ghetto: construire un concept sociologique.' *Actes de la recherche en sciences sociales* 160 (December): 4–21. Shorter English version: 'Ghetto', in Neil J. Smelser and Paul B. Baltes (eds), *International Encyclopedia of the Social and Behavioural Sciences* (London: Pergamon Press, 2004).

Wacquant, Loïc and William Julius Wilson. 1989. 'Poverty, Joblessness, and the Social Transformation of the Inner City.' In David Ellwood and Phoebe Cottingham (eds), *Welfare Policy for the 1990s* (Cambridge, MA: Harvard University Press), pp. 70–102.

Waldinger, Roger. 1996. *Still the Promised City? African Americans and New Immigrants in Postindustrial New York*. Cambridge, MA: Harvard University Press.

Waldinger, Roger and Thomas Bailey. 1991. 'The Continuing Significance of Race: Racial Conflict and Racial Discrimination in Construction.' *Politics and Society* 19/3 (September): 291–324.

Waley, Paul. 2000. 'Tokyo: Patterns of Familiarity and Partitions of Difference.' In Peter Marcuse and Ronald Van Kempen (eds), *Globalizing Cities: A New Spatial Order?* (Oxford: Blackwell), 127–56.

Walker, Gillian and Sippio Small. 1991. 'AIDS, Crack, Poverty, and Race in the African-American Community: The Need for an Ecosystemic Approach.' *Journal of Independent Social Work* 5/3–4: 69–91.

Wallace, Rodrick and Deborah Wallace. 1990. 'Origins of Public Health Collapse in New York City: The Dynamics of Planned Shrinkage, Contagious Urban Decay and Social Disintegration.' *Bulletin of the New York Academy of Science* 66/5 (September): 391–434.

Wallerstein, Immanuel. 1983. *Historical Capitalism*. London: Verso.

Walters, Pamela Barnhouse. 1993. 'Education.' In Craig Calhoun and George Ritzer (eds), *Social Problems* (New York: McGraw-Hill), pp. 571–96.

Walton, John. 1990. 'Urban Sociology: The Contribution and Limits of Political Economy.' *Annual Review of Sociology* 19: 301–20.

Ward, David. 1989. *Poverty, Ethnicity, and the American City: Changing Conceptions of the Slum and the Ghetto*. Cambridge: Cambridge University Press.

Wassenberg, Frank (ed.). 2004. 'Large Social Housing Estates: From Stigma to Demolition?' *Journal of Housing and the Built Environment* 19/3, thematic issue.

Weber, Max. 1949. *Methodology of the Social Sciences*. Glencoe, IL: Free Press.

Weber, Max. [1918–20] 1968. *Economy and Society*. Berkeley: University of California Press.

Weir, Margaret. 1993. 'Race and Urban Poverty: Comparing Europe and America.' *The Brookings Review* 11/3 (Summer): 23–7.

Weir, Margaret. 1994. 'Urban Poverty and Defensive Localism.' *Dissent* 41 (Summer): 337–42.

Weiß, Anja. 2001. *Rassismus wider Willen. Ein anderer Blick auf eine Struktur sozialer Ungleichheit*. Berlin: VS Verlag für Sozialwissenschaften.

Weiss, Linda. 1998. *The Myth of the Powerless State*. Ithaca: Cornell University Press.

West, Cornel. 1994. *Race Matters*. Boston: Beacon Press.

Westergaard, John. 1992. 'About and Beyond the "Underclass": Some Notes on Influences of Social Climate on British Sociology Today.' *Sociology* 26/4 (November): 575–87.

Whiteis, D. J. 1992. 'Hospital and Community Characteristics in Closures of Urban Hospitals, 1980–1987.' *Public Health Reports* 107: 409–16.

Wieviorka, Michel. 1993. 'Racism and Modernity in Present-Day Europe.' *Thesis Eleven* 35: 51–61.

Wihtol de Wenden, Catherine and Zakya Daoud (eds). 1994. *Intégration ou explosion? Banlieues . . .* Saint-Denis: Corlet.

Wilkinson, Daniel. 1992. 'Isolating the Poor: Work and Community in the Inner City.' Unpublished BA Honors thesis, Harvard University.

Williams, Bruce. 1987. *Black Workers in an Industrial Suburb: The Struggle Against Discrimination*. New Brunswick, NJ: Rutgers University Press.

Williams, Terry. 1989. *Cocaine Kids: The Inside Story of a Teenage Drug Ring*. Reading, MA: Addison-Wesley.

Williams, Terry. 1992. *The Crackhouse: Notes from the End of the Line*. Reading, MA: Addison-Wesley.

Williams, Terry and William Kornblum. 1985. *Growing Up Poor*. Lexington, MA: Lexington Books.

Williamson, John B. 1974. 'Beliefs about the Motivation of the Poor and Attitudes Toward Poverty Policy.' *Social Problems* 21/5 (June): 634–47.

Willis, Paul. 1981. *Learning to Labor: How Working-Class Kids Get Working-Class Jobs*. New York: Columbia University Press.

Willmott, Peter. 1963. *The Evolution of a Community: A Study of Dagenham after Forty Years*. London: Routledge.

Wilson, William Julius. 1980. *The Declining Significance of Race: Blacks and Changing American Institutions*, 2nd rev. edn. Chicago: University of Chicago Press.

Wilson, William Julius. 1987. *The Truly Disadvantaged: The Inner City, the Underclass and Public Policy*. Chicago: University of Chicago Press.

Wilson, William Julius. 1988. 'The American Underclass: Inner-City Ghettos and the Norms of Citizenship.' The Godkin Lecture, John F. Kennedy School of Government, Harvard University.

Wilson, William Julius. 1991. 'Studying Inner-City Social Dislocations: The Challenge of Public Agenda Research.' *American Sociological Review* 56/1 (February): 1–14.

Wilson, William Julius (ed.). 1993. *The Urban Underclass: Social Science Perspectives*. Newbury Park, CA: Sage Publications.

Wilson, William Julius. 1996. *When Work Disappears: The World of the New Urban Poor*. New York: Knopf.

Wilson, William Julius and Robert Aponte. 1985. 'Urban Poverty.' *Annual Review of Sociology* 11: 231–58.

Winant, Howard. 1994. *Racial Conditions: Politics, Theory, Comparisons*. Minneapolis: University of Minnesota Press.

Wintermute, Wendy. 1983. *Recession and Recovery: Impact on Black and White Workers in Chicago*. Chicago: Chicago Urban League.

Wirth, Louis. 1927. 'The Ghetto.' *American Journal of Sociology* 33/1 (July): 57–71.

Wirth, Louis. 1964. *On Cities and Social Life: Selected Papers*. Chicago: University of Chicago Press.

Witte, Rob. 1996. *Racist Violence and the State: A Comparative Analysis of Britain, France and the Netherlands*. London: Routledge.

Wittgenstein, Ludwig. 1977. *Vermischte Bemerkungen*. Frankfurt: Syndicat Verlag.

Wrench, John and John Solomos (eds). 1993. *Racism and Migration in Western Europe*. New York: Berg.

Wright, Erik Olin. 1985. *Classes*. New York: Verso.

Wright, Erik Olin. 1997. *Class Counts: Comparative Studies in Class Analysis*. Cambridge: Cambridge University Press.

Wu, Fulong. 2004. 'Urban Poverty and Marginalization under Market Transition: The Case of Chinese Cities.' *International Journal of Urban and Regional Research* 28/2 (June): 401–23.

Yinger, John. 1997. *Closed Doors, Opportunities Lost: The Continuing Costs of Housing Discrimination*. New York: Russell Sage Foundation.

Young, Alford A. Jr. 2004. *The Minds of Marginalized Black Men: Making Sense of Mobility, Opportunity, and Future Life Chances*. Princeton: Princeton University Press.

Young, Jock. 1999. *The Exclusive Society: Social Exclusion, Crime, and Difference in Late Modernity*. London: Sage.

Young, Michael and Peter Willmott. [1954] 1986. *Family and Kinship in East London*. Berkeley: University of California Press.

Young, Richard P. (ed.). 1970. *Roots of Rebellion: The Evolution of Black Politics and Protest Since World War II*. New York: Harper & Row.

Zaluar, Alba and Marcos Alvito (eds). 1998. *Um século de favela*. Rio de Janeiro: Fundação Getúlio Vargas Editora.

Zinn, Maxine Baca. 1989. 'Family, Race, and Poverty in the Eighties.' *Signs: Journal of Women in Culture and Society* 14/4: 856–74.

Zolberg, Aristide. 1991. 'Bounded States in a Global Market: The Uses of International Labor Migrations.' In Pierre Bourdieu and James S. Coleman (eds), *Social Theory for a Changing Society* (Boulder, CO: Westview Press), pp. 301–25.

Index